EYEWITNESS TRAVEL

PRAGUE

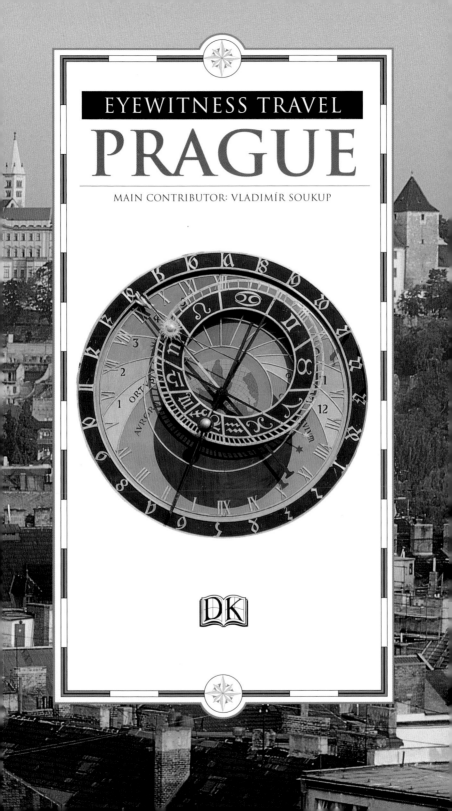

EYEWITNESS TRAVEL
PRAGUE

MAIN CONTRIBUTOR: VLADIMÍR SOUKUP

DK

LONDON, NEW YORK,
MELBOURNE, MUNICH AND DELHI
www.dk.com

PROJECT EDITOR Heather Jones
ART EDITOR Lisa Kosky
EDITORS Ferdie McDonald, Carey Combe
US EDITOR Mary Ann Bruchac Lynch
DESIGNERS Louise Parsons, Nicki Rawson

CONTRIBUTORS
Petr David, Vladimír Dobrovodský, Nicholas Lowry,
Polly Phillimore, Joy Turner-Kadéčková, Craig Turp

PHOTOGRAPHERS
Jiří Doležal, Jiří Kopřiva, Vladimír Kozlík, František Přeučil,
Milan Posselt, Stanislav Tereba, Peter Wilson

ILLUSTRATORS
Gillie Newman, Chris Orr, Otakar Pok, Jaroslav Staněk

This book was produced with the assistance of
Olympia Publishing House, Prague.

Reproduced by Colourscan, Singapore
Printed and bound in China by South China Printing Co., Ltd

First American Edition, 1994
10 11 12 13 10 9 8 7 6 5 4 3 2 1

Published in the United States by DK Publishing,
375 Hudson street, New York, New York 10014

Reprinted with revisions 1996, 1997, 2001, 2002, 2003,
2004, 2005, 2006, 2008, 2009, 2010

Copyright © 1994, 2010 Dorling Kindersley Limited, London
A Penguin Company

Published in Great Britain by Dorling Kindersley Limited

A catalog record for this book is available from the Library of Congress

ISSN 1542-1554
ISBN 978-0-75666-049-9

FLOORS ARE REFERRED TO THROUGHOUT IN ACCORDANCE WITH EUROPEAN USAGE;
IE THE "FIRST FLOOR" IS THE FLOOR ABOVE GROUND LEVEL.

*Front cover main image: the Church of Our Lady before Týn towers above
the houses of Staré Město*

We're trying to be cleaner and greener:

- we recycle waste and switch things off
- we use paper from responsibly managed
forests whenever possible
- we ask our printers to actively reduce
water and energy consumption
- we check out our suppliers' working
conditions – they never use child labour

**Find out more about our values and
best practices at www.dk.com**

**The information in this
DK Eyewitness Travel Guide is checked annually.**
Every effort has been made to ensure that this book is as up-to-date
as possible at the time of going to press. Some details, however,
such as telephone numbers, opening hours, prices, gallery hanging
arrangements and travel information, are liable to change. The
publishers cannot accept responsibility for any consequences arising
from the use of this book, nor for any material on third-party
websites, and cannot guarantee that any website address in this
book will be a suitable source of travel information. We value the
views and suggestions of our readers very highly. Please write to:
Publisher, DK Eyewitness Travel Guides,
Dorling Kindersley, 80 Strand, London WC2R 0RL, Great Britain.

◁ **View over the rooftops to Prague Castle**

CONTENTS

Rudolph II (1576–1612)

INTRODUCING
PRAGUE

Outdoor café tables

Wallenstein Palace and Garden in the Little Quarter

Church of Our Lady before Týn

TRAVELLERS'
NEEDS

SURVIVAL GUIDE

Czech beer-bottle cap

Fiacre, Old Town Square

Baroque façades
of houses at the
southern end of
Old Town Square

HOW TO USE THIS GUIDE

This Eyewitness Travel Guide helps you get the most from your stay in Prague with the minimum of difficulty. The opening section, *Introducing Prague*, locates the city geographically, sets modern Prague in its historical context and describes events through the entire year. *Prague at a Glance* is an overview of the city's main attractions, including a feature on the River Vltava. Section two, *Prague Area by Area*, starts on page 58. This is the main sightseeing

Planning the day's itinerary in Prague

section, which covers all the important sights, with photographs, maps and drawings. It also includes day trips from Prague and four guided walks around the city. Carefully researched tips for hotels, restaurants, shops and markets, cafés and bars, enter- tainment and sports are found in *Travellers' Needs*. The last section, the *Survival Guide*, contains useful practical advice on all you need to know, from making a telephone call to using the public transport system.

FINDING YOUR WAY AROUND THE SIGHTSEEING SECTION

Each of the five sightseeing areas in the city is colour-coded for easy reference. Every chapter opens with an introduction to the part of Prague it covers, describing its history and character, followed by a Street-by-Street

map illustrating the heart of the area. Finding your way around each chapter is made simple by the numbering system used throughout. The most important sights are covered in detail in two or more full pages.

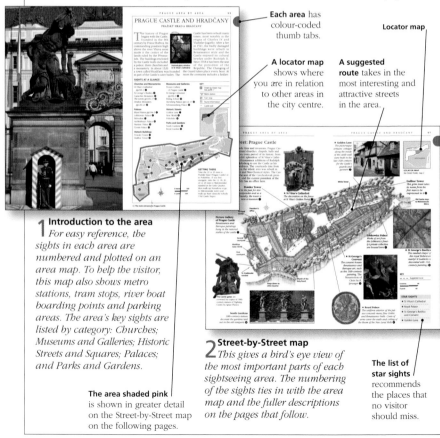

Each area has colour-coded thumb tabs.

Locator map

A locator map shows where you are in relation to other areas in the city centre.

A suggested route takes in the most interesting and attractive streets in the area.

1 Introduction to the area
For easy reference, the sights in each area are numbered and plotted on an area map. To help the visitor, this map also shows metro stations, tram stops, river boat boarding points and parking areas. The area's key sights are listed by category: Churches; Museums and Galleries; Historic Streets and Squares; Palaces; and Parks and Gardens.

The area shaded pink is shown in greater detail on the Street-by-Street map on the following pages.

2 Street-by-Street map
This gives a bird's eye view of the most important parts of each sightseeing area. The numbering of the sights ties in with the area map and the fuller descriptions on the pages that follow.

The list of star sights recommends the places that no visitor should miss.

PRAGUE AREA MAP

The coloured areas shown on this map *(see inside front cover)* are the five main sightseeing areas of Prague – each covered in a full chapter in *Prague Area by Area (pp58–157)*. They are highlighted on other maps throughout the book. In *Prague at a Glance (pp36–57)*, for example, they help locate the top sights. They are also used plot the routes of the river trip *(pp56–7)* and the four guided walks *(p172)*.

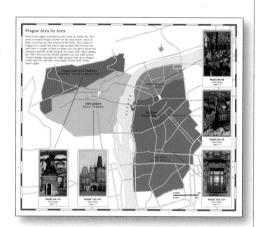

Numbers refer to each sight's position on the area map and its place in the chapter.

Practical information lists all the information you need to visit every sight, including a map reference to the *Street Finder (pp252–7)*.

Façades of important buildings are often shown to help you recognize them quickly.

The visitors' checklist provides all the practical information needed to plan your visit.

3 Detailed information on each sight

All the important sights in Prague are described individually. They are listed in order, following the numbering on the area map. Practical information on opening hours, telephone numbers, admission charges and facilities available is given for each sight. The key to the symbols used can be found on the back flap.

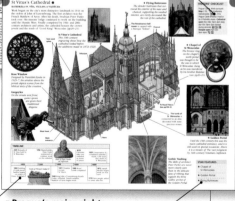

4 Prague's major sights

Historic buildings are dissected to reveal their interiors; and museums and galleries have colour-coded floorplans to help you find important exhibits.

A timeline charts the key events in the history of the building.

Stars indicate the features no visitor should miss.

INTRODUCING PRAGUE

FOUR GREAT DAYS IN PRAGUE

ew cities have as much to offer as Prague, so it can be difficult to decide how best to spend your time. The Old Town is a joy in itself, and you could amble around here admiring its old houses for days. Yet, with some planning you can see much more of

Astronomical clock

what makes this historic city special. Here are four distinct days packed with the best that Prague has to offer. Feel free to mix and match: leaving out a museum or sight will not alter the overall effect. The price guides include cost of travel, food and admission fees.

NATIONAL TREASURES

- Hradčany Square guards
- Lunch in the Little Quarter
- Cross the Charles Bridge
- Watch the Town Hall clock
- Majestic art or church

TWO ADULTS allow at least Kč2,400

Morning
Starting at **Hradčany Square**, admire the Prague Castle guards in their elaborate costumes then walk through První nádvoří to **St Vitus's Cathedral** *(see pp100–3)*, the soul of the Castle. Take a short tour around here before moving on to look at the Baroque art collection in **St George's Convent** *(see pp106–7)*. If you fancy some souvenir shopping, go for the artisans' cottages on **Golden Lane** *(see p99)*. Alternatively, head to **Lobkowicz Palace**, and tour the exhibition

The sumptuous interior of the Spanish synagogue

inside *(see p99)*. Take the easy route along Nerudova to **Little Quarter Square**. Here, enjoy a late lunch and admire the architectural gems of the **Little Quarter** *(see pp124–5)*.

Afternoon
It is a short walk from here to **Charles Bridge** *(see pp136–9)*, and on to Old Town Square. Time your arrival on the hour to see the **Old Town Square's Astronomical Clock** *(see pp72–4)* in action. The **Old Town Hall Tower** *(see p73)* is well worth a visit for amazing views of Prague Castle and the Little Quarter. Next, choose between seeing the art in the Rococo **Kinský Palace** *(see p70)* or the bare majesty of **St Nicholas' Church** *(see pp70–1)*. The narrow streets and shops of the Týn courtyard now await exploration. Enjoy dinner at the **Staroměstská** restaurant, which serves traditional Czech food in elegant surroundings *(see p203)*.

A little respite for visitors at an outdoor café in Old Town Square

LITERARY, ART AND RELIGIOUS LANDMARKS

- "Kafka's café"
- The Jewish Quarter
- Decorative and Medieval Art collections
- Quality shopping

TWO ADULTS allow at least Kč4,560

Morning
Jewish Prague and Franz Kafka are inseparable, so you may want to start the day with a coffee at **Café Grand Praha** *(see p209)* in Old Town Square. Kafka lived above here and the café was once named after his journalist girlfriend, Milena. Refreshed, head along Pařížská into the **Jewish Quarter** *(see pp80–9)*. Stop at the **Maisel Synagogue** *(see p90)*, then cross the road to the historic **Old Jewish Cemetery** *(see pp86–7)*. A good walk around here, as well as a look inside the **Klausen Synagogue** *(see p85)* will set you up for lunch. Try one of the local Jewish restaurants or the non-Jewish **Les Moules** *(see p204)*.

Afternoon

Admire the Gobelin tapestries at the **Museum of Decorative Arts** *(see p84)*. Stroll along to the **Jewish Town Hall** *(see p85)*, and the **Old-New Synagogue** *(see pp88–9)*. The eastern side of the Jewish Quarter is home to two must-see sights: the glorious **Spanish Synagogue** *(see p90)* and the medieval art in **St Agnes of Bohemia Convent** *(see pp92–3)*. After a day of high cultural input, it's time for a little quality shopping on Pařížská – a large thoroughfare in the Jewish Quarter. Eat at **King Solomon,** one of Prague's best Jewish restaurants *(see p204)*.

FAMILY DAY

- **Funicular ride and tower**
- **Mirror Maze**
- **Peacocks and caves**
- **Church of St James**

FAMILY OF 4 allow at least Kč2,900

Morning

Take the funicular railway up **Petřín Hill** *(see p141)*, to see Prague's mini-Eiffel Tower – the **Observation Tower** *(see p140)* which has a spiral staircase to the top. The Mirror Maze *(see p140)*, a short walk away, will keep youngsters happy for a little while, as will the nearby **Observatory** *(see p140)*. Take the funicular halfway back down the hill for lunch at the **Nebozízek** *(see p205)* with its outdoor patio and panoramic views.

The Mirror Maze, great fun for young and old alike

Wenceslas Square and monument in front of the National Museum

Afternoon

Take a stroll on Střelecký Ostrov, where the swans await the remnants of your lunchtime bread. There's more wildlife to be seen at the **Wallenstein Palace** *(see p126)*, home to peacocks and a bizarre replica of a limestone cave. Walk or take the metro over the river to catch the Old Town Square's **Astronomical Clock** *(see pp72–4)* in action. Eat at one of the cafés on the square. Then on to the **Church of St. James** *(see p65)*. Children will be intrigued by the mummified arm, which is hanging above the church entrance for 400 years.

HISTORY AND HEROES

- **Wenceslas Square – the rise and fall of Communism**
- **Lunch in splendid style**
- **Wartime history**
- **Shopping for antiques**

TWO ADULTS allow at least Kč3,060

Morning

Start the day with a walk along **Wenceslas Square** *(see pp144–5)* to see where the communist regime was toppled. Walk the length of the square and imagine it lined with people as it was for weeks in 1989. Pay your respects at the **Monument to the Victims of Communism** *(see p145)*, and to anti-communist martyr Jan Palach, who set himself alight here in 1969 in protest at the Soviet invasion. Just off the Square is the former Gestapo HQ on Politických vězňů (now the national trade office) where thousands of Czechs were imprisoned during WWII. Stop for lunch at the Art Nouveau **Evropa Hotel** *(see p206)* on Wenceslas Square.

Afternoon

Walk to the Baroque **Church of St Cyril and St Methodius** *(see p152)*, where Czech resistance fighters took their own lives in 1942. Bullet holes can still be seen on the wall of the crypt, where a fascinating museum chronicles the events. End the day with a bit of antique browsing. **Military Antiques** in Charvátova *(see p214)*, is a treasure trove of relics from the Nazi and Soviet occupations, and military bric-a-brac from all periods.

Putting Prague on the Map

Prague has a population of just over 1 million and covers 500 sq km (200 sq miles) at its outer limits. It is the capital of the Czech Republic and head of the region of Bohemia. Prague's geographical position at the centre of Europe makes it a convenient base from which to visit both the Bohemian countryside and many other major cities, such as Nuremberg, Vienna, Bratislava and Budapest.

View looking southwest over the Vltava

GERMANY

Berlin

Dresden

Terezín

Praha (PRAGUE)

Karlovy Vary (Karlsbad)

Karlštejn (Karlstein)

Kutná Hora

Plzeň (Pilsen)

Nuremberg

Paris

EUROPE

NORWAY
SWEDEN
FINLAND
ESTONIA
RUSSIAN FEDERATION
UNITED KINGDOM
REP. OF IRELAND
DENMARK
LATVIA
LITHUANIA
NETHERLANDS
POLAND
BELORUSSIA
BELGIUM
GERMANY
Prague
CZECH REPUBLIC
UKRAINE
SLOVAKIA
FRANCE
SWITZ.
AUSTRIA
HUNGARY
MOLDOVA
SLOVENIA
CROATIA
ROMANIA
BOSNIA HERZ.
SERBIA
SPAIN
MONTENEGRO
KOSOVO
BULGARIA
ITALY
ALBANIA
MACEDONIA
GREECE
TURKEY

České Budějovice (Budweis)

Danube

Linz

Salzburg

AUSTRIA

Graz

Europe

The Czech Republic, right at the heart of continental Europe, is completely landlocked. Prague, the capital, has one airport and road and rail links to neighbouring countries.

ITALY

Verona

Drava

PRAGUE AND ENVIRONS

Veltrusy
Neratovice
Slaný
Kralupy n. Vltavou
Brandýs n. Labem-Stará Boleslav
Lysá n. Labem
Švermov
Kladno
Roztoky
Čelákovice
Horní Počernice
Ruzyně
Unhošt
Úvaly
Český Brod
Rudná
Zbraslav
Říčany

0 km 10
0 miles 5

Beroun
Karlštejn
Jilové u Prahy
Řevnice

Prague and Environs

Most sights are in the central, historic area of Prague. These are covered in detail on pages 58–157. Important sights outside the centre and day trips can be found on pages 159–71. For road and rail networks, see pages 238–9.

POLAND

Oder
Warsaw
Wrocław

CZECH REPUBLIC

Elbe

Cracow
Ostrava
48
46
Brno
Morava

Aerial view of Greater Prague

VIENNA
BRATISLAVA
SLOVAKIA
Váh

HUNGARY
Rába
BUDAPEST

Lake Balaton
Zagreb

KEY

☐	Greater Prague
✈	Airport
▬	Motorway
▬	Major road
—	Railway line
–·–	Country boundary

0 kilometres 50
0 miles 30

Central Prague

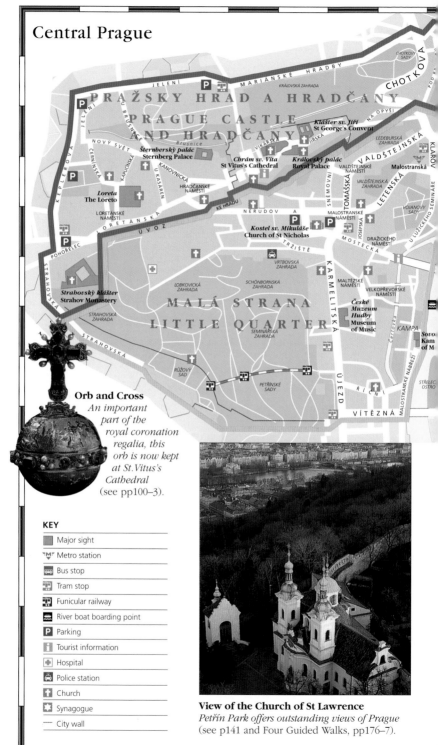

PRAŽSKÝ HRAD A HRADČANY
PRAGUE CASTLE AND HRADČANY

Klášter sv. Jiří
St George's Convent

Šternberský palác
Sternberg Palace

Chrám sv. Víta
St Vitus's Cathedral

Královský palác
Royal Palace

Malostranská

Loreta
The Loreto

Kostel sv. Mikuláše
Church of St Nicholas

Strahovský klášter
Strahov Monastery

MALÁ STRANA
LITTLE QUARTER

České Muzeum Hudby
Museum of Music

Orb and Cross
An important part of the royal coronation regalia, this orb is now kept at St.Vitus's Cathedral (see pp100–3).

KEY

▪	Major sight
Ⓜ	Metro station
🚌	Bus stop
🚊	Tram stop
🚡	Funicular railway
🚢	River boat boarding point
P	Parking
ℹ	Tourist information
✚	Hospital
👮	Police station
✝	Church
✡	Synagogue
—	City wall

View of the Church of St Lawrence
Petřín Park offers outstanding views of Prague (see p141 and Four Guided Walks, pp176–7).

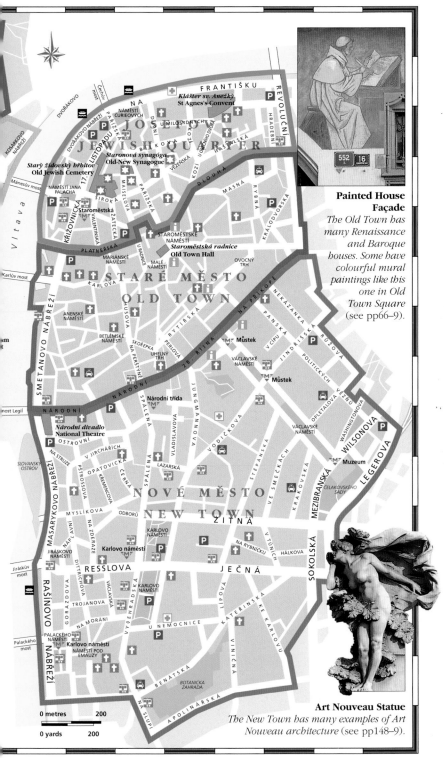

FRANTIŠKU

Klášter sv. Anežky
St Agnes's Convent

NA

JOSEFOV
JEWISH QUARTER

Staronová synagóga
Old-New Synagogue

Starý židovský hřbitov
Old Jewish Cemetery

NÁMĚSTÍ JANA
PALACHA

Staroměstská

STAROMĚSTSKÉ
NÁMĚSTÍ

Staroměstská radnice
Old Town Hall

MARIÁNSKÉ
NÁMĚSTÍ

MALÉ
NÁMĚSTÍ

OVOCNÝ
TRH

STARÉ MĚSTO
OLD TOWN

ANENSKÉ
NÁMĚSTÍ

NA PŘÍKOPĚ

BETLÉMSKÉ
NÁMĚSTÍ

Můstek

UHELNÝ
TRH

VÁCLAVSKÉ
NÁMĚSTÍ

Můstek

Národní třída

Národní divadlo
National Theatre

VÁCLAVSKÉ
NÁMĚSTÍ

Muzeum

NOVÉ MĚSTO
NEW TOWN

ŽITNÁ

KARLOVO
NÁMĚSTÍ

Karlovo náměstí

RESSLOVA

JEČNÁ

KARLOVO
NÁMĚSTÍ

U NEMOCNICE

PALACKÉHO
NÁMĚSTÍ

Karlovo náměstí

NÁMĚSTÍ POD
EMAUZY

BOTANICKÁ
ZAHRADA

| 0 metres | 200 |
| 0 yards | 200 |

Painted House Façade
The Old Town has many Renaissance and Baroque houses. Some have colourful mural paintings like this one in Old Town Square (see pp66–9).

Art Nouveau Statue
The New Town has many examples of Art Nouveau architecture (see pp148–9).

THE HISTORY OF PRAGUE

Prague's position at the crossroads of Europe has made it a magnet for foreign traders since prehistoric times. By the early 10th century Prague had become a thriving town with a large market place, the Old Town Square, and two citadels, Prague Castle and Vyšehrad, from where its first rulers, the Přemyslids, conducted their many family feuds. These were often bloody: in AD 935, Prince Wenceslas was murdered by his brother Boleslav. Wenceslas was later canonized and became the Czechs' best-known patron saint.

Prague coat of arms

During the Middle Ages Prague prospered, especially during the reign of the Holy Roman Emperor, Charles IV. Under the government of this wise and cultured ruler, Prague grew into a magnificent city, larger than Paris or London. Charles instigated the founding and building of many institutions in Prague, including the first university in Central Europe, Charles University. One of the University's first Czech rectors was Jan Hus, the reforming preacher whose execution for alleged heresy in 1415 led to the Hussite wars. The radical wing of the Hussites, the Taborites, were finally defeated at the Battle of Lipany in 1434. During the 16th century, after a succession of weak kings, the Habsburgs gained control, beginning a rule that would last for almost 400 years. One of the more enlightened of all the Habsburg Emperors was Rudolph II. He brought the spirit of the Renaissance to Prague through his love of the arts and sciences. Soon after his death, in 1618, Prague was the setting for the Protestant revolt which led to the Thirty Years' War. The war's aftermath caused a serious decline in the fortunes of the city that would revive only in the 18th century. Prague's many fine Baroque churches and palaces date from this time.

The 19th century saw a period of national revival and the burgeoning of civic pride. The great public monuments – the National Museum, the National Theatre and Rudolfinum – were built. But the Habsburgs still ruled the city, and it was not until 1918 that Prague became the capital of an independent Republic. World War II brought occupation by the German army, followed by four decades of Communism. After the "Velvet Revolution" of 1989, Prague is today on the threshold of a new era.

View of Prague Castle and Little Quarter, 1493

◁ *St Wenceslas and St Vitus*, by Bartholomaeus Spränger, about 1600

Rulers of Prague

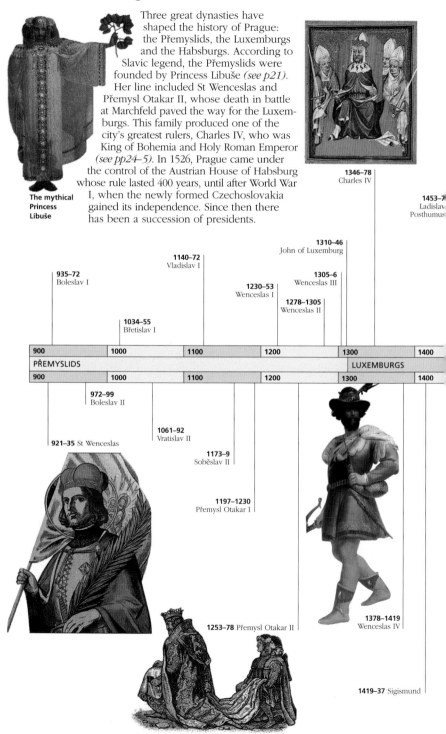

Three great dynasties have shaped the history of Prague: the Přemyslids, the Luxemburgs and the Habsburgs. According to Slavic legend, the Přemyslids were founded by Princess Libuše *(see p21)*. Her line included St Wenceslas and Přemysl Otakar II, whose death in battle at Marchfeld paved the way for the Luxemburgs. This family produced one of the city's greatest rulers, Charles IV, who was King of Bohemia and Holy Roman Emperor *(see pp24–5)*. In 1526, Prague came under the control of the Austrian House of Habsburg whose rule lasted 400 years, until after World War I, when the newly formed Czechoslovakia gained its independence. Since then there has been a succession of presidents.

The mythical Princess Libuše

1346–78
Charles IV

1453–7
Ladislav Posthumus

1310–46
John of Luxembourg

1140–72
Vladislav I

1305–6
Wenceslas III

935–72
Boleslav I

1230–53
Wenceslas I

1278–1305
Wenceslas II

1034–55
Břetislav I

900	1000	1100	1200	1300	1400
PŘEMYSLIDS				LUXEMBURGS	
900	1000	1100	1200	1300	1400

972–99
Boleslav II

1061–92
Vratislav II

921–35 St Wenceslas

1173–9
Soběslav II

1197–1230
Přemysl Otakar I

1253–78 Přemysl Otakar II

1378–1419
Wenceslas IV

1419–37 Sigismund

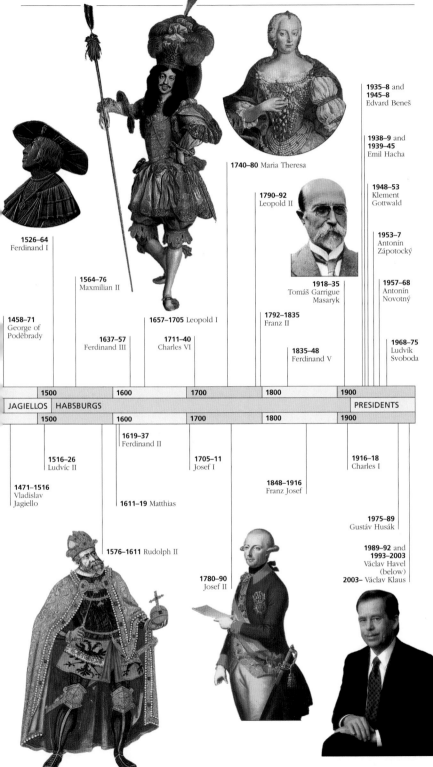

1935–8 and
1945–8
Edvard Beneš

1938–9 and
1939–45
Emil Hacha

1740–80 Maria Theresa

1948–53
Klement
Gottwald

1790–92
Leopold II

1953–7
Antonín
Zápotocký

1526–64
Ferdinand I

1957–68
Antonín
Novotný

1564–76
Maxmilian II

1918–35
Tomáš Garrigue
Masaryk

1458–71
George of
Poděbrady

1657–1705 Leopold I

1792–1835
Franz II

1968–75
Ludvík
Svoboda

1637–57
Ferdinand III

1711–40
Charles VI

1835–48
Ferdinand V

1500	1600	1700	1800	1900

JAGIELLOS	HABSBURGS			PRESIDENTS

1500	1600	1700	1800	1900

1619–37
Ferdinand II

1516–26
Ludvíc II

1705–11
Josef I

1916–18
Charles I

1471–1516
Vladislav
Jagiello

1848–1916
Franz Josef

1611–19 Matthias

1975–89
Gustáv Husák

1576–1611 Rudolph II

1989–92 and
1993–2003
Václav Havel
(below)
2003– Václav Klaus

1780–90
Josef II

Prague under the Přemyslids

Early Celtic tribes, from 500 BC, were the first inhabitants of the area around the Vltava valley. The Germanic Marcomans arrived in 9–6 BC, and gradually the Celts left. The first Slavic tribes came to Bohemia in about 500 AD. Struggles for supremacy led to the emergence of a ruling dynasty, the Přemyslids, around 800 AD. They built two fortified settlements: the first at Prague Castle *(see pp94–111)*, the second at Vyšehrad, a rocky headland on the right bank of the Vltava *(see pp180–1)*. These remained the seats of Czech princes for hundreds of years. One prince crucial to the emerging Czech State was the pious Wenceslas. He enjoyed only a brief reign but left an important legacy in the founding of St Vitus's rotunda *(see p102)*.

EXTENT OF THE CITY

☐ *1000 AD*   ☐ *Today*

Boleslav's henchman raises his sword to strike the fatal blow.

St Cyril and St Methodius
Originally Greeks from Salonica, these two brothers brought Christianity to Moravia in about 863. They baptized early Přemyslid, Bořivoj, and his wife Ludmilla, grandmother of St Wenceslas.

Second assassin grapples with the Prince's companion.

Early Coin
Silver coins like this denar were minted in the royal mint of Vyšehrad during Boleslav II's reign from 967–99.

Wild Boar Figurine
Celtic tribes made small talismans of the wild animals that they hunted for food in the forested areas around Prague.

TIMELINE

Bronze head of a Celtic goddess

623–658 Bohemia is part of an empire formed by Frankish merchant, Samo

| 500 BC | 600 AD | 700 |

500 BC Celts in Bohemia. Joined by Germanic Marcomans in 1st century AD

6th century Slavs settle alongside Germanic tribes in Bohemia

8th century Tribe of Czechs settle in central Bohemia

Vyšehrad acropolis – first Czech settlement on the right bank of the Vltava

Sword and Helmet
St Wenceslas was buried in the southern apse of the rotunda of St Vitus. His sword and helmet were preserved as relics and today form part of the Cathedral's treasure.

Wenceslas seeks sanctuary.

A monk closes the door against Wenceslas.

PRINCESS LIBUŠE
The legendary founder of the Přemyslids was Princess Libuše, head of a West Slavic tribe. She took notice of the discord among her clansmen, and succeeded her father to become the first woman ruler. Choosing a humble plough-man (*Přemysl-Oráč*) as consort and ruler, she began a dynasty that was to last 400 years.

Princess Libuše foresaw the glory of Prague in a vision

Rotunda of St Vitus
Founded by Wenceslas in the early 10th century, the rotunda became a place of pilgrimage after the saint's death in 935. It stood where St Wenceslas Chapel is today.

Roman-arched windows

Curving stone walls

ASSASSINATION OF PRINCE WENCESLAS
In 935, the young Wenceslas was murdered on the orders of his brother, Boleslav. This manuscript illustration of 1006 shows the moment when the assassins caught up with the prince as he was about to enter the church for the morning mass.

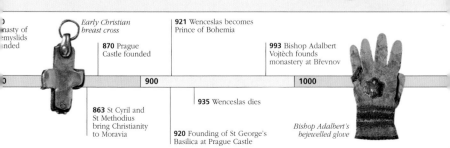

…nasty of …emyslids …nded

Early Christian breast cross

870 Prague Castle founded

921 Wenceslas becomes Prince of Bohemia

993 Bishop Adalbert Vojtèch founds monastery at Břevnov

900

1000

863 St Cyril and St Methodius bring Christianity to Moravia

935 Wenceslas dies

920 Founding of St George's Basilica at Prague Castle

Bishop Adalbert's bejewelled glove

Early Medieval Prague

EXTENT OF THE CITY

☐ *1230*　　☐ *Today*

Prague Castle steadily grew in importance from the beginning of the 9th century onwards. Prone to frequent fires, its wooden buildings were gradually replaced by stone and the area developed into a sturdy Romanesque fortress with a palace and religious buildings. Clustered around the original outer bailey was an area inhabited by skilled craftsmen and German merchants, encouraged to come and stay in Prague by Vladislav II and, later, Přemysl Otakar II. This came to be known as the "Little Quarter" and achieved town status in 1257. It was joined to the Old Town by a bridge, known as the Judith Bridge.

Initial letter D from the Vyšehrad Codex

St George's Convent and Basilica *(see pp106–9 and p98)*

PRAGUE CASTLE IN 1230

Sited on a high ridge, the Romanesque fortress had protective stone walls and easily-guarded gates.

The Prince's Palace grew into the Royal Palace *(see pp104–5).*

The White Tower gave access from the west.

Entrance from Old Town

Decorative Comb
This ornate, bone, fine-toothed comb was one of the relics of St Adalbert.

Site of Hradčany Square

External staircase

Living room

Vaulted ceiling

Romanesque Stone House
These three-storeyed houses were based around a very simple floor plan.

Ground floor

St Vitus's Basilica and Chapter House *(see pp100–3)*

Stone houses were built on what is now Nerudova Street in the Little Quarter *(see p130).*

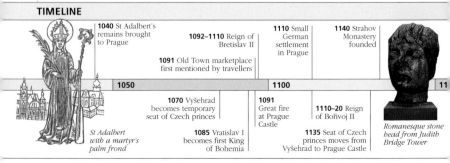

TIMELINE

1040 St Adalbert's remains brought to Prague

1092–1110 Reign of Bretislav II

1110 Small German settlement in Prague

1140 Strahov Monastery founded

1091 Old Town marketplace first mentioned by travellers

1050

1100

11

1070 Vyšehrad becomes temporary seat of Czech princes

1091 Great fire at Prague Castle

1110–20 Reign of Bořivoj II

St Adalbert with a martyr's palm frond

1085 Vratislav I becomes first King of Bohemia

1135 Seat of Czech princes moves from Vyšehrad to Prague Castle

Romanesque stone head from Judith Bridge Tower

St Agnes of Bohemia
Sister of Wenceslas I, this devout woman built a convent for the order of the Poor Clares (the female counterparts of the Franciscans) (see pp92–3). She was not canonized until 1989.

WHERE TO SEE ROMANESQUE PRAGUE

Remains can be seen in the crypt of St Vitus's *(pp100–3)*, the basements of the Palace of the Lords of Kunštát *(p78)* and the Royal Palace *(pp104–5)*.

St George's Basilica
The vaulting in the crypt dates from the 12th century (p98).

St Martin's Rotunda
This well-preserved building is in Vyšehrad (p180).

The Black Tower was the exit to Bohemia's second town, Kutná Hora *(see p168).*

Vratislav II
The Vyšehrad Codex, an illuminated selection from the gospels, was made to mark Vratislav's coronation in 1061.

Little Quarter Square

Little Quarter Coat of Arms
Vladislav II's portrait was incorporated into this 16th-century miniature painting.

Přemysl Otakar II
The last great Přemyslid king was killed in battle after trying to carve out a huge empire.

1233 Founding of St Agnes's Convent

1182 Romanesque construction of Prague Castle completed

1257 Little Quarter receives town status

1258–68 Strahov Monastery rebuilt in Gothic style after fire

1200

1250

1290

1212 Přemysl Otakar I receives the Sicilian Golden Bull, confirming the sovereignty of Bohemian kings

Sicilian Golden Bull

1278 Přemysl Otakar II dies at Marchfeld

1158 Judith Bridge built *(see pp136–9)*

Prague's Golden Age

Gift from Pope Urban V in 1368

In the late Middle Ages, Prague attained the height of its glory. The Holy Roman Emperor Charles IV chose Prague as his Imperial residence and set out to make the city the most magnificent in Europe. He founded a university (the Carolinum) and built many fine churches and monasteries in the Gothic style. Of major importance were his town-planning schemes, such as the reconstruction of Prague Castle, the building of a new stone bridge to replace the Judith Bridge, and the foundation of a new quarter, the New Town. A devout Catholic, he owned a large collection of relics which were kept, along with the Crown Jewels, at Karlstein Castle *(see pp168–9)*.

EXTENT OF THE CITY
- 1350
- Today

Charles IV wears the Imperial crown, set with sapphires, rubies and pearls.

St Wenceslas Chapel
Proud of his direct descent from the Přemyslids, Charles had this shrine to St Wenceslas built in St Vitus's Cathedral (see pp100–3).

The Emperor places the piece of the cross in its reliquary.

St Wenceslas Crown
Worn by Charles at his coronation in 1347, the Bohemian crown was based on early Přemyslid insignia.

TIMELINE

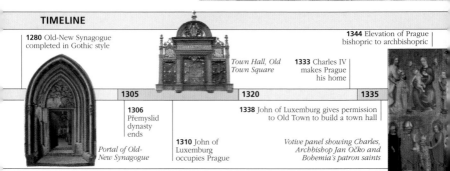

1280 Old-New Synagogue completed in Gothic style

Town Hall, Old Town Square

1333 Charles IV makes Prague his home

1344 Elevation of Prague bishopric to archbishopric

1305	1320	1335

1306 Přemyslid dynasty ends

Portal of Old-New Synagogue

1310 John of Luxemburg occupies Prague

1338 John of Luxemburg gives permission to Old Town to build a town hall

Votive panel showing Charles, Archbishop Jan Očko and Bohemia's patron saints

St Vitus by Master Theodoric
This is one of a series of paintings of saints by the great Bohemian artist for the Holy Rood Chapel at Karlstein Castle (c1365).

University Seal, 1348
The seal depicts the Emperor offering the foundation documents to St Wenceslas.

A jewelled reliquary cross was made to house the new relic.

Building the New Town
This manuscript records Charles IV supervising the building of the New Town during the 14th century.

CHARLES IV AND HIS RELICS

Charles collected holy relics from all over the Empire. In about 1357 he received a part of Christ's cross from the Dauphin. This mural in Karlstein Castle is thought to be the best likeness of the Emperor.

WHERE TO SEE GOTHIC PRAGUE

Prague's rich Gothic legacy includes three of its best-known sights – St Vitus's Cathedral *(pp100–3)*, Charles Bridge *(pp136–9)* and the Old-New Synagogue *(pp88–9)*. Another very important building from Charles IV's reign is the Carolinum *(p65)*. Churches that have retained most of their original Gothic features include the Church of Our Lady before Týn *(p70)*.

Carolinum
This fine oriel window was part of the university (p65).

Old Town Bridge Tower
The sculptural decoration is by Peter Parler (p139).

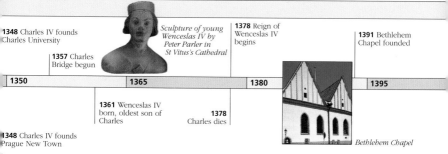

1348 Charles IV founds Charles University

1357 Charles Bridge begun

Sculpture of young Wenceslas IV by Peter Parler in St Vitus's Cathedral

1378 Reign of Wenceslas IV begins

1391 Bethlehem Chapel founded

| 1350 | 1365 | 1380 | 1395 |

1361 Wenceslas IV born, oldest son of Charles

1378 Charles dies

1348 Charles IV founds Prague New Town

Bethlehem Chapel

Hussite Prague

In the early 15th century, Europe shook in fear of an incredible fighting force – the Hussites, followers of the reformist cleric, Jan Hus. Despite simple weapons, they achieved legendary military successes against the Emperor's Catholic crusades, due largely to their religious fervour and to the discipline of their brilliant leader, Jan Žižka, who

George of Poděbrady

invented mobile artillery. The Hussites split into two camps, the moderate "Utraquists" *(see p75)* and the radical "Taborites" who were finally defeated at the Battle of Lipany in 1434, paving the way for the moderate Hussite king, George of Poděbrady.

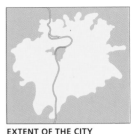

EXTENT OF THE CITY

☐ 1500   ☐ Today

Nobles' Letter of Protest
Several hundred seals of the Bohemian nobility were affixed to a letter protesting about the execution of Jan Hus.

GOD'S WARRIORS

The early-16th-century Codex of Jena illustrated the Hussite successes. Here the Hussites, who included artisans and barons, are shown singing their hymn, with their blind leader, Jan Žižka.

Jan Žižka

The priest held a gilded monstrance.

War Machine
For maximum effect, farm waggons were tied together to form a shield. A chilling array of weapons were unleashed including crossbows, flails and an early form of howitzer.

TIMELINE

Jan Hus preaching

1402–13 Jan Hus preaches at Bethlehem Chapel *(see p75)*

1415 Jan Hus burned at the stake at Constance

1419 Defenestration of councillors from New Town Hall

1434 Battle of Lipany

The Taborites made lethal weapons from simple farm tools

1400	1420	1440

1410 Jan Hus excommunicated. Building of Old Town Clock

The chalice, symbol of the Utraquists

1420 Hussites victorious under Jan Žižka at Vitkov and Vyšehrad

1424 Jan Žižka dies

1448 Prague conquered by troops of George of Poděbrady

Satan Dressed as the Pope
Lurid images satirizing the corruption of the church were painted on placards and carried through the streets.

The banner was decorated with the Hussite chalice.

A variety of farm implements were used as makeshift weapons by the peasants.

Hussite Shield
Wooden shields like this one that bears the arms of the city of Prague, were used to fill any gaps in the waggon fortress's tight formation.

The peasant army marched behind Jan Žižka.

REFORMER, JAN HUS

Born to poor parents in a small Bohemian town, Jan Hus became one of the most important religious thinkers of his day. His objections to the Catholic Church's corrupt practices, opulent style and wealth were shared by many Czechs – nobles and peasants alike. His reformist preaching in Prague's Bethlehem Chapel earned him a huge following, noticed by the Roman Papacy, and Hus was excommunicated. In 1412 Wenceslas IV, brother of the Emperor Sigismund, asked him to leave Prague. In October 1414, Hus decided to defend his teaching at the Council of Constance. Even though he had the Emperor's safe conduct, he was put in prison. The following year he was declared a heretic and burned at the stake.

Jan Hus at the Stake in 1415
After suffering death at the hands of the Church on 6 July 1415, Jan Hus became a revered martyr of the Czech people.

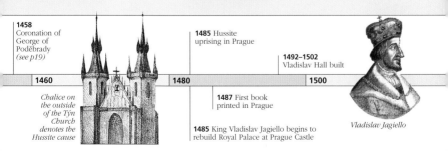

1458 Coronation of George of Poděbrady *(see p19)*

Chalice on the outside of the Týn Church denotes the Hussite cause

1485 Hussite uprising in Prague

1492–1502 Vladislav Hall built

1460   **1480**   **1500**

1487 First book printed in Prague

1485 King Vladislav Jagiello begins to rebuild Royal Palace at Prague Castle

Vladislav Jagiello

The Renaissance and Rudolph II

With the accession of the Habsburgs, the Renaissance reached Prague. Art and architecture were dominated by the Italians who enjoyed the patronage of the Imperial court, especially that of Rudolph II. The eccentric Rudolph often neglected politics, preferring to indulge his passions for collecting and science. His court was a haven for artists, astrologers, astronomers and alchemists, but his erratic rule led to revolts and an attempt by his brother Matthias to usurp him. In the course of the Thirty Years' War *(see pp30–31)* many works of art from Rudolph's collection were looted.

Renaissance tankard

EXTENT OF THE CITY

☐ *1550*   ☐ *Today*

Fish pond

Dalibor Tower

Belvedere

Pergola

Rudolph II
A connoisseur of the bizarre, Rudolph was delighted by this vegetable portrait by Giuseppe Arcimboldo (1590).

Orchard

Formal flower beds

Lion House

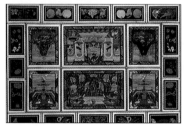

Mosaic Desk Top
Renaissance table tops with Florentine themes of fountains and gardens were made at Rudolph's court in semi-precious stones.

Rabbi Löw
A revered Jewish sage, he was said to have invented an artificial man (see pp88–9).

TIMELINE

1502 Vladislav Hall built	**1526** Habsburg rule begins with Ferdinand I	**1541** Great fire in Little Quarter, the Castle and Hradčany	**1556** Ferdinand I invites Jesuits to Prague
1520		**1540**	**1560**

Ferdinand I

1538–63 Belvedere built

1547 Unsuccessful uprising of towns of Prague against Ferdinand I

Vladislav Hall

Charter for manglers and dyers

Sense of Sight
Jan Brueghel's allegorical painting shows the extent of Rudolph II's huge collection – from globes to paintings, jewels and scientific instruments.

Tycho Brahe
The Danish astronomer spent his last years living in Prague.

Ball Game Hall

A covered bridge connected the Palace to the garden.

ROYAL PALACE GARDENS

No longer a medieval fortress, Prague Castle and its gardens were given over to the pleasure of the King. Here Rudolph enjoyed ball games, exotic plants and his menagerie.

WHERE TO SEE RENAISSANCE PRAGUE

The Royal Garden *(p111)* preserves much of the spirit of Renaissance Prague. Paintings and objects from Rudolph's collections can be seen in the Sternberg Palace *(pp112–15)*, the Picture Gallery of Prague Castle *(p98)* and the Museum of Decorative Arts *(p84)*.

At the Two Golden Bears
Built in 1590, the house is famous for its symmetrical, carved doorway, one of the most graceful in Prague (p71).

Belvedere
The palace is decorated with stone reliefs by Italian architect, Paolo della Stella (p110).

Ball Game Hall
Beautiful Renaissance sgraffito covers the façade of this building in the Royal Garden, but it has been heavily restored (p111).

1583 Prague becomes seat of Imperial court of Rudolph II; great art collection begun

1614 Matthias Gate at Prague Castle built

1618 Defenestration of two royal governors from Royal Palace *(see p105)*

1580

1600

1620

A ten-ducat coin (1603)

1609 Publication of Rudolph's Imperial Charter on religious freedom

1612 Rudolph II dies

Baroque Prague

In 1619 the Czech nobles deposed Habsburg Emperor Ferdinand II as King of Bohemia and elected instead the Protestant ruler Frederick of the Palatinate. The following year they paid for their defiance at the Battle of the White Mountain, the beginning of the Thirty Years' War. There followed a period of persecution of all non-Catholics, accompanied by the Germanization of the country's institutions. The leaders in the fight against Protestantism were the Jesuits and one of their most powerful weapons was the restoration of Prague's churches in Baroque style. Many new churches also adopted this style.

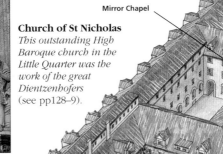

EXTENT OF THE CITY

◻	*1750*	◻	*Today*

A sculpture of Atlas (1722) adorns the top of the tower.

Mirror Chapel

Church of St Nicholas
This outstanding High Baroque church in the Little Quarter was the work of the great Dientzenhofers (see pp128–9).

Grape Courtyard

Measuring the World
Some monasteries were seats of learning. Strahov (see pp120–21) had two libraries built, decorated with Baroque painting. This fresco detail is in the Philosophical Hall.

Holy Saviour Church

TIMELINE

1620 Battle of the White Mountain		*Old Town coat of arms – embellished with the Imperial eagle and 12 flags in recognition of the defence of the city against the Swedes*		**1706–14** Decoration of Charles Bridge with statues
	1627 Beginning of Counter-Reformation committee in Prague			

1625	**1645**	**1665**	**1685**	**1705**

1621 Execution in Old Town Square of 27 Protestant leaders	**1634** Wallenstein killed by Irish mercenaries	**1648** Swedes occupy Prague Castle. Treaty of Westphalia and end of Thirty Years' War			**1704–53** Building of Church of St Nicholas in the Little Quarter
	1631 Saxon occupation of Prague		**1676–8** New bastions built to fortify Vyšehrad		

Battle of the White Mountain
In 1620 the Czech army was defeated by Habsburg troops at Bílá Hora (White Mountain), a hill northwest of Prague (see p163). After the battle, Bohemia became a de facto province of Austria.

Observatory Tower

St Clement's Church gave its name to the whole complex.

Italian Chapel

Monstrance
Baroque monstrances – used to display the communion host – became increasingly elaborate and ornate (see pp116–17).

CLEMENTINUM
The Jesuits exercised enormous power over education. Between 1653 and 1723 they built this College. It was the largest complex of buildings after Prague Castle and included three churches, smaller chapels, libraries, lecture halls and an observatory.

WHERE TO SEE BAROQUE PRAGUE
The Baroque is everywhere in Prague. Almost all the churches were built or remodelled in Baroque style, the finest being St Nicholas *(pp128–9)*. There are also the grand palaces and smaller houses of the Little Quarter *(pp122–41)*, the façades in the Old Town *(pp60–79)*, and statues on churches, street corners and along the parapets of Charles Bridge.

Nerudova Street
At the Golden Cup, No. 16, has preserved its typical Baroque house sign (p130).

Charles Bridge
This statue of St Francis Borgia by Ferdinand Brokof was added in 1710 (pp136–9).

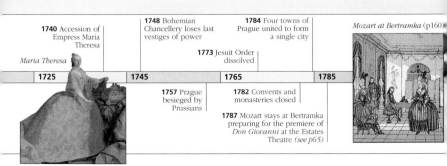

1740 Accession of Empress Maria Theresa

Maria Theresa

1748 Bohemian Chancellery loses last vestiges of power

1773 Jesuit Order dissolved

1784 Four towns of Prague united to form a single city

Mozart at Bertramka (p160)

1725 1745 1765 1785

1757 Prague besieged by Prussians

1782 Convents and monasteries closed

1787 Mozart stays at Bertramka preparing for the premiere of *Don Giovanni* at the Estates Theatre *(see p65)*

The National Revival in Prague

Emperor Franz Josef

The 19th century was one of the most glorious periods in the history of Prague. Austrian rule relaxed, allowing the Czech nation to rediscover its own history and culture. Silent for so long, Czech was re-established as an official language. Civic pride was rekindled with the building of the capital's great showpieces, such as the National Theatre, which utilized the talents of Czech architects and artists. The Jewish Quarter and New Town underwent extensive redevelopment and, with the introduction of public transport, Prague grew beyond its ancient limits.

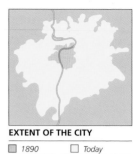

EXTENT OF THE CITY

☐ 1890   ☐ Today

Smetana's Libuše
Written for the scheduled opening of the National Theatre in 1881, the opera drew on early Czech legend (see pp20–21).

Rudolfinum
A major concert venue beside the Vltava, the building (see p84) is richly decorated with symbols of the art of music.

Days of the year

Months and zodiac signs revolve around the centre.

Old Town coat of arms

OLD TOWN CLOCK TOWER CALENDAR
In 1866, the revolving dial on Prague's most enduring landmark was replaced by a new one by celebrated artist, Josef Mánes. His studies of Bohemian peasant life are incorporated into pictures symbolizing the months of the year.

TIMELINE

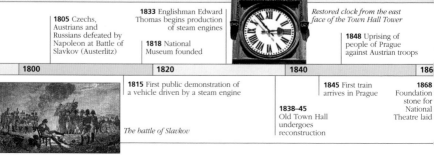

1805 Czechs, Austrians and Russians defeated by Napoleon at Battle of Slavkov (Austerlitz)

1833 Englishman Edward Thomas begins production of steam engines

1818 National Museum founded

Restored clock from the east face of the Town Hall Tower

1848 Uprising of people of Prague against Austrian troops

1800	1820	1840	186

The battle of Slavkov

1815 First public demonstration of a vehicle driven by a steam engine

1838–45 Old Town Hall undergoes reconstruction

1845 First train arrives in Prague

1868 Foundation stone for National Theatre laid

Expo 95 Poster
Vojtěch Hynais designed this poster for the ethnographic exhibition of folk culture in 1895. In the Art Nouveau style, it reflected the new appreciation of regional traditions.

WHERE TO SEE THE NATIONAL REVIVAL

Many of Prague's remarkable monuments, the National Museum for example, were built around this period. One fine example of Art Nouveau architecture is the Municipal House *(p64)*, where the Mayor's Room has murals by Mucha. The Rudolfinum *(p84)* and the National Theatre *(pp156–7)* have gloriously-decorated interiors by great artists of the day. The Prague Museum has many objects from the late 19th and early 20th centuries as well as the original painting for Mánes' Old Town Clock.

December   Sagittarius

Municipal House
Allegories of civic virtues painted by Alfons Mucha adorn this Art Nouveau interior.

Jewish Quarter
From 1897 onwards, the slum housing of the ghetto was replaced with new apartment blocks.

National Museum
The Neo-Renaissance façade dominates the skyline (p147).

National Theatre
The décor has murals by Czech artists, including Aleš (pp156–7).

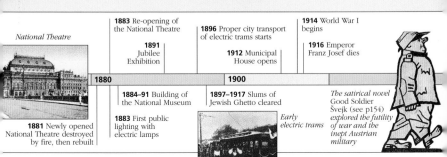

National Theatre

1883 Re-opening of the National Theatre

1891 Jubilee Exhibition

1896 Proper city transport of electric trams starts

1912 Municipal House opens

1914 World War I begins

1916 Emperor Franz Josef dies

1880   **1900**

1884–91 Building of the National Museum

1883 First public lighting with electric lamps

1897–1917 Slums of Jewish Ghetto cleared

Early electric trams

The satirical novel Good Soldier Švejk (see p154) explored the futility of war and the inept Austrian military

1881 Newly opened National Theatre destroyed by fire, then rebuilt

Prague after Independence

Letná Park metronome

Just 20 years after its foundation in 1918, the Czechoslovak Republic was helplessly caught up in the political manoeuvring that preceded Nazi domination of Europe. Prague emerged from World War II almost unscathed by bombings, no longer part of a Nazi protectorate but of a Socialist republic. Any resistance was brutally suppressed. Ultimately, the intellectuals spoke out, demanding observance of civil rights. Denial of such rights led these dissidents to unite and prepare for the "Velvet Revolution". In the end, it was a playwright, Václav Havel, who was swept into power at Prague Castle to lead the country at the start of a long and often difficult return to independence.

1968 Alexander Dubček elected to post of First Secretary

1966 Jiří Menzel's *Closely Observed Trains* wins Oscar for Best Foreign Film, drawing the world's attention to Czech cinema

1935 Edvard Beneš succeeds Masaryk as President. Nazi-funded Sudeten German Party, led by Konrad Henlein, makes election gains

1920 Avant-garde left-wing artists form Devětsil movement in Prague's Union Café

Edvard Beneš

1938 Munich Agreement hands over parts of Republic to Hitler. Beneš flees country

1945 Soviet Red Army enters Prague on 9 May to rapturous welcome, following four days of uprisings. In October, provisional National Assembly set up under Beneš

1952 Most famous of many show trials under Gottwald, Slánský Trial sends 11 senior politicians to gallows as Trotskyites and traitors

1962 Statue of Stalin in Letná Park demolished (replaced, in 1991, by a giant metronome)

1918	1930	1945	1960

1918	1930	1945	1960

1924 Death of Franz Kafka, author of *The Trial*

1918 Foundation of Czechoslovak Republic. Tomáš Masaryk first democratically-elected President

1932 Traditional gymnastic rally or *slet* takes place at Strahov stadium

1942 Tyrannical Nazi "Protector" for only eight months, Reinhard Heydrich assassinated by Czech resistance

1948 Communist Party assumes power under Klement Gottwald; announces 89% support in May elections

1958 Premiere of innovative animated film, *The Invention of Destruction* directed by Karel Zeman

1955 Largest statue of Stalin in the world unveiled in Letná Park, overlooking city

1960 Czechoslovak Socialist Republic (ČSSR) proclaimed

1967 First Secretary and President, Antonín Novotný, imprisons dissident writers

1968 Moderate Alexander Dubček adopts the programme of liberal reforms known as "Prague Spring". On 21 August, Warsaw Pact occupies Czechoslovakia and over 100 protesters are killed as troops enter Prague

POZDRAV

TOMÁŠI G. MASARYKOVI

Welcome Home poster, to mark the President's return on 21 December 1918

1939 German troops march into Prague; city declared capital of Nazi Protectorate of Bohemia and Moravia. Emil Hácha is President under the German protectorate

1969 Jan Palach burns to death in protest at Soviet occupation

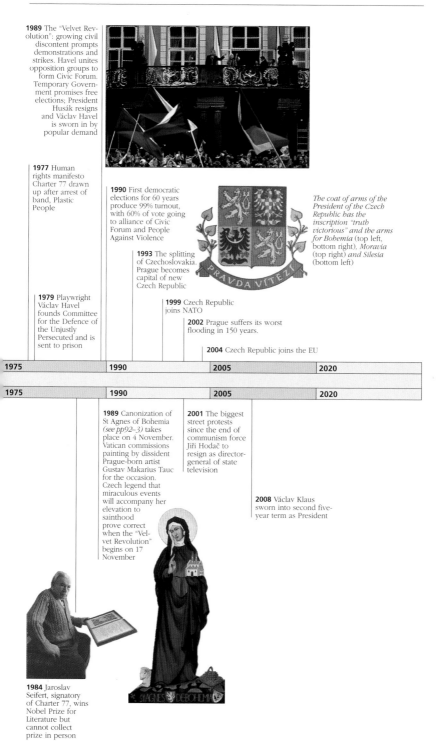

1989 The "Velvet Revolution": growing civil discontent prompts demonstrations and strikes. Havel unites opposition groups to form Civic Forum. Temporary Government promises free elections; President Husák resigns and Václav Havel is sworn in by popular demand

1977 Human rights manifesto Charter 77 drawn up after arrest of band, Plastic People

1990 First democratic elections for 60 years produce 99% turnout, with 60% of vote going to alliance of Civic Forum and People Against Violence

1993 The splitting of Czechoslovakia. Prague becomes capital of new Czech Republic

The coat of arms of the President of the Czech Republic has the inscription "truth victorious" and the arms for Bohemia (top left, bottom right), Moravia (top right) and Silesia (bottom left)

1979 Playwright Václav Havel founds Committee for the Defence of the Unjustly Persecuted and is sent to prison

1999 Czech Republic joins NATO

2002 Prague suffers its worst flooding in 150 years.

2004 Czech Republic joins the EU

1975	1990	2005	2020

1975	1990	2005	2020

1989 Canonization of St Agnes of Bohemia *(see pp92–3)* takes place on 4 November. Vatican commissions painting by dissident Prague-born artist Gustav Makarius Tauc for the occasion. Czech legend that miraculous events will accompany her elevation to sainthood prove correct when the "Velvet Revolution" begins on 17 November

2001 The biggest street protests since the end of communism force Jiří Hodač to resign as director-general of state television

2008 Václav Klaus sworn into second five-year term as President

1984 Jaroslav Seifert, signatory of Charter 77, wins Nobel Prize for Literature but cannot collect prize in person

PRAGUE AT A GLANCE

There are almost 150 places of interest described in the *Area by Area* section of this book. A broad range of sights is covered: from the ancient Royal Palace, which was the site of the Defenestration of 1618 *(see p105)*, to cubist houses built in the Jewish Quarter in the 1920s *(see p91)*; from the peaceful oasis of Petřín Park *(see p141)*, to the bustle of Wenceslas Square *(see pp144–5)*. To help you make the most of your stay, the following 12 pages are a time-saving guide to the best Prague has to offer visitors. Museums and galleries, churches and synagogues, palaces and gardens all have their own sections. Each sight has a cross reference to its own full entry. Below are the attractions that no visitor should miss.

PRAGUE'S TOP TEN SIGHTS

Old Town Square
See pp66–9.

National Theatre
See pp156–7.

Church of St Nicholas
See pp128–9.

Charles Bridge
See pp136–9.

Old Town Hall
See pp72–4.

St Vitus's Cathedral
See pp100–3.

Wallenstein Palace and Garden See p126.

Old Jewish Cemetery
See pp86–7.

Prague Castle
See p96–7.

St Agnes's Convent
See pp92–3.

◁ Mucha's allegory of Vigilance in the Mayor's Room in the Municipal House *(see p64)*

Prague's Best: Museums and Galleries

With more than 20 museums and almost 100
galleries and exhibition halls, Prague is a city
of unexpected and rare delights. Here, religious
masterpieces of the Middle Ages vie with the more
recent opulence of Art Nouveau and the giants of
modern art. New galleries have opened since 1989
with many more temporary exhibitions. There are
museums devoted to the history of the state, the
city of Prague and
its people, many
of them housed
in buildings that
are historical land-
marks and works
of art in them-
selves. This map
gives some of the
highlights, with a
detailed overview
on pages 40–41.

St George's Convent
*Among the 19th-century art
on display is the historical
painting of King George of
Poděbrady and Matthias
Corvinus of Hungary by
Czech artist Mikoláš Aleš.*

Sternberg Palace
*The collection of European
art here is outstanding,
represented in works such as
The Feast of the Rosary
by Albrecht Dürer (1506).*

*Prague Castle
and Hradčany*

The Loreto
*The offerings of
devout local
aristocrats form
the basis of this
collection of reli-
gious decorative
art. In 1721 this jewel-
encrusted, tree-shaped
monstrance was given to
the treasury by Countess
Wallenstein.*

*Little
Quarter*

VLTAVA

Smetana Museum
*The life and work of this 19th-
century Czech composer are
remembered beside the river that
inspired one of his most famous
pieces – the Vltava.*

Schwarzenberg Palace
*The ornate Renaissance palace, formerly the
home of the Museum of Military History, is now
a gallery exhibiting Baroque art.*

Museum of Decorative Arts

Five centuries of arts and crafts are represented here, with particularly impressive collections of Bohemian glass, graphic art and furniture. This carved and painted chest dates from 1612.

St Agnes of Bohemia Convent
This collection includes the 14th-century Resurrection of Christ *by the Master of the Třeboň Altar.*

Maisel Synagogue
One of the most important collections of Judaica in the world is housed in the Maisel Synagogue and other buildings of the State Jewish Museum. The displays include religious artefacts, furnishings and books. This illuminated page is from the manuscript of the Pesach Haggadah of 1728.

Jewish Quarter

Old Town

| 0 metres | 500 |
| 0 yards | 500 |

National Museum
The vast skeleton of a whale dominates the other exhibits in one of seven grand halls devoted to zoology. The museum's other displays include fine collections of minerals and meteorites.

New Town

Dvořák Museum
This viola, which belonged to the influential 19th-century Czech composer, is among the personal effects and musical scores on display in the charming Michna Summer Palace.

Exploring the Museums and Galleries

The city's museums give a fascinating insight into the history of the Czechs and of Prague's Jewish population. Also a revelation to visitors unfamiliar with the culture is the art of the Gothic and Baroque periods and of the 19th-century Czech National Revival. The major museums and galleries are cramped for space, but plans are under way to put more of their collections on show in the near future.

Carved figure on façade of the Museum of Decorative Arts

14th-century *Madonna Aracoeli*, St Vitus Treasure, Prague Castle

CZECH PAINTING AND SCULPTURE

The most important and wide-ranging collection in Prague is that of the National Gallery. Its holdings of Czech art are shown at three venues: medieval art at **St Agnes's Convent**; works dating from the 19th century at **St George's Convent**; and 20th- to 21st-century art at the Trade Fair Palace.

The **Picture Gallery of Prague Castle** is a reminder of Emperor Rudolph II's once-great collection. Alongside the paintings are documents

Commerce by Otto Gutfreund (1923), Trade Fair Palace

and other evidence of just how splendid the original collection must have been.

For some of the best Bohemian art, you must visit the Baroque works at the **Schwarzenberg Palace**, just outside the main gate of the Castle. These include examples by Baroque masters Karel Škréta and Petr Brandl. Within the Castle but currently without a permanent display space is the St Vitus Treasure, a collection of religious pieces including a Madonna from the School of Master Theodoric.

Centuries of Czech sculpture are housed in the Lapidarium at the **Exhibition Ground**. Among its exhibits is statuary formerly found on the Charles Bridge, and the Marian pillar that used to stand in the Old Town Square.

The collection at the **St Agnes of Bohemia Convent** includes Bohemian and central European Gothic painting and sculpture, including panels painted for Charles IV by Master Theodoric. Works by 19th- and 20th-century Prague artists can be seen at the Prague Gallery. Its branches include the Baroque **Troja Palace**, where the architecture makes a great backdrop. Exhibitions are drawn from the gallery's 3,000 paintings, 1,000 statues and 4,000 prints.

The superb museum of 20th- and 21st-century art at the **Trade Fair Palace** represents almost every 20th-century artistic movement. Cubism and Art Nouveau are both represented, as are the 1920s figures of Otto Gutfreund. The development of such ground breaking groups as Osma, Devětsil, Skupina 42 and the 12.15 group is also well documented.

EUROPEAN PAINTING AND SCULPTURE

On view at **Sternberg Palace** is an exceptional range of masterpieces by Europe's finest artists from antiquity to the 18th century.

The most treasured work in the collection is the *Feast of the Rosary* by Albrecht Dürer. Works by 17th-century Dutch masters such as Rubens and Rembrandt also feature.

The museum of 20th- and 21st-century art at the **Trade Fair Palace** has a fine collection of Picassos and Rodin bronzes, as well as works from almost every Impressionist, Post-Impressionist and Fauvist. Three notable self-portraits are those of Paul Gauguin (*Bonjour Monsieur Gauguin*, 1889), Henri Rousseau (1890) and Pablo Picasso (1907). Modern German and Austrian painting is also on show, with works by Gustav Klimt and Egon Schiele. The *Dance of Life*, by Norwegian Edvard Munch, is considered greatly influential upon Czech avant-garde art.

The other main venue for European art is the **Picture Gallery of Prague Castle**, which focuses on European painters of the 16th to 18th centuries. As well as Titian's superb *The Toilet of a Young Lady*, there are also works in the collection by Rubens and Tintoretto. The exquisite building of **Schwarzenberg Palace** now houses a gallery of Baroque art.

MUSIC

Two Czech composers merit their own museums, as does Prague's much-loved visitor, Mozart. The **Smetana Museum, Dvořák Museum**, housed in the Michna Summer Palace, and **Mozart Museum** all contain personal memorabilia, musical scores and correspondence. In the summer, concerts are held on the terrace of the Mozart Museum, a delightful 17th-century villa.

The **Museum of Music** has many rare and historic instruments, and a number of scores by famous composers.

HISTORY

The historical collections of the **National Museum** are held at the main Wenceslas Square building. The **Prague Museum** centres on the history of the city, with period rooms, historical prints and a model of Prague in the 19th century, made of paper and wood by the lithographer Antonín Langweil.

Bohemian Baroque glass goblet (1730), Museum of Decorative Arts

A branch of the museum at Výtoň, on the banks of the Vltava, depicts the way of life of a former settlement. Another at Vyšehrad records the history of this royal seat.

The Museum of Military History, housed in the Schwarzenberg Palace since 1945 but now on U Pamatniku 3, displays battle charts, weaponry, uniforms and other military regalia. The Lobkowicz Collection, housed in the 16th century **Lobkowicz Palace** at Prague Castle, includes rare books and manuscripts.

The Jewish Museum is made up of various sites in the Jewish Quarter, including the **High Synagogue, Maisel Synagogue** and the **Old Jewish Cemetery**. Among its collections are holy artefacts taken from other Jewish communities and brought to Prague by the Nazis as part of a chilling plan for a museum of "an extinct race". Another moving display is of drawings made by children from the Terezín concentration camp.

DECORATIVE ARTS

With glassware spanning centuries, from medieval to modern, porcelain and pewterware, furniture and textiles, books and posters, the **Museum of Decorative Arts** in the Jewish Quarter is one of Prague's best, but only a small selection of its holdings is on show. Look out for specialized temporary exhibitions mounted either at the museum itself or at other venues in Prague.

Many other museums have examples of the decorative arts, ranging from grandiose monstrances – including one with 6,222 diamonds – in the treasury of **The Loreto** to simple everyday furnishings in the **Prague Museum**. There is also a fascinating collection of pre-Columbian artefacts from Central America in the **Náprstek Museum**.

16th-century astrolabe from the National Technical Museum

SCIENCE AND TECHNOLOGY

A vast exhibition hall holds the transport section of the **National Technical Museum**. Ranks of vintage cars, motorcycles and steam engines fill the space, and over them hang examples of early flying machines. Other sections in the museum trace the progress of sciences such as electronics. Closed for several years to allow for long-overdue renovation, the museum is expected to reopen by 2010.

FINDING THE MUSEUMS AND GALLERIES

Prague's Best: Churches and Synagogues

The religious buildings of Prague vividly record the city's changing architectural styles, and many are treasure houses of religious art. But they also reflect Prague's times of religious and political strife, the lives of its people, its setbacks and growth as a city. This map features highlights of their architecture and art, with a more detailed overview on pages 44–5.

St George's Basilica
St George, sword raised to slay the dragon, is portrayed in this late-Gothic relief, set above the doorway of the magnificent early Renaissance south portal.

St Vitus's Cathedral
The jewel of the cathedral is the Chapel of St Wenceslas. Its walls are decorated with semi-precious stones, gilding and frescoes. Elizabeth of Pomerania, the fourth and last wife of Charles IV, is shown at prayer in the fresco above the Gothic altar.

Prague Castle and Hradčany

The Loreto
This shrine to the Virgin Mary has been a place of pilgrimage since 1626. Each hour, its Baroque clock tower chimes a hymn on the carillon of 27 bells.

Little Quarter

V L T A V A

Church of St Thomas
The skeleton of the martyr St Just rests in a glass coffin below a Crucifixion by Antonín Stevens, one of several superb works of religious art in this church.

Church of St Nicholas
In the heart of the Little Quarter, this is Prague's finest example of High Baroque. The dome over the high altar is so lofty that early worshippers feared it would collapse.

Church of Our Lady before Týn

Set back behind a row of arcaded buildings, the many-spired twin towers of the church dominate the eastern end of Old Town Square. The Gothic, Renaissance and Baroque features of the interior create striking contrasts.

Old-New Synagogue

Prague's oldest synagogue dates from the 13th century. Its Gothic main portal is carved with a vine which bears twelve bunches of grapes symbolizing the tribes of Israel.

Jewish Quarter

Old Town

Church of St James

Consecrated in 1374, this church was restored to new Baroque glory after a fire in 1689. Typical of its grandeur is this 18th-century monument to chancellor Jan Vratislav of Mitrovice. Fine acoustics and a superb organ make the church a popular venue for concerts.

Slavonic Monastery Emauzy

These cloisters hold a series of precious frescoes from three Gothic masters depicting scenes from the Old and New Testaments.

New Town

| 0 metres | 500 |
| 0 yards | 500 |

Church of St Peter and St Paul

Remodelled many times since the 11th century, the design of this church is now 1890s Neo-Gothic. This striking relief of the Last Judgment marks the main entrance.

Exploring Churches and Synagogues

Religious building began in Prague in the 9th century, reaching its zenith during the reign of Charles IV

(see pp24–5). The remains of an 11th-century synagogue have been found, but during the 19th-century clearance of the overcrowded Jewish ghetto three synagogues were lost. Many churches were damaged during the Hussite rebellions *(see pp26–7)*. The political regime of the 20th century also took its toll, but now churches and synagogues have been reclaimed and restored, with many open to visitors.

Altar, Capuchin Monastery

ROMANESQUE

Three reasonably well-preserved Romanesque rotundas, dating from the 11th and 12th centuries, still exist in Prague. The oldest is the **St Martin's Rotunda**; the others are the rotundas of the Holy Rood and of St Longinus. All three are tiny, with naves only 6 m (20 ft) in diameter.

By far the best-preserved and most important Romanesque church is **St George's Basilica**, founded in 920 by

11th-century Romanesque Rotunda of St Martin in Vyšehrad

Prince Vratislav I. Extensive reconstruction was carried out after a fire in 1142, but its chancel, with some exquisite frescoes on its vaulting, is a Late-Romanesque gem.

The **Strahov Monastery**, founded in 1142 by Prince Vladislav II *(see pp22–3)*, has retained its Romanesque core in spite of fire, wars and extensive renovation.

GOTHIC

Gothic architecture, with its ribbed vaulting, flying buttresses and pointed arches, reached Bohemia in about 1230 and was soon adopted into religious architecture.

The first religious building in Gothic style was the **St Agnes of Bohemia Convent**, founded in 1233 by Wenceslas I's sister, Agnes. Prague's oldest synagogue, the **Old-New Synagogue**, built in 1270, is rather different in style to the churches but is still a superb example of Early-Gothic.

The best example of Prague Gothic is **St Vitus's Cathedral**. Its fine tracery and towering

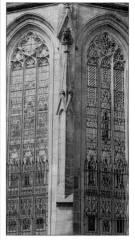

High, Gothic windows at the east end of St Vitus's Cathedral

nave epitomize the style. Other notable Gothic churches are **Our Lady before Týn** and **Our Lady of the Snows**.

Important for its historical significance is the reconstructed Gothic **Bethlehem Chapel** where Jan Hus *(see p27)* preached for 10 years.

The superb Gothic frescoes found in abundance at the **Slavonic Monastery Emauzy**, were badly damaged in World War II, but have been restored.

RENAISSANCE

In the 1530s the influence of Italian artists living in Prague sparked the city's Renaissance movement. The style is more clearly seen in secular than religious building. The Late-Renaissance period, under Rudolph II (1576–1611), offers the best remaining examples.

DOMES AND SPIRES

The domes and spires of Prague's churches are the city's main landmarks, as the view from the many vantage points will confirm. You will see a variety of spires, towers and domes: Gothic and Neo-Gothic soar skywards, while Baroque often have rounded cupolas and onion domes. The modern top of the 14th-century Slavonic Monastery, added after the church was struck in a World War II air raid, is a rare example of modernist religious architecture in Prague. Its sweeping, intersecting twin spires are a bold reinterpretation of Gothic themes, and a striking addition to the city's skyline.

Gothic

Church of Our Lady before Týn (1350–1511)

Baroque

Church of St Nicholas in t[h]e Little Quarter (1750)

The **High Synagogue** and the **Pinkas Synagogue** retain strong elements of the style: the former in its 1586 exterior, the latter in the reworking of an original Gothic building.

The Church of St Roch in the **Strahov Monastery** is probably the best example of Late-Renaissance "Mannerism".

Renaissance-influenced vaulting, Pinkas Synagogue (1535)

BAROQUE

The Counter-Reformation (see pp30–31) inspired the building of new churches and the revamping of existing ones for a period of 150 years. Prague's first Baroque church

was **Our Lady Victorious**, built in 1611–13. **St Nicholas** in the Little Quarter took almost 60 years to build. Its lush interior and frescoed vault make it Prague's most important Baroque building, followed by **The Loreto** (1626–1750), adjoining the **Capuchin Monastery**. The father-and-son team, Christoph and Kilian Ignaz Dientzenhofer designed both buildings, and **St John on the Rock** and **St Nicholas** in the Old Town.

A special place in Prague's history was occupied by the Jesuit **Clementinum**. This influential university's church was the **Holy Saviour**. The Baroque style is closely linked with Jesuit teachings: Kilian Ignaz Dientzenhofer was educated here.

Klausen Synagogue (now the Jewish Museum) was built in 1689 with Baroque stuccoed barrel vaults.

Many early buildings were given Baroque facelifts. The Gothic nave of **St Thomas** has Baroque vaulting, and the once-Gothic **St James** went Baroque after a fire in 1689.

19th-century Neo-Gothic portal, Church of St Peter and St Paul

NEO-GOTHIC

During the height of the 19th-century Gothic Revival (see pp32–3), **St Vitus's Cathedral** was completed, in accordance with the original Gothic plan. Work by Josef Mocker, the movement's leader, aroused controversy but his **St Peter and St Paul** at Vyšehrad is a well-loved landmark. The triple-naved basilica of **St Ludmila** in Náměstí Míru was also designed by Mocker.

Nave ceiling of the Church of St Nicholas in the Little Quarter

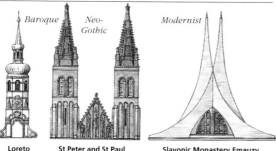

Baroque — Loreto (1725)

Neo-Gothic — St Peter and St Paul (1903)

Modernist — Slavonic Monastery Emauzy (1967)

Prague's Best: Palaces and Gardens

Prague's palaces and gardens are among the most important historical and architectural monuments in the city. Many palaces house museums or galleries (*see pp38–41*), and some are concert venues.

The gardens range from formal, walled oases with fountains and grand statuary, to open spaces beyond the city centre. This map features some of the best palaces and gardens, with a detailed overview on pages 48–9.

Belvedere
The Singing Fountain (1568) stand in front of the exquisite Renaissanc summer palace.

Royal Garden
Though redesigned in the 19th century, the Renaissance garden preserves much of its original character. Historic statues still in place include a pair of Baroque lions (1730) guarding the entrance.

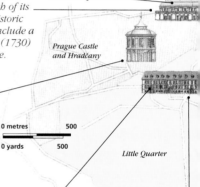

Prague Castle and Hradčany

| 0 metres | 500 |
| 0 yards | 500 |

Little Quarter

South Gardens
Starting life as the Castle's defensive bastions, these gardens afford a wonderful view of Prague. First laid out as a park in 1891, their present design was landscaped by Josip Plečnik 40 years later.

Wallenstein Palace
Built in 1624–30 for Duke Albrecht of Wallenstein, this vast Baroque palace was intended to outshine Prague Castle. Over 20 houses and a town gate were demolished to make room for the palace and garden. This Fountain of Venus (1599), stands in front of the arches of the sala terrena.

Wallenstein Garden
The garden statues are copies of 17th-century bronzes. The originals were plundered by the Swedes in 1648.

Palace Gardens
In the Baroque period, five palace gardens with spectacular terraces were laid out on the hillside below Prague Castle.

Kinský Palace
The Kinský coat of arms adorns the pink and white stuccoed façade designed by Kilian Ignaz Dientzenhofer. The Rococo palace is now part of the National Gallery.

Clam-Gallas Palace
Four giant statues of Hercules (c.1715) by Matthias Bernard Braun show the hero straining to support the weight of the massive Baroque front portals of the palace.

Jewish Quarter

Old Town

New Town

VLTAVA

Michna Summer Palace
This charming villa was designed by Kilian Ignaz Dientzenhofer in 1712. It now houses the Dvořák Museum. The garden's sculptural decorations are from the workshop of Antonín Braun.

Kampa Island
A tranquil waterside park was created on the island after the destruction of its original gardens in World War II.

Exploring the Palaces and Gardens

Prague boasts an amazing number of palaces and gardens, spanning centuries. Comparatively few palaces were lost to the ravages of war. Instead, they tended to evolve in style during restoration or enlargement. Palace gardens became fashionable in the 17th century, but could only be laid out where there was space, such as below Prague Castle. More vulnerable to change, most have been relandscaped several times. In the 19th century, and again after 1989, many of the larger parks and private gardens were opened up to the public.

Statue on Kampa Island

Bronze Singing Fountain in the Royal Garden by the Belvedere

MEDIEVAL PALACES

The oldest palace in Prague is the **Royal Palace** at Prague Castle. In the basement is the Romanesque ground floor, started in about 1135. It has been rebuilt many times, particularly between the 14th and 16th centuries. The heart of the Palace, Vladislav Hall, dates from the 1490s and is late Gothic in structure. Less well known is the **Palace of the Lords of Kunštát**. Here, the vaulted ground floor of the 13th-century building survives as the basement of a later Gothic structure.

RENAISSANCE PALACES

One of the most beautiful Renaissance buildings in Prague is the 16th-century **Schwarzenberg Palace**. The work of Italian architects, its façade is entirely covered with geometric, two-tone *sgraffito* designs. Italians also worked on the **Belvedere**. Its graceful arcades and columns, all covered with rich reliefs, make this one of the finest Renaissance buildings north of the Alps. The **Martinic Palace**, built in 1563, was the first example of late-Renaissance building in Prague. Soon after came the **Lobkowicz Palace**. Its terracotta relief-decorated windows and plaster *sgraffito* have survived later Baroque modifications. The huge **Archbishop's Palace** was given a later Rococo façade over its Renaissance structure.

BAROQUE PALACES

Many palaces were built in the Baroque style, and examples of all its phases still exist in Prague. A handsome, if ostentatious, early Baroque

Southern façade of Troja Palace and its formal gardens

DECORATIVE PORTALS AND GATES

The elaborate gates and portals of Prague's palaces are among the most beautiful and impressive architectural features in the city. Gothic and Renaissance portals have often survived, even where the buildings themselves have been destroyed or modified by renovations in a later architectural style. The period of most prolific building was the Baroque, and distinctive portals from this time can be seen framing many a grand entrance around the city. Statues of giants, heroes and mythological figures are often depicted holding up the doorways. These were not merely decorative but acted as an integral element of support.

Gateway to Court of Honour of Prague Castle (1768)

example is the **Wallenstein Palace**. Similar ostentation is evident in the **Černín Palace**, one of Prague's most monumental buildings. The mid-Baroque had two strands, one opulent and Italianate, the other formal and French or Viennese in influence. **Troja Palace** and **Michna Summer Palace** are in Italian villa style while the **Sternberg Palace** on Hradčanské náměstí is more Viennese in style. Troja was designed in 1679 by Jean-Baptiste Mathey, who, like the Dientzenhofers *(see p129)*, was a master of the Baroque. The pairs of giants on the portals of the **Clam-Gallas Palace**, and the **Morzin Palace** in Nerudova Street, are a popular Baroque motif. The **Kinský Palace** is a superb Rococo design by Kilian Ignaz Dientzenhofer.

The Royal Garden of Prague Castle, planted with spring flowers

GARDENS

The finest of Prague's palace gardens, such as the **Wallenstein Garden**, are in the Little Quarter. Though the style of Wallenstein Palace is Early Baroque, the garden still displays the geometric formality of the Renaissance, also preserved in the **Royal Garden** behind Prague Castle. The **South Gardens** on the Castle's old ramparts were redesigned in the 1920s.

Many more gardens were laid out in the 17th and 18th centuries, when noble families vied with each other to have fine winter residences in the Little Quarter below the Castle. Many are now the grounds of embassies, but others have been opened to the public. The Ledebour Garden has been combined with several neighbouring gardens. Laid out on a steep hillside, the **Palace Gardens**, in particular, make ingenious use of pavilions, stairs and terraces from which there are wonderful views of the city. The **Vrtba Garden**, landscaped on the site of former vineyards, is a similar Baroque creation with statues and splendid views. Former palace gardens were also used to create a park on **Kampa Island**.

The many old gardens and orchards on Petřín Hill have

Ancient trees in Stromovka

been transformed into the large public area of **Petřín Park**. Another former orchard is **Vojan Park**, laid out by archbishops in the 13th century. The **Botanical Gardens** are one of the few areas of green open to the public in the New Town.

Generally, the larger parks are situated further out of the city. **Stromovka** was a royal deer park, while **Letná Park** was developed in 1858 on the open space of Letná Plain.

WHERE TO FIND THE PALACES AND GARDENS

Troja Palace (c.1703)

Clam-Gallas Palace (c.1714)

PRAGUE THROUGH THE YEAR

Painted Easter egg

Springtime in Prague sees the city burst into colour as its gardens start to bloom. Celebrations begin with the Prague Spring Music Festival. In summer, visitors are entertained by street performers and the city's glorious gardens come into their own. When the weather begins to turn cooler, Prague hosts the International Jazz Festival.

The year often draws to a close with snow on the streets. The ball season starts in December, and in the coldest months, most events are held indoors. At Prague Castle, an all-year-round attraction is the changing of the guard around midday. For details of activities, check the listings magazines (see p219) or the Prague Information Service (see p218).

Concert at Wallenstein Palace during the Prague Spring Music Festival

SPRING

As Prague sees its first rays of spring sunshine, the city comes alive. A mass of colours, blooms and cultural events makes this one of the most exciting times of the year to visit. The city's blossoming parks and gardens open their gates again, after the colder months of winter. During April the temperatures rise and an entertainment programme begins – dominated by the Prague Spring Music Festival.

EASTER

Easter Monday (dates vary) is a public holiday. Easter is observed as a religious holiday but it is also associated with a bizarre pagan ritual in which Czech men beat their women with willow sticks in order to keep them fertile during the coming year. The women retaliate by throwing water over their male tormentors. Peace is finally restored when the women present the men with a painted egg. Church services are held during the entire Easter period (see p235).

MARCH

The Prague-Prčice March (third Saturday of March). Thousands of people walk to the small town of Prčice in celebration of spring.

APRIL

Boat trips (1 April). A number of boats begin trips up and down the Vltava.
Witch-burning (30 April), at the Exhibition Ground (see p162). Concerts accompany this 500-year-old tradition where old brooms are burnt on bonfires, in a symbolic act to rid nature of evil spirits.

MAY

Labour Day (1 May). Public holiday celebrated with numerous cultural events.
Opening day of Prague's gardens (1 May). Regular summer concerts are held in many parks and gardens.
Anniversary of Prague Uprising (5 May). At noon sirens are sounded for one minute. Flowers are laid at the commemorative plaques of those who died (see p34).
Day of Liberation from Fascism (8 May). Public holiday for VE day. Wreaths are laid on the graves of soldiers at Olšany cemeteries.
Prague International Book Fair (second week in May), Palace of Culture (see p176). The best of Czech and international authors.
Prague International Marathon (third week in May).

THE PRAGUE SPRING MUSIC FESTIVAL

This international festival presents a busy programme of concerts, ballet and opera from 12 May to 3 June. Music lovers can hear a huge selection of music played by some of the best musicians in the world. The main venue is the Rudolfinum (see p84) but others include churches and palaces – some of which are only open to the public on these occasions. The festival begins on the anniversary of Bedřich Smetana's death (see p79). A service is held at his grave in Vyšehrad (see p180), and in the evening there is a concert at the Municipal House (see p64) where musicians perform his most famous work, Má Vlast (My Country). Municipal House is also where the festival ends.

Bedřich Smetana

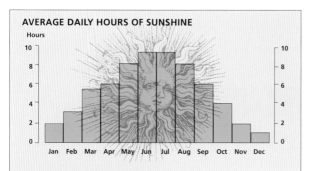

AVERAGE DAILY HOURS OF SUNSHINE

Hours

Jan Feb Mar Apr May Jun Jul Aug Sep Oct Nov Dec

Sunshine Chart
Prague's longest and hottest days fall between May and August. At the height of summer, daylight starts at 5am. The snow-covered city looks stunning on a sunny winter's day. But sunny days can be spoiled by thick smog (see p53).

Czechs and tourists enjoying the beauty of Vyšehrad Park on a sunny afternoon

SUMMER

Summer arrives with high temperatures, frequent, sometimes heavy, showers and thousands of visitors. This is a beautiful, if busy, time to visit. Every weekend, Czechs set out for the country to go hiking in the surrounding hills or stay in country cottages. Those remaining in Prague visit the reservoirs and lakes *(see p213)*, just outside the city to try and escape the heat. There is a wealth of entertainment on offer as culture moves into the open air taking over the squares, streets and gardens. Street performers, buskers and classical orchestras all help to keep visitors entertained. Many cafés have tables outside allowing you to quench your thirst while watching the fun.

JUNE

Mayoral Boat Race *(first weekend in June)*. Rowing races are held on the river Vltava, just below Vyšehrad.

Summer Concerts *(throughout the summer)*. Prague's gardens *(see pp46–9)* are the attractive and popular setting for a large number of free classical and brass-band concerts. One of the most famous, and spectacular, outdoor classical concerts is held by Křižík Fountain at the Exhibition Ground *(see p162)*. Full orchestras play to the stunning backdrop of coloured lights and water, synchronized to the music by computer.

Anniversary of the Murder of Reinhard Heydrich's Assassins *(18 June)*. A mass is held in remembrance at the Church of St Cyril and St Methodius *(see p152)* for those who died there.

Golden Prague *(first week of June)*, Kaiserstein Palace. International TV festival of prize-winning programmes.

Battle Re-enactments *(throughout summer)*, held in Prague's palaces and gardens.

Mozart's Prague *(mid-June to first week in July)*. Celebration of Mozart. International orchestras perform his works at Bertramka *(see p160)* and Lichtenstein Palace.

Dance Prague *(last week in June)*. An international festival of contemporary dance at the National Theatre *(see p156)*.

JULY

Remembrance of the Slavonic Missionaries *(5 July)*. Public holiday in honour of St Cyril and St Methodius *(see p152)*.

Anniversary of Jan Hus's Death *(6 July)*. A public holiday when flowers are laid on his memorial *(see pp26–7)*.

AUGUST

Theatre Island *(all of August)*, Střelecký Island. Czech theatre and puppet festival.

Changing of the Guard at Prague Castle

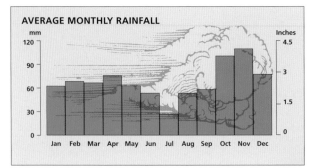

AVERAGE MONTHLY RAINFALL

Rainfall Chart
Prague has plenty of rain throughout the year. The wettest months are October and November, but there are frequent light showers in the summer months as well. Winter snowfalls can be quite heavy, but they are rarely severe.

AUTUMN

When the gardens below Prague Castle take on the shades of red and gold, and visitors start to leave, the city gets ready for the cold winter months. This is also the traditional mushroom-gathering season when you encounter people with baskets full of freshly-picked mushrooms. Market places are flooded with fruit and vegetables. The tree-lined slopes above the Vltava take on the beautiful colours of autumn. September and October still have a fair number of warm and sunny days, although November often sees the first snowfalls. Football fans fill the stadiums and the popular steeplechase course at Pardubice reverberates to the cheers of fans.

SEPTEMBER

Prague Autumn *(early September)*, at the Rudolfinum *(see p84)*. An international classical music festival.
The Autumn Fair *(dates vary)*, at the Exhibition Ground *(see p162)*. Fairground, food stalls, puppet shows and theatrical and musical performances.
Kite competitions *(third Sunday in September)*, on Letná Plain in front of Sparta Stadium. Very popular competition for children but open to anyone with a kite.
St Wenceslas *(28 September)*. A sacred music festival is held for the feast of the patron saint.
Bohemia Championship *(last Sunday in September)*. This 10-km (6-mile) road race has been run since 1887. Starts from Běchovice, a suburb of Prague, and ends in Žižkov.

Jazz musicians playing at the International Jazz Festival

OCTOBER

The Great Pardubice Steeple-chase *(second Sunday in October)*, held at Pardubice, east of Prague. This horse race has been run since 1874 and is considered to be the most difficult in Europe.
The Locking of the Vltava *(early October)*. Symbolic conclusion of the water sports season, during which the Vltava is locked with a key until the arrival of spring.
International Jazz Festival *(date varies)*, Lucerna Palace. A famous jazz festival, held since 1964, attracts musicians from around the world.
The Day of the Republic *(28 October)*. Despite the splitting up of Czechoslovakia into two separate republics, the founding of the country in 1918 is still a public holiday.

NOVEMBER

Velká Kunratická *(second Sunday in November)*. Popular, but gruelling, cross-country race in Kunratice forest. Anyone can enter.
Celebration of the Velvet Revolution *(17 November)*. Peaceful demonstrations take place around Wenceslas Square *(see pp144–5)*.

A view of St Vitus's Cathedral through autumn trees

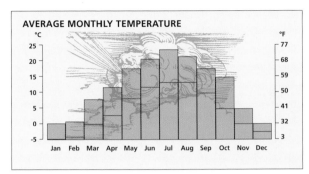

AVERAGE MONTHLY TEMPERATURE

Temperature Chart
The chart shows the average minimum and maximum temperatures for each month in Prague. The summer usually remains comfortably warm, while the winter months can get bitterly cold and temperatures often drop below freezing.

WINTER

If you are lucky enough to catch Prague the morning after a snowfall with the sun shining, the effect is magical. The view over the Little Quarter rooftops with their pristine white covering is a memorable sight. Unfortunately Prague is rarely at its best during the winter months. The weather is changeable. Foggy days with temperatures just above freezing can quickly go down to -5° C (23° F). Pollution and Prague's geographical position in the Vltava basin, lead to smog being trapped just above the city.

As if to try and make up for the winter weather's shortcomings, the theatre season reaches its climax and there are a number of premieres. Balls and dances are held in these cold months. Just before Christmas Eve large barrels containing live carp – which is the traditional Czech Christmas delicacy – appear on the streets. Christmas trees adorn the city, and carol singers can be heard on street

View of the Little Quarter rooftops covered in snow

corners. Christmas mass is held in most churches and New Year's Eve is celebrated, in time-honoured style, throughout the entire city.

DECEMBER

Christmas markets
(throughout December), Můstek metro station, 28. října, Na příkopě, Old Town Square. Stalls sell Christmas decorations, gifts, hot wine, punch and the traditional Czech carp *(see p213).*
Christmas Eve, Christmas Day and Boxing Day *(24, 25 and 26 December).* Public holidays. Mass is held in churches throughout the city.
Swimming competitions in the Vltava *(26 December).* Hundreds of hardened and determined swimmers gather together at the Vltava to swim in temperatures of around 3° C (37° F).
New Year celebrations *(31 December).* Crowds of people congregate around Wenceslas and Old Town Square.

JANUARY

New Year's Day
(1 January). Public holiday.

FEBRUARY

Dances and Balls
(early February).
Matthew Fair *(end of February to beginning of April),* the Exhibition Ground *(see p176).* Fairground, stalls and various entertainments.

Barrels of the traditional Christmas delicacy, carp, on sale in Prague

A RIVER VIEW OF PRAGUE

The Vltava river has played a vital part in the city's history *(see pp20–21)* and has provided inspiration for artists, poets and musicians throughout the centuries.

Up until the 19th century, parts of the city were exposed to the danger of heavy flooding. To try and alleviate the problem, the river's embankments have been strengthened and raised many times, in order to try to prevent the water penetrating too far (the foundations of today's embankments are made of stone or concrete). During the Middle Ages, year after year of disastrous flooding led to the decision to bury the areas affected under 2 m (6 ft) of earth to try to minimize the damage. Although this strategy was only partially effective, it meant that the ground floors of many Romanesque and Gothic buildings were preserved and can still be seen today *(see*

Statues on the wrought-iron Čechův Bridge

pp78–9). In 2002 however, a state of emergency was declared as flooding devastated large parts of the city. Despite its destructive side, the Vltava has provided a vital method of transport for the city, as well as a source of income. As technology improved, the river became increasingly important; water mills, weirs and water towers were built. In 1912 a large hydroelectric power plant was built on Štvanice Island, supplying almost a third of Prague's electricity. To make the river navigable, eight dams, a large canal and weirs were constructed along the Slapy-Prague-Mělník stretch, where the Vltava flows into the river Elbe. For the visitor, an excursion on one of the many boats and paddle steamers that travel up and down the river is well worth it. There are trips to Troja *(see pp166–7)* and as far as Slapy Lake. Catching a boat from one of the piers on the river is one of the best ways of seeing the city.

A view of the steamboat landing stage (přístaviště parníků) on Rašínovo nábřeží

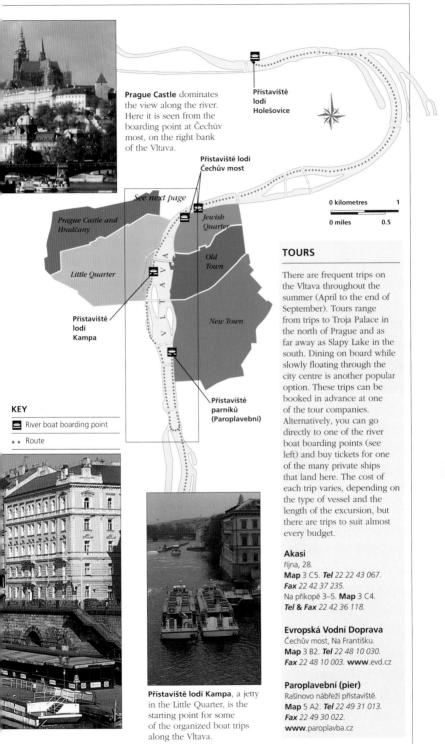

Prague Castle dominates the view along the river. Here it is seen from the boarding point at Čechův most, on the right bank of the Vltava.

Přístaviště lodí Holešovice

Přístaviště lodí Čechův most

See next page

Prague Castle and Hradčany

Jewish Quarter

Old Town

Little Quarter

V L T A V A

New Town

Přístaviště lodí Kampa

Přístaviště parníků (Paroplavebni)

0 kilometres 1

0 miles 0.5

KEY

🚢 River boat boarding point

•• Route

TOURS

There are frequent trips on the Vltava throughout the summer (April to the end of September). Tours range from trips to Troja Palace in the north of Prague and as far away as Slapy Lake in the south. Dining on board while slowly floating through the city centre is another popular option. These trips can be booked in advance at one of the tour companies. Alternatively, you can go directly to one of the river boat boarding points (see left) and buy tickets for one of the many private ships that land here. The cost of each trip varies, depending on the type of vessel and the length of the excursion, but there are trips to suit almost every budget.

Akasi
října, 28.
Map 3 C5. **Tel** *22 22 43 067.*
Fax *22 42 37 235.*
Na příkopě 3–5. **Map** 3 C4.
Tel & Fax *22 42 36 118.*

Evropská Vodní Doprava
Čechův most, Na Františku.
Map 3 B2. **Tel** *22 48 10 030.*
Fax *22 48 10 003.* **www**.evd.cz

Paroplavební (pier)
Rašinovo nábřeží přístaviště.
Map 5 A2. **Tel** *22 49 31 013.*
Fax *22 49 30 022.*
www.paroplavba.cz

Přístaviště lodí Kampa, a jetty in the Little Quarter, is the starting point for some of the organized boat trips along the Vltava.

Prague River Trip

Taking a trip on the Vltava gives you a unique view of many of the city's historic monuments. Although the left bank was the site of the first Slavonic settlement in the 9th century, it was the right bank, heavily populated by merchants and traders, that developed into a thriving and bustling commercial centre, and the tradition continues today. The left bank was never developed as intensively and much of it is still an oasis of parks and gardens. The river's beauty is enhanced by the numbers of swans which have made it their home.

Hanavský Pavilion
This flamboyant cast-iron staircase is part of a pavilion built for the Jubilee Exhibition of 1891.

Little Quarter Bridge Towers
The smaller tower was built in 1158 to guard the entrance to the original Judith Bridge, while the larger one was built on the site of an old Romanesque tower in 1464 (see p136).

Vltava Weir
The thickly-wooded slopes of Petřín Hill tower above one of several weirs on the Vltava. During the 19th century this weir, along with others on this stretch, were built to make the river navigable to ships.

The Vltava Statue on the northern tip of Children's Island is where, every year, wreaths are placed in memory of the drowned.

Little Quarter Water Tower
Built in 1560, the tower supplied river water to 57 fountains throughout the Little Quarter.

Apartment buildings of Art Nouveau design

Kampa

Přístaviště lodi Kampa

Grand Priory Mill

Střelecký ostrov

Plavební kanál

Karlův

most Legii

Jiráskův most

Palackého most

Železniční most

0 metres		500
0 yards		500

KEY

🚋 Tram

🚤 River boat boarding point

• • Boat trip

Rudolfinum
This allegorical statue of music by Antonín Wagner is one of two which decorate the imposing entrance to the Neo-Renaissance concert hall (see p84).

The Clementinum, a former Jesuit college, is one of the largest buildings in the city *(see p79).*

The Old Town Bridge Tower was built as part of the city's 14th-century fortifications *(see p139).*

Smetana Museum

Weir

The Šítka Tower, with its late-18th-century Baroque roof, was originally built in 1495 and pumped water to the New Town.

Slovanskýo strov

National Theatre
This symbol of the Czech revival, with its spectacularly-decorated roof, has dominated the skyline of the right bank since the 1860s (see pp156–7).

"Ginger and Fred" Building
This charming, quirky office building has become a symbol of post-Velvet Revolution modern architecture.

The Memorial to František Palacký commemorates the life of this eminent 19th-century Czech historian and was built in 1905.

Přístaviště parníků

The Na Slovanech Monastery was built in 1347 by Charles IV. Its two modern steeples are easily recognizable from the river.

Výtoň Excise House
The coat of arms on this 16th-century house – built to collect duty on timber transpored along the river – is of the New Town from 1671.

Church of St Peter and St Paul
The Neo-Gothic steeples on this much-rebuilt church were designed by František Mikeš and erected in 1903. They are the dominant feature of Vyšehrad rock (see pp180–81).

PRAGUE AREA
BY AREA

OLD TOWN

STARÉ MĚSTO

The heart of the city is the Old Town and its central square. In the 11th century the settlements around the Castle spread to the right bank of the Vltava. A marketplace in what is now Old Town Square (Staroměstské náměstí) was mentioned for the first time in 1091. Houses and churches sprang up

Physician, Jan Marek (1595–1667)

around the square, determining the random network of streets, many of which survive. The area gained the privileges of a town in the 13th century, and, in 1338, a Town Hall. This and other great buildings, such as Clam-Gallas Palace and the Municipal House, reflect the importance of the Old Town.

SIGHTS AT A GLANCE

Churches
Church of St James ❹
Church of Our Lady
  before Týn ❽
Church of St Nicholas ⓫
Church of St Gall ⓮
Church of St Martin
  in the Wall ⓯
Church of St Giles ⓱
Bethlehem Chapel ⓲

Museums and Galleries
Náprstek Museum ⓰
Smetana Museum ㉔

Historic Streets and Squares
Celetná Street ❸
*Old Town Square
  pp66–9* ❼
Mariánské Square ⓴
Charles Street ㉑
Knights of the Cross Square ㉕

Historic Monuments and Buildings
Powder Gate ❶
Municipal House ❷
Carolinum ❻
Jan Hus Monument ❿
Old Town Hall pp72–4 ⓬
House at the Two Golden
  Bears ⓭
Clementinum ㉓

Theatres
Estates Theatre ❺

Palaces
Clam-Gallas Palace ⓳
Kinský Palace ❾
Palace of the Lords
  of Kunštát ㉒

GETTING THERE
Můstek on metro lines A and B and Staroměstská on line A are both handy for the area. Trams do not cross the Old Town, but from Charles Bridge or Náměstí Republiky it is only a short walk to Old Town Square and the other sights.

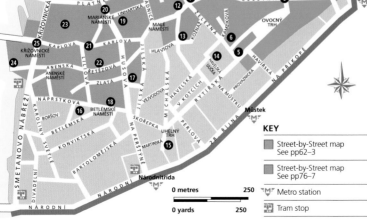

KEY

Street-by-Street map
See pp62–3

Street-by-Street map
See pp76–7

Ⓜ Metro station

Tram stop

0 metres 250

0 yards 250

◁ Café tables and strolling pedestrians in Old Town Square

Street-by-Street: Old Town (East)

Free of traffic (except for a few horse-drawn carriages) and ringed with historic buildings, Prague's Old Town Square (Staroměstské náměstí) ranks among the finest public spaces in any city. Streets like Celetná and Ovocný trh are also pedestrianized. In summer, café tables spill out onto the cobbles, and though the area draws tourists by the thousands, the unique atmosphere has not yet been destroyed.

Kinský Palace
This stunning Rococo palace now serves as an art gallery **9**

Church of St Nicholas
The imposing façade of this Baroque church dominates one corner of Old Town Square **11**

★ **Old Town Square**
This late-19th-century watercolour by Václav Jansa shows how little the Square has changed in 100 years **7**

S T A R O M Ě S T S K É
N Á M Ě S T Í

M A L É
N Á M Ě S T Í

Ž E L E Z N Á

Jan Hus Monument
Religious reformer Hus is a symbol of integrity, and the monument brings together the highest and lowest points in Czech history **10**

U Rotta is a former ironmonger's shop, decorated with colourful paintings by the 19th-century artist Mikuláš Aleš.

House at the Two Golden Bears
The carved Renaissance portal is the finest of its kind in Prague **13**

★ **Old Town Hall**
The famous astronomical clock draws a crowd of visitors every hour **12**

The Štorch house has painted decoration based on designs by Mikuláš Aleš showing St Wenceslas on horseback.

0 metres	100
0 yards	100

KEY

– – – Suggested route

Church of Our Lady before Týn
The church's Gothic steeples are the Old Town's most distinctive landmark ❽

LOCATOR MAP
See Street Finder, maps 3–4

Týn courtyard

Church of St James
This wooden Pietà, on the main altar, was made in the 15th century ❹

★ Municipal House
This Art Nouveau building is a popular concert venue ❷

Powder Gate
This much-restored Gothic gate stands at one of the 13 original 11th-century entry-ways into the Old Town ❶

House at the Black Madonna

Estates Theatre
The theatre featured in director Miloš Forman's film Amadeus ❺

Ovocný trh was Prague's fruit market.

Carolinum
A magnificently carved Oriel window projects from the oldest surviving part of the Carolinum university – founded by Charles IV in the 14th century ❻

Celetná Street
This ornamental Baroque plaque is the sign of the House at the Black Sun ❸

STAR SIGHTS

★ Old Town Square

★ Old Town Hall

★ Municipal House

Powder Gate ❶

PRAŠNÁ BRÁNA

Náměstí Republiky. **Map** 4 D3.
Tel 72 40 63 723.  Náměstí
Republiky. 5, 8, 14. **Open**
Apr–Oct: 10am–6pm daily.

There has been a gate here
since the 11th century, when
it formed one of the 13
entrances to the Old Town.
In 1475, King Vladislav II laid
the foundation stone of the
New Tower, as it was to be
known. A coronation gift
from the city council, the
gate was modelled on Peter
Parler's Old Town bridge
tower built a century earlier.
The gate had little defensive
value; its rich sculptural
decoration was intended to
add prestige to the adjacent
palace of the Royal Court.
Building was halted eight
years later when the king
had to flee because of riots.
On his return in 1485 he
opted for the safety of the
Castle. Kings never again
occupied the Royal Court.

The gate acquired its
present name when it was
used to store gunpowder in
the 17th century. The
sculptural decoration, badly
damaged during the Prussian
occupation in 1757 and mostly
removed soon afterwards,
was replaced in 1876.

**The Powder Gate viewed from
outside the Old Town**

Karel Špillar's mosaic _Homage to Prague_ on Municipal House's façade

Municipal House ❷

OBECNÍ DŮM

Náměstí Republiky 5. **Map** 4 D3.
Tel 22 20 02 101.  Náměstí
Republiky. 5, 8, 14. **Gallery
open** for exhibitions only, 10am–
6pm daily. by arrangement.
www.obecnidum.cz

Prague's most prominent Art
Nouveau building stands on
the site of the former Royal
Court palace, the King's residence between 1383 and 1485.
Abandoned for centuries, what
remained was used as a seminary and later as a military
college. It was demolished in
the early 1900s to be replaced
by the present cultural centre
(1905–11) with its exhibition
halls and auditorium, designed
by Antonín Balšánek assisted
by Osvald Polívka.

The exterior is embellished
with stucco and allegorical
statuary. Above the main
entrance there is a huge semicircular mosaic entitled
Homage to Prague by Karel
Špillar. Inside, topped by an
impressive glass dome, is
Prague's principal concert
venue and the core of the
entire building, the
Smetana Hall, sometimes

also used as a ballroom. The
interior of the building is
decorated with works by
leading Czech artists of the
first decade of the century,
including Alfons Mucha
(see p149).

There are numerous smaller
halls, conference rooms and
offices that are normally
closed but for which you can
arrange a guided tour, or you
can simply relax in one of the
cafés or res-
taurants. On
28 October,
1918, Prague's
Municipal
House was the
scene of the
momentous
proclamation
of the new
independent
state of
Czechoslovakia.

**Decorative detail
by Alfons Mucha**

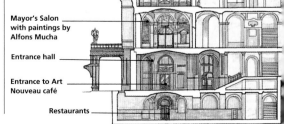

Hollar
Hall

Foyer

Mayor's Salon
with paintings by
Alfons Mucha

Entrance hall

Entrance to Art
Nouveau café

Restaurants

Celetná Street ❸
CELETNÁ ULICE

Map 3 C3. Ⓜ *Náměstí Republiky, Můstek.* **House of the Black Madonna** *Tel 22 42 11 746.* **Open** *10am–6pm Tue–Fri.* 🚻 📷 www.ngprague.cz

One of the oldest streets in Prague, Celetná follows an old trading route from eastern Bohemia. Its name comes from the plaited bread rolls that were first baked here in the Middle Ages. It gained prestige in the 14th century as a section of the Royal Route *(see p172)* used for coronation processions. Foundations of Romanesque and Gothic buildings can be seen in some of the cellars, but most of the houses with their picturesque signs are Baroque remodellings.

At No. 34, the House of the Black Madonna is home to a small collection of Czech Cubism, including paintings, sculpture, furniture, architectural plans and applied arts.

Church of St James ❹
KOSTEL SV. JAKUBA

Malá Štupartská. **Map** 3 C3. Ⓜ *Můstek, Náměstí Republiky.* **Open** *9:30am–noon, 2–4pm Mon–Sat.* ✝ 📷

This attractive Baroque church was originally the Gothic presbytery of a Minorite monastery. The order (a branch of the Franciscans) was invited to Prague by King Wenceslas I in 1232. It was

Baroque organ loft in the Church of St James

rebuilt in the Baroque style after a fire in 1689, allegedly started by agents of Louis XIV. Over 20 side altars were added, decorated with works by painters such as Jan Jiří Heinsch, Petr Brandl and Václav Vavřinec Reiner. The tomb of Count Vratislav of Mitrovice(1714–16), designed by Johann Bernhard Fischer von Erlach and executed by sculptor Ferdinand Brokof, is the most beautiful Baroque tomb in Bohemia. The count is said to have been accidentally buried alive – his corpse was later found sitting up in the tomb. Hanging on the right of the entrance is a mummified forearm. It has been there for over 400 years, ever since a thief tried to steal the jewels from the Madonna on the high altar. But the Virgin grabbed his arm and held on so tightly it had to be cut off.

Because of its long nave, the church's acoustics are excellent and many concerts and recitals are given here. There is also a magnificent organ built in 1702.

Estates Theatre ❺
STAVOVSKÉ DIVADLO

Ovocný trh 1. **Map** 3 C4. **Tel** *22 49 01 448 (tickets), 22 49 02 231 (guided tours).* Ⓜ *Můstek.* **Open** *for guided tours and performances only.* www.narodni-divadlo.cz

Built by Count Nostitz in 1783, this opera theatre is one of Prague's finest examples of Neo-Classical elegance. It is a mecca for Mozart fans *(see p220).* On 29 October 1787, Mozart's opera, *Don Giovanni* had its debut here with Mozart conducting. In 1834 the musical *Fidlovačka* premiered here; one of the songs, "Where is my Home?", became the Czech national anthem.

Carolinum ❻
KAROLINUM

Ovocný trh 3. **Map** 3 C4. **Tel** *22 44 91 111.* Ⓜ *Můstek.* **Closed** to the public. **Open** *for special exhibitions.*

At the core of the university-founded by Charles IV in 1348 is the Carolinum. The chapel, arcade and walls still survive, together with a fine oriel window, but in 1945 the courtyard was reconstructed in Gothic style. In the 15th and 16th centuries the university played a leading role in the movement to reform the church. After the Battle of the White Mountain *(see pp30–31),* the university was taken over by the Jesuits.

Old Town Square ❼
STAROMĚSTSKÉ NÁMĚSTÍ

See pp66–9.

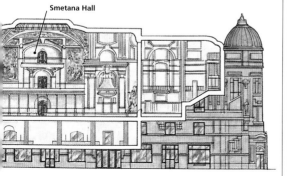

Smetana Hall

Old Town Square: East and North Sides ❼

STAROMĚSTSKÉ NÁMĚSTÍ

Some of Prague's colourful history is preserved around the Old Town Square in the form of its buildings. On the north side of the Square, the Pauline Monastery is the only surviving piece of original architecture. The east side boasts two superb examples of the architecture of their times: the House at the Stone Bell, restored to its former appearance as a Gothic town palace, and the Rococo Kinský Palace. An array of pastel-coloured buildings completes the Square.

★ **House at the Stone Bell**
At the corner of the building, the bell is the sign of this medieval town palace.

Statues by Ignaz Platzer from 1760–65

Kinský Palace
C G Bossi created the elaborate stucco decoration on the façade of this Rococo palace (see p70).

EAST SIDE

Rococo stucco work

NORTH SIDE

★ **Church of St Nicholas**
Besides its original purpose as a parish church and, later, a Benedictine monastery church, this has served as a garrison church and a concert hall (see p70).

STAR SIGHTS

★ Church of Our Lady before Týn

★ House at the Stone Bell

★ Church of St Nicholas

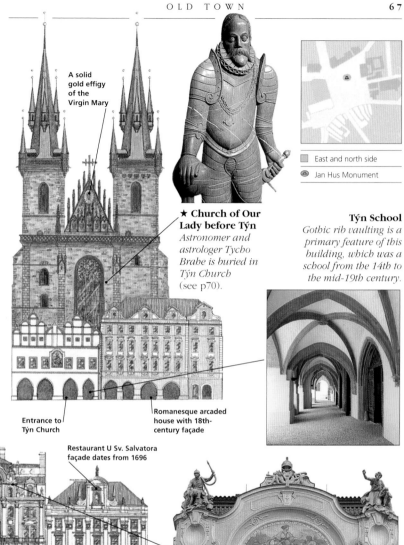

A solid gold effigy of the Virgin Mary

East and north side

Jan Hus Monument

★ Church of Our Lady before Týn
Astronomer and astrologer Tycho Brahe is buried in Týn Church (see p70).

Týn School
Gothic rib vaulting is a primary feature of this building, which was a school from the 14th to the mid-19th century.

Entrance to Týn Church

Romanesque arcaded house with 18th-century façade

Restaurant U Sv. Salvatora façade dates from 1696

Ministerstvo pro místní rozvoj
Architect Osvald Polívka designed this Art Nouveau building in 1898, with figures of firefighters on the upper façade. It houses the Ministry of Local Development.

Staroměstské náměstí, 1793
The engraving by Filip and František Heger shows the Old Town Square teeming with people and carriages. The Old Town Hall is on the left.

Old Town Square: South Side ❼
STAROMĚSTSKÉ NÁMĚSTÍ

A colourful array of houses of Romanesque or Gothic origin, with fascinating house signs, graces the south side of the Old Town Square. The block between Celetná Street and Železná Street is especially attractive. The Square has always been a busy focal point, and today offers visitors a tourist information centre, as well as a number of restaurants, cafés, shops, and galleries.

FRANZ KAFKA (1883–1924)

The author of two of the most influential novels of the 20th century, *The Trial* and *The Castle*, Kafka spent most of his short life in the Old Town. From 1893 to 1901 he studied in the Golz-Kinský Palace (*see p70*), where his father later had a shop. He worked as an insurance clerk, but frequented Berta Fanta's literary salon at the Stone Ram, Old Town Square, along with others who wrote in German. Hardly any of his work was published in his lifetime.

U Lazara (At Lazarus's)
Romanesque barrel vaulting testifies to the house's early origins, though it was rebuilt during the Renaissance. The ground floor houses the Staroměstská restaurace.

At the
Stone Table

At the Golden
Unicorn

Železná
Street

SOUTH SIDE

★ **At the Stone Ram**
The early-16th-century house sign shows a young maiden with a ram. The house has been referred to as At the Unicorn due to the similarity between the one-horned ram and a unicorn.

★ **Štorch House**
The late-19th-century painting of St Wenceslas on horseback by Mikuláš Aleš appears on this ornate Neo-Renaissance building, also known as At the Stone Madonna.

STAR SIGHTS

★ Štorch House

★ At the Stone Ram

Melantrichova Passage
*Václav Jansa's painting (1898)
shows the narrow passageway
leading to the Old Town Square.*

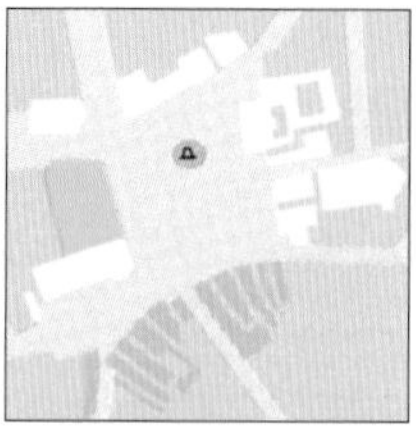

At the Red Fox
*A golden Madonna and Child
look down from the Baroque
façade of an originally
Romanesque building.*

South side

Jan Hus Monument

At The Ox
*Named after its
15th-century owner,
the burgher Ochs,
this house features an
early-18th-century
stone statue of
St Anthony of Padua.*

At the Storks

At the
Blue Star

The arcade houses the
Grand Café Praha.

U Orloje
restaurant

Melantrichova
Passage

TIMELINE

1338 Old Town
becomes
municipality

*Leopold II's Royal Procession through the
Old Town Square in 1791*

1735 Church of
St Nicholas completed

1948 Klement
Gottwald proclaims
Communist state
from balcony of
Golz-Kinský Palace

1300	1450	1600	1750	1900

1200 Square is
meeting point of
trade routes and
important market

1365
Building of
present Týn
Church

1621 Execution
of 27 anti-Habsburg
leaders in square
(see p31)

1689 Fire destroys
large part of Old Town

1784 Unification
of Prague towns

1915 Unveiling of
Jan Hus Monument

Hus Monument (detail)

Statue of the Madonna on Our Lady before Týn

Church of Our Lady before Týn ❽

KOSTEL MATKY BOŽÍ PŘED TÝNEM

Týnská, Štupartská. **Map** 3 C3. *Tel 60 22 04 213.* Ⓜ *Staroměstská, Můstek.* **Open** *10am–1pm, 3–5pm Tue–Sun.* ✝ *6pm Tue–Thu, 8am Sat, 9:30am & 9pm Sun.* ⌀

Dominating the Old Town Square are the magnificent multiple steeples of this historic church. The present Gothic church was started in 1365 and soon became associated with the reform movement in Bohemia. From the early 15th century until 1620 Týn was the main Hussite church in Prague. The Hussite king, George of Poděbrady, took Utraquist communion *(see Church of St Martin in the Wall p73)* here and had a gold chalice – the Utraquist symbol – mounted on the façade. After 1621 the chalice was melted down to become part of the statue of the Madonna that replaced it.

On the northern side of the church is a beautiful entrance portal (1390) decorated with scenes of Christ's passion. The dark interior has some notable features, including Gothic sculptures of *Calvary*, a pewter font (1414) and a 15th-century Gothic pulpit. Behind the church is the Týn Courtyard, with its numerous architectural styles.

Kinský arms on Golz-Kinský Palace

Kinský Palace ❾

PALÁC KINSKÝCH

Staroměstské náměstí 12. **Map** 3 C3. *Tel 22 48 10 758.* Ⓜ *Staroměstská.* **Open** *10am–6pm Tue–Sun.* 🖼 ⌀ 🍴 www.ngprague.cz

This lovely Rococo palace, designed by Kilian Ignaz Dientzenhofer, has a pretty pink and white stucco façade crowned with statues of the four elements by Ignaz Franz Platzer. It was bought from the Golz family in 1768 by Štěpán Kinský, an Imperial diplomat. In 1948 Communist leader, Klement Gottwald, used the balcony to address a huge crowd of party members – a key event in the crisis that led up to his *coup d'état*. The National Gallery now uses the Kinský Palace for art exhibitions.

Jan Hus Monument ❿

POMNÍK JANA HUSA

Staroměstské náměstí. **Map** 3 B3. Ⓜ *Staroměstská.*

At one end of the Old Town Square stands the massive monument to the religious reformer and Czech hero, Jan Hus *(see pp26–7)*. Hus was burnt at the stake after being pronounced a heretic by the Council of Constance in 1415. The monument by Ladislav Šaloun was unveiled in 1915 on the 500th anniversary of his death. It shows two groups of people, one of victorious Hussite warriors, the other of Protestants forced into exile 200 years later, and a young mother symbolizing national rebirth. The dominant figure of Hus emphasizes the moral authority of the man who gave up life rather than his beliefs.

Church of St Nicholas ⓫

KOSTEL SV. MIKULÁŠE

Staroměstské náměstí. **Map** 3 B3. *Tel 22 41 90 991.* Ⓜ *Staroměstská.* **Open** *10am–4pm daily and for evening concerts Apr–Nov.* ✝ *10:30am Sun.* www.svmikulas.cz

There has been a church here since the 12th century. It was the Old Town's parish church and meeting place until Týn Church was completed in the 14th century. After the Battle of the White Mountain in 1620 *(see pp30–31)* the church became part of a Benedictine monastery. The present church by Kilian Ignaz Dientzenhofer, was completed in 1735. Its dramatic white façade is studded with statues by Antonín Braun.

Defiant Hussites on the Jan Hus Monument in Old Town Square

Church of St Nicholas in the Old Town

When in 1781 Emperor Joseph II closed all monasteries not engaged in socially useful activities, the church was stripped bare. In World War I the church was used by the troops of Prague's garrison. The colonel in charge took the opportunity to restore the church with the help of artists who might otherwise have been sent to the front. The dome has frescoes of the lives of St Nicholas and St Benedict by Kosmas Damian Asam. In the nave is a huge crown-shaped chandelier. At the end of the war, the church of St Nicholas was given to the Czechoslovak Hussite Church. The church is now a popular concert venue.

Old Town Hall ⑫
STAROMĚSTSKÁ RADNICE

See pp72–3.

House at the Two Golden Bears ⑬
DŮM U DVOU ZLATÝCH MEDVĚDŮ

Kožná 1. **Map** 3 B4. Můstek.
Closed to the public.

If you leave the Old Town Square by the narrow Melantrichova Street, make a point of turning into the first alleyway on the left to see the portal of the house called "At the Two Golden Bears". The present Renaissance building was constructed from two earlier houses in 1567. The portal was added in 1590, when a wealthy merchant, Lorenc Štork, secured the services of court architect Bonifaz Wohlmut, who had designed the spire on the tower of St Vitus's Cathedral *(see pp100–3).* His ornate portal with reliefs of two bears is one of the most beautiful Renaissance portals in Prague. Magnificent arcades, also dating from the 16th century, have been preserved in the inner courtyard. In 1885 Egon Erwin Kisch, known as the "Furious Reporter", was born here. He was a German-speaking Jewish writer and journalist, feared for the force of his left-wing rhetoric.

Church of St Gall ⑭
KOSTEL SV. HAVLA

Havelská. **Map** 3 C4. Můstek.
Tel 22 42 13 475. **Open** only for services. 12:15pm Mon–Fri, 8am Sun.

Dating from around 1280, this church was built to serve an autonomous German community in the area known as Gall's Town (Havelské Město). In the 14th century this was merged with the Old Town. In the 18th century the church was given a Baroque facelift by Giovanni Santini-Aichel, who created a bold façade decorated with statues of saints by Ferdinand Brokof. Rich interior furnishings include paintings by the leading Baroque artist Karel Škréta, who is buried here. Prague's best-known market has been held in Havelská Street since the middle ages, selling flowers, vegetables, toys, and clothes.

One of nine statues on façade of St Gall's

Carved Renaissance portal of the House at the Two Golden Bears

Old Town Hall **⑫**

STAROMĚSTSKÁ RADNICE

One of the most striking buildings in Prague is the Old Town Hall, established in 1338 after King John of Luxemburg agreed to set up a town council. Over the centuries a number of old houses were knocked together as the Old Town Hall expanded, and it now consists of a row of colourful Gothic and Renaissance buildings, most of which have been carefully restored after heavy damage inflicted by the Nazis in the 1945 Prague Uprising. The tower is 69.5 m (228 ft) high and offers a spectacular view of the city.

Old Council Hall
This 19th-century engraving features the well-preserved 15th-century ceiling.

Old Town Coat of Arms
Above the inscription, "Prague, Head of the Kingdom", is the coat of arms of the Old Town, which was adopted in 1784 for the whole city.

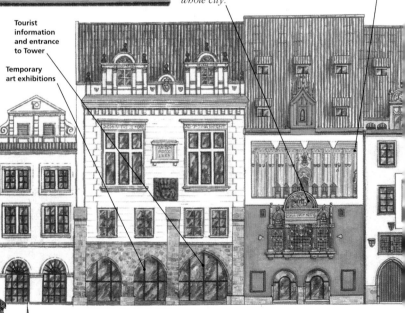

Tourist information and entrance to Tower

Temporary art exhibitions

EXECUTIONS IN THE OLD TOWN SQUARE

A bronze tablet below the Old Town Hall chapel records the names of the 27 Protestant leaders executed here by order of the Catholic Emperor Ferdinand on 21 June 1621. This was the humiliating aftermath of the Battle of the White Mountain *(see pp30–31)*. This defeat led to the emigration of Protestants unwilling to give up their faith, a Counter-Reformation drive and Germanization.

★ **Old Town Hall Tower**
In 1364 the tower was added to what was the private house of Volflin of Kamen. Its gallery provides a fine city view.

Viewing gallery

Former house of Volflin of Kamen

Steps to gallery

Entrance hall decorated with mosaics

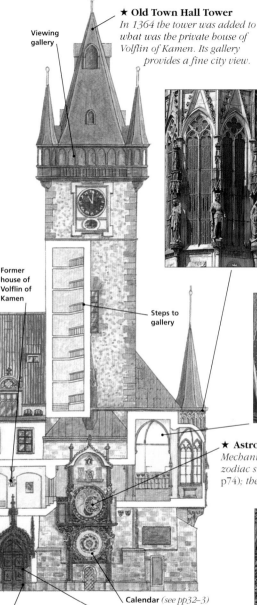

VISITORS' CHECKLIST

Staroměstské náměstí 1. **Map** 3 C3. **Tel** 72 45 08 584.
Staroměstská (line A), Můstek (A & B). 17, 18. **Open** 9am– 6pm daily (from 11am Mon).

Oriel Chapel
The original stained-glass windows on the five-sided chapel were destroyed in the last days of World War II, but were replaced in 1987.

Oriel Chapel Ceiling
The chapel, which was built on the first floor of the tower in 1381, has an ornate, recently restored ceiling.

★ **Astronomical Clock**
Mechanical figures perform above the zodiac signs in the upper section (see p74); the lower section is a calendar.

Calendar *(see pp32–3)*

Gothic Door
This late Gothic main entrance to the Town Hall and Tower was carved by Matthias Rejsek. The entrance hall is filled with wall mosaics after designs by the Czech painter Mikuláš Aleš.

STAR FEATURES

★ Astronomical Clock

★ Old Town Hall Tower

Town Hall Clock

ORLOJ

Jan Táborský

The Town Hall acquired its first clock at the beginning of the 15th century. According to legend, in 1490, when it was rebuilt by a master clockmaker called Hanuš (real name Jan Z Růže), the councillors were so anxious to prevent him from re-creating his masterpiece elsewhere, that they blinded the poor man. Though the clock has been repaired many times since, the mechanism was perfected by Jan Táborský between 1552 and 1572.

The Apostles

APOSTLES

The centrepiece of the show that draws a crowd of spectators every time the clock strikes the hour is the procession of the 12

Vanity and Greed

Arabic numerals 1–24

Astronomical Clock with the sun in Aries

Death

Vojtěch Sucharda's Apostles, sculpted after the last set was burnt in 1945

Blue, representing the daylight hours

Calendar by Josef Mánes (see pp32–3)

The Turk, a symbol of lust

Apostles. First the figure of Death, the skeleton on the right of the clock, gives a pull on the rope that he holds in his right hand. In his left hand is an hourglass, which he raises and inverts. Two windows then open and the clockwork Apostles (or to be precise 11 of the Apostles plus St Paul) move slowly round, led by St Peter.

At the end of this part of the display, a cock crows and the clock chimes the hour. The other moving figures are a Turk, who shakes his head from side to side, Vanity, who looks at himself in a mirror and Greed, adapted from the original medieval stereotype of a Jewish moneylender.

ASTRONOMICAL CLOCK

The clockmaker's view of the universe had the Earth fixed firmly at the centre. The purpose of the clock was not to tell you the exact time but to imitate the supposed orbits of the sun and moon about the Earth. The hand with the sun, which points to the hour, in fact records three different kinds of time. The outer ring of medieval Arabic numerals measures Old Bohemian time, in which a day of 24 hours was reckoned from the setting of the sun. The ring of Roman numerals indicates time as we know it. The blue part of the dial represents the

visible part of the sky. This is divided into 12 parts. In so-called Babylonian time, the period of daylight was divided into 12 hours, which would vary in length from summer to winter.

The clock also shows the movement of the sun and moon through the 12 signs of the zodiac, which were of great importance in 16th-century Prague.

The figures of Death and the Turk

Church of St Martin in the Wall ⓯

KOSTEL SV. MARTINA VE ZDI

Martinská. **Map** 3 B5. Ⓜ️ *Národní třída, Můstek.* 🚊 *6, 9, 17, 18, 22.* **Open** *for concerts.*

This 12th-century church became part of the newly erected town wall during the fortification of the Old Town in the 13th century, hence its name. It was the first church where blessed wine, usually reserved for the clergy, was offered to the congregation as well as bread. This was a basic tenet of belief of the moderate Hussites *(see pp26–7)*, the Utraquists, who took their name from the Latin *sub utraque specie*, "in both kinds". In 1787 the church was converted into workshops, but rebuilt in its original form in the early years of this century.

Náprstek Museum ⓰

NÁPRSTKOVO MUZEUM

Betlémské náměstí. **Map** 3 B4. **Tel** *22 44 97 511.* Ⓜ️ *Národní třída, Staroměstská.* 🚊 *6, 9, 17, 18, 22.* **Open** *10am–6pm Tue–Sun.* 🖼️ **www.**nm.cz

Vojta Náprstek, art patron and philanthropist, created this museum as a tribute to modern industry following a decade of exile in America after the 1848 revolution *(see pp32–3)*. On his return in 1862, inspired by London's Victorian museums, he began his collection. He created the Czech Industrial Museum by joining five older buildings together, and in the process virtually destroyed the family brewery and home – an 18th-century house called At the Haláneks (U Halánků). He later turned to ethnography and the collection now consists of artefacts from Asian, African and Native American cultures, including weapons and ritual objects from the Aztecs, Toltecs and Mayas. The museum is part of the National Museum. Regular temporary exhibitions on a range of subjects are also staged here.

Ceiling fresco by Václav Vavřinec Reiner in Church of St Giles

Church of St Giles ⓱

KOSTEL SV. JILJÍ

Husova. **Map** 3 B4. **Tel** *22 42 20 235.* Ⓜ️ *Národní třída.* 🚊 *6, 9, 17, 18, 22.* **Open** *for services only.* 🕐 *7am & 6:30pm Mon–Fri, 6:30pm Sat, 9:30am, 6:30pm Sun.* 📷 **www.**jilji.op.cz

Despite a beautiful Gothic portal on the southern side, the inside of this church is essentially Baroque. Founded in 1371 on the site of an old Romanesque church, it became a Hussite parish church in 1420. Following the Protestant defeat in 1620 *(see pp30–31)*, Ferdinand II presented the church to the Dominicans, who built a huge friary on its southern side. It has now been returned to the Dominicans, religious orders having been abolished under the Communists.

The vaults of the church are decorated with frescoes by the painter Václav Vavřinec Reiner, who is buried in the nave before the altar of St Vincent. The main fresco, a glorification of the Dominicans, shows St Dominic and his friars helping the pope defend the Catholic Church from non-believers.

Bethlehem Chapel ⓲

BETLÉMSKÁ KAPLE

Betlémské náměstí 4. **Map** 3 B4. Ⓜ️ *Národní třída, Staroměstská.* 🚊 *6, 9, 17, 18, 22.* **Open** *10am–6pm Tue–Sun.* 🖼️📷♿️📷 *organized by the Prague Information Service* (see p227).

The present "chapel" is a reconstruction of a hall built by the followers of the radical preacher Jan Milíč z Kroměříže in 1391–4. The hall was used for preaching in Czech. Between 1402 and 1413 Jan Hus *(see pp26–7)* preached in the Chapel. Influenced by the teachings of the English religious reformer John Wycliffe, Hus condemned the corrupt practices of the Church, arguing that the Scriptures should be the sole source of doctrine. After the Battle of the White Mountain in 1620 *(see pp30–31)*, when Protestant worship was outlawed, the building was handed over to the Jesuits, who rebuilt it with six naves. In 1786 it was almost demolished. After World War II the chapel was reconstructed following old illustrations.

16th-century illustration showing Jan Hus preaching in Bethlehem Chapel

Street-by-Street: Old Town (West)

The narrow streets near Charles Bridge follow
Prague's medieval street plan. For centuries Charles
Street (Karlova) was the main route across the Old
Town. The picturesque, twisting street is lined with
shops and houses displaying Renaissance and Baroque
façades. In the 17th century the Jesuits bought up a
vast area of land to the north of the street to house
the complex of the Clementinum university.

★ **Clementinum**
*This plaque records the
founding in 1783 of a state-
supervised seminary in place
of the old Jesuit university* ㉓

**Knights of the
Cross Square**
*From the façade of
the Church of the
Holy Saviour, black-
ened statues overlook
the small square* ㉕

Church of
St Francis

★ **Smetana Museum**
*A museum devoted to the life
and work of composer Bedřich
Smetana is housed in this Neo-
Renaissance building set on the
riverfront, which was once
an old waterworks* ㉔

A N E N S K A

The Old Town Bridge Tower
*dates from 1380. The Gothic
sculptural decoration on the
eastern façade was from Peter
Parler's workshop. The kingfisher
was the favourite personal symbol
of Wenceslas IV (son of Charles
IV) in whose reign the tower was
completed (see p139).*

St Anne's Convent
was abolished in 1782.
Some of its buildings
are now used by the
National Theatre
(see pp156–7).

Charles Street
*Among the many decorated houses
along the ancient street, be sure to
look out for this Art Nouveau
statue of the legendary Princess
Libuše (see p21) surrounded by
roses at No. 22/24* ㉑

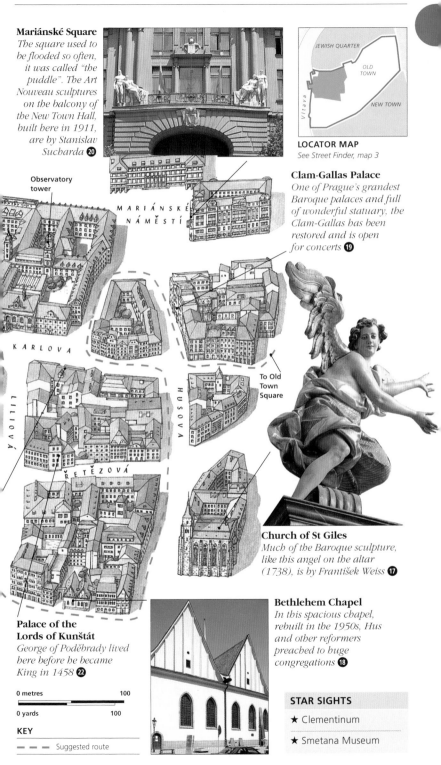

Mariánské Square
The square used to be flooded so often, it was called "the puddle". The Art Nouveau sculptures on the balcony of the New Town Hall, built here in 1911, are by Stanislav Sucharda ⑳

Observatory tower

MARIÁNSKÉ NÁMĚSTÍ

KARLOVA

LILIOVÁ

ŘETĚZOVÁ

HUSOVA

LOCATOR MAP
See Street Finder, map 3

JEWISH QUARTER
OLD TOWN
NEW TOWN
Vltava

Clam-Gallas Palace
One of Prague's grandest Baroque palaces and full of wonderful statuary, the Clam-Gallas has been restored and is open for concerts ⑲

To Old Town Square

Church of St Giles
Much of the Baroque sculpture, like this angel on the altar (1738), is by František Weiss ⑰

Palace of the Lords of Kunštát
George of Poděbrady lived here before he became King in 1458 ⑫

Bethlehem Chapel
In this spacious chapel, rebuilt in the 1950s, Hus and other reformers preached to huge congregations ⑱

| 0 metres | 100 |
| 0 yards | 100 |

KEY

– – – Suggested route

STAR SIGHTS

★ Clementinum

★ Smetana Museum

Clam-Gallas Palace ⑲

CLAM-GALLASŮV PALÁC

Husova 20. **Map** 3 B4. *No tel.* Ⓜ *Staroměstská.* **Open** *for concerts and temporary exhibitions only.*

The interior of this magnificent Baroque palace had suffered during its use as a store for the city archives, but has now been lovingly restored and can be seen if you attend a concert here. The palace, designed by Viennese court architect Johann Bernhard Fischer von Erlach, was built in 1713–30 for the Supreme Marshal of Bohemia, Jan Gallas de Campo. Its grand portals, each flanked by two pairs of Hercules sculpted by Matthias Braun, give a taste of what lies within. The main staircase is also decorated with Braun statues, set off by a

ceiling fresco, *The Triumph of Apollo* by Carlo Carlone. The palace has a theatre, where Beethoven performed.

Mariánské Square ⑳

MARIÁNSKÉ NÁMĚSTÍ

Map 3 B3. Ⓜ *Staroměstská, Můstek.*

Two statues dominate the square from the corners of the forbidding Town Hall, built in 1912. One illustrates the story of the long-lived Rabbi Löw *(see p88)* finally being caught by the Angel of Death. The other is the Iron Man, a local ghost condemned to roam the Old Town after murdering his mistress. A niche in the garden wall of the Clam-Gallas Palace houses a statue of the River Vltava, depicted as a nymph pouring water from a jug. There is a story that an old soldier once made the nymph sole beneficiary of his will.

Charles Street ㉑

KARLOVA ULICE

Map 3 A4. Ⓜ *Staroměstská.*

A 19th-century sign on the House at the Golden Snake

Dating back to the 12th century, this narrow, winding street was part of the Royal Route *(see pp174–5)*, along which coronation processions passed on the way to Prague Castle. Many original Gothic and Renaissance houses remain, most converted into shops to attract tourists.

A café at the House at the Golden Snake (No. 18) was established in 1714 by an Armenian, Deodatus Damajan, who handed out slanderous pamphlets from here. It is now a restaurant. Look out for At the Golden Well (No. 3), which has a magnificent Baroque façade and stucco reliefs of saints including St Roch and St Sebastian, who are believed to offer protection against plagues.

Palace of the Lords of Kunštát ㉒

DŮM PÁNŮ Z KUNŠTÁTU

Řetězová 3. **Map** 3 B4. *Tel* 22 22 21 240. Ⓜ *Národní třída, Staroměstská.* 🚋 6, 9, 17, 18, 22. **Open** Apr–Oct: 11am–9pm daily. 📷

The basement of the palace, dating from around 1200, contains three of the best-preserved Romanesque rooms in Prague. It was originally the ground floor, but over the years the surrounding ground level was raised by 3m (10 ft) to prevent flooding. In the 15th century the house was enlarged in Gothic style by its owners, the Lords of Kunštát and Poděbrady. The palace

Matthias Braun's statues on a portal of the Clam-Gallas Palace (c.1714)

houses a historical exhibition devoted to Bohemia's only Hussite king, George of Poděbrady *(see pp26–7)*, who lived here for a time.

Clementinum ㉓
KLEMENTINUM

Křižovnické náměstí 4, Mariánské náměstí 5, Seminářská 1. **Map** 3 A4. **Tel** 22 22 20 879 (tours). **Ⓜ** Staroměstská. ▥ 17, 18. **Library open** 9am–10pm Mon–Fri, 8am–2pm Sat. **Church open** only for services. ✚ 7pm Tue, 2pm & 8pm Sun. ☒ ♿ ✪ Mar–Oct: every hour from 10am–6pm daily. **www**.klementinum.cz

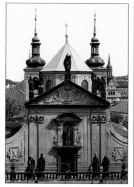
Former Jesuit Church of the Holy Saviour in the Clementinum

In 1556 Emperor Ferdinand I invited the Jesuits to Prague to help bring the Czechs back into the Catholic fold. They established their headquarters in the former Dominican monastery of St Clement, hence the name Clementinum. This soon became an effective rival to the Carolinum *(see p65)*, the Utraquist university. Prague's first Jesuit church, the Church of the Holy Saviour (Kostel sv. Salvátora) was built here in 1601. Its façade, with seven large statues of saints by Jan Bendl (1659), is dramatically lit up at night.

Expelled in 1618, the Jesuits were back two years later more determined than ever to stamp out heresy. In 1622 the two universities were merged, resulting in the Jesuits gaining a virtual monopoly on higher education in Prague. They searched for books in Czech and then burnt them by the thousand. Between 1653 and 1723 the Clementinum expanded eastwards. Over 30 houses and three churches were pulled down to make way for the new complex.

When in 1773 the pope dissolved their order, the Jesuits had to leave Prague and education was secularized. The Clementinum became the Prague University library, today the National Library. Look out for classical concerts performed in the beautiful Chapel of Mirrors (Zrcadlová kaple). You can also take a tour of the library and Chapel of Mirrors.

Smetana Museum ㉔
MUZEUM BEDŘICHA SMETANY

Novotného lávka 1. **Map** 3 A4. **Tel** 22 22 20 082. **Ⓜ** Staroměstská. ▥ 17, 18. **Open** 10am–noon, 12:30–5pm Wed–Mon. ☒ ✪ **www**.nm.cz

On a spit of land beside the Vltava, a former Neo-Renaissance waterworks has been turned into a memorial to Bedřich Smetana, the father of Czech music. The museum contains documents, letters, scores and musical instruments detailing the composer's life and work. Smetana was a fervent patriot and his music helped inspire the Czech national revival. Deaf towards the end of his life, he never heard his cycle of symphonic poems *Má Vlast* (My Country), being performed.

Statue of Charles IV(1848) in Knights of the Cross Square

Knights of the Cross Square ㉕
KŘIŽOVNICKÉ NÁMĚSTÍ

Map 3 A4. **Tel** 23 60 33 680. **Ⓜ** Staroměstská. ▥ 17, 18. ▤ 133. **Church of St Francis open** for services and concerts. ✚ 7am Mon–Fri, 9am Sun. ☒ ♿

This small square in front of the Old Town Bridge Tower offers fine views across the Vltava. On the north side is the Church of St Francis (kostel sv. Františka), once part of the monastery of the crusading Knights of the Cross with the Red Star. In summer, concerts of popular Classical and Baroque music take place in this beautiful Baroque church most evenings at 8pm. To the east is the Church of the Holy Saviour, part of the huge Clementinum complex. In the square stands a large bronze Neo-Gothic statue of Charles IV.

Sgraffitoed façade of the Smetana Museum

JEWISH QUARTER

JOSEFOV

In the Middle Ages there were two distinct Jewish communities in Prague's Old Town: Jews from the west had settled around the Old-New Synagogue, Jews from the Byzantine Empire around the Old Shul (on the site of today's Spanish Synagogue). The two settlements gradually merged and were confined in an enclosed ghetto. For centuries Prague's Jews suffered from oppressive laws – in the 16th century they had to wear a yellow circle as a mark of shame. Rudolph II's

Art Nouveau detail on house in Kaprova

more enlightened reign saw the Jewish Mayor Mordechai Maisel (see p90) appointed chief financial advisor. Discrimination was further relaxed by Joseph II, and the Jewish Quarter was named Josefov after him. In 1850 the area was officially incorporated as part of Prague. In the 1890s the city authorities decided to raze the ghetto slum because the lack of sanitation made it a health hazard. However, the Town Hall, a number of synagogues and the Old Jewish Cemetery were saved.

SIGHTS AT A GLANCE

Synagogues and Churches

Pinkas Synagogue ➍
Klausen Synagogue ➎
Old-New Synagogue pp88–9 ➏
High Synagogue ➐
Maisel Synagogue ➒
Church of the Holy Ghost ➓
Spanish Synagogue ⓫
Church of St Simon and St Jude ⓭
Church of St Castullus ⓮

Concert Hall

Rudolfinum ➊

Museums and Galleries

Museum of Decorative Arts ➋
St Agnes of Bohemia Convent pp92–3 ⓯

Historic Buildings

Jewish Town Hall ➑
Cubist Houses ⓬

Cemeteries

Old Jewish Cemetery pp86–7 ➌

GETTING THERE

Staroměstská station on metro line A is close to all the major sights in the Jewish Quarter. The alternative is to take tram 17 or 18 to Náměstí Jana Palacha. For St Agnes of Bohemia Convent, bus 133 is convenient.

0 metres   250
0 yards   250

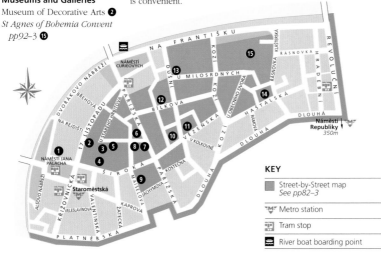

KEY

▨	Street-by-Street map See pp82–3
Ⓜ	Metro station
🚋	Tram stop
⛴	River boat boarding point

◁ **Densely-packed gravestones in the Old Jewish Cemetery**

Street-by-Street: Jewish Quarter

Though the old ghetto has disappeared, much of the area's fascinating history is preserved in the synagogues around the Old Jewish Cemetery, while the newer streets are lined with many delightful Art Nouveau buildings. The old lanes to the east of the former ghetto lead to the quiet haven of St Agnes's Convent, beautifully restored as a branch of the National Gallery.

Cubist Houses
One of the new architectural styles used in the rebuilding of the old Jewish Quarter was based on the ideas of Cubism 12

★ **Old Jewish Cemetery**
Thousands of gravestones are crammed into the ancient cemetery 3

★ **Old-New Synagogue**
The Gothic hall with its distinctive crenellated gable has been a house of prayer for over 700 years 6

Klausen Synagogue
The exhibits of the Jewish Museum include this alms box, dating from about 1800 5

High Synagogue
The interior has splendid Renaissance vaulting 7

★ **Museum of Decorative Arts**
Stained glass panels on the staircase depict the crafts represented in the museum's wide-ranging collection 2

Pinkas Synagogue
The walls are now a moving memorial to the Czech Jews killed in the Holocaust 4

To Metro Staroměstská

Jewish Town Hall
The 16th-century building still serves the Czech Jewish community 8

Maisel Synagogue
The original synagogue was built for Mayor Mordechai Maisel in 1591 9

BŘEHOVÁ

17. LISTOPADU

ELIŠKY KRÁSNOHORSKÉ

PAŘÍŽSKÁ

★ **St Agnes of Bohemia Convent**
Christ on Clouds, by the Czech Master, is one of the Medieval and Gothic works on show in the converted convent 15

Na Františku Hospital

LOCATOR MAP
See Street Finder, map 3

Former Charnel House

Church of St Castullus
Some fine mid-14th-century Gothic vaulting has been preserved in this restored parish church 14

Parsonage of St Castullus

Church of St Simon and St Jude
Part of the Na Františku Hospital since the 17th century, the church is now a popular venue for concerts 13

Spanish Synagogue
The newest of the synagogues in this part of Prague, it was built in flamboyant imitation Moorish style in 1868 11

Church of the Holy Ghost
This Baroque statue of St John Nepomuk by Ferdinand Brokof (1727) stands in front of the church 10

0 metres 50
0 yards 50

KEY

- - - Suggested route

STAR SIGHTS

★ Museum of Decorative Arts

★ Old Jewish Cemetery

★ Old-New Synagogue

★ St Agnes's Convent

Stage of the Dvořák Hall in the Rudolfinum

Rudolfinum ❶

Alšovo nábřeží 12. **Map** 3 A3.
Ⓜ *Staroměstská.* 🚊 *17, 18.*
🚌 *133.* **Philharmonic** *Tel 22 70 59
270.* **Galerie Rudolphinum** *Tel 22
70 59 205.* **Open** *10am–6pm Tue–
Sun.* 🏛 ♿ 🖵 www.rudolfinum.cz

Now the home of the Czech
Philharmonic Orchestra, the
Rudolfinum is one of the most
impressive landmarks on the
Old Town bank of the Vltava.
Many of the major concerts of
the Prague Spring music festi-
val *(see p50)* are held here.
There are several concert halls,
and the sumptuous Dvořák
Hall is one of the finest
creations of 19th-century
Czech architecture.

The Rudolfinum was built
between 1876 and 1884 to a
design by Josef Zítek and Josef
Schulz and named in honour
of Crown Prince Rudolph of
Habsburg. Like the National
Theatre *(see pp156–7)*, it is an
outstanding example of Czech
Neo-Renaissance style. The
curving balustrade is decorated
with statues of distinguished
Czech, Austrian and German
composers and artists.

Also known as the House of
Artists (Dům umělců), the
building houses the Galerie

Rudolphinum, a collection of
modern art. Between 1918
and 1939, and for a brief
period after World War II, the
Rudolfinum was the seat of
the Czechoslovak parliament.

Museum of
Decorative Arts ❷

UMĚLECKOPRŮMYSLOVÉ
MUZEUM

17. listopadu 2. **Map** 3 B3. **Tel** 25 10
93 111. Ⓜ *Staroměstská.* 🚊 *17,
18.* 🚌 *133.* **Open** *10am–6pm Tue–
Sun.* 🏛 🏛 🖵 www.upm.cz

For some years after its
foundation in 1885, the
museum's collections were
housed in the Rudolfinum.
The present building, designed
by Josef Schulz in French
Neo-Renaissance style, was
completed in 1901.

The museum's glass collection
is one of the largest in the
world, but only a fraction
of it is ever on display.
Pride of place goes to the
Bohemian glass, of which
there are many fine Baroque
and 19th- and 20th-century
pieces. Medieval and Venetian
Renaissance glass are also
well represented.

Among the permanent
exhibitions of other crafts are
Meissen porcelain, the Gobelin
tapestries and displays
covering fashion, textiles,
photography and printing.
The furniture collection has
exquisitely carved escritoires
and bureaux from the Renaissance. On the mezzanine
floor are halls for temporary
exhibitions and an extensive
art library housing more than
100,000 publications.

Old Jewish
Cemetery ❸

STARÝ ŽIDOVSKÝ HŘBITOV

See pp86–7.

Pinkas
Synagogue ❹

PINKASOVA SYNAGÓGA

Široká 3. **Map** 3 B3. **Tel** 22 23 17
191. Ⓜ *Staroměstská.* 🚊 *17, 18.*
🚌 *133.* **Open** *Apr–Oct:
9am–6pm Sun–Fri; Nov–Mar:
9am–4:30pm.* 🏛 🏛 ♿
www.jewishmuseum.cz

The synagogue was founded
in 1479 by Rabbi Pinkas and
enlarged in 1535 by his great-
nephew Aaron Meshulam
Horowitz. It has been rebuilt
many times over the centuries.
Excavations have turned up
fascinating relics of life in the
medieval ghetto, including a
mikva or ritual bath. The
core of the

Names of Holocaust victims on Pinkas Synagogue wall

present building is a hall with Gothic vaulting. The gallery for women was added in the early 17th century.

The synagogue now serves as a memorial to all the Jewish Czechoslovak citizens who were imprisoned in Terezín concentration camp and later deported to various Nazi extermination camps. The names of the 77,297 who did not return are inscribed on the synagogue walls. The building now houses an exhibition of children's drawings from the Terezín concentration camp.

Klausen Synagogue ❺

KLAUSOVÁ SYNAGÓGA

U starého hřbitova 3a. **Map** 3 B3. *Tel 22 23 17 191.* Ⓜ *Staroměstská.* 🚋 *17, 18.* 🚌 *133.* **Open** *Apr–Oct: 9am–6pm daily; Nov–Mar: 9am–4:30pm.* 📷 🚫 **www**.jewishmuseum.cz

Before the fire of 1689, this site was occupied by a number of small Jewish schools and prayer houses known as *klausen*. The name was preserved in the Klausen Synagogue, built on the ruins and completed in 1694. The High Baroque structure has a fine barrel-vaulted interior with rich stucco decorations. It now houses Hebrew prints and manuscripts and an exhibition of Jewish tradi-

19th-century Torah pointer in Klausen Synagogue

tions and customs, tracing the history of the Jews in Central Europe back to the early Middle Ages. Many exhibits relate to famous figures in the city's Jewish community including the 16th-century Rabbi Löw *(see p88)*, who, according to legend, created an artificial man out of clay.

Adjoining the synagogue is a building that looks like a tiny medieval castle. It was built in 1906 as the ceremonial hall of the Jewish Burial

18th-century silver-gilt Torah shield in the High Synagogue

Society. In 1944 an exhibition was put on here detailing the history of the Prague ghetto.

Old-New Synagogue ❻

STARONOVÁ SYNAGÓGA

See pp88–9.

High Synagogue ❼

VYSOKÁ SYNAGÓGA

Červená 4. **Map** 3 B3. *Tel 22 48 00 813.* Ⓜ *Staroměstská.* 🚋 *17, 18.* 🚌 *133.* **Open** *for services only: 8am & 2pm Sun–Fri, 9am & 12:45pm Sat.* **www**.kehila.cz

Like the Jewish Town Hall, the building of the High Synagogue was financed by Mordechai Maisel, mayor of the Jewish Town, in the 1570s. Originally the two buildings formed a single complex and to facilitate communi-cation with the Town Hall, the main hall of the synagogue was on the first floor. It was not until the 19th century that the two buildings were sep-arated and the syna-gogue was given a staircase and street entrance. You can still see the original Renaissance vault-ing and stucco decoration.

Jewish Town Hall ❽

ŽIDOVSKÁ RADNICE

Maislova 18. **Map** 3 B3. *Tel & Fax 22 48 00 813.* Ⓜ *Staroměstská.* 🚋 *17, 18.* 🚌 *133.* **Closed** *to the public.*

The core of this attractive pink and white building is the original Jewish Town Hall, built in 1570–77 by architect Panacius Roder at the expense of the immensely rich mayor, Mordechai Maisel. In 1763 it acquired a new appearance in the flowery style of the Late Baroque. The last alterations date from 1908, when the southern wing was enlarged.

The building is one of the few monuments that survived far-reaching sanitation of this medieval part of Prague at the beginning of the 20th century. On the roof stands a small wooden clock tower with a distinctive green steeple. The right to build the tower was originally granted to the Jewish community after their part in the defence of Charles Bridge against the Swedes in 1648 *(see pp30–31)*. On one of the gables there is another clock. This one has Hebrew figures and, because Hebrew reads from right to left, hands that turn in an anti-clockwise direction. The Town Hall is now the seat of the Council of Jewish Religious Communities in the Czech Republic.

Façade and clock tower of the Jewish Town Hall

Old Jewish Cemetery ❸

STARÝ ŽIDOVSKÝ HŘBITOV

This remarkable site was, for over 300 years, the only burial ground permitted to Jews. Founded in 1478, it was slightly enlarged over the years but still basically corresponds to its medieval size. Because of the lack of space people had to be buried on top of each other, up to 12 layers deep. Today you can see over 12,000 gravestones crammed into the tiny space, but several times that number are thought to have been buried here. The last burial was of Moses Beck in 1787.

View across the cemetery towards the western wall of the Klausen Synagogue

David Gans' Tombstone
The tomb of the writer and astronomer (1541–1613) is decorated with the symbols of his name – a star of David and a goose (Gans in German).

The Pinkas Synagogue is the second-oldest in Prague *(see p84).*

Jewish printers, Mordechai Zemach (d 1592) and his son Bezalel (d 1589), are buried under this square gravestone.

The oldest tomb is that of the writer Rabbi Avigdor Kara (1439).

Rabbi David Oppenheim (1664–1736)
The chief rabbi of Prague owned the largest collection of old Hebrew manuscripts and prints in the city.

Klausen Synagogue *(see p85)*

The gravestone of Moses Beck

The Nephele Mound was where infants who died under a year old were buried.

STAR SIGHTS

- ★ Tombstone of Rabbi Löw
- ★ Tombstone of Hendela Bassevi
- ★ 14th-Century Tombstones

★ **14th-Century Tombstones**
Embedded in the wall are fragments of Gothic tombstones brought here from an older Jewish cemetery discovered in 1866 in Vladislavova Street in the New Town.

Prague Burial Society
Founded in 1564, the group carried out ritual burials and performed charitable work in the community. Members of the society wash their hands after leaving the cemetery.

The Museum of Decorative Arts *(see p84)*

★ **Tombstone of Rabbi Löw**
The most visited grave in the cemetery is that of Rabbi Löw (1520–1609). Visitors place hundreds of pebbles and wishes on his grave as a mark of respect.

The Neo-Romanesque Ceremonial Hall

Mordechai Maisel (1528–1601) was Mayor of Prague's Jewish Town and a philanthropist.

★ **Tombstone of Hendela Bassevi**
The highly-decorated tomb (1628) was built for the beautiful wife of Prague's first Jewish nobleman.

UNDERSTANDING THE GRAVESTONES

From the late 16th century onwards, tombstones in the Jewish cemetery were decorated with symbols denoting the background, family name or profession of the deceased person.

Blessing hands: Cohen family

A pair of scissors: tailor

A stag: Hirsch or Zvi family

Grapes: blessing or abundance

Old-New Synagogue ❻

STARONOVÁ SYNAGOGA

Star of David in Červená Street

Built around 1270, this is the oldest synagogue in Europe and one of the earliest Gothic buildings in Prague. The synagogue has survived fires, the slum clearances of the 19th century and many Jewish pogroms. Residents of the Jewish Quarter have often had to seek refuge within its walls and today it is still the religious centre for Prague's Jews. It was originally called the New Synagogue until another synagogue was built nearby – this was later destroyed.

The synagogue's eastern side

The 14th-century stepped brick gable

★ **Jewish Standard**
The historic banner of Prague's Jews is decorated with a Star of David and within it the hat that had to be worn by Jews in the 14th century.

These windows formed part of the 18th-century extensions built to allow women a view of the service.

RABBI LÖW AND THE GOLEM

The scholar and philosophical writer Rabbi Löw, director of the Talmudic school (which studied the Torah) in the late 16th century, was also thought to possess magical powers. He was supposed to have created a figure, the Golem, from clay and then brought it to life by placing a magic stone tablet in its mouth. The Golem went berserk and the Rabbi had to remove the tablet. He hid the creature among the Old-New Synagogue's rafters.

Rabbi Löw and the Golem

Candlestick holder

★ **Five-rib Vaulting**
Two massive octagonal pillars inside the hall support the five-rib vaults.

Right-hand Nave
The glow from the bronze chandeliers provides light for worshippers using the seats lining the walls.

VISITORS' CHECKLIST

Pařížská and Červená. **Map** 3 B2.
***Tel** 22 23 17 191.* **M** Staro-
městská. 17, 18 to Staroměstská, 17 to Law Faculty (Právnická
fakulta). **Open** 9:30am–6pm
Sun–Fri (to 5pm Nov–Mar).
Closed Jewish holidays.
8am Mon–Fri, 9am Sat.
www.jewishmuseum.cz

The tympanum above the Ark is decorated with 13th-century leaf carvings.

★ **Rabbi Löw's Chair**
A star of David marks the chair of the Chief Rabbi, placed where the distinguished 16th-century scholar used to sit.

The cantor's platform and its lectern is surrounded by a wrought-iron Gothic grille.

Entrance to the Synagogue in Červená Street

The Ark
This shrine is the holiest place in the synagogue and holds the sacred scrolls of the Torah.

Entrance Portal
The tympanum above the door in the south vestibule is decorated with clusters of grapes and vine leaves growing on twisted branches.

STAR FEATURES

★ Rabbi Löw's Chair

★ Five-rib Vaulting

★ Jewish Standard

18th-century silver Torah crown in the Maisel Synagogue

Maisel Synagogue ❾

MAISELOVA SYNAGÓGA

Maiselova 10. **Map** 3 B3. **Tel** 22 23 17 191. ᛟ Staroměstská. 🚊 17, 18. 🚌 133. **Open** Apr–Oct: 9am–6pm Sun–Fri; Nov–Mar: 9am–4.30pm Sun–Fri. 📷 📵 ♿ www.jewishmuseum.cz

When it was first built, at the end of the 16th century, this was a private house of prayer for the use of mayor Mordechai Maisel and his family. Maisel had made a fortune lending money to Emperor Rudolph II to finance wars against the Turks, and his synagogue was the most richly decorated in the city. The original building was a victim of the fire that devastated the Jewish Town in 1689 and a new synagogue was built in its place. Its present crenellated, Gothic appearance dates from the start of the 20th century. Since the 1960s the Maisel Synagogue has housed a fascinating collection of Jewish silver and other metalwork dating from Renaissance times to the 20th century. It includes many Torah crowns, shields and finials. Crowns and finials were used to decorate the rollers on which the text of the Torah (the five books of Moses) was kept. The shields were hung over the mantle that was draped over the

Torah and the pointers were used to follow the text so that it was not touched by readers' hands. There are also objects such as wedding plates, lamps and candlesticks. By a tragic irony, nearly all these Jewish treasures were brought to Prague by the Nazis from synagogues throughout Bohemia and Moravia with the intention of founding a museum of a vanished people.

Church of the Holy Ghost ❿

KOSTEL SV. DUCHA

Dušní, Široká. **Map** 3 B3. ᛟ Staroměstská. 🚊 17. 🚌 133. **Open** only for services. ⛪ 9:30am Sun. 📵 ♿

This church stands on the narrow strip of Christian soil which once separated the two Jewish communities of the Middle Ages – the Jews of the eastern and western rites. Built in the mid-14th century, the single-naved Gothic church was originally part of a convent of Benedictine nuns. The convent was destroyed in 1420 during the Hussite Wars (see pp26–7) and not rebuilt.

The church was badly damaged in the Old Town fire of 1689. The exterior preserves the original Gothic buttresses and high windows, but the vault of the nave was rebuilt in Baroque style after the fire. The furnishings too

are mainly Baroque. The high altar dates from 1760, and there is an altar painting of St Joseph by Jan Jiří Heintsch (c1647–1712). In front of the church stands a stone statue of St John Nepomuk (see p83) distributing alms (1727) by the prolific sculptor of the Czech Baroque Ferdinand Maximilian Brokof. Inside the church there are a few earlier statues, including a 14th-century Pietà (the heads of the figures are later, dating from 1628), a Late Gothic statue of St Ann and busts of St Wenceslas and St Adalbert from the early 16th century.

Church of the Holy Ghost

Spanish Synagogue ⓫

ŠPANĚLSKÁ SYNAGÓGA

Vězeňská 1. **Map** 3 B2. **Tel** 22 23 17 191. ᛟ Staroměstská. 🚊 17, 18. 🚌 133. **Open** Apr–Oct: 9am–6pm Sun–Fri; Nov–Mar: 9am–4.30pm Sun–Fri. 📷 ♿ www. jewishmuseum.cz

Prague's first synagogue, known as the Old School (Stará škola), once stood on this site. In the 11th century the Old School was the centre of the community of Jews of the eastern rite, who lived strictly apart from Jews of the western rite, who were concentrated round the Old-New Synagogue. The present building dates from the second half of the 19th century. The exterior and interior are both pseudo-Moorish in

Motif of the Ten Commandments on the Spanish Synagogue's façade

appearance. The rich stucco decorations on the walls and vaults are reminiscent of the Alhambra in Spain, hence the name. Once closed to the public, the Spanish Synagogue now houses a permanent exhibition dedicated to the history of the Jews of Bohemia.

Cubist Houses ⑫
KUBISTICKÉ DOMY

Elišky Krásnohorské, 10–14. **Map** 3 B2. "M̃" *Staroměstská.* 17, 18. **Closed** to the public.

The rebuilding of the old Jewish Quarter at the turn of the 20th century gave Prague's architects scope to experiment with many new styles. Most of the blocks in this area are covered with flowing Art Nouveau decoration, but on the corner of Bílkova and Elišky Krásnohorské there is a plain façade with a few simple repeated geometrical shapes. This is an example of Cubist architecture, a fashion that did not really catch on in the rest of Europe, but was very popular with the avant-garde in Bohemia and Austria before and after World War I. This block was built for a cooperative of teachers in 1919–21.

At No. 7 Elišky Krásnohorské you can see the influence of Cubism in the curiously flattened atlantes supporting the windows. Another interesting Cubist building is the House of the Black Mother of God in Celetná *(see pp174–5).*

Church of St Simon and St Jude ⑬
KOSTEL SV. ŠIMONA A JUDY

U milosrdných. **Map** 3 B2. "M̃" *Staroměstská.* 17, 18. 133. **Open** for concerts. **www**.fok.cz

Members of the Bohemia Brethren built this church with high Late Gothic windows in 1615–20. The Brethren, founded in the mid-15th century, agreed with the Utraquists *(see p75)* in directing the congregation to receive both bread and wine

Cubist-style atlantes framing a window in Elišky Krásnohorské Street

at Holy Communion. In other respects they were more conservative than other Protestant sects, continuing to practise celibacy and Catholic sacraments such as confession. After the Battle of the White Mountain *(see pp30–31),* the Brethren were expelled from the Empire.

The church was then given to a Catholic order, the Brothers of Mercy, becoming part of a monastery and hospital. Tradition has it that the monastery's wooden steps were built from the scaffold on which 27 Czechs were executed in 1621 *(see p72).* In the 18th century the city's first anatomy lecture hall was established here and the complex continues to serve as a hospital – the Na Františku. The church is now used as a venue for concerts.

Detail of Baroque façade of Church of St Simon and St Jude

Church of St Castullus ⑭
KOSTEL SV. HAŠTALA

Haštalské náměstí. **Map** 3 C2. 5, 8, 14. 133. Open *irregularly.* 5pm Sun.

This peaceful little corner of Prague takes its name – Haštal – from the parish church of St Castullus. One of the finest Gothic buildings in Prague, the church was erected on the site of an older Romanesque structure in the second quarter of the 14th century. Much of the church had to be rebuilt after the fire of 1689, but fortunately the double nave on the north side survived. It has beautiful slender pillars supporting a delicate ribbed vault.

The interior furnishings are mainly Baroque, though there are remains of wall paintings of about 1375 in the sacristy and a metal font decorated with figures dating from about 1550. Standing in the Gothic nave is an impressive sculptural group depicting *Calvary* (1716) from the workshop of Ferdinand Maximilian Brokof.

St Agnes of Bohemia Convent ⑮
KLÁŠTER SV. ANEŽKY ČESKÉ

See pp92–3.

St Agnes of Bohemia Convent ⑮

KLÁŠTER SV. ANEŽKY ČESKÉ

In 1234 a convent of the Poor Clares was founded here by Agnes, sister of King Wenceslas I. She was not canonized until 1989. The convent, one of the very first Gothic buildings in Bohemia, was abolished in 1782 and used to house the poor and as storage space, later falling into disrepair. Following painstaking restoration in the 1960s, it has recovered much of its original appearance and is now used by the National Gallery to display a large collection of medieval painting and sculpture from Bohemia and Central Europe, dating from 13th–16th centuries.

Head of statue of St Agnes by Josef Myslbek

First floor

★ **Votive panel of Archbishop Jan Očko of Vlašim**
This detailed panel, painted around 1370 by an anonymous artist, shows Charles IV kneeling before the Virgin in Heaven.

Ground floor

★ **The Annunciation of Our Lady**
Painted around 1350 by the renowned Master of the Vyšší Brod Altar, this panel is one of the oldest and finest works in the museum.

★ **Strakonice Madonna**
This 700-year-old statue evokes the Classical French sculpture found in such places as Reims Cathedral.

Steps to first-floor gallery

Terrace café

STAR EXHIBITS

★ The Annunciation by the Master of the Vyšší Brod Altarpiece

★ Strakonice Madonna

★ Votive panel of Archbishop Jan Očko of Vlašim

GALLERY GUIDE

The permanent exhibition is housed on the first floor of the old convent in a long gallery and smaller rooms around the cloister. The works are arranged chronologically.

VISITORS' CHECKLIST

U Milosrdných 17. **Map** 3 C2.
Tel 22 48 10 628. ꔛ Náměstí Republiky, Staroměstská. 🚊 17 to Law faculty, 5, 8, 14 to Dlouhá třída. 🚌 133 to Řásnovka. **Open** 10am–6pm Tue–Sun (last guided tour:5pm). 🎧 📷 ♿ 🎫 💻 **www**.ngprague.cz

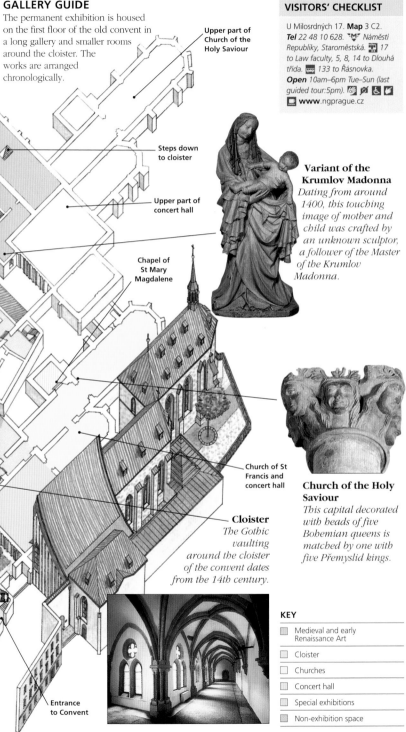

Upper part of Church of the Holy Saviour

Steps down to cloister

Upper part of concert hall

Chapel of St Mary Magdalene

Variant of the Krumlov Madonna
Dating from around 1400, this touching image of mother and child was crafted by an unknown sculptor, a follower of the Master of the Krumlov Madonna.

Church of St Francis and concert hall

Cloister
The Gothic vaulting around the cloister of the convent dates from the 14th century.

Church of the Holy Saviour
This capital decorated with heads of five Bohemian queens is matched by one with five Přemyslid kings.

Entrance to Convent

KEY

🟦	Medieval and early Renaissance Art
⬜	Cloister
⬜	Churches
⬜	Concert hall
⬜	Special exhibitions
🟦	Non-exhibition space

PRAGUE CASTLE AND HRADČANY

PRAŽSKÝ HRAD A HRADČANY

The history of Prague begins with the Castle, founded in the 9th century by Prince Bořivoj. Its commanding position high above the river Vltava soon made it the centre of the lands ruled by the Přemyslids. The buildings enclosed by the Castle walls included a palace, three churches and a monastery. In about 1320 a town called Hradčany was founded in part of the Castle's outer bailey. The

Stained-glass window in St Vitus's Cathedral

Castle has been rebuilt many times, most notably in the reigns of Charles IV and Vladislav Jagiello. After a fire in 1541, the badly damaged buildings were rebuilt in Renaissance style and the Castle enjoyed its cultural heyday under Rudolph II. Since 1918 it has been the seat of the president of the Republic. The Changing of the Guard takes place every hour. At noon the ceremony includes a fanfare.

SIGHTS AT A GLANCE

Churches and Monasteries
St Vitus's Cathedral pp100–3 **2**
St George's Basilica **5**
Capuchin Monastery **19**
The Loreto pp116–17 **20**
Strahov Monastery pp120–21 **23**

Palaces
Royal Palace pp104–5 **4**
Belvedere **11**
Archbishop's Palace **14**
Martinic Palace **16**
Černín Palace **21**

Historic Buildings
Powder Tower **3**
Dalibor Tower **9**

Museums and Galleries
Picture Gallery of Prague Castle **1**
St George's Convent pp106–9 **6**
Lobkowicz Palace **8**
Riding School **13**
Sternberg Palace pp112–15 **15**
Schwarzenberg Palace **17**

Historic Streets
Golden Lane **7**
New World **18**
Pohořelec **22**

Parks and Gardens
South Gardens **10**
Royal Garden **12**

KEY

	Street-by-Street map See pp96–7
M	Metro station
	Tram stop
i	Tourist Information
—	Castle wall

GETTING THERE
Take the 22 tram to Pražský hrad (Prague Castle) or to Pohořelec. If you feel energetic, take the 12, 18, 20 or 22 tram to Malostranské náměstí in the Little Quarter, then walk up Nerudova or go to Malostranská metro and walk up Staré zámecké schody (Old Castle Steps).

◁ **The main entrance to Prague Castle**

Street-by-Street: Prague Castle

Despite periodic fires and invasions, Prague Castle has retained churches, chapels, halls and towers from every period of its history, from the the Gothic splendour of St Vitus's Cathedral to the Renaissance additions of Rudolph II, the last Habsburg to use the Castle as his principal residence. The courtyards date from 1753–75 when the whole area was rebuilt in Late Baroque and Neo-Classical styles. The Castle became the seat of the Czechoslovak president in 1918, and the current president of the Czech Republic has an office here.

★ St Vitus's Cathedral
The decoration on the fence at St Vitus's Golden Portal ❷

Powder Tower
Used in the past for storing gunpowder and as a bell foundry, the tower is now a museum ❸

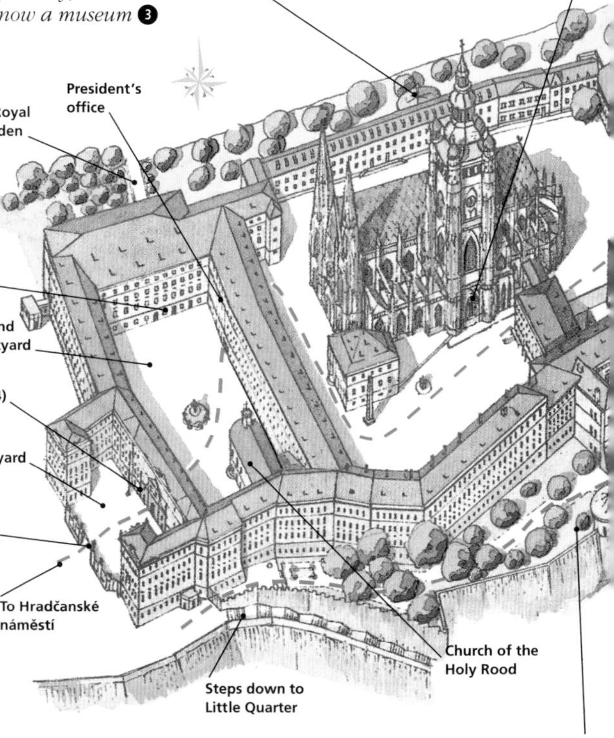

Gothic reliquary of St George's arm in St Vitus's Cathedral

To Royal Garden

President's office

Picture Gallery of Prague Castle
Renaissance and Baroque paintings hang in the restored stables of the castle ❶

Second courtyard

Matthias Gate (1614)

First courtyard

To Hradčanské náměstí

Church of the Holy Rood

Steps down to Little Quarter

The Castle gates are crowned by copies of 18th-century statues of Fighting Giants by Ignaz Platzer.

South Gardens
18th-century statues decorate the gardens laid out in the old ramparts ❿

★ Golden Lane
The picturesque artisans' cottages along the inside of the castle wall were built in the late 16th century for the Castle's guards and gunners **7**

LOCATOR MAP
See Street Finder, map 2

White Tower

Dalibor Tower
This grim tower is named for a prisoner who played his violin in return for food **9**

Old Castle steps to Malostranská Metro

JIŘSKÁ

Lobkowicz Palace
Works of art from the Lobkowicz family's private collection are housed here **8**

★ St George's Basilica
The vaulted chapel of the royal Bohemian martyr St Ludmilla is decorated with 16th-century paintings **5**

KEY

– – – Suggested route

0 metres   60

0 yards   60

★ St George's Convent
The convent houses 19th-century Czech art such as this piece titled Summer Countryside with Chapel *by Adolf Kosárek* **6**

★ Royal Palace
The uniform exterior of the palace conceals many fine Gothic and Renaissance halls. Coats of arms cover the walls and ceiling of the Room of the New Land Rolls **4**

STAR SIGHTS

★ St Vitus's Cathedral

★ Royal Palace

★ St George's Basilica and Convent

★ Golden Lane

Picture Gallery of Prague Castle ❶

OBRAZÁRNA PRAŽSKÉHO HRADU

Prague Castle, the second courtyard.
Map 2 D2. **Tel** 22 43 73 368.
Ⓜ Malostranská, Hradčanská.
🚊 22 **Open** 9am–4pm daily in
winter, 9am–6pm daily in summer.
📷 ♿ www.obrazarna-hradu.cz

The gallery was created in
1965 to hold works of art
collected since the reign of
Rudolph II *(see pp28–9)*.
Though most of the collection
was looted by the Swedes in
1648, many interesting paintings remain. Paintings from
the 16th–18th centuries form
the bulk of the collection, but
there are also sculptures,
among them a copy of a bust
of Rudolph by Adriaen de
Vries. Highlights include
Titian's *The Toilet of a Young
Lady*, Rubens' *The Assembly
of the Olympic Gods* and
Guido Reni's *The Centaur
Nessus Abducting Deianeira*.
Master Theodoric, Paolo
Veronese, Tintoretto and the
Czech Baroque artists Jan
Kupecký and Petr Brandl are
among other artists
represented. The Picture
Gallery houses many of
Rudolph's best paintings.

You can also see the
remains of the Castle's first
church, the 9th-century Church
of our Lady, thought to have
been built by Prince Bořivoj,
the first Přemyslid prince to
be baptized a Christian *(see
pp20–21)*. The site was discovered during reconstruction.

St Vitus's Cathedral ❷

CHRÁM SV. VÍTA

See pp100–3.

Powder Tower ❸

PRAŠNÁ VĚŽ

Prague Castle, Vikářská.
Map 2 D2. **Tel** 22 43 73 368.
Ⓜ Malostranská, Hradčanská.
🚊 22. **Open** Apr–Oct: 9am–6pm;
Nov–Mar: 9am–4pm daily.
📷 🚫 🎫

A tower was built here in
about 1496 by the King
Vladislav II's architect Benedikt
Ried as a cannon bastion overlooking the Stag Moat. The
original was destroyed in the
fire of 1541, but it was rebuilt
as the home and workshop of
gunsmith and bell founder
Tomáš Jaroš. In 1549 he made
Prague's largest bell, the 18-
tonne Sigismund, for the bell
tower of St Vitus's Cathedral.

During Rudolph II's reign
(1576–1612), the tower
became a laboratory for

**View of the Powder Tower from
across the Stag Moat**

alchemists. It was here that
adventurers such as Edward
Kelley performed experiments
that convinced the emperor
they could turn lead into gold.

In 1649, when the Swedish
army was occupying the
Castle, gunpowder exploded
in the tower, causing serious
damage. Nevertheless it
was used as a gunpowder
store until 1754, when it
was converted into flats
for the sacristans of St
Vitus's Cathedral. Today,
the tower houses a perma-
nent exhibition of Czech
military history.

Royal Palace ❹

KRÁLOVSKÝ PALÁC

See pp104–5.

St George's Basilica ❺

BAZILIKA SV. JIŘÍ

Jiřské náměstí. **Map** 2 E2. **Tel** 22 43 73
368. Ⓜ Malostranská, Hradčanská.
🚊 22. **Open** Apr–Oct: 9am–6pm
daily; Nov–Mar: 9am–4pm daily.
📷 🚫 ♿ www.hrad.cz

Founded by Prince Vratislav
(915–21), the basilica
predates St Vitus's Cathedral

Titian's *The Toilet of a Young Lady* in the Castle Picture Gallery

and is the best-preserved Romanesque church in Prague. It was enlarged in 973 when the adjoining St George's Convent was established here, and rebuilt following a fire in 1142. The massive twin towers and austere interior have been scrupulously restored to give a good idea of the church's original appearance. However, the rusty red façade was a 17th-century Baroque addition.

Buried in the church is St Ludmila, widow of the 9th-century ruler Prince Bořivoj *(see pp20–21)*. She became Bohemia's first female Christian martyr when she was strangled on the orders of Drahomíra, her daughter-in-law, as she knelt at prayer. Other members of the Přemyslid dynasty buried here include Vratislav. His austere tomb stands on the right-hand side of the nave at the foot of the curving steps that lead up to the choir. The impressive Baroque grille opposite encloses the tomb of Boleslav II (973–99).

St George's Convent ❻
KLÁŠTER SV. JIŘÍ

See pp106–9.

Golden Lane ❼
ZLATÁ ULIČKA

Map 2 E2. ᴹ⸍ *Malostranská, Hradčanská.* 🚊 *22.* 🏛

Named after the goldsmiths who lived here in the 17th century, this short, narrow street is one of the most picturesque in Prague. One side of the lane is lined with tiny, brightly

One of the tiny houses in Golden Lane

Façade and towers of St George's Basilica

painted houses which were built right into the arches of the Castle walls. They were constructed in the late 1500s for Rudolph II's 24 Castle guards. A century later the goldsmiths moved in and modified the buildings. But by the 19th century the area had degenerated into a slum and was populated by Prague's poor and the criminal community. In the 1950s all the remaining tenants were moved and the area restored to something like its original state. Most of the houses were converted into shops selling books, Bohemian glass and other souvenirs for tourists, who flock to the narrow lane.

Golden Lane has been home to some well-known writers, including the Nobel prize-winning poet, Jaroslav Seifert, and Franz Kafka *(see p68)* who stayed at No. 22 with his sister for a few months in 1916–17. Because of its name, legends have spread about the street being filled with alchemists huddled over their bubbling alembics trying to produce gold for Rudolph II. In fact the alchemists had laboratories in Vikářská, the lane between St Vitus's Cathedral and the Powder Tower.

Lobkowicz Palace ❽
LOBKOVICKÝ PALÁC

Jiřská 3. **Map** 2 E2. *Tel 23 33 12 925.* ᴹ⸍ *Hradčanská.* 🚊 *22.* **Open** *10:30am–6pm daily.* 🏛 📷 ♿ 💻 www.lobkowiczevents.cz **Toy Museum** *Tel 22 43 72 294.* **Open** *9:30am–5:30pm daily.* www.ivan-steiger.de

This is one of the palaces that sprang up after the fire of 1541, when Hradčany was almost totally destroyed. It dates from 1570, and some original *sgraffito* on the façade has been preserved, but most of the present palace is Carlo Lurago's 17th-century reconstruction for the Lobkowicz family, who had inherited it in 1627. The most splendid room is the 17th-century banqueting hall with mythological frescoes by Fabian Harovník.

The palace once formed part of Prague's National Museum but has since been returned to the Lobkowicz family. It now houses the valuable Princely Collections, an exhibition of paintings, decorative arts, original music scores annotated by Beethoven and Haydn, and musical instruments.

Opposite the palace, at No. 6, is a delightful toy museum claiming to be the world's second largest, with toys from ancient Greece to the present.

Detail of 16th-century *sgraffito* on façade of Lobkowicz Palace

St Vitus's Cathedral ❷

KATEDRÁLA SV. VÍTA, VÁCLAVA A VOJTĚCHA

Work began on the city's most distinctive landmark in 1344 on the orders of John of Luxembourg. The first architect was the French Matthew of Arras. After his death, Swabian Peter Parler took over. His masons' lodge continued to work on the building until the Hussite Wars. Finally completed by 19th- and 20th-century architects and artists, the cathedral houses the crown jewels and the tomb of "Good King" Wenceslas *(pp20–21)*.

St Vitus's Cathedral
This 19th-century engraving shows how the cathedral looked before the additions made in 1872–1929.

Twin west spires

Triforium

Rose Window
Designed by František Kysela in 1925–7, the window above the portals depicts scenes from the biblical story of the creation.

Gargoyles
On the ornate west front, gutter spouts are given their traditional disguise.

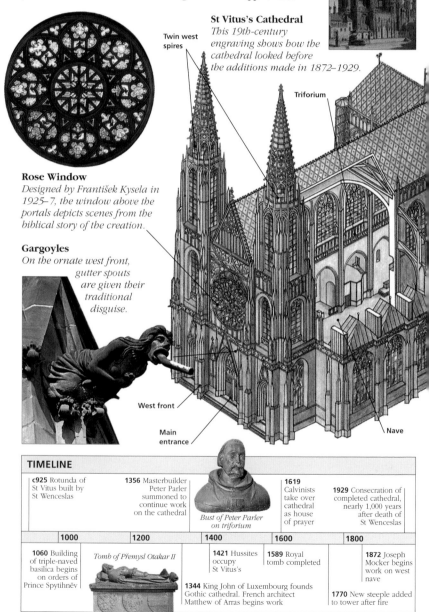

West front

Main entrance

Nave

TIMELINE

c925 Rotunda of St Vitus built by St Wenceslas	**1356** Masterbuilder Peter Parler summoned to continue work on the cathedral		**1619** Calvinists take over cathedral as house of prayer	**1929** Consecration of completed cathedral, nearly 1,000 years after death of St Wenceslas	

Bust of Peter Parler on triforium

1000	1200	1400	1600	1800

1060 Building of triple-naved basilica begins on orders of Prince Spytihněv	*Tomb of Přemysl Otakar II*	**1421** Hussites occupy St Vitus's	**1589** Royal tomb completed	**1872** Joseph Mocker begins work on west nave
		1344 King John of Luxembourg founds Gothic cathedral. French architect Matthew of Arras begins work		**1770** New steeple added to tower after fire

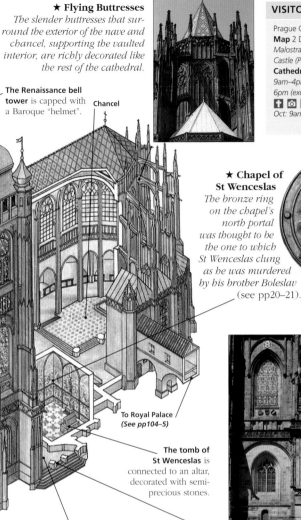

★ Flying Buttresses
The slender buttresses that surround the exterior of the nave and chancel, supporting the vaulted interior, are richly decorated like the rest of the cathedral.

The **Renaissance bell tower** is capped with a Baroque "helmet".

Chancel

VISITORS' CHECKLIST

Prague Castle, third courtyard.
Map 2 D2. 🚇 Hradčanská,
Malostranská. 🚊 22 to Prague
Castle (Pražský hrad).
Cathedral open Nov–Mar:
9am–4pm daily; Apr–Oct: 9am–
6pm (except during services).
🕇 📷 ♿ **Steeple open** Apr–
Oct: 9am–5pm. 📷 📷

★ Chapel of St Wenceslas
The bronze ring on the chapel's north portal was thought to be the one to which St Wenceslas clung as he was murdered by his brother Boleslav (see pp20–21).

To Royal Palace
(See pp104–5)

The tomb of St Wenceslas is connected to an altar, decorated with semi-precious stones.

★ Golden Portal
Until the 19th century this was the main cathedral entrance, and it is still used on special occasions. Above it is a mosaic of The Last Judgment *by 14th-century Venetian craftsmen.*

Gothic Vaulting
The skills of architect Peter Parler are never more clearly seen than in the delicate fans of ribbing that support the three Gothic arches of the Golden Portal.

STAR FEATURES

★ Chapel of
    St Wenceslas

★ Golden Portal

★ Flying Buttresses

A Guided Tour of St Vitus's Cathedral

West door: St Wenceslas' murder

A walk around St Vitus's takes you back through a thousand years of history. Go in through the west portal to see some of the best elements of the modern, Neo-Gothic style and continue past a succession of side chapels to catch glimpses of religious artefacts such as saintly relics, and works of art from Renaissance paintings to modern statuary. Allow plenty of time to gaze at the richly decorated, jewel-encrusted St Wenceslas Chapel before you leave.

② Chancel
The chancel was built by Peter Parler from 1372. It is remarkable for the soaring height of its vault, counterpointed by the intricacy of the webbed Gothic tracery.

Cathedral organ (1757)

New sacristy

① Alfons Mucha Window
The cathedral contains many superb examples of 20th-century Czech stained glass, notably St Cyril and St Methodius.

Main entrance (West Portal)

Thun Chapel

Chapel of St Ludmilla

THE FOUR ERAS OF ST VITUS'S

Excavations have revealed sections of the northern apse of St Wenceslas's original rotunda, and architectural and sculptural remains of the later basilica, beneath the existing cathedral. The western, Neo-Gothic end is a faithful completion of the 14th-century plan.

KEY

☐ Rotunda, 10th century

■ Basilica, 11th century

☐ Gothic cathedral, 14th century

☐ 19th- and 20th-century additions to cathedral

Leopold II is shown in a contemporary engraving being crowned King of Bohemia at the cathedral in September 1791. Mozart composed an opera, *La Clemenza di Tito*, in honour of the occasion.

③ **Flight of Frederick of the Palatinate**
In depicting the sad aftermath of the Battle of the White Mountain in 1620 (see p31), this carved wooden panel shows 17th-century Prague in fascinating detail.

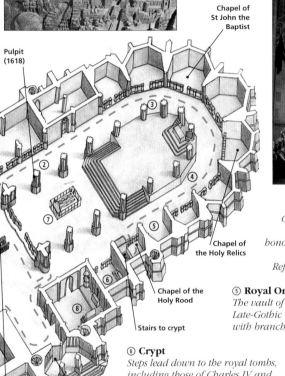

Chapel of
St John the
Baptist

Pulpit
(1618)

Chapel of
the Holy Relics

Chapel of the
Holy Rood

Stairs to crypt

Golden
Portal

Exit from
crypt

④ **Tomb of
St John Nepomuk**
Crafted from solid silver in 1736, this elaborate tomb honours the saint who became the focus of a Counter-Reformation cult (see p137).

⑤ **Royal Oratory**
The vault of the 15th-century Late-Gothic oratory is carved with branches instead of ribs.

⑥ **Crypt**
Steps lead down to the royal tombs, including those of Charles IV and his four wives, as well as vestiges of the early rotunda and basilica.

⑧ **St Wenceslas
Chapel**
Gothic frescoes with scenes from the Bible and the life of the saint cover the walls, interspersed with a patchwork of polished gemstones and fine gilding. Every object is a work of art – this golden steeple held the wafers and wine for Holy Communion.

⑦ **Royal Mausoleum**
Ferdinand I died in 1564. His beloved wife and son, Maximilian II, are buried alongside him in the mausoleum.

KEY

– – – Tour route

Royal Palace ❹

KRÁLOVSKÝ PALÁC

From the time Prague Castle was first fortified in stone in the 11th century *(see pp22–3)*, the palace was the seat of Bohemian princes. The building consists of three different architectural layers. A Romanesque palace built by Soběslav I around 1135 forms the cellars of the present building. Přemysl Otakar II and Charles IV then added their own palaces above this, while the top floor, built for Vladislav Jagiello, contains the massive Gothic Vladislav Hall. During the period of Habsburg rule the palace housed government offices, courts and the old Bohemian Diet (parliament). In 1924 it was extensively restored.

Riders' Staircase
These wide and gently sloping steps, with their Gothic rib vault, were used by knights on horseback to get to Vladislav Hall for indoor jousting competitions.

The Diet, the medieval parliament, was also the throne room. Destroyed by fire in 1541, it was rebuilt by Bonifaz Wohlmut in 1563.

An overhead passage from the palace leads to the Royal Oratory in St Vitus's Cathedral *(see p103).*

14

4

3

2

5

1

Entrance

Vladislav Hall
The 17th-century painting by Aegidius Sadeler shows that the Royal Court was very like a public market. The hall's magnificent rib vaulting was designed by Benedikt Ried in the 1490s.

TIMELINE

Přemysl Otakar II, 1230–78

1253 Palace reconstructed by Přemysl Otakar II

1618 Defenestration from Bohemian Chancellery

1041 Castle besieged and palace burnt

1541 Fire destroys large part of Castle

1766–8 Building of Theresian Wing

900	1100	1300	1500	1700	1900

Late 9th century Founding of Prague Castle by Prince Bořivoj

1340 Charles IV rebuilds palace

1370s Peter Parler rebuilds All Saints' Chapel

Decorated door of office in Royal Palace

1135 Rebuilding undertaken by Soběslav I

1502 Completion of Vladislav Hall by Benedikt Ried after nine years

1924 Palace undergoes extensive restoration

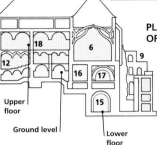

PLAN AND CROSS SECTION OF ROYAL PALACE

The cross section of the palace shows the three distinct levels of the building, all constructed at different times. The plan shows how Vladislav Hall dominates the entire palace structure.

Upper floor

Ground level

Lower floor

VISITORS' CHECKLIST

Prague Castle, third courtyard.
Map 2 D2. **Tel** 22 43 73 368.
🚇 *Hradčanská, up K Brusce, then through the Royal Garden; Malostranská, left up Klárov, then up Old Castle Steps.* 🚌 22 to Prague Castle (Pražský hrad). **Open** Apr–Oct: 9am–6pm daily; Nov–Mar: 9am–4pm daily; last adm: 1hr before closing. 📷 🚫 ♿

All Saints' Chapel was built by Peter Parler for Charles IV. After the 1541 fire, its vault had to be rebuilt and it was redecorated in the Baroque style.

KEY TO ROYAL PALACE

☐ Romanesque and Early Gothic

☐ Late Gothic

☐ Rebuilt after 1541 fire

☐ Baroque and later

1 Eagle Fountain	**10** All Saints' Chapel
2 Vestibule	**11** Diet Hall
3 Green Chamber	**12** Ride taircase
4 King's Bedchamber	**13** Court of Appeal
5 Romanesque tower	**14** Palace courtyard
6 Vladislav Hall	**15** Hall of the
7 Bohemian	Romanesque palace
Chancellery	**16** Old Land Rolls
8 Imperial Council	**17** Palace of
Room steps	Charles IV
9 Terrace	**18** New Land Rolls

The Theresian Way was built to house the office registers.

Bohemian Chancellery
This 17th-century Dutch-style stove decorates the former royal offices of the Habsburgs. The chancellery is the site of the 1618 defenestration.

DEFENESTRATION OF 1618

Painting by Václav Brožík, 1889

On 23 May, 1618, more than 100 Protestant nobles, led by Count Thurn, marched into the palace to protest against the succession to the throne of the intolerant Habsburg Archduke Ferdinand. The two Catholic Governors appointed by Ferdinand, Jaroslav Martinic and Vilém Slavata, were confronted and, after a row, the Protestants threw both the Governors and their secretary, Philipp Fabricius, out of the eastern window. Falling some 15 m (50 ft), they survived by landing in a dung heap. This event signalled the beginning of the Thirty Years' War. The Catholics attributed the survival of the Governors to the intervention of angels.

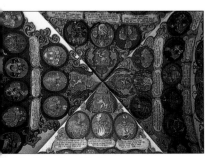

The New Land Rolls
These rooms are decorated with the crests of clerks who worked here from 1561 to 1774.

St George's Convent ⑥

KLÁŠTER SV. JIŘÍ

The first convent in Bohemia was founded here close to the Royal Palace in 974 by Prince Boleslav II. His sister Mlada was its first abbess. Rebuilt over the centuries, the convent was finally abolished in 1782 and converted into barracks. In 1962–74 it was reconstructed and today it houses the National Gallery's collection of 19th-century Czech art. The collection, chosen as an artistic mirror to 19th-century Bohemian society, features paintings from luminaries such as Josef Navrátil, the Mánes family and Jakub Schikaneder plus sculpture from Josef Václav Myslbek. The collection is interspersed with pieces of decorative art from the period.

★ **George of Poděbrady and Matthius Corvinus**
Mikoláš Aleš painted many patriotic historical scenes. Here, Corvinus King of Hungary, signs a treaty with King George in 1469.

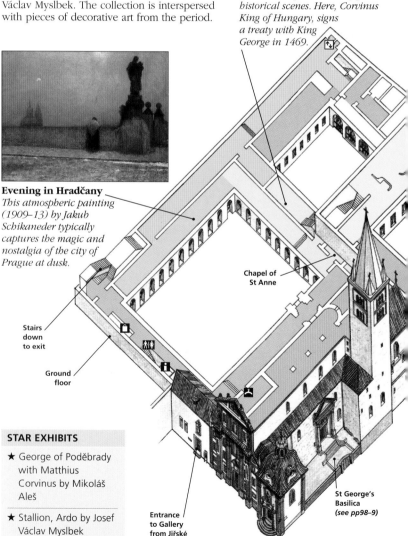

Evening in Hradčany
This atmospheric painting (1909–13) by Jakub Schikaneder typically captures the magic and nostalgia of the city of Prague at dusk.

Chapel of St Anne

Stairs down to exit

Ground floor

STAR EXHIBITS

★ George of Poděbrady with Matthius Corvinus by Mikoláš Aleš

★ Stallion, Ardo by Josef Václav Myslbek

Entrance to Gallery from Jiřské náměstí

St George's Basilica
(see pp98–9)

Summer Country with a Chapel
One of Adolf Kosárek's final paintings before his untimely death in 1859, the Romantic motif is a composite of landscape views.

VISITORS' CHECKLIST

Prague Castle, Jiřské náměstí 33.
Map 2 E2. **Tel** 25 75 35 829.
🚊 Hradčanská or Malostranská, then 10 mins up steep steps. 🚋 22, 23 to Prague Castle (Pražský hrad) **Open** 10am–6pm daily. 📷 Ø 💻
www.ngprague.cz

Josefina
Josef Mánes's evocative portrait (1855) asks the eternal question: who is Josefina? Was she the mother of Mánes's daughter or an actress?

Upper floor

★ **Stallion, Ardo**
Perfectionist Josef Václav Myslbek created many drafts of the iconic mounted statue of St Wenceslas (see p146). As with the others, this bronze (1898–99) was modeled on a seven-year-old Oldenburg stallion named Ardo.

Fox Hunt
This striking landscape from the 1850s illustrates the aesthetic traits of the Romantic movement. Josef Navrátil highlights the gloom with one hunter's red scarf and glowing cigarette.

KEY

⬜	Late Baroque, Neo-Classicism and Early Romanticism
⬜	Onset of Romanticism
⬜	The Mánes family
⬜	Romanticism: Hausofer & landscape
⬜	Romanticism: Ruben & history painting
⬜	The Realists
⬜	Generation of the National Theatre
⬜	Neo-Romanticism, Symbolism and Naturalism
⬜	St George's Basilica
⬜	Special exhibitions
⬜	Non-exhibition space

GALLERY GUIDE

The permanent exhibition is located on both the upper and lower floors of the convent. The collection is laid out chronologically, beginning on the upper floor, and thematically and spans the years 1790–1910. The paintings and sculptures illustrate the progression of Czech art and the changes occurring in Bohemian society through this period. There are also examples of religious art in the Chapel of St Anne.

Exploring the St George's Collection

This fine collection of 19th-century Czech art is produced in collaboration with the Museum of Decorative Art in Prague, which has interspersed the artworks with various items of furniture, jewellery and clothing from the day. The collection spans the period of 1790 to 1910, when Prague witnessed a renewed interest in art and a growth in communication between artists and the public. The burgeoning influence of the middle classes is evident in portraits of artistic patrons, members of the intelligentsia and, latterly, the National Revival movement. The cultural climate of Bohemia and specifically Prague has been beautifully mapped by this collection of paintings, sculptures, sketches and monuments.

Detail from *Goldsmith* (1861) by Quido Mánes

Still Life with Lizard and Flowers (1826) by Jenny Salmová

LATE BAROQUE, NEO-CLASSICISM AND EARLY ROMANTICISM

The drama and exuberant religious motifs of the Late-Baroque period are evident in the masterful compositional style of *St Bernard's Dream* (c.1830) by Josef Führich as well as *Pietà* (1837) by František Tkadlík.

Antonín Machek was a key artist of this genre, as illustrated by his whimsical labour of love, *Cycle of Rulers* (1828–35). His portraits also interestingly demonstrate the societal emergence of the middle class intelligentsia as patrons of the arts.

Elsewhere in this section are Romantic pastorals by master landscape painter Norbert Grund and Neo-Classical scenes from Ludvík Kohl and Kryštof Seckel. Also of note are some religious sculptures by Václav Prachner and Václav Levý.

ONSET OF ROMANTICISM

The aesthetic experience and emphasis on high emotions and untamed nature that epitomises Romanticism is beautifully demonstrated by this vast collection of landscapes, portraits and even shop signs by master painter Josef Navrátil. The contemporaneous lure of western Europe is evident in his Alpine landscapes, but it is Navrátil's dedication to homespun subjects that truly delights; an example is the beloved, relaxed nature of *In Chumlecký's Wine Cellar* (1850s).

Other artists here include Jenny Salmová who couples the exotic and the mundane in *Still Life with Lizard and Flowers* (1826) and Charlotta Piepenhagenová who is appropriately rugged in, *A Lake in the Mountains* (1870s).

THE MÁNES FAMILY

Unsurprisingly, the influential Mánes family of painters take up a whole section. Father Antonín Mánes was a forerunner of Romantic Czech landscape painting, even though he took much of his inspiration from western Europe. *Landscape with Church Ruins* (1827–28), for example, was sketched, fairly accurately, from literary discriptions of Kelso Abbey in Scotland.

Antonín's son Quido's ability grew with experience and his *Goldsmith* (1861) is exemplary of his evocative paintings of workers and peasants. It is Quido's brother Josef who is undoubtedly the most successful of the family and his cabinet-sized *Red Umbrella* (1855) is one of the more familiar exhibits in the collection. Josef Václav Mylsbek was much inspired by Josef and a draft (1916) of his monument to the artist is on show here.

Landscape With Church Ruins (1827–28) by Antonín Mánes

Deserted Countryside (1858) by Adolf Kosárek

ROMANTICISM: HAUSOFER & LANDSCAPE

The 19th century is often considered the golden age of landscape painting in Prague, with Romanticism being the principal style. Master painters such as Josef Navrátil and Antonín Mánes made names for themselves but it was Max Haushofer, professor of landscape painting at the Prague Academy of Fine Arts from 1845 to 1866, who influenced many young painters of the time. Here, the legacy of his mammoth landscape, *A Lake in the Alps* (1860), for example, is evident in Alois Bubák's *Summer Afternoon* (1863). Other students of his include Bedřich Havránek, Václav Prachner and Adolf Kosárek. Note the typically Romantic stormy landscape in the latter's *Deserted Countryside* (1858).

ROMANTICISM: RUBEN & HISTORY PAINTING

Christian Ruben was appointed director of the Prague Academy of Fine Arts in 1841 and his monumental visions of a brave new world formed the basis of his teachings. The human quest and trepidation is palpable in his *Columbus Discovering America* (1846) and also resonates in *Kriemhild's Accusation* (1879) by his student Emil Jan Lauffer.

Early Christian scenes and Bohemia's past are the predominant subjects within this genre. Another student of Ruben, Jaroslav Čermák, however, found much inspiration from the history and people, particularly women, of Montenegro, as displayed in the atmospheric *Captives* (1870).

THE REALISTS

Jaroslav Čermák's talent crossed genres into the Realist style as illustrated by *Still Life with Fish* (1873). However, it is the prolific Karel Purkyně who dominates this section. Faithful to the Realist aesthetic, his *Snowy Owl* (1862), actually records where the owl was killed. Purkyně's portraits are typically peopled with ordinary folk at work; a blacksmith and woodcarver for instance.

Elsewhere look out for Soběslav Hippolyt Pinkas's compositional skills in *Interior of a Farmhouse with Girl* (1867) and landscapes by Antonín Chittussi; the latter's *Bohemian Moravian Highlands* (1882) contains almost Impressionistic touches.

Captives (1870) by Jaroslav Čermák

GENERATION OF THE NATIONAL THEATRE

The Czech nation acquired some of its most exceptional buildings during the period of the National Revival *(see pp32–3)*, including the National Theatre and National Museum, which were embellished by many of the great painters, sculptors and architects of the day. Here, sketches of the interior and exterior decorations to the National Theatre are on display as well as other works by the artists involved. The spirit of the time is particularly captured in portraits of contemporary cultural personalities by J V Myslbek.

Master academic painter Václav Brožík is represented by some excellent snapshots of country life as well as a study for the 7 m- (23 ft-) long painting *Tu, Felix Austria, Nube* (1897), commissioned by the Emperor Franz Josef I. The Chapel of St Anne contains drafts of the four saints that flank Myslbek's St Wenceslas Monument *(see p146)* and Emanuel Max's sublime *Christ on the Cross* (1843).

J V Myslbek's Music (c.1895)

NEO-ROMANTICISM, SYMBOLISM AND NATURALISM

The end of the 19th century saw artistic style veer toward the heightened emotional traits of Neo-Romanticism, here beautifully illustrated by Lev Lerch's *Will-o'-the-Wisp* (before 1890) and Maximilían Pirner's emotive *Frenzy, Hatred and Death* (1886–93). Beneš Knüpfer more subtly symbolises the despair and remorse felt by Judas in his eponymous painting (1900).

Also in this section are some interesting Naturalistic street scenes from Jakub Schikaneder, whose works capture the solitary mood of the city so well, blurring Realism with Impressionism and foreshadowing more modern techniques to come.

Old prison in the Dalibor Tower

Dalibor Tower ❾

DALIBORKA

Prague Castle, Zlatá ulička. **Map** 2 E2.
Ⓜ *Malostranská.* 🚋 *12, 18, 20,
22.* **Open** *9am–5pm daily (to 4pm
Nov–Mar).* 📷 🚫

This 15th-century tower with
a conical roof was part of the
fortifications built by King
Vladislav Jagiello (see p26–7).
His coat of arms can be seen
on the outer wall. The tower
also served as a prison and is
named after its first inmate,
Dalibor of Kozojedy, a young
knight sentenced to death for
harbouring some outlawed
serfs. While awaiting execution, he was kept in an
underground dungeon, into
which he had to be lowered
through a hole in the floor.
    According to legend, while
in prison he learnt to play the
violin. People sympathetic to
his plight came to listen to his
playing and provided him
with food and drink, which

they lowered on a rope from a
window – prisoners were often
left to starve to death. The
story was used by Bedřich
Smetana in his opera *Dalibor.*
The tower ceased to serve as
a prison in 1781. Visitors can
see part of the old prison.

South Gardens ❿

JIŽNÍ ZAHRADY

Prague Castle (access from Hradčanské
náměstí). **Map** 2 D3. Ⓜ
Malostranská, Hradčanská. 🚋 *12, 18,
20, 22.* **Open** *Apr–Oct: 10am–6pm
daily (to 7pm May & Sep, 9pm Jun,
Jul & Aug).* 📷 www.hrad.cz

The gardens occupy the long
narrow band of land below the
Castle overlooking the Little
Quarter. Several small gardens
have been linked to form
what is now known as the
South Gardens. The oldest,
the Paradise Garden (Rajská
zahrada), laid out in 1562,
contains a circular pavilion
built for Emperor Matthias in
1617. Its carved wooden ceiling
shows the coloured emblems
of the 39 countries of the
Habsburg Empire. The Garden
on the Ramparts (Zahrada Na
valech) dates from the 19th
century. It occupies a former
vegetable patch and is famous
as the site of the defenestration
of 1618 (see p105), when two
Imperial governors were
thrown from a first-floor window. Two obelisks were subse-
quently erected by Ferdinand
II to mark the spots where

they landed. Modifications
were carried out in the 1920s
by Josip Plečnik, who built
the Bull Staircase leading to
the Paradise Garden and the
observation terrace. Below the
terrace, in the former Hartig
Garden, is a Baroque music
pavilion designed by Giovanni
Battista Alliprandi. Beside it
stand four statues of Classical
gods by Antonín Braun.

**Alliprandi's music pavilion in
the South Gardens**

Belvedere ⓫

BELVEDÉR

Prague Castle, Royal Garden. **Map** 2
E1. Ⓜ *Malostranská, Hradčanská.*
🚋 *12, 18, 20, 22.* **Open** *10am–6pm
Tue–Sun during exhibitions only.* 📷
♿ www.hrad.cz

Built by Ferdinand I for his
beloved wife Anne, the
Belvedere is one of the finest
Italian Renaissance buildings
north of the Alps. Also known
as the Royal Summer Palace

The Belvedere, Emperor Ferdinand I's summer palace in the Royal Garden beside Prague Castle

Antonín Braun's statue of *The Allegory of Night* in front of the *sgraffito* decoration of the Ball Game Hall in the Royal Garden

(Královský letohrádek), it is an arcaded summerhouse with slender Ionic columns topped by a roof shaped like an inverted ship's hull clad in blue-green copper. The main architect was Paolo della Stella, who was also responsible for the ornate reliefs inside the arcade. Work began in 1538, but was interrupted by the great Castle fire of 1541. The Belvedere was eventually completed in 1564.

In the middle of the small geometrical garden in front of the palace stands the Singing Fountain. Dating from 1568, it owes its name to the musical sound the water makes as it hits the bronze bowl, though you have to listen closely to appreciate the effect. The fountain was cast by Tomáš Jaroš, the famous bell founder, who lived and worked in the Powder Tower (see p98).

Many of the Belvedere's works of art were plundered by the occupying Swedish army in 1648. The statues stolen included Adriaen de Vries's 16th-century bronze of *Mercury and Psyche*, which is now in the Louvre in Paris. The Belvedere is now used as an art gallery.

Royal Garden ⓬
KRÁLOVSKÁ ZAHRADA

Prague Castle, U Prašného mostu. **Map** 2 D2. ⁔Ⓜ⁔ *Malostranská, Hradčanská.* 🚋 22. **Open** May–Oct: 10am–6pm daily (to 7pm May & Sep, 9pm Jun, Jul & Aug). 📷 🅿️ ♿ **www**.hrad.cz

The garden was created in 1535 for Ferdinand I. Its appearance has been altered over time, but some examples of 16th-century garden architecture have survived, notably the Belvedere and the Ball Game Hall (Míčovna), built by Bonifaz Wohlmut in 1569. The building is covered in beautiful, though much re-stored, Renaissance *sgraffito*, a form of decoration created by cutting a design through the wet top layer of plaster on to a contra-sting undercoat. The garden is beautiful in spring when thousands of tulips bloom. This is where tulips were first acclimatized to Europe.

Riding School ⓭
JÍZDÁRNA

Prague Castle. **Map** 2 D2. **Tel** *22 43 73 368.* ⁔Ⓜ⁔ *Malostranská, Hradčanská.* 🚋 22. **Open** 10am–6pm during exhibitions.

The 17th-century Riding School forms one side of U Prašného mostu, a road which runs to the northern side of Prague Castle via Deer Moat. In the 1920s it was converted into an exhibition hall, which now holds important exhibitions of painting and sculpture. A garden provides excellent views of St. Vitus's Cathedral and the northern fortifications of the castle.

Archbishop's Palace ⓮
ARCIBISKUPSKÝ PALÁC

Hradčanské náměstí 16. **Map** 2 D3. **No tel.** ⁔Ⓜ⁔ *Malostranská, Hradčanská.* 🚋 22. **Not open** to the public.

Ferdinand I bought this sumptuous palace in 1562 for the first Catholic Archbishop since the Hussite Wars (see pp26–7). It replaced the old Archbishop's Palace in the Little Quarter, which had been destroyed during the wars, and has remained the Archbishop's seat in Prague ever since. In the period after the Battle of the White Mountain (see p30–31), it was a powerful symbol of Catholic domination of the city and the Czech lands. Its spectacular cream-coloured Rococo façade was designed by Johann Joseph Wirch in the 1760s for Archbishop Antonín Příchovský, whose coat of arms sits proudly above the portal.

Příchovský coat of arms

Sternberg Palace ⓯
ŠTERNBERSKÝ PALÁC

See pp112–15.

Sternberg Palace ⓯

ŠTERNBERSKÝ PALÁC

Franz Josef Sternberg founded the Society of Patriotic Friends of the Arts in Bohemia in 1796. Fellow noblemen would lend their finest pictures and sculpture to the society, which had its headquarters in the early-18th-century Sternberg Palace. Since 1949, the fine Baroque building has been used to house the National Gallery's collection of European art, with its superb range of Old Masters.

The Lamentation of Christ
The frozen, sculptural figures make this one of the finest paintings by Lorenzo Monaco (1408).

First floor

Cardinal Cesi's Garden in Rome
Henrick van Cleve's painting (1548) provides a valuable image of a Renaissance collections of antiquities. The garden was later destroyed.

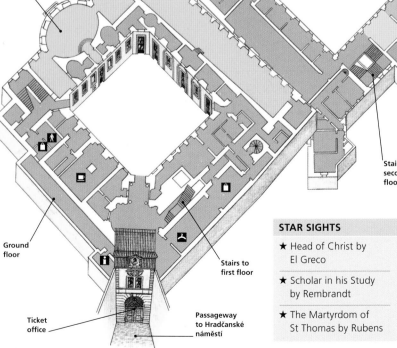

Garden Room

Stairs to second floor

Ground floor

Stairs to first floor

Ticket office

Passageway to Hradčanské náměstí

STAR SIGHTS

★ Head of Christ by El Greco

★ Scholar in his Study by Rembrandt

★ The Martyrdom of St Thomas by Rubens

★ **Scholar in his Study**
*In this painting from
1634 Rembrandt used
keenly observed detail
to convey wisdom
in the face of the
old scholar.*

VISITORS' CHECKLIST

Hradčanské náměstí 15.
Map 1 C2. **Tel** 22 05 14 634.
Hradčanská, Malostranská.
22 to Prague Castle (Pražský
hrad) or Pohořelec. **Open** 10am–
6pm Tue–Sun (last tour: 5pm).
www.ngprague.cz
30 minutes' walk from centre
(old town).

**Chinese
Cabinet**

Paradise *(1618)*
*Roelandt Savery studied models of exotic
animals, brought to Prague by Persian
nobles, at the court of Emperor Rudolf II.
He was then able to paint real animals.*

**Second
floor**

GALLERY GUIDE
*The gallery is arranged on
three floors around the
central courtyard of the
palace. The ground floor,
reached from the courtyard,
houses German and Austrian
art from the 15th to 19th
centuries. The stairs to the
collections on the upper floors
are just beyond the ticket
office at the main entrance.*

**Stairs down to
other floors
and exit**

★ **Head of Christ**
*Painted by El Greco in the
1590s, this portrait
emphasizes the humanity
of Christ. At the same time
the curious square halo
framing the head gives the
painting the qualities of an
ancient icon.*

★ **The Martyrdom of
St Thomas**
*This magnificent work is
by Peter Paul Rubens, the
foremost Flemish painter
of the 17th century.*

KEY

- German and Austrian Art 1400–1800
- Flemish and Dutch Art 1400–1600
- Italian Art 1400–1500
- Flemish and Dutch Art 1600–1800
- French Art 1400–1800
- Icons, Classical and Ancient Art
- Venice 1700–1800 and Goya
- Spanish Art 1400–1800
- Naples and Venice 1600–1700
- Italian Art 1500–1600
- Non-exhibition space

Exploring the Sternberg Collections

The National Gallery's collection of European art at the Sternberg Palace ranks among the country's best collections. The museum is divided into three separate viewing areas. Its extensive holdings of German and Austrian art of the 15th–19th centuries are exhibited just off the courtyard on the ground floor. A small collection of art from antiquity and religious icons, as well as a larger display of early Italian and Dutch art, occupy the first floor. Most of the real treasures are on the second floor, where the museum displays works of Italian, Spanish, French and Dutch masters from the 16th–18th centuries.

ICONS, CLASSICAL AND ANCIENT ART

Two small rooms on the first floor are occupied by an odd assortment of paintings that do not quite fit in with the rest of the collection. These include a *Portrait of a Young Woman* dating from the 2nd century AD, which was discovered during excavations at Fayoum in Egypt in the 19th century.

The second room, on the left as you enter the main viewing area, holds icons of the Orthodox church – some are Byzantine, some Italo-Greek and some Russian. A fine example on show here is a later 16th-century work, *Christ's Entry Into Jerusalem* from Russia. The collection of icons on display offers examples from a variety of the most important Mediterranean and Eastern European centres.

Christ's Entry into Jerusalem, a 16th-century Russian icon

GERMAN AND AUSTRIAN ART (1400–1800)

This collection is massive and it could take half a day to see everything. One of the most celebrated paintings in the Sternberg's collection is Albrecht Dürer's *The Feast of the Rosary*, painted during the artist's stay in Venice in 1506. The work has a particular significance for Prague since it

was bought by Emperor Rudolph II. The two figures in front of the Virgin and Child are Maximilian I (Rudolph's great-great-grandfather) and Pope Julius II.

The collection also includes works by several other important German painters of the Renaissance, including Hans Holbein the Elder and the Younger and Lucas Cranach the Elder. Cranach is represented by a striking *Adam and Eve* whose nudes show the spirit of the Renaissance, tempered by Lutheran Reform.

ITALIAN ART (1400–1700)

When you enter the gallery of early Italian art on the first floor, you are greeted by a splendid array of richly gilded early diptychs and triptychs from the churches of Tuscany and northern Italy. Most came originally from the d'Este collection at Konopiště Castle *(see p169)*. Of particularly high quality are the two triangular panels of saints by the 14th-century Sienese painter Pietro Lorenzetti and a moving *Lamentation of Christ* by Lorenzo Monaco.

A fascinating element of the collection is the display of Renaissance bronze statuettes. Fashionable amongst Italian nobility of the 15th century, these little bronzes were at first cast from famous or newly-discovered works of antiquity. Later, sculptors began to use the medium more freely – Padua, for example, specialized in the depiction of small animals – and producers also adapted items for use as decorative household goods such as oil lamps, ink pots and door knockers. This small collection has representative works from all the major Italian producers except Mantua and, while many variations can be found in other museums throughout the world, there are some pieces here that are both unique and outstanding examples of the craft.

The Feast of the Rosary by Dürer (1506)

is in complete contrast to the spiritual calm of *St Augustine*. Two other fine portraits are those of Rembrandt's *Scholar in His Study* and Frans Hals' *Portrait of Jasper Schade*.

Also on display is a wide assortment of paintings by other, less-prominent, artists who nonetheless represent the enormous range and quality of this period.

Don Miguel de Lardizábal (1815), by Francisco Goya

On the second floor, among the 16th-century Italian works on display, are some delightful surprises. These include *St Jerome* by the Venetian painter, Tintoretto, and *The Annunciation to the Shepherds* and *Portrait of an Elderly Man* by another Venetian, Jacopo Bassano. There is also an expressive portrait by the Florentine mannerist, Bronzino, of *Eleanor of Toledo*, the wife of Cosimo de' Medici.

FLEMISH AND DUTCH ART (1400–1800)

The collections of Flemish and Dutch art on the first and second floors are rich and varied, ranging from rural scenes by Pieter Brueghel the Elder to portraits by Rubens and Rembrandt. Highlights of the former include an altarpiece showing the *Adoration of the Magi* by Geertgen tot Sint Jans. Other early works of great interest include *St Luke Drawing the Virgin* by Jan Gossaert (c1515), one of the first works of art from the Netherlands to show the clear

influence of the Italian Renaissance. The collection from the 17th century on the second floor includes several major works, notably by Peter Paul Rubens who, in 1639, sent two paintings to the Augustinians of the Church of St Thomas *(see p127)* in the Little Quarter. The originals were lent to the gallery in 1896 and replaced by copies. The violence and drama of *The Martyrdom of St Thomas*

Eleanor of Toledo (1540s) by the Florentine Mannerist painter Agnolo Bronzino

SPANISH AND FRENCH ART (1400–1800)

French art on the second floor is represented chiefly by the 17th-century painters Simon Vouet *(The Suicide of Lucretia)*, Sébastien Bourdon and Charles Le Brun. Spanish painting is even less well represented, but two of the collection's finest works are a haunting *Head of Christ* by El Greco, which is the only work by this important artist on display in the Czech Republic, and a noble half-length portrait of the politician *Don Miguel de Lardizábal by* Goya.

THE CHINESE CABINET

After several years of difficult restoration this curiosity on the second floor is once again open to the public. The richly decorated little chamber was part of the original furnishings of the Sternberg Palace, and was designed as an intimate withdrawing room away from the bustle of the grand state rooms. In its plethora of decorative styles, Baroque mingles with Far Eastern motifs and techniques, which were fashionable at the turn of the 18th century. The vaulted ceiling features the Star of the Sternbergs among its geometric decorations. Black lacquered walls are embellished with cobalt blue and white medallions in golden frames, while gilded shelves once held rare Oriental porcelain.

The Loreto ❷⓿

LORETA

Ever since its construction in 1626, the Loreto has been an important place of pilgrimage. It was commissioned by Kateřina of Lobkowicz, a Czech aristocrat who was very keen to promote the legend of the Santa Casa of Loreto *(see opposite)*. The heart of the complex is a copy of the house believed to be the Virgin Mary's. The Santa Casa was enclosed by cloisters in 1661, and a Baroque façade 60 years later by Christoph and Kilian Ignaz Dientzenhofer. The grandiose design and miraculous stories about the Loreto were part of Ferdinand II's campaign to recatholicize the Czechs *(see pp30–31)*.

Kateřina Lobkowicz, founder of the Santa Casa

Bell Tower
Enclosed in this large Baroque tower is a set of 30 bells cast 1683–91 in Amsterdam by Claudy Fremy.

Chapel of St Joseph

Fountain decorated with a sculpture of the Resurrection

Chapel of St Francis Seraphim

Chapel of St Ann

Entrance from Loretánské náměstí

★ **Loreto Treasury**
This gold-plated, diamond-encrusted monstrance, for displaying the host, is one of the valuable liturgical items in the Loreto treasury, most of which originated in the 16th–18th centuries.

Baroque Entrance
The balustrade above the Loreto's front entrance is decorated with statues of St Joseph and St John the Baptist by Ondřej Quitainer.

STAR SIGHTS

★ Loreto Treasury

★ Santa Casa

★ Church of the Nativity

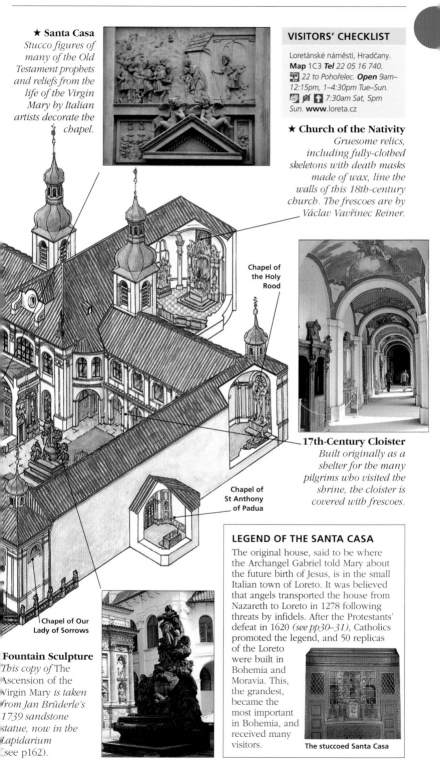

★ **Santa Casa**
Stucco figures of many of the Old Testament prophets and reliefs from the life of the Virgin Mary by Italian artists decorate the chapel.

VISITORS' CHECKLIST

Loretánské náměstí, Hradčany.
Map 1C3 **Tel** 22 05 16 740.
🚊 22 to Pohořelec. **Open** 9am–12:15pm, 1–4:30pm Tue–Sun.
📷 🚫 🕖 7:30am Sat, 5pm
Sun. www.loreta.cz

★ **Church of the Nativity**
Gruesome relics, including fully-clothed skeletons with death masks made of wax, line the walls of this 18th-century church. The frescoes are by Václav Vavřinec Reiner.

Chapel of the Holy Rood

17th-Century Cloister
Built originally as a shelter for the many pilgrims who visited the shrine, the cloister is covered with frescoes.

Chapel of St Anthony of Padua

Chapel of Our Lady of Sorrows

LEGEND OF THE SANTA CASA

The original house, said to be where the Archangel Gabriel told Mary about the future birth of Jesus, is in the small Italian town of Loreto. It was believed that angels transported the house from Nazareth to Loreto in 1278 following threats by infidels. After the Protestants' defeat in 1620 *(see pp30–31)*, Catholics promoted the legend, and 50 replicas of the Loreto were built in Bohemia and Moravia. This, the grandest, became the most important in Bohemia, and received many visitors.

The stuccoed Santa Casa

Fountain Sculpture
This copy of The Ascension of the Virgin Mary *is taken from Jan Brüderle's 1739 sandstone statue, now in the Lapidarium (see p162).*

Martinic Palace 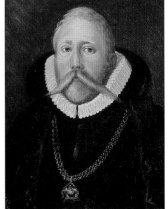⓰
MARTINICKÝ PALÁC

Hradčanské náměstí 8. **Map** 1 C2.
Tel 23 33 26 722. ⫶Ⓜ⫶
Malostranská, Hradčanská. 🚊 *22.*
Open *10am–6pm daily.* 📷
www.martinickypalac.cz

In the course of the palace's
restoration in the early 1970s,
workmen uncovered the
original 16th-century façade
decorated with ornate cream
and brown *sgraffito (see p111).*
It depicts Old Testament
scenes, including the story of
Joseph and Potiphar's wife.
More *sgraffito* in the courtyard
shows the story of Samson
and the Labours of Hercules.
  Martinic Palace was enlarged
by Jaroslav Bořita of Martinice,
who was one of the imperial
governors thrown from a
window of the Royal Palace
in 1618 *(see p105).*
  According to an old legend,
between 11pm and midnight
the ghost of a fiery black dog
appears at the palace and acc-
ompanies walkers as far as the
Loreto *(see pp116–17).* You can
tour the palace or visit a small
museum of musical machines,
such as gramophones.

Schwarzenberg Palace ⓱
SCHWARZENBERSKÝ PALÁC

Hradčanské náměstí 2. **Map** 2 D3.
Tel 23 48 10 758.
⫶Ⓜ⫶ *Malostranská, Hradčanská*
🚊 *22.* **Open** *10am–6pm*
Tue–Sun. 📷 🚫 **www**.ngprague.cz

From a distance, the façade of
this grand Renaissance palace
appears to be clad in project-
ing pyramid-shaped stone-
work. On closer inspection,
this turns out to be an
illusion created
by *sgraffito*
patterns incised

on a flat wall. Built
originally for the
Lobkowicz family by
the Italian architect
Agostino Galli in
1545–76, the gabled
palace is Florentine
rather than Bohemian
in style. It passed
through several hands
before the Schwarzen-
bergs, a leading family
in the Habsburg
Empire, bought it in
1719. Much of the
interior decoration has
survived, including
four painted ceilings
on the second floor
dating from 1580. The
palace once housed
the Museum of Military
History, now at U Pamatniku
3. Following renovation, the
palace is now home to the
National Gallery's collection
of Baroque art.
  In the square outside is the
statue of Tomáš G Masaryk,
Czechoslovakia's first president.

New World ⓲
NOVÝ SVĚT

Map 1 B2. 🚊 *22.*

Now a charming street of
small cottages, Nový Svět
(New World) used to be the
name of this area of Hradčany.
Developed in the mid-14th
century to provide houses for
the castle workers, the area
was twice destroyed by fire,
the last time being in 1541.
Most of the cottages date from
the 17th century. They have
been spruced up, but are
otherwise unspoilt and very
different in character from the

Tycho Brahe, Rudolph II's astronomer

rest of Hradčany. In defiance
of their poverty, the inhabitants
chose golden house signs to
identify their modest houses –
you will see a Golden Pear,
a Grape, a Foot, a Bush and
an Acorn. Plaques identify
No. 1 as the former home of
Rudolph II's brilliant court
astronomer, Tycho Brahe, and
No. 25 as the 1857 birthplace
of the great Czech violinist
František Ondříček.

Capuchin Monastery ⓳
KAPUCÍNSKÝ KLÁŠTER

Loretánské náměstí 6. **Map** 1 B3
🚊 *22.* **Closed** *to the public except
the church.*

Bohemia's first Capuchin
monastery was founded here
in 1600. It is connected to the
neighbouring Loreto *(see
pp116–17)* by an overhead
roofed passage. Attached to the
monastery is the Church of
Our Lady Queen of Angels, a
single-naved building with
plain furnishings, typical of
the ascetic Capuchin order.
  The church is famous for
its miraculous statue of the
Madonna and Child. Emperor
Rudolph II liked the statue so
much he asked the Capuchins
to give it to him to place in
his private chapel. The monks
agreed, but then the statue
somehow found its way back
to the church. Three times
Rudolph had the Madonna
brought back but each time

The Carmelite monastery next to the Schwarzenberg Palace

she returned to her original position. The Emperor eventually gave up, left her where she was and presented her with a gold crown and a robe. Each year at Christmas the church attracts crowds of visitors to see its delightful Baroque nativity scene of life-sized figures dressed in costumes from the period.

Church of the Capuchin Monastery

The Loreto ⑳
LORETA

See pp116–17.

Černín Palace ㉑
ČERNÍNSKÝ PALÁC

Loretánské náměstí 5. **Map** 1 B3.
Tel *22 41 81 111* 🚋 *22.*
Closed *to the public.* **www**.*mzv.cz*

Built in 1668 for Count Černín of Chudenice, the Imperial Ambassador to Venice, the Černín Palace is 150 m (500 ft) long with a row of 30 massive Corinthian half-columns running the length of its upper storeys. The palace towers over the attractive, small, grassy square that lies between it and the Loreto.

The huge building suffered as a result of its prominent position on one of Prague's highest hills. It was looted by the French in 1742 and badly damaged in the Prussian bombardment of the city in 1757. In 1851 the impoverished Černín family sold the palace to the state and it became a

barracks. After the creation of Czecho-slovakia in 1918 the palace was restored to its original design and became the Ministry of Foreign Affairs. A few days after the Communist Coup in 1948 the Foreign Minister, Jan Masaryk, the popular son of Czechoslovakia's first President, Tomáš Masaryk, died as the result of a fall from a top-floor window of the Palace. He was the only non-Communist in the government that had just been formed. No-one really knows whether he was pushed or jumped, but he is still widely mourned.

Capital on Černín Palace

Pohořelec ㉒

Map 1 B3. 🚋 *22.*

First settled in 1375, this is one of the oldest parts of Prague. The name is of more recent origin: Pohořelec means "place destroyed by fire", a fate the area has suffered three times in the course of its history – the last time being in 1741. It is now a large open square on a hill high over the city and part of the main access route to Prague Castle. In the centre stands a large monument to St John Nepomuk (1752) *(see p137)*, thought to be by Johann Anton Quitainer. The houses around the square are mainly Baroque and Rococo. In front of the Jan Kepler grammar school stands a monument to Kepler and his predecessor as astronomer at the court of Rudolph II, Tycho Brahe, who died in a house on the school site in 1601.

Strahov Monastery ㉓
STRAHOVSKÝ KLÁŠTER

See pp120–21.

Kučera Palace, a Rococo building in Pohořelec

Strahov Monastery ㉓

STRAHOVSKÝ KLÁŠTER

Statue of St John
A Late-Gothic, painted statue of St John the Evangelist situated in the Theological Hall, has the saint's prayer book held in a small pouch.

When it was founded in 1140 by an austere religious order, the Premonstratensians, Strahov rivalled the seat of the Czech sovereign in size. Destroyed by fire in 1258, it was rebuilt in the Gothic style, with later Baroque additions. Its famous library, in the theological and philosophical halls, is over 800 years old and despite being ransacked by many invading armies, is one of the finest in Bohemia. Strahov also escaped Joseph II's 1783 dissolution of the monasteries by changing its library into a research institute. It is now a working monastery and museum.

The bust of Joseph II over entrance gate

Baroque tower

The Museum of National Literature is devoted to Czech literature.

Refectory

Entrance to main courtyard of the monastery

Baroque organ on which Mozart played

★ **Church of Our Lady**
The interior of this Baroque church is highly decorated. Above the arcades of the side naves, there are 12 paintings with scenes from the life of St Norbert, founder of the Premonstratensian order, by Jiří Neunhertz.

Entrance to Church of Our Lady

Church Façade
The elaborate statues, by Johann Anton Quitainer, were added to the western façade of the church when it was remodelled by the architect Anselmo Lurago in the 1750s.

STAR FEATURES

★ Church of Our Lady

★ Philosophical Hall

★ Theological Hall

View from Petřín Hill
*A gate at the eastern end of the first
courtyard leads to Petřín Hill, part of
which was once the monastery's orchards.*

VISITORS' CHECKLIST

Královská Kanonie Premonstrátů
na Strahově. Strahovské nádvoří 1.
Map 1 B4. **Tel** 23 31 07 711.
22 to Pohořelec **Open** 9am–
noon, 12:30–5pm Tue–Sun. **Philosophical Hall, Theological
Hall, Church of Our Lady, Picture Gallery open** 9am–noon, 1–
5pm daily, **closed** Easter Sun, 25
Dec.

★ Theological Hall
*One of the 17th-century
astronomical globes by
William Blaeu that line the
hall. The stucco and wall
paintings relate to
librarianship.*

The façade of the
Philosophical
Hall is decorated
with vases and a
gilded medallion
of Joseph II by
Ignaz Platzer.

Entrance
libraries

★ Philosophical Hall
*The ceiling fresco depicts
the* Struggle of Mankind to
Know Real History *by
Franz Maulbertsch. It was
built in 1782 to hold the
Baroque bookcases and
their valuable books from
a dissolved monastery
near Louka, in Moravia.*

Strahov Gospel Book
*A facsimile of this superb
and precious 9th-century
volume, is now on display
in the Theological Hall.*

LITTLE QUARTER

MALÁ STRANA

The Little Quarter is the part of Prague least affected by recent history. Hardly any new building has taken place here since the late 18th century and the quarter is rich in splendid Baroque palaces and old houses with attractive signs. Founded in 1257, it is built on the slopes below the Castle hill with magnificent views across the river to the Old Town.

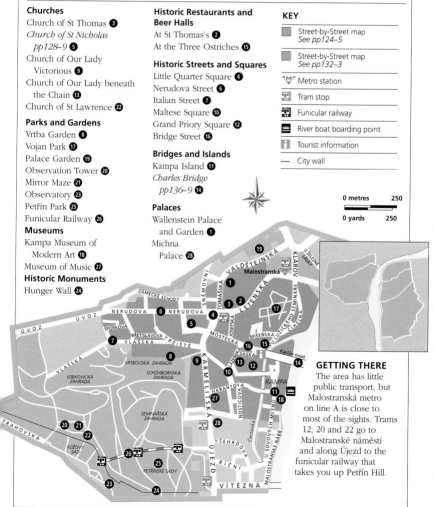

Sign from At the Golden Horseshoe in Nerudova

The centre of the Little Quarter has always been Little Quarter Square (Malostranské náměstí), dominated by the Church of St Nicholas. The Grand Prior's millwheel at Kampa Island still turns, pilgrims still kneel before the Holy Infant of Prague in the Church of Our Lady Victorious, and music rings out from churches and palaces as it did when Mozart stayed here.

SIGHTS AT A GLANCE

Churches
Church of St Thomas ❸
Church of St Nicholas pp128–9 ❺
Church of Our Lady Victorious ❾
Church of Our Lady beneath the Chain ❸
Church of St Lawrence ㉒

Parks and Gardens
Vrtba Garden ❽
Vojan Park ⑰
Palace Garden ⑲
Observation Tower ⑳
Mirror Maze ㉑
Observatory ㉓
Petřín Park ㉕
Funicular Railway ㉖

Museums
Kampa Museum of Modern Art ⑱
Museum of Music ㉗

Historic Monuments
Hunger Wall ㉔

Historic Restaurants and Beer Halls
At St Thomas's ❷
At the Three Ostriches ⑮

Historic Streets and Squares
Little Quarter Square ❹
Nerudova Street ❻
Italian Street ❼
Maltese Square ❿
Grand Priory Square ⑫
Bridge Street ⑯

Bridges and Islands
Kampa Island ⑪
Charles Bridge pp136–9 ⑭

Palaces
Wallenstein Palace and Garden ❶
Michna Palace ㉘

KEY

▨	Street-by-Street map *See pp124–5*
▨	Street-by-Street map *See pp132–3*
Ⓜ	Metro station
🚊	Tram stop
🚠	Funicular railway
🚤	River boat boarding point
ℹ	Tourist information
----	City wall

0 metres 250
0 yards 250

GETTING THERE
The area has little public transport, but Malostranská metro on line A is close to most of the sights. Trams 12, 20 and 22 go to Malostranské náměstí and along Újezd to the funicular railway that takes you up Petřín Hill.

◁ **Charles Bridge and the Little Quarter Bridge Towers**

Street-by-Street: Around Little Quarter Square

The Little Quarter, most of whose grand Baroque palaces now house embassies, has preserved much of its traditional character. The steep, narrow streets and steps have an air of romantic mystery and you will find fascinating buildings decorated with statues and house signs at every turn. Some smart new restaurants have been established in the old buildings.

At the Three Little Fiddles, now a restaurant, acquired its house sign when it was the home of a family of violin makers around 1700.

Thun-Hohenstein Palace (1721–6) has a doorway crowned with two sculpted eagles by Matthias Braun. The palace is now the seat of the Italian embassy.

★ Nerudova Street
This historic street leading up to Prague Castle is named after the 19th-century writer Jan Neruda ❻

Morzin Palace has a striking Baroque façade with a pair of sculpted moors.

Italian Street
From the 16th to the 18th century, houses in the street, like the House at the Golden Scales, were occupied by Italian craftsmen ❼

STAR SIGHTS

★ Wallenstein Palace

★ Church of St Nicholas

★ Nerudova Street

Vrtba Garden
Laid out in about 1725 by František Maximilián Kaňka, these fine Baroque terraces provide good views over the rooftops of the Little Quarter ❽

★ **Wallenstein Palace**
On the main hall ceiling, Albrecht von Wallenstein, the great general of the 30 Years' War, appears as the god Mars ❶

To Malostranská Metro

Czech National Assembly

Plague Column

LOCATOR MAP
See Street Finder, map 2

Wallenstein Gardens

Little Quarter Town Hall

At St Thomas's
This traditional beer hall occupies the cellars of a medieval monastery brewery ❷

Church of St Thomas
A statue of St Augustine by Hieronymus Kohl (1684) decorates the church's dramatic Baroque façade ❸

Little Quarter Square
This 18th-century view shows the lower half of the square between the church of St Nicholas and the Town Hall ❹

★ **Church of St Nicholas**
The cupola and bell tower of this Baroque church are the best-known landmarks of the Little Quarter ❺

Schönborn Palace, now the American Embassy, is decorated with caryatids from the 17th century.

0 metres	100
0 yards	100

KEY

– – – Suggested route

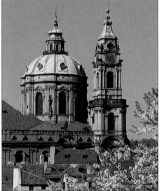

Wallenstein Palace and Garden ❶
VALDŠTEJNSKÝ PALÁC

Valdštejnské náměstí 4. **Map** 2 E3.
Ⓜ *Malostranská.* **Tel** 25 70 75
707. 🚋 *12, 18, 20, 22.* **Palace
open** *10am–4pm Sat & Sun
(to 5pm Apr–Oct).* **Riding school
open** *for exhibitions 10am–6pm
Tue–Sun.* 🚫 ♿ *from Valdštejnská.*
Garden open *Apr–Oct: 10am–6pm
daily (to 8pm in Aug).* 📷 ♿ *from
Valdštejnské náměstí.* 💻
www.senat.cz

The first large secular
building of the Baroque era
in Prague, the palace stands
as a monument to the fatal
ambition of imperial military
commander Albrecht von
Wallenstein (1581–1634). His
string of victories over the
Protestants in the 30 Years'
War *(see pp30–31)* made him
vital to Emperor Ferdinand II.
Already showered with titles,
Wallenstein soon started to
covet the crown of
Bohemia. Finally
he dared to begin
to negotiate inde-
pendently with the
enemy, and he
was killed on the
emperor's orders
by mercenaries
in 1634.

Wallenstein

The main hall of Wallenstein Palace

Wallenstein's intention was to
overshadow even Prague Castle with his palace, built
between 1624 and 1630. To
obtain a suitable site, he had
to purchase 23 houses, three
gardens and the municipal
brick kiln. The magnificent
main hall rises to a height of
two storeys with a ceiling
fresco of Wallenstein himself
portrayed as Mars, the god of
war, riding in a triumphal
chariot. The architect,
Andrea Spezza, and
nearly all the artists
employed in the
decoration of the
palace were Italians.
   Today the palace is
used as the home of
the Czech Senate, and
following restoration
is now open to the
public. The gardens
are laid out as they

were when Wallenstein dined
in the huge *sala terrena*
(garden pavilion) that looks
out over a fountain and rows
of bronze statues. These are
copies of works by Adriaen
de Vries that were stolen
by the Swedes in 1648 *(see
pp30–31).* There is also a
pavilion with fine frescoes
showing scenes from the
legend of the Argonauts
and the Golden Fleece.
Wallenstein was a holder
of the Order of the
Golden Fleece, the
highest order of
chivalry of the Holy
Roman Empire. At the
far end of the garden
is a large ornamental
pond with a central
statue. Behind this
stands the old Riding
School, now used
to house special
exhibitions by the
National Gallery.
Both gardens and
riding school have
undergone sub-
stantial restoration.

**Copy of a bronze statue of
Eros by Adriaen de Vries**

Palace

**Sala
terrena**

Avenue of sculptures

Riding School

**Valdštejnská
Street
entrance**

The grotesquery is a curious imitation
of the walls of a limestone cave,
covered in stalactites.

**Letenská
Street
entrance**

**Statue of
Hercules**

Klárov entrance

At St Thomas's ❷

U SV. TOMÁŠE

Letenská 12. **Map** 2 E3. **Tel** 25 75 33 466. Ⓜ *Malostranská.* 🚊 12, 20, 22. **Open** from summer 2009. 📷

No other beer hall in Prague can match the antiquity of At St Thomas's. Beer was first brewed here in 1352 by Augustinian monks. The brewery gained such renown that it was appointed sole pur-veyor of beer to Prague Cas-tle. It remained in operation until 1951. A five-star hotel spanning five floors opens on the premises in 2009, retain-ing the historical features of the beer hall. Guests can also enjoy stunning views of the neighbouring St Thomas monastery.

Church of St Thomas ❸

KOSTEL SV. TOMÁŠE

Josefská 8. **Map** 2 E3. **Tel** 25 75 32 675. Ⓜ *Malostranská.* 🚊 12, 20, 22. **Open** for services. ✝ 6:45am, 12:15pm Mon–Sat (and 6pm Sat in English), 9:30am, 11am (in English), 12:30pm Sun. 📷 ♿

Founded by Wenceslas II in 1285 as the monastery church of the Augustinians, the original Gothic church was completed in 1379. In the Hussite period *(see pp26–7)* this was one of the few churches to remain Catholic. As a result it suffered serious fire damage. During the reign of Rudolph II *(see pp28–9)*, St Thomas's developed strong links with the Imperial court. Several prominent members of Rudolph's entourage were buried here, including court architect Ottavio Aostalli and the sculptor Adriaen de Vries.

In 1723 the church was struck by lightning and Kilian Ignaz Dientzenhofer was called in to rebuild it. The shape of the original church was preserved in the Baroque reconstruction but, apart from the spire, the church today betrays little of its Gothic ori-gins. The interior of the dome and the curving ceiling frescoes in the nave were painted by

Václav Vavřinec Reiner. Above the altar are copies of paintings by Rubens – *The Martyrdom of St Thomas* and a picture of St Augustine. The originals are in the Sternberg Palace *(see pp112–15)*. The English-speaking Catholic community of Prague meets in this church.

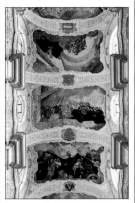

Baroque ceiling in the nave of the Church of St Thomas

Little Quarter Square ❹

MALOSTRANSKÉ NÁMĚSTÍ

Map 2 E3. Ⓜ *Malostranská.* 🚊 12, 20, 22.

The square has been the centre of life in the Little Quarter since its foundation in 1257. It had started life as a large marketplace in the outer bailey of Prague Castle. Buildings sprang up in the middle of the square dividing

it in half – a gallows and pillory stood in its lower part.

Most of the houses around the square have a medieval core, but all were rebuilt in the Renaissance and Baroque periods. The centre of the square is dominated by the splendid Baroque church of St Nicholas. The large building beside it was a Jesuit college. Along the upper side of the square, facing the church, runs the vast Neo-Classical façade of Lichtenstein Palace. In front of it stands a column raised in honour of the Holy Trinity to mark the end of a plague epidemic in 1713.

Other important buildings include the Little Quarter Town Hall with its splendid Renaissance façade and the Sternberg Palace, built on the site of the outbreak of the fire of 1541, which destroyed most of the Little Quarter. Beside it stands the Smiřický; Palace. Its turrets and hexagonal towers make it an unmistakable landmark on the northern side of the lower square. The Baroque Kaiserstein Palace is situated at the eastern side. On the façade is a bust of the great Czech soprano Emmy Destinn, who lived there between 1908 and 1914. She often sang with the famous Italian tenor Enrico Caruso.

Church of St Nicholas ❺

KOSTEL SV. MIKULÁŠE

See pp128–9.

Arcade in front of buildings on the north side of Little Quarter Square

Church of St Nicholas ⑤

KOSTEL SV. MIKULÁŠE

The Church of St Nicholas divides and dominates the two sections of Little Quarter Square. Building began in 1703, and the last touches were put to the glorious frescoed nave in 1761. It is the acknowledged masterpiece of father-and-son architects Christoph and Kilian Ignaz Dientzenhofer, Prague's greatest exponents of High Baroque *(see opposite)*, although neither lived to see the completion of the church. The statues, frescoes and paintings inside the church are by leading artists of the day, and include a fine *Crucifixion* of 1646 by Karel Škréta. Extensive renovation in the 1950s reversed the damage caused by 200 years of leaky cladding and condensation.

★ Pulpit
Dating from 1765, the ornate pulpit is by Richard and Peter Prachner. It is lavishly adorned with golden cherubs.

Altar Paintings
The side chapels hold many works of art. This painting of St Michael is by Francesco Solimena.

Baroque Organ
A fresco of St Cecilia, patron saint of music, watches over the superb organ. Built in 1746, the instrument was played by Mozart in 1787.

Entrance from west side of Little Quarter Square

Chapel of St Ann

Chapel of St Catherine

STAR FEATURES

★ Dome Fresco

★ Pulpit

★ Statues of the Church Fathers

Façade
St Paul, by John Frederick Kohl, is one of the statues that grace the curving façade. It was completed in 1710 by Christoph Dientzenhofer, who was influenced by Italian architects Borromini and Guarini.

The dome was completed by Kilian Ignaz Dientzenhofer in 1751, shortly before his death.

The belfry, added in 1751–6, was the last part to be built. It houses a small museum of musical instruments.

VISITORS' CHECKLIST

Malostranské náměstí. **Map** 2 E3. Malostranská. **Tel** 25 75 34 215. 12, 20, 22 to Malostranské náměstí. **Open** Apr–Oct: 9am–5pm daily; Nov–Mar: 9am–4pm daily. **Concerts**. www.psalterium.cz

★ **Dome Fresco**
František Palko's fresco, The Celebration of the Holy Trinity *(1752–3), fills the 70 m (230 ft) high dome.*

High Altar
A copper statue of St Nicholas by Ignaz Platzer surmounts the high altar. Below it, the painting of St Joseph is by Johann Lukas Kracker, who also painted the nave fresco.

Entrance to Belfry

★ **Statues of the Church Fathers**
The great teachers by Ignaz Platzer stand at the four corners of the crossing. St Cyril dispatches the devil with his crozier.

Chapel of St Francis Xavier

THE DIENTZENHOFER FAMILY

Christoph Dientzenhofer (1655–1722) came from a family of Bavarian master builders. His son Kilian Ignaz (1689–1751) was born in Prague and educated at the Jesuit Clementinum *(see p79).* They were responsible for the greatest treasures of Jesuit-influenced Prague Baroque architecture. The Church of St Nicholas, their last work, was completed by Kilian's son-in-law, Anselmo Lurago.

Kilian Ignaz Dientzenhofer

Nerudova Street ❻
NERUDOVA ULICE

Map 2 D3. ꟷ*M* *Malostranská.*
꠸ *12, 20, 22.*

A picturesque narrow street
leading up to Prague Castle,
Nerudova is named after the
poet and journalist Jan
Neruda, who wrote many
short stories set in
this part of Prague. He lived
in the house called At the
Two Suns (No. 47) between
1845 and 1857.
　Up until the introduction
of house numbers in 1770,
Prague's houses were distinguished by signs. Nerudova's
houses have a splendid selection of heraldic beasts and
emblems. As you make your
way up Nerudova's steep
slope, look out in particular
for the Red Eagle (No. 6), the
Three Fiddles (No. 12), the
Golden Horseshoe (No. 34),
the Green Lobster (No. 43)
and the White Swan (No. 49)
as well as the Old Pharmacy
museum (No. 32).
　There are also a number
of grand Baroque buildings
in the street, including the
Thun-Hohenstein Palace (No.
20, now the Italian embassy)
and the Morzin Palace (No. 5,
the Rumanian palace).
The latter has a façade with
two massive statues of moors
(a pun on the name Morzin)
supporting the semicircular
balcony on the first floor.
Another impressive façade is
that of the Church of Our
Lady of Unceasing Succour,
the church of the Theatines,
an order founded during the
Counter-Reformation.

**Italian Street, heart of the former
colony of Italian craftsmen**

Italian Street ❼
VLAŠSKÁ ULICE

Map 1 C4 ꟷ*M* *Malostranská.*
꠸ *12, 20, 22.*

Italian immigrants started to
settle here in the 16th
century. Many were artists or
craftsmen employed to rebuild
and redecorate the Castle. If
you approach the street from
Petřín, on the left you will see
the former Italian Hospital, a
Baroque building with an
arcaded courtyard. Today it
maintains its traditional
allegiance as the cultural
section of the Italian embassy.
　The grandest building in the
street is the former Lobkowicz
Palace, now the German
embassy. One of the finest
Baroque palaces in Prague, it
has a large oval hall on the
ground floor leading out onto
a magnificent garden. Look
out too for the pretty stucco
sign on the house called At
the Three Red Roses, dating
from the early 18th century.

Vrtba Garden ❽
VRTBOVSKÁ ZAHRADA

Karmelitská 25. **Map** 2 D4. **Tel** *25
75 31 480.* ꟷ*M* *Malostranská.* ꠸ *12,
20, 22.* **Open** *Apr–Oct: 10am–6pm
daily.* 📷 🎦 **www**.vrtbovska.cz

Behind Vrtba Palace lies a
beautiful Baroque garden
with balustraded terraces.
From the highest part of the
garden there are magnificent
views of Prague Castle and
the Little Quarter. The Vrtba
Garden was designed by
František Maximilián Kaňka in
about 1720. The statues of
Classical gods and stone vases
are the work of Matthias Braun
and the paintings in the *sala
terrena* (garden pavilion) in
the lower part of the garden
are by Václav Vavřinec Reiner.

**View of the Little Quarter from the
terrace of the Vrtba Garden**

Church of Our
Lady Victorious ❾
KOSTEL PANNY MARIE VÍTĚZNÉ

Karmelitská. **Map** 2 E4. **Tel** *25 75 33
646.* ꠸ *12, 20, 22.* **Open** *9am–
6pm daily.* ⬛ *9am, 6pm Mon–Fri,
9am, 6pm Sat, 10am, noon (English),
5pm (French), 6pm (Italian), 7pm Sun.*
www.pragjesu.info

The first Baroque building in
Prague was the Church of the
Holy Trinity, built for the
German Lutherans by Giovanni
Maria Filippi. It was finished in
1613 but after the Battle of the
White Mountain *(see p31)* the
Catholic authorities gave the
church to the Carmelites, who
rebuilt it and renamed it in

Sign of Jan Neruda's house, At the Two Suns, 47 Nerudova Street

honour of the victory. The fabric has survived including the portal. Enshrined on a marble altar in the right aisle is a glass case containing the Holy Infant Jesus of Prague (better-known by its Italian name – *il Bambino di Praga*). This wax effigy has a record of miracle cures and is one of the most revered images in the Catholic world. It was brought from Spain and presented to the Carmelites in 1628 by Polyxena of Lobkowicz. A small museum adjacent to the church traces its history.

Maltese Square ❿
MALTÉZSKÉ NÁMĚSTÍ

Map 2 E4. 🚋 *12, 20, 22.*

The square takes its name from the Priory of the Knights of Malta, which used to occupy this part of the Little Quarter. At the northern end stands a group of sculptures featuring St John the Baptist by Ferdinand Brokof – part of a fountain erected in 1715 to mark the end of a plague epidemic.

Most of the buildings were originally Renaissance houses belonging to prosperous townspeople, but in the 17th and 18th centuries the Little Quarter was taken over by the Catholic nobility and many were converted to flamboyant Baroque palaces. The largest, Nostitz Palace, stands on the southern side. It was built in the mid-17th century, then in about 1720 a balustrade was added with Classical vases and statues of emperors. The palace now houses the Ministry of Culture and in summer, concerts are held here. The Japanese embassy is housed in the Turba Palace (1767), an attractive pink Rococo building designed by Joseph Jäger.

Čertovka (the Devil's Stream) with Kampa Island on the right

Ferdinand Brokof's statue of John the Baptist in Maltese Square

Kampa Island ⓫
KAMPA

Map 2 F4. 🚋 *6, 9, 12, 20, 22.*

Kampa, an island formed by a branch of the Vltava known as the Devil's Stream (Čertovka), is a delightfully peaceful corner of the Little Quarter. The stream got its name in the 19th century, allegedly after the diabolical temper of a lady who owned a house nearby in Maltese Square. For centuries the stream was used as a millrace and from Kampa you can see the remains of three old mills. Beyond the Grand Prior's Mill the stream disappears under a small bridge below the piers of Charles Bridge. From here it flows between rows of houses. Predictably, the area has become known as "the Venice of Prague", but instead of gondolas you will see canoes.

For most of the Middle Ages there were only gardens on Kampa, though the island was also used for washing clothes and bleaching linen. In the 17th century the island became well-known for its pottery markets. There are some enchanting houses from this period around Na Kampě Square. Most of the land from here to the southern tip of the island is a park, created from several old palace gardens.

The island all but vanished beneath the Vltava during the floods of 2002, which caused widespread devastation to homes, businesses and historic buildings, many of which are still being rebuilt and restored.

Grand Priory Square ⓬
VELKOPŘEVORSKÉ NÁMĚSTÍ

Map 2 F4. 🚇 *Malostranská.* 🚋 *12, 20, 22.*

On the northern side of this small leafy square stands the former seat of the Grand Prior of the Knights of Malta. In its present form the palace dates from the 1720s. The doorways, windows and decorative vases were made at the workshop of Matthias Braun. On the opposite side of the square is the Buquoy Palace, now the French embassy, a delightful Baroque building roughly contemporary with the Grand Prior's Palace.

The only incongruous feature is a painting of John Lennon with "give peace a chance" graffitied alongside. The "Lennon Peace Wall" has graced the Grand Prior's garden since Lennon's death.

Street-by-Street: Little Quarter Riverside

On either side of Bridge Street lies a delightful half-hidden world of gently decaying squares, picturesque palaces, churches and gardens. When you have run the gauntlet of the trinket-sellers on Charles Bridge, escape to Kampa Island to enjoy a stroll in its informal park, the views across the Vltava weir to the Old Town and the flocks of swans gliding along the river.

The Church of St Joseph dates from the late 17th century. The painting of *The Holy Family* (1702) on the gilded high altar is by the leading Baroque artist Petr Brandl.

The House at the Golden Unicorn in Lázeňská Street has a plaque commemorating the fact that Beethoven stayed here in 1796.

Bridge Street
A major thoroughfare for 750 years, the narrow street leads to Little Quarter Square **16**

To Little Quarter Square

Grand Priory Square
The Grand Prior's Palace is the former seat of the Knights of Malta and dates from the 1720s. Its street wall features colourful murals and graffitti **12**

Church of Our Lady beneath the Chain
Two massive towers survive from when this was a fortified priory **13**

Museum of Music
This museum houses a vast collection of beautifully hand-crafted musical instruments **27**

Church of Our Lady Victorious
This Baroque church houses the famous effigy, the Holy Infant of Prague **9**

MOSTECKÁ

LÁZEŇSKÁ

KARMELITSKÁ

NEBOVIDSKÁ

Maltese Square
Grand palaces surround the oddly-shaped square. This coat of arms decorates the 17th-century Nostitz Palace, a popular venue for concerts **10**

| 0 metres | | 100 |
| 0 yards | | 100 |

KEY

- - - - Suggested route

Vojan Park
Quiet shady paths have been laid out under the apple trees of this former monastery garden ⓱

LOCATOR MAP
See Street Finder, map 2

At the Three Ostriches
A restaurant and hotel have kept the sign of a seller of ostrich plumes ⓯

U LUŽICKÉHO SEMINÁŘE

★ Charles Bridge
The approach to this magnificent 14th-century bridge, with its files of Baroque statues, passes under an arch below a Gothic tower ⓮

Čertovka (the Devil's Stream)

NA KAMPĚ

Lichtenstein Palace

The Grand Priory Mill has had its wheel meticulously restored, though it now turns very slowly in the sluggish water of the Čertovka, the former millrace.

★ Kampa Island
This 19th-century painting by Soběslav Pinkas shows boys playing on Kampa. The island's park is still a popular place for children ⓫

STAR SIGHTS

★ Charles Bridge

★ Kampa Island

Church of Our Lady beneath the Chain ⓭

KOSTEL PANNY MARIE POD ŘETĚZEM

Lázeňská. **Map** 2 E4. **Tel** *25 75 30 876.* Ⓜ *Malostranská.* 🚋 *12, 20, 22.* **Open** *for concerts and services.* 🕗 *9:30am Sat & Sun.*

This church, the oldest in the Little Quarter, was founded in the 12th century. King Vladislav II presented it to the Knights of St John, the order which later became known as the Knights of Malta. It stood in the centre of the Knights' heavily fortified monastery that guarded the approach to the old Judith Bridge. The church's name refers to the chain used in the Middle Ages to close the monastery gatehouse.

A Gothic presbytery was added in the 13th century, but in the following century the original Romanesque church was demolished. A new portico was built with a pair of massive square towers, but work was then abandoned and the old nave became a courtyard between the towers and the church. This was given a Baroque facelift in 1640 by Carlo Lurago. The painting by Karel Škréta on the high altar shows the Virgin Mary and John the Baptist coming to the aid of the Knights of Malta in the famous naval victory over the Turks at Lepanto in 1571.

Charles Bridge ⓮

KARLŮV MOST

See pp136–9.

Fresco that gave At the Three Ostriches its name

View along Bridge Street through the tower on Charles Bridge

At the Three Ostriches ⓯

U TŘÍ PŠTROSŮ

Dražického náměstí 12. **Map** 2 F3. **Tel** *25 75 32 410.* Ⓜ *Malostranská.* 🚋 *12, 20, 22. See* **Where to Stay** *p192,* **Restaurants, Cafés and Pubs** *p205.*

Many of Prague's colourful house signs indicated the trade carried on in the premises. In 1597 Jan Fux, an ostrich-feather merchant, bought this house by Charles Bridge. At the time ostrich plumes were very fashionable as decoration for hats among courtiers and officers at Prague Castle. Fux even supplied feathers to foreign armies. So successful was his business that in 1606 he had the house rebuilt and decorated with a large fresco of ostriches. The building is now an expensive hotel and restaurant.

Bridge Street ⓰

MOSTECKÁ ULICE

Map 2 E3. Ⓜ *Malostranská.* 🚋 *12, 20, 22.*

Since the Middle Ages this street has linked Charles Bridge with the Little Quarter Square. Crossing the bridge from the Old Town you can see the doorway of the old customs house built in 1591 in front of the Judith Tower. On the first floor of the tower there is a 12th-century relief of a king and a kneeling man.

Throughout the 13th and 14th centuries the area to the north of the street was the Court of the Bishop of Prague. This was destroyed during the Hussite Wars *(see pp26–7)*, but one of its Gothic towers is preserved in the courtyard of the house called At the Three Golden Bells. It can be seen from the higher of the two bridge towers. The street is lined with a mixture of Renaissance and Baroque houses. As you walk up to Little Quarter Square, look out for the house called At the Black Eagle on the left. It has rich sculptural decoration and a splendid Baroque wrought-iron grille. Kaunic Palace, also on the left, was built in the 1770s. Its Rococo façade has striking stucco decoration and sculptures by Ignaz Platzer.

Vojan Park  ❼

VOJANOVY SADY

U lužického semináře. **Map** 2 F3.
✝️ *Malostranská.* 🚊 *12, 18, 20,
22.* **Open** *8am–5pm daily (to 7pm in
summer).*

A tranquil spot hidden behind
high white walls, the park
dates back to the 17th century,
when it was the garden of the
Convent of Barefooted Carmelites. Two chapels erected
by the Order have survived
among the park's lawns and
fruit trees. One is the Chapel
of Elijah, who, because of his
Old Testament associations
with Mount Carmel, is regarded
as the founder of the Order.
His chapel takes the form of a
stalagmite and stalactite cave.
The other chapel, dedicated
to St Theresa, was built in the
18th century as an expression
of gratitude for the convent's
preservation during the Prussian siege of Prague in 1757.

Kampa Museum of Modern Art ❽

MUZEUM KAMPA

U Sovových mlýnů 2. **Map** 2 F4.
Tel *25 72 86 147.* 🚊 *6, 9, 22.*
Open *10am–6pm daily.* 🍴 📷 ♿
www.museumkampa.cz

Housed in the historic Sova
mill in the heart of the city, the
Kampa Museum of Modern Art
boasts an impressive collection
of Central European art. The
museum was founded by the
Czech-American couple Jan
and Meda Mládek to house
their private collection of
drawings, paintings and
sculptures. Among the artists
on display are abstract painter
Frantisek Kupka and Czech
cubist sculptor Otto Gutfreund.

Palace Gardens ❾

PALÁCOVÉ ZAHRADY

Valdštejnská. **Map** 2 F2. **Tel** *25 70 10
401.* ✝️ *Malostranská.* 🚊 *12, 18, 20,
22.* **Open** *Apr & Oct: 10am–6pm;
May & Sep: 9am–7pm; Jun& Jul:
9am–9pm; Aug: 9am–8pm daily.* ♿
📷 **www**.palacovezahrady.cz

The steep southern slope
below Prague Castle was
covered with vineyards and

gardens during the Middle
Ages. But in the 16th century,
when nobles started building
palaces here, they laid out
larger formal terraced gardens
based on Italian Renaissance
models. Most of these gardens
were rebuilt during the 18th
century and decorated with
Baroque garden statuary and
fountains. Five of the gardens
– including those belonging
to the former Ledebour,
Černín and Pálffy Palaces –
have been linked together.
They have recently under-
gone a much-needed pro-
gramme of restoration work,
and they again are delighting
visitors with their elegant land-
scaping and attractive plants.

From their terraces, the gardens boast magnificent views
of Prague. The Ledebour Garden, designed in the early
18th century, has a fine *sala
terrena* (garden pavilion) by
Giovanni Battista Alliprandi.
The Pálffy Garden was laid
out in the mid-18th century
with terraces (the second still
has its original sundial) and
loggias. The most beautiful of

**18th-century statue of Hercules
located in the Palace Gardens**

the five and architecturally the
richest is the Kolowrat-Černín
Garden, created in 1784 by
Ignaz Palliardi. The highest
terrace has a *sala terrena*
decorated with statues and
Classical urns. Below this there
is a wonderful assortment of
staircases, archways and balu-
strades, and the remains of
Classical statuary and fountains.

The foot of the Palace Gardens

Charles Bridge (Little Quarter Side) ⑭

KARLŮV MOST

Prague's most familiar monument connects the Old Town with the Little Quarter. It is now pedestrianised but at one time could take four carriages abreast. The bridge is undergoing renovation so some parts may not be accessible. Many of the statues on the bridge are copies; the originals are kept in the Lapidarium of the National Museum *(see p162)* and at Vyšehrad *(see p181)*. The Gothic Old Town Bridge Tower *(see p139)* is one of the finest buildings of its kind.

★ **View from Little Quarter Bridge Tower**
The tall pinnacled wedge tower, gives a superb view of the city of 100 spires. The shorter tower is the remains of Judith Bridge.

St Adalbert, 1709
Adalbert, Bishop of Prague, founded the Church of St Lawrence (see p140) *on Petřín Hill in 991. He is known to the Czechs as Vojtěch.*

Little Quarter Bridge Tower

Tower entrance

St Wenceslas, 1858

St Philip Benizi, 17

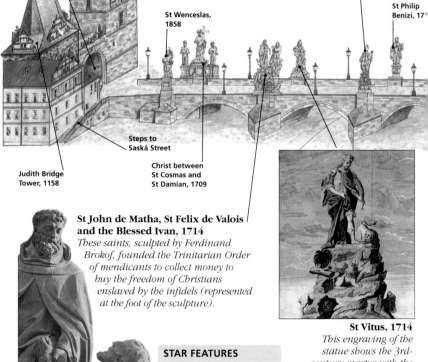

Judith Bridge Tower, 1158

Steps to Saská Street

Christ between St Cosmas and St Damian, 1709

St John de Matha, St Felix de Valois and the Blessed Ivan, 1714
These saints, sculpted by Ferdinand Brokof, founded the Trinitarian Order of mendicants to collect money to buy the freedom of Christians enslaved by the infidels (represented at the foot of the sculpture).

St Vitus, 1714
This engraving of the statue shows the 3rd-century martyr with the lions which were supposed to maul him, but licked him instead. St Vitus is the patron saint of dancers and often invoked against convulsive disorders.

STAR FEATURES

★ Little Quarter Bridge Tower and View

★ St John Nepomuk

★ St Luitgard

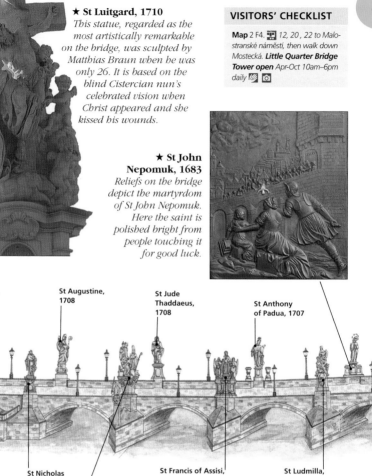

★ St Luitgard, 1710
This statue, regarded as the most artistically remarkable on the bridge, was sculpted by Matthias Braun when he was only 26. It is based on the blind Cistercian nun's celebrated vision when Christ appeared and she kissed his wounds.

VISITORS' CHECKLIST

Map 2 F4. 🚈 12, 20, 22 to Malostranské náměstí, then walk down Mostecká. **Little Quarter Bridge Tower open** Apr–Oct 10am–6pm daily

★ St John Nepomuk, 1683
Reliefs on the bridge depict the martyrdom of St John Nepomuk. Here the saint is polished bright from people touching it for good luck.

St Cajetan, 1709

St Augustine, 1708

St Jude Thaddaeus, 1708

St Anthony of Padua, 1707

Steps to Kampa Island

St Nicholas Tolentino, 1708

St Francis of Assisi, with two angels, 1855

St Ludmilla, 1710

St Vincent Ferrer and St Procopius, 1712
This detail shows a rabbi saddened by St Vincent's success in converting many Jews to Christianity. St Procopius is one of Bohemia's patron saints.

ST JOHN NEPOMUK
The cult of St John Nepomuk, canonized in 1729, was promoted by the Jesuits to rival the revered Jan Hus *(see p27)*. Jan Nepomucký, vicar-general of the Archdiocese of Prague, was arrested in 1393 by Wenceslas IV along with the archbishop and others who had displeased him. The king had St John thrown off Charles Bridge, where he drowned. Statues modelled on the one placed here in 1683 are seen throughout central Europe, especially on bridges. Catholics would later argue that St John was killed for failing to reveal the confessions of the queen.

Charles Bridge (Old Town Side) ⑭

KARLŮV MOST

Until 1741, Charles Bridge was the only crossing over the Vltava. It is 520 m (1,706 ft) long and is built of sandstone blocks, rumoured to be strengthened by mixing mortar with eggs. The bridge was commissioned by Charles IV in 1357 to replace the Judith Bridge and built by Peter Parler. The bridge's original decoration was a simple cross. The first statue – of St John Nepomuk – was added in 1683, inspired by Bernini's sculptures on Rome's Ponte Sant'Angelo.

St Francis Xavier, 1711
The Jesuit missionary is supported by three Moorish and two Oriental converts. The sculptor Brokof is seated on the saint's left.

★ 17th-Century Crucifixion
For 200 years, the wooden crucifix stood alone on the bridge. The gilded Christ dates from 1629 and the Hebrew words "Holy, Holy, Holy Lord", were paid for by a Jew as punishment for blasphemy.

St Norbert, St Wenceslas and St Sigismund, 1853

St Francis Borgia, 1710

St John the Baptist, 1857

St Cyril and St Methodius, 1938

St Christopher, 1857

St Ann, 1707

St Joseph, 1854

Thirty Years' War
In the last hours of this war, the Old Town was saved from the Swedish army. The truce was signed in the middle of the bridge in 1648.

STAR FEATURES

★ Old Town Bridge Tower

★ 17th-Century Crucifixion

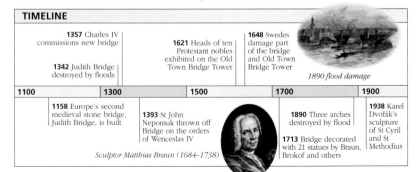

TIMELINE

1357 Charles IV commissions new bridge

1342 Judith Bridge destroyed by floods

1621 Heads of ten Protestant nobles exhibited on the Old Town Bridge Tower

1648 Swedes damage part of the bridge and Old Town Bridge Tower

1890 flood damage

1100	1300	1500	1700	1900

1158 Europe's second medieval stone bridge, Judith Bridge, is built

1393 St John Nepomuk thrown off Bridge on the orders of Wenceslas IV

Sculptor Matthias Braun (1684–1738)

1890 Three arches destroyed by flood

1713 Bridge decorated with 21 statues by Braun, Brokof and others

1938 Karel Dvořák's sculpture of St Cyril and St Methodius

**The Madonna,
St Dominic and
St Thomas, 1708**
*The Dominicans,
(known in a Latin pun
as* Domini canes, *the
dogs of God), are shown
with the Madonna and
their emblem, a dog.*

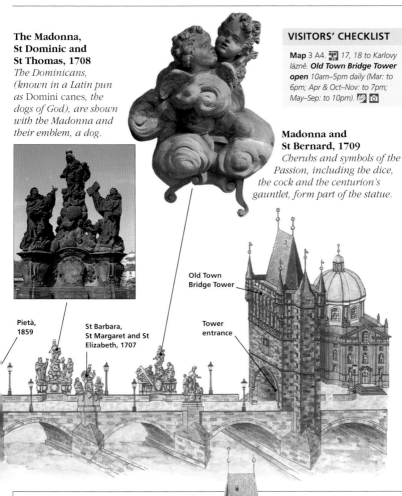

VISITORS' CHECKLIST

Map 3 A4. 🚋 17, 18 to Karlovy
lázně. **Old Town Bridge Tower
open** 10am–5pm daily (Mar: to
6pm; Apr & Oct–Nov: to 7pm;
May–Sep: to 10pm). 📷 ⬚

**Madonna and
St Bernard, 1709**
*Cherubs and symbols of the
Passion, including the dice,
the cock and the centurion's
gauntlet, form part of the statue.*

Old Town
Bridge Tower

Tower
entrance

Pietà,
1859

St Barbara,
St Margaret and St
Elizabeth, 1707

★ OLD TOWN BRIDGE TOWER

This magnificent Gothic tower, designed by Peter Parler, was built at the
end of the 14th century. An integral
part of the Old Town's fortifications,
it was badly damaged in 1648 and
the west side still bears the scars.

Pinnacled
wedge spire

Roof viewing point

The viewing gallery is a
rib-vaulted room, on the
tower's first floor. It
provides a wonderful
view of Prague Castle
and the Little Quarter.

Bridge Tower sculptures
by Peter Parler include
St Vitus, the bridge's patron saint,
Charles IV (left) and Wenceslas IV.

Observation Tower ⑳

PETŘÍNSKÁ ROZHLEDNA

Petřín. **Map** 1 C4. **Tel** *25 73 20 112.*
🚋 *6, 9, 12, 20, 22, then take
funicular railway.* 🚌 *143, 149, 176,
217.* **Open** *May–Sep: 10am–10pm
daily but subject to change; Oct–Apr:
10am–6pm daily.* 🖼 ▢ 📷
www.petrinska-rozhledna.cz

The most conspicuous
landmark in Petřín Park is an
imitation of the Eiffel Tower,
built for the Jubilee Exhibition
of 1891. The octagonally
shaped tower is only 60 m
(200 ft), a quarter the height
of the Eiffel Tower. A spiral
staircase of 299 steps leads up
to the viewing platform. A lift
is also available. On a clear
day, you can see as far as
Bohemia's highest peak,
Sněžka in the Krkonoše
(Giant) Mountains, 150 km
(100 miles) to the northeast.

Mirror Maze ㉑

ZRCADLOVÉ BLUDIŠTĚ

Petřín. **Map** 1 C4. **Tel** *25 73 15 212.*
🚋 *6, 9, 12, 20, 22, then take
funicular railway.* 🚌 *143, 149, 176,
217.* **Open** *May–Aug: 10am–10pm
daily; Sep–Apr: 10am–6pm daily.* 🖼
🚫 ♿

Like the Observation Tower,
the maze, which has walls
lined with distorting mirrors,
is a relic of the Exhibition of
1891. It is in a wooden pavilion
in the shape of the old Špička
Gate, part of the Gothic
fortifications of Vyšehrad
(see pp180–81). This amuse-

The 100-year-old Observation
Tower overlooking the city

ment house moved to Petřín
at the end of the exhibition.
When you have navigated
your way through the maze
and laughed at your reflection,
your reward is to view the
vivid diorama of *The Defence
of Prague against the Swedes*,
which took place on Charles
Bridge *(see p138)* in 1648,
badly damaging the tower.

Church of St Lawrence ㉒

KOSTEL SV. VAVŘINCE

Petřín. **Map** 1 C5. 🚋 *6, 9, 12, 20, 22,
then take funicular railway.*
🚌 *143, 149, 176, 217.* **Closed** *to
the public.*

According to legend, the
church was founded in the
10th century by the pious
Prince Boleslav II and St
Adalbert on the site of a pagan
shrine. The ceiling of the

sacristy is decorated with a
painting illustrating this legend. The painting dates from
the 18th century when the
Romanesque church was
swallowed up by a large new
Baroque structure, featuring a
cupola flanked by two onion-
domed towers. The small
Calvary Chapel, which dates
from 1735, is situated to the
left of the church entrance.

Observatory ㉓

HVĚZDÁRNA

Petřín 205. **Map** 2 D5. **Tel** *25 73 20
540.* 🚋 *6, 9, 12, 20, 22, then
funicular.* **Open** *Tue–Sun year-round;
opening hours vary monthly, so phone
ahead.* 🖼 🚫 **www**.observatory.cz

Since 1930, Prague's amateur
astronomers have been able
to enjoy the facilities of this
observatory on Petřín Hill.
You can use its telescopes to
view anything from the craters
of the moon to unfamiliar
distant galaxies. There is an
exhibition of old astronomical
instruments and special
events for children are held
on Saturdays and Sundays.

Hunger Wall ㉔

HLADOVÁ ZED'

Újezd, Petřín, Strahovská. **Map** 2 D5.
🚋 *6, 9, 12, 20, 22, then take funicular
railway.* 🚌 *143, 149, 176, 217.*

The fortifications built around
the southern edge of the Little
Quarter on the orders of
Charles IV in 1360–62 have
been known for centuries as
the Hunger Wall. Nearly 1,200 m
(1,300 yards) of the wall have
survived, complete
with crenellated battlements
and a platform for marksmen
on its inner side. It runs from
Újezd across Petřín Park to
Strahov. The story behind the
name is that Charles commissioned its construction with
the aim of giving employment
to the poor during a period of
famine. It is true that a great
famine did break out in
Bohemia in the 1360s and
the two events, the famine
and the building of the wall,
became permanently linked
in the people's memory.

Diorama of *The Defence of Prague against the Swedes* in the Mirror Maze

Nebozízek, the station halfway up Petřín's funicular railway

Petřín Park ㉕
PETŘÍNSKÉ SADY

Map 2 D5. 🚋 *6, 9, 12, 20, 22, then take funicular railway. See* **Four Guided Walks** *pp176–7.*

To the west of the Little Quarter, Petřín hill rises above the city to a height of 318 m (960 ft). The name derives either from the Slavonic god Perun, to whom sacrifices were made on the hill or from the Latin name Mons Petrinus, meaning "rocky hill". A forest used to stretch from here as far as the White Mountain *(see p31)*. In the 12th century the southern side of the hill was planted with vineyards, but by the 18th century most of these had been transformed into gardens and orchards.

Today a path winds up the slopes of Petřín, offering fine views of Prague. In the park is the *Monument to the Victims of Communism* (2002) by the sculptor Olbram Zoubek and a monument to Romantic poet Karel Hynek Mácha.

Statue of Karel Hynek Mácha in Petřín Park

Funicular Railway ㉖
LANOVÁ DRÁHA

Újezd. **Map** 2 D5. 🚋 *6, 9, 12, 20, 22.* **In operation** *summer: 9am– 11:30pm daily; winter: 9am– 11:20pm daily.* 📷 ♿

Built to carry visitors to the 1891 Jubilee Exhibition up to the Observation Tower at the top of Petřín hill, the funicular was originally powered by water. In this form, it remained in operation until 1914, then between the wars was converted to electricity. In 1965 it had to be shut down because part of the hillside collapsed – coal had been mined here during the 19th century. Shoring up the slope and rebuilding the railway took 20 years, but since its reopening in 1985 it has proved a reliable way of getting up Petřín Hill. At the halfway station, Nebozízek, there is a restaurant *(see p205)* with fine views of the Castle and the city.

Museum of Music ㉗
ČESKÉ MUZEUM HUDBY

Karmelitská 2, Praha 1, Malá Strana. **Map** 2 E4. *Tel 25 72 57 777.* Ⓜ *Malostranská.* 🚋 *12, 20, 22.* **Open** *10am–6pm Mon, Wed–Sun.* 📷 ♿ **www.nm.cz**

Housed in the former 17th century Baroque Church of St Magdalene, the Museum of Music seeks to present musical instruments not only as fine specimens of craftsmanship and artistry but also as mediators between man and music.

The museum is run by the National Museum *(see p147)* and boasts a magnificent atrium. Exhibits include a look at the diversity of popular 20th century music as preserved in film, television, photographs and sound recordings. Also examined is the production of handcrafted instruments, the history of musical notation and the social occasions linked to certain instruments. Earphones offer high-quality sound reproduction of original recordings made on the instruments displayed. The museum's collections can be accessed via the study room and there is a listening studio for the library of recordings.

Michna Palace ㉘
MICHNŮV PALÁC

Újezd 40. **Map** 2 E4. *Tel 25 73 11 831.* 🚋 *12, 20, 22.*

In about 1580 Ottavio Aostalli built a summer palace here for the Kinský family on the site of an old Dominican convent. In 1623 the building was bought by Pavel Michna of Vacínov, a supply officer in the Imperial Army, who had grown rich after the Battle of the White Mountain. He commissioned a new Baroque building that he hoped would rival the palace of his late commander, Wallenstein *(see p126)*.

In 1767 the Michna Palace was sold to the army and over the years it became a crumbling ruin. After 1918 it was bought by Sokol (a physical culture association) and converted into a gym and sports centre with a training ground in the old palace garden. The restored palace was renamed Tyrš House in honour of Sokol's founder.

Restored Baroque façade of the Michna Palace (Tyrš House)

NEW TOWN
NOVÉ MĚSTO

The New Town, founded in 1348 by Charles IV, was carefully planned and laid out around three large central market-places: the Hay Market (Senovážné Square), the Cattle Market (Charles Square) and the Horse Market (Wenceslas Square). Twice as large as

Art Nouveau decoration on No. 12 Wenceslas Square

the Old Town, the area was mainly inhabited by tradesmen and craftsmen such as blacksmiths, wheelwrights and brewers. During the late 19th century, much of the New Town was demolished and completely redeveloped, giving it the appearance it has today.

SIGHTS AT A GLANCE

Churches and Monasteries
Church of Our Lady of the Snows **2**
Church of St Ignatius **8**
Church of St Cyril and St Methodius **11**
Church of St John on the Rock **13**
Slavonic Monastery Emauzy **14**
Church of St Catherine **16**
Church of St Stephen **19**
Church of St Ursula **22**

Historic Buildings
Hotel Europa **4**
Jesuit College **9**
Faust House **12**
New Town Hall **20**

Theatres and Opera Houses
State Opera **6**
National Theatre pp156–7 **23**

Historic Squares
Wenceslas Square **1**
Charles Square **10**

Museums and Galleries
National Museum **5**
Mucha Museum **7**
Dvořák Museum **18**

Historic Restaurants and Beer Halls
Chalice Restaurant **17**
U Fleků **21**

Parks and Gardens
Franciscan Garden **3**
Botanical Gardens **15**

GETTING THERE
The entire area is well served by the metro with two main stations, Můstek and Muzeum in Wenceslas Square, and others at Karlovo náměstí and Národní třída (possible closures here from 2009). Most of the city's tram routes pass through Karlovo náměstí.

KEY

▣	Street-by-Street map *See pp144–5*
▣	Street-by-Street map *See pp150–51*
Ⓜ	Metro station
🚋	Tram stop
ℹ	Tourist information
🚢	River boat boarding point

◁ **Art Nouveau sculptures on the Hlahol Choir Building (1905) on Masarykovo nábřeží**

Street-by-Street: Wenceslas Square

Hotels and restaurants occupy many of the buildings around Wenceslas Square, though it remains an important commercial centre – the square began life as a medieval horse market. As you walk along, look up at the buildings, most of which date from the turn of last century, when the square was redeveloped. There are fine examples of the decorative styles used by Czech architects of the period. Many blocks have dark covered arcades leading to shops, clubs, theatres and cinemas.

Statue of St Lawrence at U Pinkasů

U Pinkasů became one of Prague's most popular beer halls when it started serving Pilsner Urquell *(see pp200–1)* in 1843.

Church of Our Lady of the Snows

The towering Gothic building is only part of a vast church planned during the 14th century **2**

Koruna Palace (1914) is an ornate block of shops and offices. Its corner turret is topped with a crown (*koruna*).

To Powder Gate

NA PŘÍKOPĚ

Můstek

Můstek

Můstek

VODIČKOVA

Lucerna Palace

Jungmann Square is named after Josef Jungmann (1773–1847), an influential scholar of language and lexicography, and there is a statue of him in the middle. The Adria Palace (1925) used to be the Laterna Magika Theatre *(see p220)*, which was where Václav Havel's Civic Forum worked in the early days of the 1989 Velvet Revolution.

Franciscan Garden

An old monastery garden has been laid out as a small park with this fountain, rose-beds, trellises and a children's playground **3**

Wiehl House, named after its architect Antonín Wiehl, was completed in 1896. The five-storey building is in striking Neo-Renaissance style, with a loggia and colourful *sgraffito*. Mikuláš Aleš designed some of the Art Nouveau figures.

STAR SIGHTS

★ Wenceslas Square

★ Hotel Europa

★ National Museum

★ Wenceslas Square
The dominant features of the square are the bronze, equestrian statue of St Wenceslas (1912) and the National Museum behind it. St Wenceslas, a former prince who was murdered by his brother Boleslav, is the patron saint of Bohemia ❶

LOCATOR MAP
See Street Finder, maps 3, 4 & 6

The Assicurazioni Generali Building was where Franz Kafka *(see p68)* worked as an insurance clerk for 10 months in 1906–7.

The Monument to the Victims of Communism is close to the spot where Jan Palach immolated himself in 1969 in protest at the Warsaw Pact invasion. An unofficial shrine has been maintained here since 1989.

★ Hotel Europa
Both the façade and the interior of the hotel (1906) preserve most of their original Art Nouveau features ❹

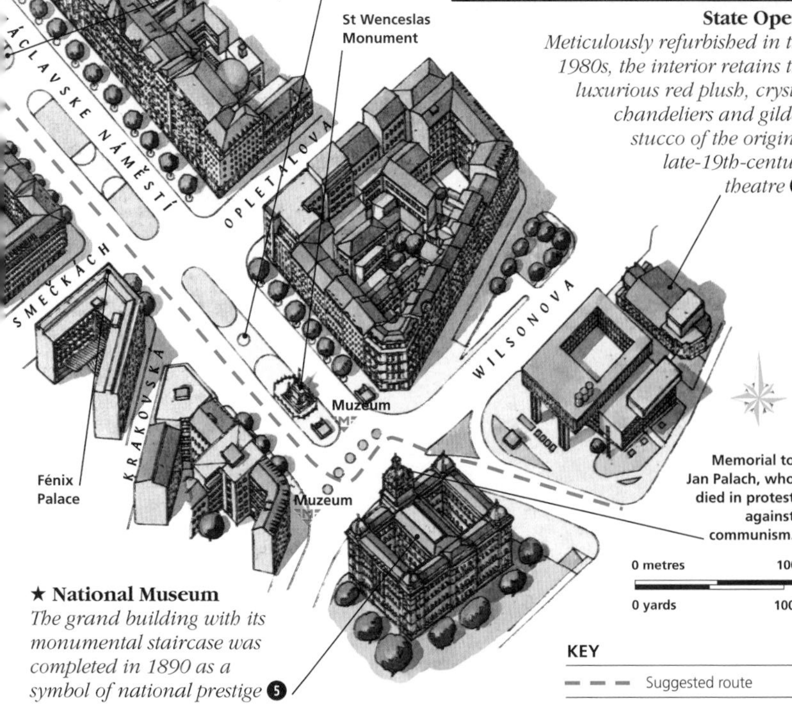

Café Tramvaj 11

St Wenceslas Monument

State Opera
Meticulously refurbished in the 1980s, the interior retains the luxurious red plush, crystal chandeliers and gilded stucco of the original late-19th-century theatre ❻

OPLETALOVA

ÁCLAVSKÉ NÁMĚSTÍ

SMEČKÁCH

KRAKOVSKÁ

WILSONOVA

Muzeum

Fénix Palace

Muzeum

Memorial to Jan Palach, who died in protest against communism.

★ National Museum
The grand building with its monumental staircase was completed in 1890 as a symbol of national prestige ❺

| 0 metres | 100 |
| 0 yards | 100 |

KEY

- - - Suggested route

Wenceslas Monument in Wenceslas Square

Wenceslas Square ❶

VÁCLAVSKÉ NÁMĚSTÍ

Map 3 C5. ᴹ Můstek, Muzeum.
🚊 *3, 9, 14, 24.*

The square has witnessed
many key events in Czech
history. It was here that the
student Jan Palach burnt himself to death in 1969, and in
November 1989 a protest rally
in the square against police
brutality led to the Velvet
Revolution and the overthrow
of Communism.
  Wenceslas "Square" is
something of a misnomer,
for it is some 750 m (825 yd)
long and only 60 m (65 yd)
wide. Originally a horse
market, today it is lined with
hotels, restaurants, clubs and
shops, reflecting the seamier
side of global consumerism.
The huge equestrian statue
of St Wenceslas that looks
the length of the square
from in front of the National
Museum was erected in
1912. Cast in bronze, it is the
work of Josef Myslbek, the
leading Czech sculptor of
the late 19th century. At the
foot of the pedestal there
are several other statues of
Czech patron saints. A
memorial near the statue
commemorates the victims
of the former regime.

Church of Our Lady of the Snows ❷

KOSTEL PANNY MARIE SNĚŽNÉ

Jungmannovo náměstí 18. **Map** 3
C5. **Tel** *22 22 46 243.* ᴹ *Můstek.*
Open *9am–7pm daily.* **Closed** *last
Sat of month.* ✝ *7am, 8am, 6pm
Mon–Fri, 9am, 10:15am, 11:30am,
6pm Sun.* 📷 ♿ www.*pms.ofm.cz*

Charles IV founded this church
to mark his coronation in
1347. The name refers to a
4th-century miracle in
Rome, when the
Virgin Mary appeared
to the pope in a dream
telling him to build a
church to her on the
spot where snow fell
in August. Charles's
church was to have
been over 100 m (330
ft) long, but was
never completed. The
towering building we
see today was just
the presbytery of the projected
church. Over 33 m (110 ft)
high, it was finished in 1397,
and was originally part of a
Carmelite monastery. On the
northern side there is a gateway with a 14th-century pediment that marked the entrance
to the monastery graveyard.
  In the early 15th century a
steeple was added, but further
building was halted by the
Hussite Wars *(see pp26–7)*. The
Hussite firebrand Jan Želivský
preached at the church and
was buried here after his execution in 1422. The church
suffered considerable damage
in the wars and in 1434 the
steeple was destroyed. For a
long time the church was left
to decay. In 1603 Franciscans

restored the building. The
intricate net vaulting of the
ceiling dates from this period,
the original roof having
collapsed. Most of the interior
decoration, apart from the
1450s pewter font, is
Baroque. The monumental
three-tiered altar is crowded
with statues of saints, and is
crowned with a crucifix.

Franciscan Garden ❸

FRANTIŠKÁNSKÁ ZAHRADA

Jungmannovo náměstí 18. **Map** 3 C5.
ᴹ *Můstek.* **Open** *Apr–Sep: 7am–
10pm (to 8pm Oct, 7pm Nov–Mar).* ♿

Originally the garden of a
Franciscan monastery, the area
was opened to the public in
1950 as a tranquil oasis close
to Wenceslas Square. By the
entrance is a Gothic portal
leading down to a cellar restaurant – U františkánů (At
the Franciscans). In the 1980s
several of the beds were
replanted with herbs, cultivat-
ed by the Franciscans in the
17th century.

Hotel Europa ❹

HOTEL EVROPA

Václavské náměstí 29.
Map 4 D5. **Tel** *22 42 15 387.*
ᴹ *Můstek.* 🚊 *3, 9, 14, 24.* ⊘
♿ *See* **Where to Stay** *p192,*
Restaurants, Cafés and Pubs
p206. www.*evropahotel.cz*

Though a trifle shabby in
places, the Europa Hotel is
a wonderfully preserved
reminder of the golden age

Art Nouveau decoration on façade of the Hotel Europa

Façade of the State Opera, formerly the New German Theatre

of hotels. It was built in highly decorated Art Nouveau style between 1903 and 1906. Not only has its splendid façade crowned with gilded nymphs survived, but many of the interiors on the ground floor have remained virtually intact, including all the original bars, large mirrors, panelling and light fittings.

National Museum ❺
NÁRODNÍ MUZEUM

Václavské náměstí 68. **Map** 6 E1. *Tel 22 44 97 111.* Ⓜ *Muzeum.* **Open** *Oct–Apr: 9am–5pm daily; May–Sep: 10am–6pm (but closed first Tue of month).* 🎥 📷 *for a fee.* **www**.nm.cz

The vast Neo-Renaissance building at one end of Wenceslas Square houses the National Museum. Designed by Josef Schulz as a triumphal affirmation of the Czech national revival, the museum was completed in 1890. The entrance is reached by a ramp decorated with allegorical statues. Seated by the door are History and Natural History.
  Inside, the rich marbled decoration is impressive, but overwhelms the collections devoted mainly to mineralogy, archaeology, anthropology, numismatics and natural history. The museum also has a Pantheon containing busts and statues of Czech scholars, writers and artists. It is deco-rated with many paintings by František Ženíšek, Václav Brožík and Vojtěch Hy nais.

State Opera ❻
STÁTNÍ OPERA

Wilsonova 4. **Map** 4 E5. *Tel 22 42 27 266 (box office).* Ⓜ *Muzeum.* **Open** *for performances only. See* **Entertainment** *p220 & p222.* **www**.opera.cz

The first theatre built here, the New Town Theatre, was pulled down in 1885 to make way for the present building. This was originally known as the New German Theatre, built to rival the Czechs' National Theatre

(see pp156–7). A Neo-Classical frieze decorates the pediment above the columned loggia at the front of the theatre. The figures include Dionysus and Thalia, the muse of comedy. The interior is stuccoed and original paintings in the auditorium and on the curtain have been preserved. In 1945 the theatre became the city's main opera house.

Mucha Museum ❼
MUCHOVO MUZEUM

Panská 7. **Map** 4 D4. *Tel 22 14 51 333.* Ⓜ *Můstek, Náměstí Republiky.* 🚊 *3, 5, 9, 14, 24, 26.* **Open** *10am–6pm daily.* 📷 📹 💻 **www**.mucha.cz

The 18th-century Kaunicky Palace is home to the first museum dedicated to this Czech master of Art Nouveau. A selection of more than 100 exhibits include paintings and drawings, sculptures, photographs and personal memorabilia. The central courtyard becomes a terrace for the café in the summer, and there is a museum shop offering exclusive gifts with Mucha motifs.

Main staircase of the National Museum

Art Nouveau in Prague

The decorative style known as Art Nouveau originated in Paris in the 1890s. It quickly became international as most of the major European cities quickly responded to its graceful, flowing forms. In Prague it was called "Secese" and at its height in the first decade of the 20th century but died out during World War I, when it seemed frivolous and even decadent. There is a wealth of Art Nouveau in Prague, both in the fine and decorative arts and in architecture. In the New Town and the Jewish Quarter *(see pp80–93)*, entire streets were demolished at the turn of the century and built in the new style.

Façade detail, 10 Masaryk Embankment

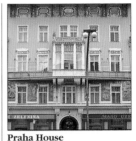

Praha House
This house was built in 1903 for the Prague Insurance Company. Its name is in gilt Art Nouveau letters at the top.

ARCHITECTURE

Art Nouveau made its first appearance in Prague at the Jubilee exhibition of 1891. Architecturally, the new style was a deliberate attempt to break with the 19th-century tradition of monumental buildings. In Art Nouveau the important aspect was ornament, either painted or sculpted, often in the form of a female figure, applied to a fairly plain surface. This technique was ideally suited to wrought iron and glass, popular at the turn of the century. These materials were light but strong. The effect of this, together with Art Nouveau decoration, created buildings of lasting beauty.

Hotel Central
Built by Alois Dryák and Bedřich Bendelmayer in 1900, the façade of this hotel has plasterwork shaped like tree branches.

Hlahol Choir Building, 1905
The architect Josef Fanta embellished this building with mosaics and sculptures by Karl Mottl and Josef Pekárek (see also p142).

Hotel Meran
Finished in 1904, this grand Art Nouveau building is notable for its fine detailing inside and out.

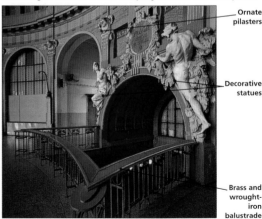

Ornate pilasters

Decorative statues

Brass and wrought-iron balustrade

Hlavní nádraží
Prague's main railway station was completed in 1901. With its huge interior glazed dome and elegant sculptural decoration, it shows many Art Nouveau features.

DECORATIVE AND FINE ARTS

Many painters, sculptors and graphic artists were influenced by Art Nouveau. One of the most successful exponents of the style was the artist Alfons Mucha (1860–1939). He is celebrated chiefly for his posters. Yet he designed stained glass (see p102), furniture, jewellery, even postage stamps. It is perhaps here, in the decorative and applied arts, that Art Nouveau had its fullest expression in Prague. Artists adorned every type of object – doorknobs, curtain ornaments, vases and cutlery – with tentacle- and plant-like forms in imitation of the natural world from which they drew their inspiration.

Postage Stamp, 1918
A bold stamp design by Alfons Mucha marked the founding of the Czechoslovak Republic.

Poster for Sokol Movement
Mucha's colour lithograph for the sixth national meeting of the Sokol gymnastic movement (1912) is in Tyrš's Museum (Physical Culture and Sports).

Záboj and Slavoj
These mythical figures (invented by a forger of old legends) were carved by Josef Myslbek for Palacký Bridge in 1895. They are now in Vyšehrad.

Glass Vase
This iridescent green vase made of Bohemian glass has relief decoration of intertwined threads. It is in the Museum of Decorative Arts.

Curtain Ornament and Candlestick
The silver and silk ornament adorns the Mayor's room of the Municipal House. The candlestick by Emanuel Novák with fine leaf design is in the Museum of Decorative Arts.

WHERE TO SEE ART NOUVEAU IN PRAGUE

Detail of doorway, Široká 9, Jewish Quarter

ARCHITECTURE
Apartment Building,
    Na příkopě 7
Hanavský Pavilion *p161*
Hlahol Choir Building,
    Masarykovo nábřeží 10
Hlavní nádraží, Wilsonova
Hotel Central, Hybernská 10
Hotel Evropa *p146*
Industrial Palace *p162* and
    Four Guided Walks *pp178–9*
Ministerstvo pro místní rozvoj
    p67
Municipal House *p64*
Palacký Bridge (Palackého most)
Praha House, Národní třída 7
Wiehl House *p144*

PAINTING
Trades Fair Palace *pp164–5*

SCULPTURE
Jan Hus Monument *p70*
Vyšehrad Garden and
    Cemetery *p160* and Four
    Guided Walks *pp180–1*
Zbraslav Monastery *p163*

DECORATIVE ARTS
Mucha Museum *p147*
Museum of Decorative Arts
    p84
Prague Museum *p161*

Street-by-Street: Charles Square

The southern part of the New Town resounds to the rattle of trams, as many routes converge in this part of Prague. Fortunately, the park in Charles Square (Karlovo náměstí) offers a peaceful and welcome retreat. Some of the buildings around the Square belong to the University and the statues in the centre represent writers and scientists, reflecting the academic environment. There are several Baroque buildings and towards the river stands the historic 14th-century Slavonic Monastery.

Detail of house in Charles Square

The Czech Technical University was founded here in 1867 in a grand Neo-Renaissance building.

Charles Square Centre

Church of St Wenceslas

RESSLOVÁ

To the river

VÁCLAVSKÁ

NA MORÁNI

KARLOVO NÁ...

To metro Karlovo náměstí

★ Church of St Cyril and St Methodius
A plaque and a bullet-scarred wall are reminders of a siege in 1942, when German troops attacked Czech and Slovak para-troopers hiding here after assassinating Nazi Reinhard Heydrich ⓫

★ Charles Square
The centre of the square is a pleasant 19th-century park with lawns, formal flowerbeds, fountains and statues ❿

Church of St Cosmas and St Damian

POD SLOVANY

VYŠEHRADSKÁ

Slavonic Monastery Emauzy
In 1965 a pair of modern concrete spires by František Černý were added to the church of the 14th-century monastery ⓮

TROJICKÁ

STAR SIGHTS

★ Charles Square

★ Church of St Cyril and St Methodius

Church of St John on the Rock
This view of the organ and ceiling shows the dynamic Baroque design of Kilian Ignaz Dientzenhofer ⓭

Church of St Ignatius
The sun rays and gilded cherubs on the side altars are typical of the gaudy decoration in this Baroque church built for the Jesuits **8**

LOCATOR MAP
See Street Finder, map 5

Eliška Krásnohorská was a 19th-century poet who wrote the libretti for Smetana's operas. A statue of her was put up here in 1931.

A statue of Jan Purkyně (1787–1869), an eminent physiologist and pioneer of cell theory, was erected in 1961. It is the most recent of the many memorials in the square.

Jesuit College
Founded in the mid-17th century, this imposing building has been a hospital since the suppression of the Jesuits in 1773 (see pp30–31) **9**

18th-century Institute of Gentlewomen (now a hospital)

Faust House
In the 18th century this house was owned by Count Ferdinand Mladota of Solopysky. The chemical experiments he performed reinforced the associations that gave the building its name **12**

Botanical Gardens
Though part of the Charles University, the gardens are open to the public and are known for their profusion of rare plants. This is an agreeable place to relax **15**

| 0 metres | 100 |
| 0 yards | 100 |

KEY

– – – Suggested route

Sculptures on the façade of the Jesuit College by Tomasso Soldati

Church of St Ignatius ❽

KOSTEL SV. IGNÁCE

Ječná 2. **Map** 5 C2. **Tel** 22 49 21 254. Ⓜ Karlovo náměstí. 🚋 3, 4, 6, 10, 14, 18, 22, 24. **Open** 6am–6:30pm daily. 🚏 frequent. 📷

With its wealth of gilding and flamboyant stucco decoration, St Ignatius is typical of the Baroque churches built by the Jesuits to impress people with the power and glamour of their faith. The architects were the same two men responsible for the adjoining Jesuit College, Carlo Lurago, who started work on the church in 1665, and Paul Ignaz Bayer, who added the tower in 1687.

The painting on the high altar of *The Glory of St Ignatius* (St Ignatius Loyola, the founder of the Jesuit order) is by Jan Jiří Heinsch.

The Jesuits continued to embellish the interior right up until the suppression of their order in 1773, adding stuccowork and statues of Jesuit and Czech saints.

Jesuit College ❾

JEZUITSKÁ KOLEJ

Karlovo náměstí 36. **Map** 5 B2. Ⓜ Karlovo náměstí. 🚋 3, 4, 6, 10, 14, 16, 18, 22, 24. **Closed** to the public.

Half the eastern side of Charles Square is occupied by the former college of the Jesuit order in the New Town. As in other parts of Prague, the Jesuits were able to demolish huge swathes of the city to put up another bastion of their formidable education system. The college was built between 1656 and 1702 by Carlo Lurago and Paul Ignaz Bayer. The two sculptured portals are the work of Johann Georg Wirch who extended the building in 1770. After the suppression of the Jesuit order in 1773 the college was converted into a military hospital. It is now a teaching hospital and part of Charles University.

Charles Square ❿

KARLOVO NÁMĚSTÍ

Map 5 B2. Ⓜ Karlovo náměstí. 🚋 3, 4, 6, 10, 14, 16, 18, 22, 24.

Since the mid-19th century the square has been a park. Though surrounded by busy roads, it is a pleasant place to sit and read or watch people exercising their dachshunds.

The square began life as a vast cattle market, when Charles IV founded the New Town in 1348. Other goods sold in the square included firewood, coal and pickled herring from barrels.

In the centre of the market Charles had a wooden tower built, where the coronation jewels were put on display once a year. In 1382 the tower was replaced by a chapel, from which, in 1437, concessions made to the Hussites by the pope at the Council of Basle were read out to the populace.

Church of St Cyril and St Methodius ⓫

KOSTEL SV. CYRILA A METODĚJE

Resslova 9. **Map** 5 B2. **Tel** 22 49 20 686. Ⓜ Karlovo náměstí. 🚋 3, 4, 6, 10, 14, 16, 18, 22, 24. **Open** Oct–Apr: 10am–4pm Tue–Sun; May–Sep: 10am–5pm Tue–Sun. 📷 🚫 ♿

This Baroque church, with a pilastered façade and a small central tower, was built in the 1730s. It was dedicated to St Charles Borromeo and served as the church of a community of retired priests, but both were closed in 1783. In the 1930s the church was restored and given to the Czechoslovak Orthodox Church, and rededicated to St Cyril and St Methodius, the 9th-century "Apostles to the Slavs" (*see pp20–21*). In May 1942 parachutists who had assassinated Reinhard Heydrich, the Nazi governor of Czechoslovakia, hid in the crypt along with members of the Czech Resistance. Surrounded by German troops, they took their own lives rather than surrender. Bullet holes made by the German machine guns during the siege can still be seen below the memorial plaque on the outer wall of the crypt, which now houses a museum of these times.

Main altar in the Church of St Cyril and St Methodius

Faust House

FAUSTŮV DŮM

Karlovo náměstí 40, 41. **Map** 5 B3.
Ⓜ Karlovo náměstí. 🚋 3, 4, 14,
16, 18. **Closed** to the public.

Prague thrives on legends of
alchemy and pacts with the
devil, and this Baroque
mansion has attracted many.
There has been a house here
since the 14th century when it
belonged to Prince Václav of
Opava, an alchemist and natural historian. In the 16th century it was owned by the
alchemist Edward Kelley. The
chemical experiments of
Count Ferdinand Mladota of
Solopysky, who owned the
house in the mid-18th century,
gave rise to its association
with the legend of Faust.

Baroque façade of Faust House

Church of St John on the Rock ⓭

KOSTEL SV. JANA NA SKALCE

Vyšehradská 49. **Map** 5 B3.
Tel 22 49 15 371. 🚋 3, 4, 14, 16,
18, 24. **Open** for services only.
✝ 8am Sun. 📷

One of Prague's smaller
Baroque churches, St John
on the Rock is one of Kilian
Ignaz Dientzenhofer's most
daring designs. Its twin
square towers are set at a
sharp angle to the church's
narrow façade and the
interior is based on an
octagonal floorplan. The
church was completed in

1738, but the double staircase
leading up to the west front
was not added until the
1770s. On the high altar there
is a wooden version of Jan
Brokof's statue of St John
Nepomuk (see p137) which
stands on the Charles Bridge.

Slavonic Monastery Emauzy ⓮

KLÁŠTER NA SLOVANECH-EMAUZY

Vyšehradská 49. **Map** 5 B3.
Tel 22 19 79 227. 🚋 3, 4, 14, 18,
24. **Monastery church open** 9am–
4pm Mon–Fri. **Cloisters open** by
appointment. ✝ 10am, 6pm daily.
📷 📷 ♿ www.emauzy.cz

Both the monastery and its
church were almost destroyed
in an American air raid in
1945. During their
reconstruction, the church
was given a pair of modern
reinforced concrete spires.
The monastery was founded
in 1347 for the Croatian
Benedictines, whose services
were held in the Old Slavonic
language, hence its name
"Na Slovanech". In the course
of Prague's tumultuous
religious history it has since
changed hands many times.
In 1446 a Hussite order was
formed here, then in 1635 the
monastery was acquired by
Spanish Benedictines. In the
18th century the complex was
given a thorough Baroque
treatment, but in 1880 it was
taken over by some German
Benedictines, who rebuilt
almost everything in Neo-
Gothic style. The monastery
has managed to preserve some
historically important 14th-
century wall paintings in the
cloister, though many were
damaged in World War II.

Remains of 14th-century wall paintings in the Slavonic Monastery

Botanical Gardens ⓯

BOTANICKÁ ZAHRADA

Na slupi 16. **Map** 5 B3. **Tel** 22 49 18
970. 🚋 18, 24. 🚌 148.
Glasshouses open 10am–4pm daily.
Gardens open Jan–Feb: 10am–5pm
daily; Mar–Oct: 10am–6pm daily;
Nov–Dec: 10am–4pm daily. 📷 📷 ♿

Charles IV founded Prague's
first botanical garden in the
14th century. This is a much
later institution. The university
garden was founded in the
Smíchov district in 1775, but
in 1897 it was moved to its
present site. The huge
greenhouses date from 1938.
Special botanical exhibitions
and shows of exotic birds and
tropical fish are often held
here. One star attraction of the
gardens is the giant water lily,
Victoria cruziana, whose huge
leaves can support a small
child. During the summer it
produces dozens of flowers
which only survive for a day.

Entrance to the university's Botanical Gardens

Octagonal steeple of St Catherine's

Church of St Catherine

KOSTEL SV. KATEŘINY

Kateřinská. **Map** 5 C3. 🚋 *4, 6, 10, 16, 22.* **Closed** *to the public.*

St Catherine's stands in the garden of a former convent, founded in 1354 by Charles IV to commemorate his victory at the Battle of San Felice in Italy in 1332. In 1420, during the Hussite revolution *(see pp26–7)*, the convent was demolished, but in the following century it was rebuilt by Kilian Ignáz Dientzenhofer as an Augustinian monastery. The monks remained here until 1787, when the monastery closed. Since 1822 it has been used as a hospital. In 1737 a new Baroque church was built, but the slender steeple of the old Gothic church was retained. Its octagonal shape has gained it the nickname of "the Prague minaret".

Chalice Restaurant 🟠

RESTAURACE U KALICHA

Na bojišti 14. **Map** 6 D3. *Tel 29 61 89 600.* IP Pavlova. 🚋 *4, 6, 10, 16, 22.* **Open** *11am–11pm daily (book ahead).* 📷 ♿ *See* **Restaurants, Cafés and Pubs** *p207.* **www.** ukalicha.cz

This Pilsner Urquell beer hall owes its fame to the novel *The Good Soldier Švejk* by Jaroslav Hašek. It was Švejk's

favourite drinking place and the establishment trades on the popularity of the best-known character in 20th-century Czech literature. The staff dress in period costume from World War I, the era of this novel.

Dvořák Museum 🔞

MUZEUM ANTONÍNA DVOŘÁKA

Ke Karlovu 20. **Map** 6 D2. *Tel 22 49 23 363.* I.P. Pavlova. 🚋 *148.* **Open** *10am–1:30pm, 2–5pm Tue–Sun and for concerts.* 📷 ♿ **www.**nm.cz

One of the most enchanting secular buildings of the Prague Baroque now houses the Antonín Dvořák Museum. On display are Dvořák scores and editions of his works, plus photographs and memorabilia of the great 19th-century Czech composer, including his piano, viola and desk.

The building is by the great Baroque architect Kilian Ignaz Dientzenhofer *(see p129)*. Just two storeys high with an elegant tiered mansard roof, the house was completed in 1720, for the Michnas of Vacínov and was originally known as the Michna Summer Palace. It later became known as Villa Amerika, after a nearby inn called Amerika. Between the two pavilions flanking the house is a fine iron

gateway, a replica of the Baroque original. In the 19th century the villa and garden fell into decay. The garden statues and vases, from the workshop of Matthias Braun, date from about 1735. They are original but heavily restored, as is the interior of the palace. The ceiling and walls of the large room on the first floor are decorated with 18th-century frescoes by Jan Ferdinand Schor.

Church of St Stephen 🔟

KOSTEL SV. ŠTĚPÁNA

Štěpánská. **Map** 5 C2. 🚋 *4, 6, 10, 16, 22.* **Open** *only for services.* 🔔 *11am Sun.* ♿

Founded by Charles IV in 1351 as the parish church of the upper New Town, St Stephen's was finished in 1401 with the completion of the multi-spired steeple. In the late 17th century the Branberg Chapel was built on to the north side of the church. It contains the tomb of the prolific Baroque sculptor Matthias Braun.

Most of the subsequent Baroque additions were removed when the church was scrupulously re-Gothicized in the 1870s by Josef Mocker.

There are several fine Baroque paintings,

The Michna Summer Palace, home of the Dvořák Museum

Renaissance painted ceiling in the New Town Hall

however, including *The Baptism of Christ* by Karel Škréta at the end of the left hand aisle and a picture of St John Nepomuk *(see p137)* by Jan Jiři Heinsch to the left of the 15th-century pulpit. The church's greatest treasure is undoubtedly a beautiful Gothic panel painting of the Madonna, known as *Our Lady of St Stephen's*, which dates from 1472.

Gothic pulpit in St Stephen's

New Town Hall ⑳
NOVOMĚSTSKÁ RADNICE

Karlovo náměstí 23. **Map** 5 B1. Karlovo náměstí. 3, 4, 6, 10, 14, 16, 18, 22, 24. **Tel** 22 49 48 229. **Tower open** May–Sep: 10am–6pm Tue–Sun.

In 1960 a statue of Hussite preacher Jan Želivský was unveiled at the New Town Hall. It commemorates the first and bloodiest of many defenestrations. On 30 July 1419 Želivský led a crowd of demonstrators to the Town Hall to demand the release of some prisoners. When they were refused, they stormed the building and threw the Catholic councillors

out of the windows. Those who survived the fall were finished off with pikes.

The Town Hall already existed in the 14th century, the Gothic tower was added in the mid-15th century and contains an 18th century chapel. In the 16th century it acquired an arcaded courtyard. After the joining-up of the four towns of Prague in 1784 the Town Hall ceased to be the seat of the municipal administration and became a courthouse and a prison. It is now used for cultural and social events, and its splendid Gothic hall can be hired for wedding receptions.

U Fleků ㉑

Křemencova 11. **Map** 5 B1. **Tel** 22 49 34 019. Národní třída, Karlovo náměstí. 6, 9, 17, 18, 22. **Museum open** 10am–4pm Mon–Fri. See **Restaurants, Cafés and Pubs** p206. **www.**ufleku.cz

Records indicate that beer was brewed here as early as 1459. This archetypal Prague beer hall has been fortunate in its owners, who have kept up the tradition of brewing as

an art rather than just a means of making money. In 1762 the brewery was purchased by Jakub Flekovský, who named it U Fleků (At the Fleks). The present brewery, the smallest in Prague, makes a special strong, dark beer, sold only here. The restaurant now also features a small museum of Czech brewing history.

Church of St Ursula ㉒
KOSTEL SV. VORŠILY

Ostrovní 18. **Map** 3 A5. **Tel** 22 49 30 502. Národní třída. 6, 9, 18, 22. 5pm daily. For visits at any other time, contact Prague Information Service (see p227).

The delightful Baroque church of St Ursula was built as part of an Ursuline convent founded in 1672. The original sculptures still decorate the façade and in front of the church stands a group of statues featuring St John Nepomuk (1747) by Ignaz Platzer the Elder. The light airy interior has a frescoed, stuccoed ceiling and on the various altars there are lively Baroque paintings. The main altar has one of St Ursula.

The adjoining convent has been returned to the Ursuline order and is now a Catholic school. For many years part of the ground floor was used as a restaurant but this area may now be redeveloped.

National Theatre ㉓
NÁRODNÍ DIVADLO

See pp156–7.

U Fleků, Prague's best-known beer hall

National Theatre ㉓

NÁRODNÍ DIVADLO

This gold-crested theatre has always been an important symbol of the Czech cultural revival. Work started in 1868, funded largely by voluntary contributions. The original Neo-Renaissance design was by the Czech architect Josef Zítek. After its destruction by fire *(see opposite)*, Josef Schulz was given the job of rebuilding the theatre and all the best Czech artists of the period contributed towards its lavish and spectacular decoration. During the late 1970s and early 80s the theatre was restored and the New Stage was built by architect Karel Prager.

The theatre from Marksmen's Island

A bronze sculpture in the foyer

A bronze three-horse chariot, designed by Bohuslav Schnirch, carries the Goddess of Victory.

Laterna Magika

The New Stage auditorium

★ Auditorium
The elaborately-painted ceiling is adorned with allegorical figures representing the arts by František Ženíšek.

STAR FEATURES

★ Auditorium

★ Lobby Ceiling

★ Stage Curtain

The five arcades of the loggia are decorated with lunette paintings by Josef Tulka, entitled *Five Songs*.

★ Lobby Ceiling
This ceiling fresco is the final part of a triptych painted by František Ženíšek in 1878 depicting the Golden Age of Czech Art.

★ Stage Curtain
This sumptuous gold and red stage curtain, showing the origin of the theatre, is the work of Vojtěch Hynais.

VISITORS' CHECKLIST

Národní 2, Nové Město. **Map** 3 A5. **Box office open** 10am–6pm daily. *Tel* 22 49 01 448. Národní třída, line B. 6, 9, 17, 18, 22 to Národní divadlo. **Auditorium open** only during performances.

Façade Decoration
This standing figure on the attic of the western façade is one of many figures representing the Arts sculpted by Antonín Wagner in 1883.

The startling sky-blue roof covered with stars, is said to symbolize the summit all artists should aim for.

The President's Box
The former royal box, lined in red velvet, is decorated with famous historical figures from Czech history by Václav Brožík.

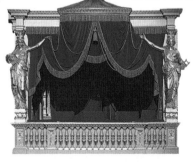

NATIONAL THEATRE FIRE

On 12 August, 1881, just days before the official opening, the National Theatre was completely gutted by fire. It was thought to have been started by metalworkers on the roof. But just six weeks later, enough money had been collected to rebuild the theatre. It was finally opened two years late in 1883 with a performance of Czech composer Bedřich Smetana's opera *Libuše* (see p79).

FURTHER AFIELD

Visitors to Prague, finding the old centre packed with sights, tend to ignore the suburbs. It is true that once you start exploring away from the centre, the language can become more of a problem. However, it is well worth the effort, firstly to escape the crowds of tourists milling around the Castle and the Old Town Square, secondly to realize that Prague is a living city as well as a picturesque time capsule. Most of the museums and other sights in the first part of this section are easily reached by Metro, tram or even on foot. If you are prepared to venture a little further, do not miss the grand palace at Troja or the former monastery at Zbraslav, which houses the Asian Art collection of the National Gallery. The Day Trips *(pp168–71)* include visits to castles close to Prague and the historic spa towns of Marienbad and Karlsbad, which attracted the first tourists to Bohemia during the 19th century.

Vaulting in Church of St Barbara, Kutná Hora

SIGHTS AT A GLANCE

Museums and Galleries
Mozart Museum **1**
Prague Museum **6**
National Technical Museum **8**
Trades Fair Palace pp164–5 **9**
Zbraslav Monastery **15**

Monasteries
Břevnov Monastery **13**

Historic Districts
Vyšehrad **2**
Žižkov **4**
Náměstí Míru **5**

Cemeteries
Olšany Cemeteries **3**

Historic Sites
White Mountain and Star Hunting Lodge **14**

Historic Buildings
Troja Palace pp166–7 **11**

Parks and Gardens
Letná Park **7**
Exhibition Ground and Stromovka Park **10**
Zoo **12**

KEY

▣	Central Prague
▢	Greater Prague
✈	Airport
▬	Motorway
▬	Major road
═	Minor road

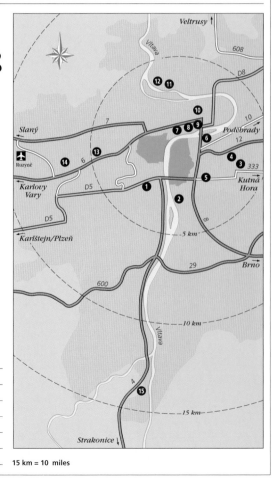

15 km = 10 miles

Bertramka, the villa that houses the Mozart Museum

Mozart Museum ❶

BERTRAMKA

Mozartova 169. **Tel** 25 73 18 461.
Ⓜ *Anděl*. 🚋 4, 7, 9, 10. **Open**
Apr–Oct: 9:30am–6pm daily; Nov–
Mar: 9:30am–4pm daily. 📷 📵
www.bertramka.com

Though slightly off the beaten
track, the museum is well
signposted because of Prague's
reverence for Mozart. Bertramka is a 17th-century farmhouse, enlarged in the second
half of the 18th century into a
comfortable suburban villa.
Mozart and his wife Constanze
stayed here as the guests of
the composer František Dušek
and his wife Josefina in 1787,
when Mozart was working on
Don Giovanni. He composed

the overture to the opera in
the garden pavilion just a few
hours before its premiere at
the Nostitz (now the Estates)
Theatre *(see p65)*. The house,
with a small exhibition on
Mozart, is at its best in the
late afternoon when it is qui-
etest. In summer, recitals take
place on the terrace.

Vyšehrad ❷

Map 5 B5. Ⓜ *Vyšehrad*. 🚋 3, 7, 16,
17, 18, 24.

A rocky outcrop above the
Vltava, Vyšehrad means
"castle on the heights" *(see
pp180–81)*. It was fortified in
the 10th century and, at
times, used as the seat of the
Přemyslid princes. The area
has great historical and
mythological significance, and
in the 1870s it became the site
of a national cemetery.

Olšany Cemeteries ❸

OLŠANSKÉ HŘBITOVY

Vinohradská 153, Jana Želivského.
Ⓜ *Želivského*. **Tel** 26 73 10 652. 🚋
5, 6, 10, 11, 16, 19, 26. **Open** Mar–
Sep: 8am–7pm; Oct–Feb: 8am–6pm.

At the northwest corner
of the main cemetery
stands the small Church of
St Roch (1682), protector
against the plague – the
first cemetery was founded
here in 1679 specifically for
the burial of plague victims.
In the course of the 19th
century, the old cemetery
was enlarged and new ones
developed, including a

Well-tended grave in the eastern
part of the Olšany Cemeteries

Russian cemetery, distin-
guished by its old-fashioned
Orthodox church (1924–5),
and a Jewish one, where
Franz Kafka *(see p68)* is
buried. Tombs include those
of painter Josef Mánes
(1820–71) who worked
during the Czech Revival
movement *(see pp32–3)*, and
Josef Jungmann (1773–1847),
compiler of a five-volume
Czech-German dictionary.

Žižkov ❹

Ⓜ *Jiřího z Poděbrad, Želivského,
Flóra*.
National Monument, *Vítkov, U
památníku*. 🚌 133. **Closed** for long-
term renovation.

Equestrian statue of Jan Žižka

This quarter of Prague was
the scene of a historic victory
for the Hussites *(see pp26–7)*
over Crusaders sent by the
Emperor Sigismund to destroy
them. On 14 July 1420 on
Vítkov hill, a tiny force of
Hussites defeated an army of
several thousand well-armed
men. The determined, hymn-
singing Hussites were led by
the one-eyed Jan Žižka.
  In 1877 the area around
Vítkov was renamed Žižkov in
honour of Žižka's victory, and
in 1950 a bronze equestrian
statue of Žižka by Bohumil
Kafka was erected on the hill.
About 9m (30 ft) high, this is
the largest equestrian statue
in the world. It stands in front
of the National Monument
(1927–32), built as a symbol of
the struggle for independence
of the Czechoslovak people.
The Monument later served as
a mausoleum for Klement
Gottwald and other Communist
leaders. Their remains have
since been removed and the
building was given to the
National Museum *(see p147)*,

Relief by Josef Myslbek on portal of St Ludmilla in Náměstí Míru

which plans to open a permanent exhibition on modern Czech history in 2010.

Nearby is a giant television transmitter, 260 m (850 ft) high. Locals are suspicious of the rays emanating from this great tube of reinforced concrete, built in 1984–8.

Náměstí Míru **⑤**

Map 6 F2. 🚇 *Náměstí Míru.* 🚊 *4, 6, 10, 16, 22.* 🚌 *135.* **Church of St Ludmila open** *only for services.*

This attractive square, with a well-kept central garden, is the focal point of the mostly residential Vinohrady quarter. At the top of its sloping lawns stands the attractive, brick Neo-Gothic Church of St Ludmila (1888–93), designed by Josef Mocker, architect of the west end of St Vitus's Cathedral *(see pp100–3).* Its twin octagonal spires are 60 m (200 ft) high. On the tympanum of the main portal is a relief of Christ with St Wenceslas and St Ludmila by the great 19th-century sculptor Josef Myslbek. Leading artists also contributed designs for the stained-glass windows.

The outside of the square is lined with attractive buildings, the most conspicuous being the Vinohrady Theatre, a spirited Art Nouveau building completed in 1907. The façade is crowned by two huge winged figures sculpted by Milan Havlíček, symbolizing Drama and Opera.

Prague Museum **⑥**

MUZEUM HLAVNÍHO MĚSTA PRAHY

Na Poříčí 52. **Map** 4 F3. **Tel** *22 48 16 773.* 🚇 *Florenc.* 🚊 *3, 8, 24, 26.* **Open** *9am–6pm Tue–Sun.* 🖼 📷 **www**.muzeumprahy.cz

The collection records the history of Prague from primeval times. A new museum was built to house the exhibits in the 1890s. Its Neo-Renaissance façade is rich with stucco and sculptures, and the interior walls are painted with historic views of the city. Some of the items on display include examples of Prague china and furniture, relics of the medieval guilds and paintings of Prague through the ages. The most

remarkable exhibit is the paper and wood model of Prague by Antonín Langweil. Completed in 1834, it covers 20 sq m (25 sq yards). The scale of the extraordinarily accurate model is 1:500.

Letná Park **⑦**

LETENSKÉ SADY

Map 3 A1. 🚇 *Malostranská, Hradčanská.* 🚊 *1, 8, 12, 14, 17, 18, 20, 22, 25, 26.*

Across the river from the Jewish Quarter, a large plateau overlooks the city. It was here that armies gathered before attacking Prague Castle. Since the mid-19th century it has been a wooded park.

On the terrace at the top of the granite steps that lead up from the embankment stands a curious monument – a giant metronome built in 1991. It was installed after the Velvet Revolution on the pedestal formerly occupied by the gigantic stone statue of Stalin leading the people, which was blown up in 1962. A far more durable monument is the Hanavský Pavilion, a Neo-Baroque cast iron structure, built for the 1891 Exhibition. It was later dismantled and erected on its present site in the park, where it houses a popular restaurant and café. The park has a popular beer garden in summer at its eastern end.

View of the Vltava and bridges from Letná Park

National Technical Museum **8**
NÁRODNÍ TECHNICKÉ MUZEUM

Kostelní 42. *Tel* 22 03 99 111. 🚋 *1, 8, 25, 26.* **Closed** *for renovation until 2010.* 🖼 🚫 📷 ♿
www.ntm.cz

Though it tries to keep abreast of all scientific developments, the museum's strength is its collection of machines from the Industrial Revolution to the present day, the largest of its kind in Europe. The section that attracts the most visitors is the History of Transportation in the vast central hall. This is filled with locomotives, railway carriages, bicycles, veteran motorcars and motorcycles, with aeroplanes and a hot-air balloon suspended overhead.

The photography and cinematography section is well worth a visit, as is the collection of astronomical instruments. The section on measuring time is also popular, especially on the hour when everything starts to chime at once. In the basement there is a huge reconstruction of a coal mine, with an assortment of tools tracing the development of mining from the 15th to the 19th century.

Trade Fair Palace **9**
VELETRŽNÍ PALÁC

See pp164–5.

Exhibition Ground and Stromovka Park **10**
VÝSTAVIŠTĚ A STROMOVKA

🚋 *12, 14, 17.* **Exhibition Ground open** *10am–11pm daily; parts may be closed for renovation until 2010.* 🖼 **Stromovka Park open** *24hrs daily.* **Lapidarium** *Tel* 23 33 75 636. **Open** *noon–5pm Tue–Fri, 10am–5pm Sat, Sun.* ♿ **www**.nm.cz

Laid out for the Jubilee of 1891, the Exhibition Ground has a lively funfair and is great for a day out with children. All kinds of exhibitions, sporting events, spectacles and concerts are staged in summer. The large park to the west

The Industrial Palace, centrepiece of the 1891 Exhibition Ground

was the former royal hunting enclosure and deer park, first established in the late 16th century. The name Stromovka means "place of trees". Opened to the public in 1804, the park is still a pleasant wooded area and an ideal place for a walk. The Lapidarium holds an exhibition of 11th–19th century sculpture, including some originals from Charles Bridge (see pp136–9). Part of the Exhibition Ground, including a wing of the Industrial Palace, was ravaged by fire in 2008 and may be inaccessible until renovation is complete.

Troja Palace **11**
TROJSKÝ ZÁMEK

See pp166–7.

Zoo **12**
ZOOLOGICKÁ ZAHRADA

U trojského zámku 3/120. *Tel* 29 61 12 111. 🚇 *Holešovice, then* 🚌 *112.* **Open** *Jun–Aug: 9am–7pm daily; Apr, May, Sep, Oct: 9am–6pm daily; Nov–Feb: 9am–4pm daily; Mar: 9am–5pm daily.* 🖼 📷 ♿ 🍴
www.zoopraha.cz

Attractively situated on a rocky slope overlooking the

right bank of the Vltava, the zoo was founded in 1924. It now covers an area of 64 hectares (160 acres) and there is a chair lift to take visitors to the upper part.

The zoo's 2,500 animals represent 500 species, 50 of them extremely rare in the wild. It is best known for its breeding programme of Przewalski's horses, the only species of wild horse in the world. It has also enjoyed success in breeding big cats, gorillas and orang-utans. In addition there are two pavilions, one for lions, tigers and other beasts of prey and one for elephants. The zoo also works on reintroducing endangered species to the wild.

Red panda, relative of the famous giant panda, in Prague Zoo

Břevnov Monastery

BŘEVNOVSKÝ KLÁŠTER

Markétská 28. **Tel** 22 04 06 111.
🚇 15, 22, 25. 🕐 only, Sat & Sun;
tour times vary. 📷 🅿
www.brevnov.cz

From the surrounding sub-urban housing, you would never guess that Břevnov is one of the oldest inhabited parts of Prague. A flourishing community grew up here around the Benedictine abbey founded in 993 by Prince Boleslav II *(see p20)* and Bishop Adalbert (Vojtěch) – the first monastery in Bohemia. An ancient well called Vojtěška marks the spot where prince and bishop are supposed to have met and decided to found the monastery.

The gateway, courtyard and most of the present monastery buildings are by the great Baroque architects Christoph and Kilian Ignaz Dientzenhofer *(see p129)*. The monastery Church of St Margaret is the work of Christoph. Completed in 1715, it is based on a floor-plan of overlapping ovals, as ingenious as any of Bernini's churches in Rome. In 1964 the crypt of the original 10th-century church was discovered below the choir and is open to the public. Of the other buildings, the most interesting is the Theresian Hall, with a painted ceiling dating from 1727.

White Mountain and Star Hunting Lodge 🄸

BÍLÁ HORA A HVĚZDA

🚇 15, 22, 25. **White Mountain enclosure open** 24hrs daily. **Star Hunting Lodge Tel** 23 53 57 938.
Open Apr, Oct: 10am–5pm Tue–Sun (to 6pm May–Sep). 📷 🅿

The Battle of the White Mountain *(see p31)*, fought on 8 November 1620, had a very different impact for the two main communities of Prague. For the Protestants it was a disaster that led to 300 years of Habsburg

Star Hunting Lodge

domination; for the Catholic supporters of the Habsburgs it was a triumph, so they built a memorial chapel on the hill. In the early 1700s this chapel was converted into the grander Church of Our Lady Victorious and decorated by leading Baroque artists, including Václav Vavřinec Reiner.

In the 16th century the woodland around the battle site had been a royal game park. The hunting lodge, completed in 1556, survives today. This fascinating building is shaped as a six-pointed star – *hvězda* means star. On site is a small exhibition about the building and its history. Also on show are exhibits relating to the Battle of

the White Mountain and temporary exhibitions about Czech culture.

Zbraslav Monastery 🄵

ZBRASLAVSKÝ KLÁŠTER

Zámek Zbraslav. **Tel** 25 79 21 638.
🚌 129, 241, 243. **Open** 10am–6pm Tue–Sun. 📷 🅿 ♿
www.ngprague.cz

In 1279 Wenceslas II founded a monastery to serve as the burial place for the royal family, though only he and Wenceslas IV were ever buried here. Destroyed during the Hussite Wars *(see pp26–7)*, the monastery was rebuilt in 1709–39, only to be abolished in 1785 and made into a factory. In the early 20th century it was restored and in 1941 was given to the National Gallery. It now houses a unique collection of Asian art with exhibits including art and artefacts from China, Japan, India, South East Asia and Tibet. A collection of Japanese sculpture is fea-tured, which visually impaired visitors are encouraged to touch. The exhibition also includes a section dedicated to Islamic art. Informative guided tours are available, and there is a pleasant tea-house on the ground floor.

Zbraslav Monastery, home to the National Gallery's Asian Art Collection

Trade Fair Palace ❾

VELETRŽNÍ PALÁC

The National Gallery in Prague opened its museum of 20th- and 21st-century art in 1995, housed in a reconstruction of a former Trade Fair building of 1929. Since 2000 it has also housed a 19th-century collection. Its vast, skylit spaces make an ideal backdrop for the paintings, which range from French 19th-century art and superb examples of Impressionism and Post-Impressionism, to works by Munch, Klimt, Picasso and Miró, as well as a splendid collection of Czech modern art. The collection is subject to rearrangment so the placement of artworks may change.

Grand Meal *(1951–5)*
Mikuláš Medek's works range from post-war Surrealism to 1960s Abstraction.

Fourth Floor

Cleopatra *(1942–57)*
This painting by Jan Zrzavý, a major representative of Czech modern art, took the artist 45 years to complete and is his best-known piece.

Third Floor

Pomona *(1910)*
Aristide Maillol was a pupil of Rodin. This work is part of an exceptional collection of bronzes.

St Sebastian *(1912)*
This self-portrait by Bohumil Kubišta takes its inspiration from the martyrdom of St Sebastian, who was persecuted by being bound to a tree and shot with arrows.

STAR SIGHTS

★ The Virgin by Gustav Klimt

★ Big Dialog by Karel Nepraš

★ Torso by Pešánek

KEY

☐	Czech Art 1900–1930
☐	19th- and 20th-century French Art
☐	Czech Art 1930–present day
☐	20th-century Foreign Art
☐	Temporary exhibition space
☐	Non-exhibition space

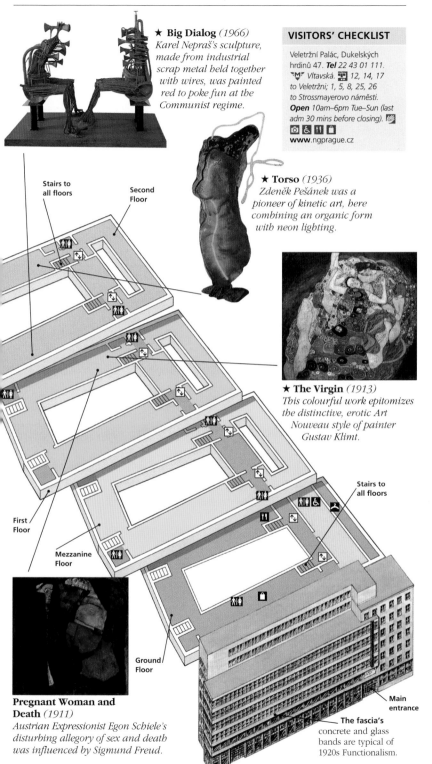

★ **Big Dialog** *(1966)*
Karel Nepraš's sculpture, made from industrial scrap metal held together with wires, was painted red to poke fun at the Communist regime.

Stairs to all floors

Second Floor

★ **Torso** *(1936)*
Zdeněk Pešánek was a pioneer of kinetic art, here combining an organic form with neon lighting.

★ **The Virgin** *(1913)*
This colourful work epitomizes the distinctive, erotic Art Nouveau style of painter Gustav Klimt.

Stairs to all floors

First Floor

Mezzanine Floor

Ground Floor

Pregnant Woman and Death *(1911)*
Austrian Expressionist Egon Schiele's disturbing allegory of sex and death was influenced by Sigmund Freud.

Main entrance

The fascia's concrete and glass bands are typical of 1920s Functionalism.

Troja Palace ⓫

TROJSKÝ ZÁMEK

One of the most striking summer palaces in Prague, Troja was built in the late 17th century by Jean-Baptiste Mathey for Count Sternberg, a member of a leading Bohemian aristocratic family. Situated at the foot of the Vltava Heights, the exterior of the palace was modelled on a Classical Italian villa, while its garden was laid out in formal French style. The magnificent interior took over 20 years to complete and is full of extravagant frescoes expressing the Sternberg family's loyalty to the Habsburg dynasty. Troja houses a good collection of 19th-century art.

Terracotta urn on the garden balustrade

Defeat of the Turks
This turbaned figure, tumbling from the Grand Hall ceiling, symbolizes Leopold I's triumph over the Turks.

Belvedere turret

Statue of Olympian God

Statues of sons of Mother Earth

Personification of Justice
Abraham Godyn's image of Justice gazes from the lower east wall of the Grand Hall.

★ **Garden Staircase**
The two sons of Mother Earth which adorn the sweeping oval staircase (1685–1703) are part of a group of sculptures by Johann Georg Heermann and his nephew Paul, depicting the struggle of the Olympian Gods with the Titans.

VISITORS' CHECKLIST

U trojského zámku 1, Prague 7. **Tel**
283 851614. ⬛ see p55. 🚌 112
from Holešovice metro station.
Open Apr–Oct: 10am–6pm Tue–
Sun; Nov–Mar: 10am–5pm Sat &
Sun. 🖼 🚫 ▢ **www**.ghmp.cz

★ Grand Hall Fresco
*The frescoes in the Grand
Hall (1691–7), by Abraham
Godyn, depict the story of the
first Habsburg Emperor,
Rudolph I, and the victories of
Leopold I over the archenemy
of Christianity, the Sublime
Porte (Ottoman Empire).*

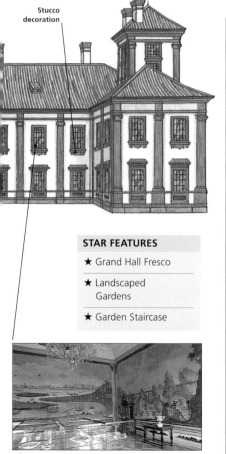

Stucco
decoration

STAR FEATURES

★ Grand Hall Fresco

★ Landscaped
Gardens

★ Garden Staircase

Chinese Rooms
*Several rooms feature 18th-century murals
of Chinese scenes. This room makes a
perfect backdrop for a ceramics display.*

★ LANDSCAPED GARDENS

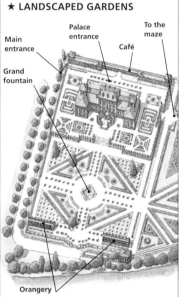

Main
entrance
Palace
entrance
Café
To the
maze
Grand
fountain
Orangery

Sloping vineyards were levelled, hill-
sides excavated and terraces built to
fulfil the elaborate and grandiose plans
of French architect, Jean-Baptiste
Mathey, for the first Baroque French-
style formal gardens in Bohemia. The
palace and its geometric network of
paths, terracing, fountains, statuary
and beautiful terracotta vases, is best
viewed from the south of the garden
between the two orangeries. The
gardens have been carefully restored
according to Mathey's original plans.

Day Trips from Prague

The sights that attract most visitors away from the city are Bohemia's picturesque medieval castles. Karlstein, for example, stands in splendid isolation above wooded valleys that have changed little since the Emperor Charles IV hunted there in the 14th century. We have chosen four castles, very varied in character. There are regular organized tours *(see p227)* to the major sights around Prague, to the historic mining town of Kutná Hora and, if you have more time to spare, to the famous spa towns of Karlsbad and Marienbad in western Bohemia.

St George and Dragon, Konopiště

SIGHTS AT A GLANCE

Castles	Historic Towns
Veltrusy ❶	Kutná Hora ❺
Karlstein ❷	Karlsbad ❻
Konopiště ❸	Marienbad ❼
Křivoklát ❹	

KEY

▢	Central Prague
▢	Greater Prague
✈	Airport
═	Motorway
▬	Major road
═	Minor road

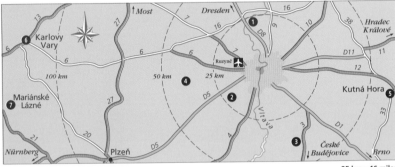

25 km = 16 miles

Veltrusy Château ❶

VELTRUSKÝ ZÁMEK

20 km (12 miles) north of Prague. **Tel** 31 57 81 144/146. 🚉 *from Masarykovo nádraží to Kralupy nad Vltavou, then local bus.* **Open** May–Sep: 9–11am, 1–4pm Tue–Sun. 🎫 ⚠ ♿ *(park only).* **Nelahozeves Castle Tel** 31 57 09 121. 🚉 *from Masarykovo to Nelahozeves – zastávka.* **Open** 9am–5pm Tue–Sun (last adm: 4pm). 🎫 🍴 ▢ ✎

Veltrusy is a small town beside the Vltava, famous for the 18th-century château built by the aristocratic Chotek family. The building is in the shape of a cross, with a central dome and a grand staircase adorned with statues representing the months of the year and the seasons.

The estate was laid out as an English-style landscaped deer park, covering an area of 300 hectares (750 acres). Near the entrance there is still an enclosure with a herd of deer. The Vltava flows along one side and dotted around the grounds are summer houses.

The Doric and Maria Theresa pavilions, the orangery and the grotto date from the late 18th century. The park is planted with some 100 different kinds of tree. The castle was damaged by floods in 2002 and ongoing repairs mean that some rooms may remain closed to the public.

Across the river, and accessible from Veltrusy by bus or train, is **Nelahozeves Castle**. This Renaissance castle houses an exhibition entitled "Private Spaces: A Noble Family At Home", depicting the life of the Lobkowicz family spanning five centuries. Some 12 rooms have been fitted out with period furnishings, including the library, where the Lobkowicz family archives are exhibited. The family's art treasures are now housed in Lobkowicz Palace *(see p99)*. The birthplace of Czech composer Antonín Dvořák is nearby.

Karlstein Castle, built by Emperor Charles IV in the 14th century

Karlstein Castle ❷

KARLŠTEJN

25 km (16 miles) southwest of Prague. *Tel 27 40 08 154.* 🚉 *from Smíchov or Hlavní nádraží to Karlštejn (1.5 km/ 1 mile from castle. The uphill walk takes around 40 minutes).* **Open** *9am–3pm Tue–Sun (to 5pm May, Jun & Sep; to 6pm Jul & Aug).* 🎫 🎟 *compulsory (book in advance).* 🅿 **www**.hradkarlstejn.cz

The castle was founded by Charles IV as a country retreat, a treasury for the crown jewels and a symbol of his divine right to rule the Holy Roman Empire. It stands on a crag above the River Berounka. The castle is largely a 19th-century reconstruction by Josef Mocker. The original building work (1348–67) was supervised by French master mason Matthew of Arras, and then by Peter Parler. You can still see the audience hall and the bed-chamber of Charles IV in the Royal Palace. On the third floor, the Emperor's quarters are below those of the Empress.

The central tower houses the Church of Our Lady, decorated with faded 14th-century wall paintings. A narrow passage leads to the tiny Chapel of St Catherine, the walls of which are adorned with semiprecious stones set into the plaster.

Konopiště Castle ❸

40 km (25 miles) southeast of Prague. *Tel 31 77 21 366.* 🚉 *from Hlavní nádraží to Benešov, then local bus.* **Open** *Apr & Oct: 9am–12:30pm, 1–3pm Tue–Sun (to 4pm Sat & Sun); May–Sep: 9am–12:30pm, 1–5pm Tue–Sun; Nov: 9am–3pm Sat & Sun (by appointment Tue–Fri).* 🎫 🅿 🍴 💻 **www**.zamek-konopiste.cz

Though it dates back to the 13th century, this moated castle is essentially a late 19th-century creation. In between, Konopiště had been rebuilt by Baroque architect František Kaňka and in front of the bridge across the moat is a splendid gate (1725) by Kaňka and sculptor Matthias Braun.

In 1887 Konopiště was bought by Archduke Franz Ferdinand, who later became heir to the Austrian throne. It

View of the castle at Křivoklát, dominated by the Great Tower

was his assassination in 1914 in Sarajevo that triggered off World War I. To escape the Habsburg court's harsh disapproval of his wife, Ferdinand spent much of his time at Konopiště. He amassed arms, armour and Meissen porcelain, all on display in the fine furnished interiors. However, the abiding memory of the castle is of the hundreds of stags' heads lining the walls.

Hunting trophies at Konopiště

Křivoklát Castle ❹

45 km (28 miles) west of Prague. *Tel 31 35 58 440.* 🚉 *from Smíchov to Křivoklát (1 km /0.6 mile) from castle).* 🚌 *from Zličín.* **Open** *Mar, Nov, Dec: 9am–noon, 1–3pm Sat, Sun; Apr, Oct: 9am–noon, 1–3pm Tue–Sun; May, Sep: 9am–noon, 1–4pm Tue–Sun; Jun–Aug: 9am–noon, 1–5pm Tue–Sun.* 🎫 🅿 💻

This castle, like Karlstein, owes its appearance to the

restoration work of Josef Mocker. It was originally a hunting lodge belonging to the early Přemyslid princes and the seat of the royal master of hounds. In the 13th century King Wenceslas I built a stone castle here, which remained in the hands of Bohemia's kings and the Habsburg emperors until the 17th century.

Charles IV spent some of his childhood here and returned from France in 1334 with his first wife Blanche de Valois. Their daughter Margaret was born in the castle. To amuse his queen and young princess, Charles ordered the local vil-lagers to trap nightingales and set them free in a wooded area just below the castle. Today you can still walk along the "Nightingale Path".

The royal palace is on the eastern side of the triangular castle. This corner is dominated by the Great Tower, 42 m (130 ft) high. You can still see some 13th-century stonework, but most of the palace dates from the reign of Vladislav Jagiello. On the first floor there is a vaulted Gothic hall, reminiscent of the Vladislav Hall in the Royal Palace at Prague Castle *(see pp104–5).* It has an oriel window and a beautiful loggia that was used by sentries. Also of interest is the chapel, which has a fine Gothic altar carving. Below the chapel lies the Augusta Prison, so-called because Bishop Jan Augusta of the Bohemian Brethren was imprisoned here for 16 years in the mid-16th century. The dungeon now houses a grim assortment of instruments of torture.

Kutná Hora ❺

70 km (45 miles) east of Prague.
Tel 32 75 12 378 (tourist information).
🚇 *from Hlavní nádraží, Masarykovo nádraží to Kutná Hora, then bus 1 to Kutná Hora-Město.* 🚌 *from Florenc.*
Church of St Barbara open *Nov– Mar: 10–noon, 1–4pm Tue–Sun; Apr & Oct: 9–noon, 1–4:30pm Tue–Sun; May–Sep: 9am–6pm.* 🏛 **Italian Court open** *10am–4pm daily (to 5pm Mar & Oct; to 6pm Apr–Sep).* 🏛 **Hrádek open** *Apr & Oct: 9am– 5pm Tue–Sun (to 6pm May, Jun & Sep); Jul–Aug: 10am–6pm Tue–Sun.* 🏛 **Stone House open** *as Hrádek.*
www.kutnahora.cz

The town originated as a small mining community in the second half of the 13th century. When rich deposits of silver were found, the king took over the licensing of the mines and Kutná Hora became the second most important town in Bohemia.

In the 14th century five to six tonnes of pure silver were extracted here each year, making the king the richest ruler in Central Europe. The Prague *groschen*, a silver coin that circulated all over Europe, was minted here in the Italian Court (Vlašský; dvůr), so-called because Florentine experts were employed to set up the mint. Strongly fortified, it was also the ruler's seat in the town.

In the late 14th century a superb palace was constructed with reception halls and the Chapel of St Wenceslas and St Ladislav, below which lay the royal treasury.

When the silver started to run out in the 16th century, the town began to lose its importance; the mint finally closed in 1727. The Italian Court later became the town hall. On the ground floor you can still see a row of forges. Since 1947 a mining museum has been housed in another building, the Hrádek, which was originally a fort. A visit includes a tour of a medieval mine. There is museum in the Stone House (Kamenný dům), a restored Gothic building of the late 15th century.

To the southwest of the town stands the Church of St Barbara, begun in 1380 by the workshop of Peter Parler, also the architect of St Vitus's Cathedral *(see pp100–3)*. The presbytery (1499) has a fine net vault and windows with intricate tracery. The slightly later nave vault is by royal architect Benedikt Ried. The murals show mining scenes. The cathedral, with its three massive and tent-shaped spires

The Italian Court, Kutná Hora's first mint

rising above a forest of flying buttresses, is a wonderful example of Bohemian Gothic.

In Sedlec, a suburb of Kutná Hora, is the Ossuary of All Saints church, where thousands of human bones have been fashioned into furnishings and decorative objects.

Karlsbad ❻

KARLOVY VARY

140 km (85 miles) west of Prague.
🚇 *from Hlavní nádraží.* 🚌 *from Florenc.* ℹ *Lázeňská 1 (35 53 21 176).*

Legend has it that Charles IV *(see pp24–5)* discovered one of the sources of mineral water that would make the town's fortune when one of his staghounds fell into a hot spring. In 1522 a medical description of the springs was published and by the end of the 16th century over 200 spa buildings had been built there. Today there are 12 hot mineral springs – *vary* means hot springs. The best-known is the Vřídlo (Sprudel), which rises to a height of 12 m (40 ft). At 72°C, it is also the hottest. The water is good for digestive disorders, but you do not have to drink it; you can take the minerals in the form of salts.

The town is also known for its Karlovy Vary china and Moser glass, and for summer concerts and other cultural

The three steeples of Kutná Hora's great Church of St Barbara

events, including an international film festival in early July. The race course is popular with the more sporting invalids taking the waters.

Outstanding among the local historic monuments is the Baroque parish church of Mary Magdalene by Kilian Ignaz Dientzenhofer (1732–6). More modern churches built for foreign visitors include a Russian church (1896) and an Anglican one (1877). The 19th-century Mill Colonnade (Mlýnská kolonáda) is by Josef Zítek, architect of the National Theatre *(see pp156–7)* in Prague.

Marienbad 🄼
MARIÁNSKÉ LÁZNĚ

170 km (105 miles) west of Prague.
🚉 *from Hlavní nádraží.* 🚌 *from Florenc.* 🛈 Hlvaní 47 *(35 46 22 474).*
www.marienbad.cz

The elegance of Marienbad's hotels, parks and gardens has faded considerably since it was the playground of kings and princes at the turn of the century. The area's health-giving waters – *lázně* means bath (or spa) – have been known since the 16th century, but the spa was not founded until the beginning of the 19th century. The waters are used to treat all kinds of disorders; mud baths are also popular.

Most of the spa buildings date from the latter half of the 19th century. The great cast-iron colonnade with frescoes by Josef Vyletěl is still an

Bronze statue of a chamois at Jeleni skok (Stag's Leap), with a view across the valley to the Imperial Sanatorium, Karlsbad

impressive sight. In front of it is a "singing fountain", its jets of water now controlled by computer. Churches were provided for visitors of all denominations, including an Evangelical church (1857), an Anglican church (1879) and the Russian Orthodox church of St Vladimír (1902). Visitors can learn the history of the spa in the house called At the Golden Grape (U zlatého hroznu),

where the German poet Johann Wolfgang von Goethe stayed in 1823. Musical visitors during the 19th century included the composers Weber, Wagner and Bruckner, while writers such as Ibsen, Gogol, Mark Twain and Rudyard Kipling also found its treatments beneficial. King Edward VII also came here and in 1905 he agreed to open the golf course (Bohemia's first), despite hating the game.

The cast-iron colonnade at Marienbad, completed in 1889

FOUR GUIDED WALKS

Prague offers some good opportunities for walking. In the centre of the city, many streets are pedestrianized and the most important sights are confined to quite a small area *(see pp14–15)*. Here are four guided walks of varied character. The first passes through a main artery of the city, from the Powder Gate on the outskirts of the Old Town to St Vitus's Cathedral in Prague Castle, crossing Charles Bridge at its mid-point. This is the Royal Coronation Route, followed for

House sign in Celetná Street
(See Royal Route Walk pp174–5)

centuries by Bohemian kings. Away from the busy centre, the second and third of the walks takes in the peace and tranquility of two of Prague's loveliest parks – Petřín and the Royal Enclosure. Petřín Park is rewarding for its spectacular views of the city. The Royal Enclosure is outside the centre in the old royal hunting park. The final walk is in Vyšehrad – an ancient fortress which is steeped in history and atmosphere. The views from Vyšehrad of the Vltava and Prague Castle are unparalleled.

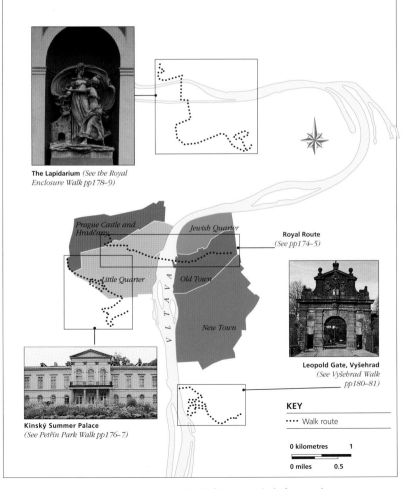

The Lapidarium *(See the Royal Enclosure Walk pp178–9)*

Prague Castle and Hradčany

Jewish Quarter

Royal Route
(See pp174–5)

Little Quarter

Old Town

VLTAVA

New Town

Leopold Gate, Vyšehrad
(See Vyšehrad Walk pp180–81)

Kinský Summer Palace
(See Petřín Park Walk pp176–7)

KEY

•••• Walk route

0 kilometres   1

0 miles   0.5

◁ **View of the New Town from Petřín Park with the Church of St Lawrence in the foreground**

A 90-Minute Walk along the Royal Route

The Royal Roue originally linked two important royal seats; the Royal Court – situated on the site of the Municipal House and where the walk starts – and Prague Castle, where the walk finishes. The name of this walk derives from the coronation processions of the Bohemian kings and queens who passed along it. Today, these narrow streets offer a wealth of historical and architecturally interesting sights, shops and cafés, making the walk one of Prague's most enjoyable. For more details on the Old Town, the Little Quarter and Hradčany turn to pages 60–79; 122–41 and 94–121 respectively.

Figural *sgraffito* covers the façade of the Renaissance House at the Minute

History of the Royal Route

The first major coronation procession to travel along this route was for George of Poděbrady *(see p26)* in 1458. The next large procession took place in 1743, when Maria Theresa was crowned with great pomp – three Turkish pavilions were erected just outside the Powder Gate. September 1791 saw the coronation of Leopold II. This procession was led by cavalry, followed by mounted drummers, trumpeters and soldiers and Bohemian lords. Some 80 carriages came next, carrying princes and bishops. The most splendid were each drawn by six pairs of horses, flanked by servants with red coats and white leather trousers, and carried the ladies-in-waiting.

The last great coronation procession along the Royal Route – for Ferdinand V – was in 1836 with over 3,391 horses and four camels.

From the Powder Gate to Old Town Square

At Náměstí Republiky turn towards the Municipal House *(see p64)* and walk under the Gothic Powder Gate ① *(see p64)*. Here, at the city gates, the monarch and a large retinue of church dignitaries, aristocrats, and foreign ambassadors were warmly welcomed by leading city representatives. The gate leads into one of Prague's oldest streets, Celetná *(see p65)*. It was here the Jewish community and the crafts guilds, carrying their insignia, greeted their king.

The street is lined with Baroque and Rococo houses. At house No. 36 was the Mint ②. It moved here after the mint at Kutná Hora *(see p170)* was occupied

The distinct Baroque façade of the House at the Golden Well in Karlova Street ⑪

by Catholic troops in the Hussite Wars *(see pp26–7)*. It minted coins from 1420 to 1784. The House of the Black Madonna ③ contains a museum of Czech Cubist art *(see p65)*. Revellers would watch processions from the taverns At the Spider ④ and At the Vulture ⑤.

House at the Black Madonna ③

At the end of Celetná Street is the Old Town Square ⑥ *(see pp66–9)*. Here, the processions halted beside Týn Church ⑦ *(see p70)* for pledges of loyalty from the university. Keep to the left of the square, past No. 17, At the Unicorn ⑧, then No. 20, Smetana House, where the composer began a music school in 1848. Proceed to the Old Town Hall ⑨ *(see pp72–4)*.

Here, the municipal guard and a band waited for the royal procession and city dignitaries cheered from the temporary balcony around the hall.

Along Karlova Street and across Charles Bridge

Walk past the sgraffitoed façade of the House at the Minute and into Malé náměstí ⑩, where merchants waited with members of the various religious orders. Bear left off the square, then turn right into

good omen. But only a few months later he died. Walk under the Old Town Bridge Tower ⑫ and over Charles Bridge ⑬ and then under the Little Quarter Towers ⑭ (see pp136–9).

The Little Quarter

The walk now follows Mostecká Street. On entering the Little Quarter the mayor handed the city keys to the king and the artillery fired a salute. At the end of this street is Little Quarter Square ⑮ (see p124) and the Baroque

The Old Town from Charles Bridge ⑬

Sculpture of Moor by Ferdinand Brokof on Morzin Palace

turn sharp right and walk up the Castle ramp, which leads you to Hradčanské Square. The route ends at the Castle's Matthias Gate (see p48) ⑲. The procession ended with the coronation held at St Vitus's Cathedral.

gallery-filled Karlova Street. Beyond Husova Street is an attractive Baroque house, At the Golden Well ⑪. Further on is the 16th-century Clementinum (see p79), where the clergy stood. You then pass into Knights of the Cross Square (see p79). When Leopold II's procession passed through here the clouds lifted, which was considered to be a

church St Nicholas's ⑯ (see pp128–9). The procession passed the church to the sound of its bells ringing.
Leave this picturesque square by Nerudova Street ⑰ (see p130). Poet and writer Jan Neruda, who immortalized hundreds of Little Quarter characters in books like *Mala Strana Tales*, grew up and worked at No. 47, The Two Suns ⑱. Cross the street,

KEY

•••	Walk route
☼	Good viewing point
Ⓜ	Metro station
🚋	Tram stop
—	City wall

0 metres   300

0 yards   300

TIPS FOR WALKERS

Starting point: Náměstí Republiky.
Length: 2.4 km (1.5 miles).
Getting there: Line B goes to Náměstí Republiky metro station. At Hradčany you can get tram 22 back into town.
Stopping-off points: Rest beneath the sunshades of the outdoor cafés on Old Town Square or Karlova Street in the summer. There are plenty of cafés and restaurants on Malostranské náměstí, as well as along Nerudova Street.

Coronation procession passing through the Knights of the Cross Square

A Two-Hour Walk through Petřín Park

Part of the charm of this walk around this large and peaceful hillside park are the many spectacular views over the different areas of Prague. The Little Quarter, Hradčany and the Old Town all take on a totally different aspect when viewed from above. The tree-covered gardens are dotted with châteaux, pavilions and statues and crisscrossed by winding paths leading you to secret and unexpected corners. For more on the sights of Petřín Hill see pages 140–41.

One of the gateways in the Hunger Wall ⑤

Actress Hana Kvapilová's statue, near Kinský Summer Palace ①

Kinský Square to Hunger Wall

The walk starts at náměstí Kinských in Smíchov. Enter Kinský Garden through a large enclosed gateway. This English-style garden was founded in 1827 and named after the wealthy Kinský family, supporters of Czech culture in the 19th century.

Take the wide cobbled and asphalt path on your left to the Kinský Summer Palace ①. This 1830s pseudo-classical building was designed by Jindřich Koch and its façade features Ionic columns terminating in a triangular tympanum. Inside the building is a large hall of columns with a triple-branched staircase beautifully decorated with statues. The Ethnographical Museum, housed here, holds a permanent exhibition of folk art.

Next to the museum is a 1913 statue of the actress Hana Kvapilová.

About 50 m (150 ft) above the palace is the lower lake ②, where a small waterfall trickles into a man-made pond. Keep going up the hill until you reach the Church of St Michael ③, on your left. This 18th-century wooden folk church was moved here from a village in the Ukraine.

Follow the path up the hill for about 20 m (60 ft), then go to the top of the steps to a wide asphalt path known as the Observation Path for its beautiful views of the city. Turn right and further on your left is the small upper lake ④ with a 1950s bronze statue of a seal at its centre. Keep following the Observation Path; ahead of you stands a Neo-Gothic gate. This allows you to pass through the city's old Baroque fortifications.

Hunger Wall to Observation Tower

Continue along the path to the Hunger Wall ⑤ *(see pp140–41)*. This was a major part of the Little Quarter's fortifications; the wall still runs from Újezd

Church of St Michael ③

Street across Petřín Hill and up to Strahov Monastery. Passing through the gate in the wall brings you to Petřín Park. Take the wide path to the left below the wall and walk up the hill beside the wall until you cross the bridge which spans the funicular railway *(see p141)*. Below on your right you can see the

Sunbathers on Petřín Hill

Nebozízek restaurant *(see p205)* famed for its views. On either side of the path are small sandstone rockeries. Most are entrances to reservoirs, built in the 18th and 19th centuries, to bring water to Strahov Monastery; others are left over from the unsuccessful attempts at mining the area. Walk up to the summit of the hill. On your right is the Mirror Maze ⑥ *(see p140)*. Facing the maze is the 12th-century St Lawrence's Church ⑦ *(see p140)*, renovated in 1740 in the Baroque style.

Observation Tower to Strahov Monastery

A little further on stands the Observation Tower ⑧ *(see p140)*. This steel replica of the Eiffel Tower in Paris is 60 m (200 ft) high. Opposite the tower is the main gate of the Hunger Wall. Pass through, turn left and follow the path to the Rose Garden ⑨.

The garden was planted by the city of Prague in 1932, and features a number of attractive sculptures. When you look down to the far end of the garden you can see The Observatory *(see p140)*. This was rebuilt from a municipal building in 1928 by the Czech Astronomical Society and was then modernized in the 1970s. It now houses a huge telescope and is open in the evenings to the public.

Returning to the Observation Tower, follow the wall on the left, passing some chapels of the Stations of the Cross dating from 1834. Then pass through a gap in the Hunger Wall, turn right, and walk past a charming Baroque house. About 50 m (150 ft) beyond this, you pass through another gap in the Hunger Wall on your right. Turn left into a large orchard above Strahov Monastery ⑩ *(see pp120–21)* for spectacular views of the city. Leave by the same hole in the wall that you came in by, turn right, and walk downhill along the wall, through the orchard and past tennis courts

Sgraffitoed façade of the Calvary Chapel next to the Church of St Lawrence ⑦

to the Strahov Monastery courtyard. You can catch tram 22 from here, or linger in the peaceful monastery grounds. If you feel energetic you can walk back down the hill.

TIPS FOR WALKERS

Starting point: náměstí Kinských in Smíchov.
Length: 2.7 km (1.7 miles). The walk includes steep hills.
Getting there: The nearest metro station to the starting point is Anděl. Trams 6, 9, 12 and 20 go to náměstí Kinských (Kinský Square). *Stopping-off points:* There is a restaurant, Nebozízek, half way up Petřín Hill and in the summer a few snack bars are open at the summit of the Hill near the Observation Tower.

KEY

••• Walk route

Good viewing point

Tram stop

Funicular railway

Hunger wall

| 0 metres | 300 |
| 0 yards | 300 |

Hradčany and the Little Quarter from the summit of Petřín Hill

A 90-Minute Walk in the Royal Enclosure

The royal enclosure, more popularly called
Stromovka, is one of the largest parks in Prague.
It was created around 1266 during the reign of
Přemysl Otakar II, who fenced the area in and
built a small hunting château in the grounds. In
1804 it was opened to the public and became
Prague's most popular recreational area. The
large park of Troja Palace and the zoological
garden are on the opposite river bank.

A bust on the Academy of Fine Arts ⑥

The Exhibition Ground (Výstaviště)

From U Výstaviště ① pass
through the gate to the old
Exhibition Ground. This was
created for the 1891 Jubilee
Exhibition. Since the late 19th
century it has been used for
exhibitions and entertainment.

The large Lapidarium of the
National Museum ② is on your
right. This Neo-Renaissance
exhibition pavilion was rebuilt
in 1907 in the Art Nouveau
style, and decorated with
reliefs of figures from
Czech history. Many
architectural monu-
ments and sculptures
from the 11th to the
19th centuries are
also housed here.

Facing you is the
Industrial Palace ③, a
vast Neo-Renaissance
building constructed of
iron which was partially
destroyed by fire in 2008.
Walk to the right of the building and you will come to
Křižík's Fountain ④. This was
restored in 1991 in honour of
the Czechoslovakia Exhibi-

The Art Nouveau Lapidarium ②

tion. It was
designed by the
great inventor
František Křižík
(1847–1941), who
established Prague's
first public electric
lighting system.
During summer the
fountain is illumi-
nated at night by
computer-control-
led lights which
synchronize with the
music (see p51).

Behind the fountain there is
a permanent fairground.
On the left of the Industrial
Palace is a circular building
which houses Marold's
Panorama ⑤. This was painted
by Luděk Marold in 1898 and
depicts the Battle of Lipany.
As you walk back to the
Exhibition Ground entrance,
you pass the Academy of Fine
Arts ⑥, decorated with 18
busts of artists. On leaving the

The summer palace created from a
medieval Hunting Château ⑩

0 metres   300

0 yards   300

KEY

••• Walk route

🔆 Good viewing point

🚊 Tram stop

═ Railway line

Exhibition Ground, turn sharp right. Following the outer edge of the Ground you will pass the Planetarium ⑦ on your left, which has interactive exhibitions; walk straight ahead, take the road down the slope, then turn left into a wide avenue of chestnut trees.

The Royal Enclosure
Continue for some way along the avenue until you reach a simple building among trees, on your left. Behind this is the Rudolph Water Tunnel ⑧, a grand monument of the age of Rudolph II (see pp28–9). Hewn into rock, the aqueduct

The grand facade of Troja Palace (see pp166–7) ⑭

is over 1,000 m (3,000 ft) long. Now sadly defaced by graffiti, it was built in 1584 to carry water from the Vltava to Rudolph's newly constructed lakes in the Royal Park.

Continue along the path until you reach the derelict Royal Hall ⑨. Built in the late 17th century, it was converted into a restaurant, then rebuilt in 1855 in Neo-Gothic style. Beyond the Royal Hall, at the bend in the main path, take a steep left fork up through woods to the former Hunting Château ⑩. This medieval building was built for the Bohemian kings who used the park as a hunting reserve. The Château was then later enlarged, and in 1805 was changed again by Jiří Fischer into a Neo-Gothic summer palace. Until 1918, this was a residence of the Governor of Bohemia. Today it is used to house the extensive library of newspapers and magazines of the National Museum.

The Industrial Palace, built in 1891 ③

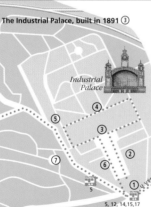

Prague Planetarium, the largest in the Czech Republic ⑦

Retrace your steps to the main path, walk ahead and take the first small path on the right which will lead you into a pleasant late-16th-century formal garden ⑪. Return to the main path and turn right. At the fork, take the path which bends to the right along the railway embankment then turn left under the railway line to a canal ⑫.

Walk over the bridge, turn left along the canal, then right across the island. Cross the Vltava ⑬ and turn left into Povltavská Street where a wall marks the boundary of Troja Park. Carry along to the south entrance of the gardens of Troja Palace ⑭ (see pp166–7), and then wander through them up to the palace itself.

TIPS FOR WALKERS

Starting point: U Výstaviště in Holešovice.
Length: 5 km (3 miles). The walk goes up a very steep inc line to the former Hunting Château.
Getting there: Trams 5, 12, 14 and 17 run to the starting point. The nearest metro stations are Vltavská or Nádraží Holešovice on line C, ten minutes walk away. At the end of the walk you can get on bus No. 112 at Troja to Nádraží Holešovice metro station.
Stopping-off points: There are a number of restaurants and kiosks in the Exhibition Ground. All the gardens are tranquil spots in which to rest. If you feel like a boat trip down the Vltava, there are often trips starting from the bridge over the canal to Palacký Bridge (see p55).

A 60-Minute Walk in Vyšehrad

According to ancient legend, Vyšehrad was the first seat of Czech royalty. It was from this spot that Princess Libuše is said to have prophesied the future glory of the city of Prague *(see pp20–21)*. However, archaeological research indicates that the first castle on Vyšehrad was not built until the 10th century. The fortress suffered a turbulent history and was rebuilt many times. Today, it is above all a peaceful place with parks and unrivalled views of the Vltava valley and Prague. The fascinating cemetery is the last resting place of many famous Czech writers, actors, artists and musicians.

Decorative sculpture on the Baroque Leopold Gate ⑤

The ruin of Libuše's Baths on the cliff face of Vyšehrad Rock ⑩

V Pevnosti

From Vyšehrad metro ① take the exit for the Congress Centre Prague ②, walk up the steps and continue straight ahead with views of Prague Castle to your right. Go down the incline and straight ahead into the quiet street Na Bučance. Cross the road, turn right at the end, and you find yourself on V Pevnosti, facing the brick walls of the original Vyšehrad Citadel. Ahead of you is the west entrance to the fortress, the mid-17th-century Tábor Gate ③. Through the gate on the right are the ruins

of the 14th-century fortifications built by Charles IV. Further on are the ruins of the original Gothic gate, Špička ④. Past that is the sculpture-adorned Leopold Gate ⑤, one of the most impressive parts of these 17th-century fortifications. It adjoins the brick walls ⑥ that were widened during the French occupation of 1742.

K rotundě to Soběslavova Street

Turn right out of the gate and just after St Martin's Rotunda, turn left into K rotundě. A few metres on your left, almost concealed behind high walls, is the New Deanery ⑦. Situated at the corner of K rotundě and Soběslavova streets is the Canon's House ⑧. Turn left down Soběslavova to see the excavations of the foundations of the

Basilica of St Lawrence ⑨. This was built by Vratislav II, the first Bohemian king, in the late 11th century, but was destroyed by the Hussites *(see pp26–7)* in 1420. About 20 m (65 ft) past the basilica, turn right on to the fortified walls for a stunning view of Prague.

KEY

••••	Walk route
✳	Good viewing point
Ⓜ	Metro station
⊞	Tram stop
—	Castle wall

0 metres	200
0 yards	200

18th-century engraving by I G Ringle, showing Vyšehrad and the Vltava

Vyšehrad Rock

The wooded outcrop of rock on which Vyšehrad was built drops in the west to form a steep rock wall to the river – a vital defensive position. On the summit of the rock are the Gothic ruins of the so-called Libuše's Baths ⑩. This was a defence bastion of the medieval castle. To the left of the bastion is a grassy patch where the remains of a 14th-century Gothic palace ⑪ have been found.

The elaborate memorial to the composer Antonín Dvořák in Vyšehrad Cemetery ⑭

Vyšehrad Park

The western part of Vyšehrad has been transformed into a park. Standing on the lawn south of the Church of St Peter and St Paul are four groups of statues ⑫ by the 19th-century sculptor Josef Myslbek. The works represent figures from early Czech history – including the legendary Přemysl and Libuše *(see pp20–21)*. The statues were originally on Palacký Bridge, but were damaged during the US bombardment of February 1945. After being restored, they were taken to Vyšehrad Park. The park was the site of a Romanesque palace, which was connected to the neighbouring church by a bridge. Another palace was built here in the reign of Charles IV *(see pp24–5)*.

The Church of St Peter and St Paul

This twin-spired church ⑬ dominates Vyšehrad. It was founded in the latter half of the 11th century by Vratislav II and was enlarged in 1129. In the mid-13th century it burned down and was replaced by an Early Gothic church. Since then it has been redecorated and restored many times in a variety of styles. In 1885, it was finally rebuilt in Neo-Gothic style, the twin steeples being added in 1902. Note the early-12th-century stone coffin, thought to be of St Longinus, and a mid-14th-century Gothic panel painting *Our Lady of the Rains* on the altar in the third chapel on the right.

Vyšehrad Cemetery and the Pantheon

The cemetery ⑭ was founded in 1869 as the burial place for some of the country's most famous figures, such as Bedřich Smetana *(see p79)*. Access is through a gate at the front. On the east side of the cemetery is the Slavín (Pantheon) – built in 1890 for the most honoured citizens of the Czech nation, including the sculptor Josef Myslbek.

Leave the cemetery by the same gate and return down K rotundě. On your left is the Devil's Column ⑮, said to be left by the devil after losing a wager with a priest. At the end is St Martin's Rotunda *(see p44)* ⑯, a small Romanesque church built in the late 11th century and restored in 1878. Turn left, walk downhill to Cihelná (Brick) Gate ⑰, built in 1741 and home to a small museum that houses six of the original statues from Charles Bridge. Go down Vratislavova Street to Výtoň tram stop on the Vltava Embankment.

The Neo-Gothic Church of St Peter and St Paul ⑬

TIPS FOR WALKERS

Starting point: Vyšehrad metro station, line C.
Length: 1.5 km (1 mile).
Getting there: The walk starts at Vyšehrad metro station and ends at Výtoň tram stop. Trams 3 and 17 go back to the city centre.
Stopping-off points: Relax in the park next to the church of St Peter and St Paul. There is a café in front of the Basilica of St Lawrence and more outdoor cafés in the summer.

Statue of Přemysl and Princess Libuše by Josef Myslbek in Vyšehrad Park ⑫

Tábor Gate

ČIKLOVA

① Vyšehrad

②

NA BUČANCE

③ NA PANKRÁCI

TRAVELLERS' NEEDS

WHERE TO STAY

Since the "Velvet Revolution" of 1989, Prague has become one of the most visited cities in Europe. Thanks to investment in new hotels, helped by huge injections of foreign capital, Prague has developed enough accommodation to meet every tourist need. Many old hotels have been rebuilt, while others have been fully re-vamped. Most of the renovated hotels are as smart as any in Europe – and they are often just as expensive. There is also a good number of mid-range hotels, many offering surprisingly reasonable rates as competition grows intense. Several are centrally located and even feature designer touches as well as much improved service. Cheaper hotels tend to be old-fashioned places in the centre of the city, or smaller, pension-type hotels located in the suburbs. Staying in a flat or a room in a private home can also save you money. This type of accommodation is usually booked by an agency *(see p186)*. Hostels and campsites offer other budget options *(see p187)*.

Doorman in livery outside a Prague hotel

The Ungelt hotel *(see p189)*

WHERE TO LOOK

As Prague is such a small city, it is best to stay near the centre close to all the main sights, restaurants and shops. Most hotels are found around Wenceslas Square. Here you are at the hub of everything, and the prices of some (but not all) of the hotels reflect this. Another popular area is the nearby Náměstí Republiky, but the best area is around Old Town Square, a few minutes' walk from Charles Bridge. Hotels here include large, international establishments, old-fashioned Czech places, and some small, much more exclusive hotels.

To the south, in the New Town, there are a few cheaper hotels only a few metro stops from Old Town Square. But the area is less picturesque and some of the streets suffer from heavy volumes of traffic.

For a view of the river Vltava, stay in the Jewish Quarter, although most hotels here are new and expensive. There are also a few botels (floating hotels) moored along the embankments away from the city centre. Many have been prettied up and improved and, if you don't mind compromising on space a little, make for unusual options worth considering for budget travellers.

Over Charles Bridge, in the Little Quarter, you will find a handful of interesting hotels in delightful surroundings, but there are far fewer by Prague Castle in Hradčany. Further north of this area, there are some large and particularly unappealing hotels. The city's suburbs too, have a number of rather nondescript places a few of these being new.

These have some good facilities, but are often as expensive as their equivalents in the centre with the added inconvenience of travelling time and cost – the metro stops at midnight and taxis can become expensive.

HOW TO BOOK

To reserve a room you can telephone, email, book online or send a letter by fax (the best deals are often done online). It is advisable to get confirmation of your booking in writing or via email and bring it with you when you check in as it can save you some time on arrival. Most hotel receptionists speak English, so you can always ring them for advice, otherwise ask your tour

Spacious room at the Grand Hotel Bohemia, Jewish Quarter *(see p190)*

◁ **Rear view of the equestrian statue of St Wenceslas on Wenceslas Square** operator for help; a number of UK operators specialize in Prague *(see p186)*. When arriving by car, try to park in the hotel garage or ask at reception about secure parking in the area.

FACILITIES

Following the large investment in many of Prague's hotels, most rooms now have en suite WC and shower or bath, Internet, telephone and TV, which may also offer video and satellite channels. Many hotels offer a reasonably-priced laundry service, and the larger hotels usually have 24-hour room service and mini bars. Guests are expected to vacate rooms by midday, but most hotels are happy to keep luggage safe if you are leaving later.

Foreign-owned hotels sometimes import managers, but the Czech staff generally speak good English so you should encounter few communication problems.

DISCOUNT RATES

The price structure for hotels in Prague is fairly flexible. One way to get a cheap rate is to check the hotel's website for Internet-only deals and special rates for weekends, which are now quite common. The popular seasons are Christmas, New Year and Easter, when rooms are often hard to find. For cheap rooms in summer it is worth looking at student houses. Most of these have two bedrooms and a kitchen on the same floor, plus a small shop selling hot and cold drinks.

HIDDEN EXTRAS

All hotels include tax (currently at 19%) and service charges in their tariff, but do check these details when you book. Telephone charges can be a shock when you receive your bill so be aware of the mark-up rate. A few surviving telephone boxes in the city take phone cards and some take credit cards but it may be more practical to use roaming facilities on your

The Pařiž is a protected monument *(see p189)*

mobile phone if your plan is affordable *(see pp232–3)*. Some expensive hotels charge an extra fee for breakfast, others include a continental breakfast, but hot dishes cost extra. Buffet-style continental breakfasts are popular, and usually offer fresh fruit, cereals, yogurt, cold meat and cheese, and juice, jugs of coffee and tea.

Tipping is common and is expected in many hotels. As in most countries, single

The modern Praha Hilton hotel dominates the area *(see p195)*

travellers receive no favours. There are few single rooms, particularly in newer hotels, and a supplement is charged for single occupancy of a double room; you'll pay about 70–80% of the standard rate.

DISABLED TRAVELLERS

Most of the newer hotels in Prague have wheelchair access. For information on accommodation suitable for the disabled, contact the **Czech Association of Persons with Disabilities**, the **Prague Association of Wheelchair-Users** *(see p234)* or the Embassy of the Czech Republic in your country.

TRAVELLING WITH CHILDREN

Children are accommodated by most hotels, either in family rooms or with extra beds. Reliable baby-sitting services are sometimes available in high-end establishments or small inns. Highchairs are common too. It is worth asking if there are discounts, or if children can stay free in parents' rooms.

DIRECTORY

UK AGENCIES

British Airways Holidays
Astral Towers
Bettsway, London Rd,
Crawley, RH10 9XA.
Tel 0870 850 9850.
www.baholidays.com

Čedok Travel
www.cedok.com

Cresta Holidays
Thomas Cook Business
Park, Conningsby,
Peterborough PE3 8SB.
Tel 0844 800 7019.
www.cresta
holidays.co.uk

Crystal Holidays
Kings Place,
Wood Street,
Kingston-upon-Thames,
Surrey KT1 1JY.
Tel 0870 166 4971.
www.crystal
holidays.co.uk

Czech Tourist Centre
13 Harley Street,
London W1G 9QG.
Tel 020 7631 0427.
www.czechtourism.com

Osprey Holidays
5 Thistle Street,
Edinburgh EH2 1DF.
Tel 0845 310 3031.
www.osprey-
holidays.co.uk

Page & Moy Ltd.
Compass House,
Rockingham Rd,
Market Harborough,
Leicestershire LE16 7QD.
Tel 08708 334 012.
Fax 01858 461 956.
www.pageandmoy.com

Prospect Cultural Tours Ltd
79 William St, Herne Bay,
Kent CT6 5NR.
Tel 01227 743 307.
Fax 01227 743 377.
www.prospecttours.com

Thomson
Thomas Cook Business
Park, Conningsby,
Peterborough PE3 8SB.
Tel 0844 800 7019.
www.thomsoncities.co.uk

US AGENCIES

Friends of Czech Greenways
Suite 1B, 515 Avenue I
Brooklyn, NY 11230.
Tel 718 258 54 68.
Fax 718 258 56 32.
www.pragueviennagreen
ways.org

FLATS AND ROOMS IN PRIVATE HOMES

IN UK
The Czechbook
Jopes Mill,
Trebrownbridge,
Nr. Liskard,
Cornwall PL14 3PX.
Tel & Fax 01503 240 629.
@ agnes.michael@
czechbook.com
www.czechbook.com

Regent Holidays
Mezzanine Suite,
Froomsgate House, Rupert
Street, Bristol BS1 2QJ.
Tel 0845 277 3317.
www.regent-
holidays.co.uk

IN PRAGUE
Akasi
října, 28.
Map 3 C5.
Tel 22 22 43 067.
Fax 22 42 37 235.

American Express Travel Service
Václavské náměstí 56.
Map 3 C5.
Tel 22 22 10 106.
www.american
express.cz

Autoturist Travel Agency
Londýnská 62.
Map 6 F4.
Tel 22 25 12 053.
Fax 22 25 20 242.
www.autoturist.cz

AVE Ltd
Pod Barvirkov 6.
Tel 25 15 51 011.
Fax 25 15 55 157.
www.praguehotel
locator.de

Čedok
Na Příkopě 18.
Map 4 D4.
Tel 22 14 47 242.
www.cedok.com

Estec
Vaníčkova 5, Prague 6.
Tel 25 72 10 410.
Fax 25 72 15 263.
www.estec.cz

Pragotur
Arbesovo náměstí 4.
Tel 22 17 14 130.
Fax 22 17 14 127.
www.prague–info.cz

Prague Information Service (PIS)
Staroměstské náměstí 1.
Map 3 B3.
Tel 22 17 14 444.
www.pis.cz
Hlavní nádraží (main
station).
Map 4 E5.
Tel 22 17 14 444.
www.pis.cz

e.travel.cz
Divadelní 24.
*Tel 22 49 90 990, 0808
120 2320 (UK), 1-877-
744-1222 (US).*
www.e.travel.cz

Top Tour
Revoluční 24.
Map 4 D2.
Tel 22 48 13 172.
Fax 22 48 12 386.
www.toptour.cz

Travel Agency of Czech Railways
Na Příkopě 31.
Map 3 C4.
Tel 97 22 43 053.
www.cdtravel.cz

HOSTELS

Dlouhá
Dlouhá 33.
Map 3 C3.
Tel 22 48 26 662.
Fax 22 48 26 665.
www.travellers.cz

Hostel Jednota
Opletalova 38.
Map 4 D5.
Tel 22 42 30 038.
www.alfatourist.cz

Petros Agency
Tel 41 56 58 580.
Fax 41 56 58 497.
www.hostel.cz

CAMPING

Aritma Džbán
Nad Lávkou 5.
Tel 23 53 58 554.
Fax 23 53 51 365.
www.campdzban.eu

Kotva Braník
U ledáren 55,
Braník.
Tel 24 44 61 712.
Fax 24 44 66 110.
www.kotvacamp.cz

Troja
Trojská 129, Troja
Tel 28 38 50 482.
Fax 28 38 52 181.
www.campdana.cz

DISABLED TRAVELLERS

Czech Association of Persons with Disabilities
Karlínské náměstí 12,
Prague 8.
Map 5 B2.
Tel 22 23 17 489.
www.svaztp.cz

Embassy of the Czech Republic
26 Kensington Palace
Gardens,
London W8 4QY.
Tel 020 7243 1115.
www.mzv.eu

Hotel in a quiet street of a historic neighbourhood

PRIVATE ROOMS AND SELF-CATERING APARTMENTS

Over the past few years, the number of private rooms to rent in Prague has grown enormously. Although cheap and popular, they may be some distance from the centre. Private rooms in homes start at about Kč1,000 per person per night, usually with breakfast. There are also self-contained apartments – a fairly central one-bedroom apartment costs about Kč2,000 per night. Most agencies that offer private rooms also rent out apartments (*see Directory opposite*).

To book a room or apartment, tell the agency exactly what you want, for how many, when and in which area. The agency will suggest places. Find out the exact location

and the nearest metro before accepting; if you are in Prague, see it yourself. Make sure you receive written, faxed or emailed confirmation of a booking to take with you. On arrival in Prague, pay the agency in cash; they give you a voucher to take to the room or apartment (sometimes you can pay the owner directly). If the agency requires advance payment by banker's draft go direct to the accommodation with your receipt. Agencies may ask for a deposit on bookings from abroad, or charge a registration fee payable in Prague.

HOSTELS

There are also many hostels in Prague, and the **Petros Agency** provides up-to-date information on availability. Useful websites include www.hoteldiscount.cz, www.bed.cz, and www.travellers.cz.

Numerous hostels throughout the city centre now operate year-round. A few hostels operate curfews, so it's worth checking this before you book. It is rarely necessary to bring your own sleeping bag as most hostels tend to provide bed sheets and blankets for free. Sometimes it can be better value to choose a hostel further away from the city centre, as some of the more central establishments can cost just as much as a cheap hotel.

If you are visiting between June and mid-September, it's

worth investigating the thousand or so very basic student rooms available to the public in the summer holidays at Prague's university, the Karolinum (Tel: 224 491 111/250). Although these do not offer much in the way of luxury, they are an excellent option for the budget traveller. Some other Czech colleges also offer a similar service.

CAMPING

Most campsites in or near Prague are closed from November to the start of April. They are very cheap with basic facilities, but are well served by transport. The largest site is at **Troja**, 3 km (1.5 miles) north of the city centre. **Aritma Džbán**, 4 km (2.5 miles) west, is open all year for tents, and **Kotva Braník** is 6 km (4 miles) south of the city on the banks of the Vltava.

PENSIONS

In the Czech Republic, pensions, or guesthouses, are a cosy, inexpensive type of accommodation. They offer guests reasonably priced standard rooms with ensuite bathrooms, and most include breakfast in the price. Look out for their signs along the roads approaching Prague – the word *pension* is usually in green. Pensions tend to be located outside the city centre and are therefore most convenient for visitors who are arriving by car.

CONCIERGES

Many hotels have a concierge who can help guests with theatre tickets and dinner reservations. A concierge with connections may be able to find you good seats for a show or secure a reservation at one of the best restaurants in Prague. You can also turn to your hotel concierge for help when making travel arrangements and sightseeing plans, and if you need to make use of local services or deal with an emergency. It is polite to tip a concierge who has helped during your stay.

Hotel entrance on a Little Quarter street

Choosing a Hotel

The hotels in this guide have been selected across a wide range of price categories for the excellence of their facilities, location or character. The chart below lists the hotels in price categories within each particular area, starting with the Old Town and moving on to hotels further outside the city centre.

PRICE CATEGORIES
The following price ranges are for a standard double room and taxes per night during the high season. Breakfast is included.
Ⓚ Under Kč3000
ⓀⓀ Kč3000–4500
ⓀⓀⓀ Kč4500–6000
ⓀⓀⓀⓀ Kč6000–8000
ⓀⓀⓀⓀⓀ Over Kč8000

OLD TOWN

Cloister Inn
Konviktská 14, Praha 1 **Tel** 22 42 11 020 **Fax** 22 42 10 800 **Rooms** 75   **Map** 3 B5

Just a few minutes' walk from Charles Bridge, the Cloister Inn is, despite the name, a modern hotel offering large, well-furnished rooms with en suite bathrooms. A good buffet breakfast is served in a high-ceilinged dining room, while tea and coffee is on offer all day in the lobby. **www.cloister-inn.com**

Hotel Černý Slon
Týnská 1, Praha 1 **Tel** 22 23 21 521 **Fax** 22 23 10 351 **Rooms** 16   **Map** 3 C3

With an incredible location next to the Týn Church just off Old Town Square, this cosy inn is in a 14th-century building on the UNESCO heritage list. Gothic stone arches, wooden floors and a charming traditional Czech restaurant go with the smallish but comfortable rooms with basic amenities. **www.hotelcernyslon.cz**

Melantrich
Melantrichova 5, Praha 1 **Tel** 22 42 35 551 **Fax** 22 42 35 778 **Rooms** 24   **Map** 3 C4

The EuroAgentur group has consolidated several local hotels, offering smart design and good value. This one is a bargain right on Old Town's main walking street near the Havelská street market, just off Wenceslas Square. Rooms are adequate, as is service, though the basement disco makes the lower floors noisy. **www.euroagentur.cz**

Prague Inn
28. října 15, Praha 1 **Tel** 22 60 14 444 **Fax** 22 60 14 555 **Rooms** 34   **Map** 3 C4

A cool, modern option with sleek decor in Japanese-influenced style, with low furniture and clean, simple designs. The great location is complemented by an excellent bar and restaurant and service is helpful too. Guests are entitled to temporary membership at the respected World Class gym nearby. **www.hotelpragueinn.cz**

Astoria
Rybná 10, Praha 1 **Tel** 22 17 75 711 **Fax** 22 17 75 712 **Rooms** 74   **Map** 4 D3

Rooms at the Astoria are clean and the hotel offers competitive value for its location, but you would hardly call it cosy or inspiring. With blue-grey office-style carpeting, the hotel's best attributes are its location, price and the great Old Town views on upper floors. **www.hotelastoria.cz**

Euroagentur Hotel Royal Esprit
Jakubská 5, Praha 1 **Tel** 22 48 00 055 **Fax** 22 48 00 056 **Rooms** 27   **Map** 3 C3

Formerly the Mejstřík, this great value hotel one block from Old Town Square is a revived classic founded in 1924. Though noise from late-night stag parties can be an issue, the individually decorated rooms and Art Deco touches help to offset the ubiquitous modern hotel decor. **www.hoteleuroagentur.com**

Floor Hotel
Na Příkopě 13, Praha 1 **Tel** 23 40 76 300 **Fax** 23 40 76 112 **Rooms** 43   **Map** 3 C4

Conveniently located on Old Town's main shopping street, half the rooms at the Floor Hotel offer luxury facilities and the rest are sleek and modern. There is an upscale Italian restaurant on site and a large, crystal-chandeliered conference room. Numerous bargain packages, including tours, can be booked via the website. **www.floorhotel.cz**

Metropol
Národní 33, Praha 1 **Tel** 24 60 22 100 **Fax** 24 60 22 200 **Rooms** 64   **Map** 3 B5

This slick hotel is striking, with nine floors of glass-walled design, though service does not always match the good looks and it attracts a steady flow of package tour groups. Still, it's a centrally located bargain with a rooftop restaurant offering amazing views. Rooms are comfortable and sleek, though small. **www.metropolhotel.cz**

Modrá Růže
Rytířská 16, Praha 1 **Tel** 22 44 04 100 **Fax** 22 42 26 106 **Rooms** 47   **Map** 3 C4

Just off Wenceslas Square, this comfortable, five-storey hotel offers old-fashioned European style, with classic interiors, parquet floors and large rooms. Luxury upgrades add nice amenities such as fluffy robes and appealing views but front-facing rooms are prone to noise from the busy pedestrian street below. **www.hotelmodraruze.cz**

Key to Symbols see back cover flap

U Červené Židle

Liliová 4, Praha 1 **Tel** *296 180 018* **Rooms** *15* **Map** *3 B4*

This small, informal option is similar to a pension and only offers minimal amenities. Nevertheless, the staff are friendly and the location boasts access to one of the Old Town's loveliest squares. Rooms are comfortable and rustic colour schemes and ceiling rafters add further charm. Free cable Internet and satellite TV. **www.redchairhotel.com**

U Medvídků

Na Perštýně 7, Praha 1 **Tel** *22 42 11 916* **Fax** *22 42 20 930* **Rooms** *33* **Map** *3 B5*

Classic Czech restaurant, beerhouse and pension. The more expensive rooms have wooden beams and a definite medieval flavour, but all are large and full of character, and have private facilities. U Medvídků is one of the few hotels which have a brewing museum in the basement. **www.umedvidku.cz**

U Zlatého Stromu

Karlova 6, Praha 1 **Tel** *22 22 20 441* **Fax** *22 22 20 441* **Rooms** *22* **Map** *3 B4*

Set in a 13th-century house, this charming hotel has smallish rooms with real character. Furniture and fittings are all tasteful and classic, including wooden, beamed ceilings. While the garden out back is a haven of peace and quiet, some of the rooms facing the busy street are not. **www.zlatystrom.com**

Metamorphis

Malá Štupartská 5, Praha 1 **Tel** *22 17 71 011* **Fax** *22 17 71 099* **Rooms** *32* **Map** *3 C3*

In the centre of Old Town, in the wonderful Týn Courtyard, the Metamorphis offers rather strangely-styled but large rooms, with en suite bathrooms. Many rooms retain original features from the 14th century, when the building was built. The hotel's restaurant makes great pizzas. **www.metamorphis.cz**

Clementin

Seminářská 4, Praha 1 **Tel** *22 22 21 798* **Fax** *22 22 21 768* **Rooms** *9* **Map** *3 B4*

Located at the crossroads of ancient and modern Prague, this hotel is an ideal starting point for discovering and enjoying the city. It is housed in the narrowest and greenest building and dates to 1360, and it has only relatively recently been converted to a hotel. Rooms are small but all have en suite bathrooms. **www.clementin.cz**

Grand Hotel Praha

Staroměstské náměstí 22, Praha 1 **Tel** *22 16 32 556* **Fax** *22 16 32 558* **Rooms** *31* **Map** *3 C3*

With marvellous views of the Old Town Square it is no wonder that the large rooms and apartments are often fully-booked. Rooms are furnished classically and simply, but all have the necessary amenities the modern world demands. Breakfast is served in the historical U Orloje restaurant and beerhouse. **www.grandhotelpraha.cz**

Ungelt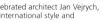

Štupartská 7, Praha 1 **Tel** *22 27 45 900* **Fax** *22 27 45 901* **Rooms** *10* **Map** *3 C3*

Tucked away in a quiet street behind the Old Town Square, this elegant hotel has more than just an air of exclusivity. The accommodation is in suites, simple yet stylish, and some rooms feature magnificent wooden ceilings. The restaurant is simple and there is a shady terrace. **www.ungelt.cz**

Four Seasons

Veleslavínova 2a, Praha 1 **Tel** *22 14 27 000* **Fax** *22 14 26 000* **Rooms** *79* **Map** *3 A3*

This luxury hotel located close to the Charles Bridge needs no introduction. There are a variety of rooms and suites to choose from, and all have stunning views over the Vltava. The hotel's Allegro restaurant is often rated the best in the Czech Republic. **www.fourseasons.com**

Pařiž

U Obecního domu 1, Praha 1 **Tel** *22 21 95 195* **Fax** *22 42 25 475* **Rooms** *86* **Map** *4 D3*

This Neo-Gothic building with a number of Art Nouveau elements was built by the celebrated architect Jan Vejrych, and was declared a historic monument in 1984. The rooms have been modernised in international style and everything is in pristine condition. **www.hotel-paris.cz**

Ventana

Celetná 7, Praha 1 **Tel** *22 17 76 600* **Fax** *22 17 76 603* **Rooms** *30* **Map** *3 C3*

Classic Prague hotel in the heart of Old Town. A narrow building that makes great use of the space available, such as the modern lift inside the old staircase. The rooms are imaginatively designed, some on two levels, and all have rather grand four-poster beds. The reception area is an Art Deco treat. **www.ventana-hotel.net**

JEWISH QUARTER

Travellers' Hostel

Dlouhá 33, Praha 1 **Tel** *22 48 26 662* **Fax** *22 48 26 665* **Rooms** *48* **Map** *3 C2*

The city's most popular hostel is a hit with backpackers, located above the most respected dance club, the Roxy, and attached to the gallery NoD and Dahab Middle Eastern café. It is run well, great value, and has a good youth scene. Additional apartment accommodation allows privacy for those who prefer it. **www.travellers.cz**

Clarion

Hradební 9, Praha 1 **Tel** *29 67 44 249* **Fax** *29 67 44 233* **Rooms** *93*   **Map** *4 D2*

A member of the Choice Hotels International chain, this small hotel offers well-appointed rooms with four-star amenities, a great location facing the Vltava river and above-average service. Pets are welcome and there are conference facilities for business travellers, plus two on-site restaurants. **www.clarionhotel.cz**

U Zlaté Studny

Karlova 3, Praha 1 **Tel** *22 22 20 262* **Fax** *22 22 20 130* **Rooms** *8*   **Map** *3 B4*

Located between Charles Bridge and Old Town Square in a 16th-century building historically known as "At the Golden Well" (the ornate water hole still stands in the cellar), this hotel features exquisite decor and Louis XIV antiques and replicas. Rooms are large and children aged up to 15 stay free. **www.uzlatestudny.cz**

Bellagio

U Milosrdných 2, Praha 1 **Tel** *22 17 78 999* **Fax** *22 17 78 900* **Rooms** *46*   **Map** *3 B2*

Wonderful, pastel-hued hotel on a quiet street minutes from the river. The tastefully decorated bedrooms are large and all have well-sized bathrooms. The lobby bar is a pleasant place to have a drink and the Isabella restaurant downstairs is becoming a popular attraction in its own right. **www.bellagiohotel.cz**

Josef

Rybná 20, Praha 1 **Tel** *22 17 00 111* **Fax** *22 17 00 999* **Rooms** *109*   **Map** *3 C3*

This ultra-modern hotel is a wonderful contrast to the historic Jewish Quarter. Well furnished rooms, with probably the best showers in Prague, are situated in two buildings: the Orange House and the Pink House, separated by a lovely courtyard with manicured lawn. Breakfast is served all morning. **www.hoteljosef.com**

Maximilian

Haštalská 14, 110 00 Praha 1 **Tel** *22 53 03 111* **Fax** *22 53 03 110* **Rooms** *71*   **Map** *3 C2*

One of the most fashionable places to stay in the city. Exquisitely furnished rooms with over-sized beds are the order of the day at the Maximilian. Each room has classical drapes from Venice, a large en suite bathroom and internet access. **www.maximilianhotel.com**

President

Curieových náměstí 100, Praha 1 **Tel** *23 46 14 111* **Fax** *23 46 14 110* **Rooms** *130*   **Map** *3 B2*

A modern hotel with a good location by the river, the President boasts an executive floor, a casino and health spa, and fabulously furnished rooms and suites. Uniquely amongst Prague's hotels, you can select from one of four great views: the Castle, river, Old Town or St Agnes's Convent. **www.hotelpresident.cz**

Grand Hotel Bohemia

Králodvorská 4, Praha 1 **Tel** *23 46 08 111* **Fax** *22 23 29 545* **Rooms** *78*   **Map** *4 D3*

A mustard-coloured Art Nouveau hotel, as grand and as imperial as the name would suggest. Rooms are enormous, staff are friendly and the hotel's café is a convenient meeting point. The buffet breakfast is equally famous amongst regular visitors to Prague. **www.austria-hotels.at**

Inter-Continental

Náměstí Curieových 43–45, Praha 1 **Tel** *29 66 31 111* **Fax** *22 48 11 296* **Rooms** *372*   **Map** *3 B2*

An imposing 1970s building set on the banks of the Vltava, this hotel has excellent health and fitness facilities and a swimming pool. There is nothing Czech about the place, but it is a good example of a five-star international hotel. WiFi in all public areas, high-speed broadband in all rooms. **www.ichotelsgroup.com**

PRAGUE CASTLE AND HRADČANY

Hotel Questenberk

Úvoz 15, Praha 1 **Tel** *22 04 07 600* **Fax** *22 04 07 601* **Rooms** *30*   **Map** *1 B3*

This 17th-century Baroque-style building, originally established as the Hospital of St Elizabeth and St Norbert, has been remodelled as a hotel but some original features including cloistered ceilings and exposed wood remain. Its restaurant has fine views and the hotel is a short walk from Prague Castle. **www.questenberk.cz**

Hoffmeister

Pod Bruskou 7, Praha 1 **Tel** *251 01 71 12* **Fax** *251 01 71 20* **Rooms** *41*   **Map** *2 F2*

The closest, quality hotel to Prague Castle, the imposing Hoffmeister offers a spa and fitness centre alongside its individually furnished rooms. Views from the rooms of the river towards the old town are terrific. The location, half-way up Chotkova, is not a great choice for the elderly or disabled, however. **www.hoffmeister.cz**

Savoy

Keplerova 6, Praha 1 **Tel** *22 43 02 430* **Fax** *22 43 02 128* **Rooms** *61*   **Map** *1 B3*

Splendid period building inside which a luxury, modern hotel plays host to the great and good. The list of famous people who have stayed here is as endless as the services that the hotel offers. Rooms are large and plush, all with what are probably the largest bathrooms in Prague. **www.hotel-savoy.cz**

Key to Price Guide *see p188* **Key to Symbols** *see back cover flap*

LITTLE QUARTER

Aureus Clavis Hotel

Nerudova 27, Praha 1 **Tel** *25 75 34 569* **Fax** *23 39 20 120* **Rooms** *26* **Map** *2 D3*

This small hotel on Malá Strana's main road to Prague Castle has been nicely refurbished, with rooms spread over three floors and an attic with a terrace restaurant. Accommodation is cosy with parquet floors, classic contemporary interiors and an airy lobby. Service is friendly and attentive. **www.aureusclavis.cz**

U Kříže

Újezd 20, Praha 1 **Tel** *25 73 12 272* **Fax** *25 73 12 542* **Rooms** *22* **Map** *2 E5*

This hotel is a good find, offering solid value for the location. "At the Cross", as the name translates, features rooms that are tidy if conventional. On the same street as the district's top nightlife spots, it's a good option for those seeking a handy and affordable place to sleep. **www.ukrize.com**

Pension Dientzenhofer

Nosticova 2, Praha 1 **Tel** *25 73 11 319* **Fax** *25 73 20 888* **Rooms** *9* **Map** *2 E4*

Book well ahead for one of the nine rooms in this charming and well-run little pension on a small back street of Malá Strana. Accommodation is basic, but rooms are bright and cheerful, and the service eager. The house was the birthplace of famous Baroque architect Kilian Ignaz Dientzenhofer. **www.dientzenhofer.cz**

Residence Malá Strana

Mělnická 9, Praha 1 **Tel** *25 15 10 372* **Fax** *25 15 10 406* **Rooms** *35* **Map** *2 F5*

Smart hotel in a lovely Neo-Classical building in the Little Quarter. Rooms are large, more like suites, and have small kitchens and a separate dining area. A filling breakfast is included in the price. There is a nice lounge with garden view on the ground floor, perfect for relaxing after a day's sightseeing. **www.hotelresidence-mala-strana.com**

U Brány

Nerudova 21, Praha 1 **Tel** *25 75 34 050* **Fax** *23 39 20 120* **Rooms** *17* **Map** *2 D3*

With one of the best addresses in Prague, U Brány is a popular spot, often full at busy times. Reserving your room well ahead is essential. The rooms, all of which are in fact two-, three- or four-roomed suites, are large and luxuriously decorated. The bathrooms are splendid. **www.ubrany.cz**

U Karlova mostů

Na Kampě 15, Praha 1 **Tel** *25 75 31 430* **Fax** *25 75 33 168* **Rooms** *26* **Map** *2 F4*

This atmospheric little inn has for years been a respected traditional pub, with a back terrace on the bank of the Vltava river. The hotel is within sight of the Charles Bridge but is not mobbed by tourists and offers great service, with rooms that mix antique touches such as ceiling beams with modern furnishings. **www.archibald.cz**

U Žluté boty

Jánský vršek 11, Praha 1 **Tel** *25 75 32 269* **Fax** *257 53 41 34* **Rooms** *9* **Map** *2 D3*

The sparsely furnished but tasteful and elegant rooms at U Žluté boty are all individually decorated, some with lots of wood, others with a more modern feel. The rooms are large and have well-sized bathrooms. The courtyard at the back is very pleasant during the summer. **www.zlutabota.cz**

Best Western Kampa

Všehrdova 16, Praha 1 **Tel** *27 10 90 847* **Fax** *25 74 04 333* **Rooms** *84* **Map** *2 E5*

A 17th-century armoury, the Kampa is minutes from Charles Bridge, tucked away on a peaceful side street surrounded by lovely gardens. In the large reception hall, a bar and restaurant are combined under a huge Baroque-vaulted ceiling. The furnishings are simple and bedrooms are clean. **www.euroagentur.cz**

Dům U Červeného lva

Nerudova 41, Praha 1 **Tel** *25 75 33 833* **Fax** *25 75 35 131* **Rooms** *21* **Map** *2 F3*

With views of the Royal Route, Prague Castle or the serene Petrin Hill Orchards, the Red Lion is absolutely ideal for sightseers. Add in the hand-painted Renaissance ceilings, original period furniture and parquet floors and you have a real historical treat. There is a traditional Czech beer hall too. **www.hotelredlion.com**

Hotel Mandarin Oriental

Nebovidská 1, Praha 1 **Tel** *23 30 88 888* **Fax** *23 30 88 668* **Rooms** *99* **Map** *2 E4*

This elegant, classy flagship of the respected Mandarin group has won rave reviews for its Eastern-influenced designs, plush rooms and excellent Asian cuisine. Just a 10-minute walk from Charles Bridge in a former 14th-century monastery, amenities include a great gym, spa and terrace dining. **www.mandarinoriental.com/prague**

Pod Věží

Mostecká 2, Praha 1 **Tel** *25 75 32 041* **Fax** *25 75 32 069* **Rooms** *12* **Map** *2 F3*

In the heart of the historical centre, this is a delightful, family-run hotel. Pod Věží offers a peaceful ambience, highlighted by the charming roof garden and the sidewalk café, which is open – and usually full – all day. Rooms are well appointed if not huge, and breakfast is included in the price. **www.podvezi.com**

Sax

🍴 📋 Ⓦ   ⓦⓦⓦ

Jánský vršek 3, Praha 1 **Tel** *25 75 31 268* **Fax** *25 75 34 101* **Rooms** *22*   **Map** *2 D3*

Easily the hippest hotel in Malá Strana, with rooms decorated in outrageous and very cool designs from the 1960s and 1970s. Alongside all the retro chic, rooms have wide-screen LCD TVs, DVD players and all the latest amenities. Close to Prague Castle, but all the steps make it unsuitable for those with impaired mobility. **www.hotelsax.cz**

U Tří Pštrosů

🅿 🍴 📋 Ⓦ   ⓦⓦⓦⓦ

Dražického náměstí 12, Praha 1 **Tel** *25 72 88 888* **Fax** *25 75 33 217* **Rooms** *52*   **Map** *2 F3*

Just beside Charles Bridge, the hotel "At The Three Ostriches" began life as the home of Jan Fux, an ostrich-feather dealer. It is one of the best-known hotel/restaurants in Prague. Family run, it has an intimate atmosphere, and children are especially welcome. The bedrooms have recently been refurbished. **www.utripstrosu.com**

U Zlaté Studně

🍴 📋 Ⓦ   ⓦⓦⓦⓦ

U Zlaté studně 166, Praha 1 **Tel** *25 70 11 213* **Fax** *25 75 33 320* **Rooms** *19*   **Map** *2 E2*

Luxury rooms in a former house which is almost as old as Prague itself, just minutes from the castle. Views of Prague from the rooftop restaurant and terrace are stunning, and the rooms are well furnished with original touches. Bathrooms, too, are comfortable, which is something of a rarity in these parts. **www.goldenwell.cz**

Aria

🅿 🍴 🛗 🅿 📋 Ⓦ   ⓦⓦⓦⓦⓦ

Tržiště 9, Praha 1 **Tel** *22 53 34 111* **Fax** *22 53 34 666* **Rooms** *52*   **Map** *2 E3*

A charming, unusual little hotel where each of the fantastic, though not large, rooms are modelled to honour a particular musical legend, be it Dizzy Gillespie, Puccini or Mozart. The hotel even has a musical director who will recommend music to suit your mood, while also advising on concerts that you may attend. **www.ariahotel.net**

NEW TOWN

Evropa

🅿 🍴   Ⓧ

Václavské náměstí 25, 110 00 Praha 1 **Tel** *22 42 28 215* **Fax** *22 42 24 544* **Rooms** *90*   **Map** *4 D5*

The Evropa is Prague's most beautiful and possibly most famous hotel, with superb Art Nouveau decor, and a ground-floor terrace-café boasting stunning glasswork that is in itself a major attraction. The rooms are in keeping with the period style but are quite bare by modern standards. Service can be a little brusque. **www.evropahotel.cz**

Jerome House

📋 ♿ Ⓦ   Ⓧ

V Jirchářích 13, Praha 1 **Tel** *22 49 33 207* **Fax** *22 49 33 212* **Rooms** *64*   **Map** *5 B1*

In an amazing location just two blocks from Wenceslas Square on a quiet, cobbled street, this clean and modern hotel offers serious value. The trade-off is very basic rooms (most en suite, but nine are a great deal for groups, with shared facilities). It is part of a network so staff can place you elsewhere if full. **www.hoteljeromehouse.cz**

987 Prague

🍴 📋 ♿ Ⓦ   ⓦⓦ

Senovážné náměstí 15, Praha 1 **Tel** *25 57 37 100* **Fax** *22 22 10 369* **Rooms** *80*   **Map** *4 E4*

Run by the group Design Hotels Collection, 987 Prague is hip but comfortable, featuring amenities such as free WiFi. Part of a recent wave of design hotels in the city, this addition pulls off the concept very successfully, without sacrificing service for looks. Handy location opposite Prague's main station. **www.designhotelscollection.com**

BW Meteor Plaza

🅿 🍴 🛗 📋 ♿ Ⓦ   ⓦⓦ

Hybernská 6, Praha 1 **Tel** *22 41 92 559* **Fax** *22 42 20 681* **Rooms** *88*   **Map** *4 D3*

This is another Best Western satellite, meaning reliable service and comfort, in this case on the edge of Old Town and next to the main shopping street. The hotel is within a charming old building with Gothic-era roots and an attractive pool and sauna, all within view of the Powder Tower. Clean, modern rooms. **www.hotel-meteor.cz**

Elysee

📋 ♿ Ⓦ   ⓦⓦ

Václavské náměstí 43, Praha 1 **Tel** *22 14 55 111* **Fax** *22 42 25 773* **Rooms** *70*   **Map** *4 D5*

Classy, old-fashioned rooms with parquet floors and ornate dark wood accents are not what you'd expect on Wenceslas Square. Great value, Elysee offers well-appointed comfort with luxury bathrooms, thoroughly insulated windows that block traffic noise, and six apartments. Secure parking is also a plus. **www.hotelelysee.cz**

Harmony

🅿 🍴 Ⓦ   ⓦⓦ

Na poříčí 31, Praha 1 **Tel** *22 23 19 807* **Fax** *22 23 10 009* **Rooms** *60*   **Map** *4 E3*

The rather bleak looking Harmony is, in fact, in pristine condition after reconstruction. A compact place, it is run by young, friendly staff. Two small restaurants, one with tables on the pavement, give a choice of cuisine. Ask for a room away from the busy central street, which can be noisy at night. **www.euroagentur.cz**

Hotel Sovereign

🍴 🛗 📋 ♿ Ⓦ   ⓦⓦ

Politických vězňů 16, Praha 1 **Tel** *24 24 54 545* **Fax** *24 24 54 511* **Rooms** *50*   **Map** *4 D5*

This elegant but relaxing hotel is one block off Wenceslas Square, with well designed rooms and suites with a homely style. Amenities include free WiFi and satellite TV, and black-and-white photography contributes to the unique decor in the rooms. Excellent fitness centre and special online-only offers add further appeal. **www.hotel-sovereign.cz**

Key to Price Guide *see p188* **Key to Symbols** *see back cover flap*

Junior

Senovážné náměstí 21, Praha 1 **Tel** *22 22 48 057* **Fax** *22 42 21 579* **Rooms** *14* **Map** *4 E4*

Expect excellent value-for-money if you stay at this cheap hotel, just a few minutes' walk from the top of Wenceslas Square. Rooms are not luxurious but are well equipped with private bathrooms. A good pizzeria downstairs does a roaring trade, and there is a bowling alley onsite too. **www.euroagentur.cz**

Luník

Londýnská 50, 120 00 Praha 2 **Tel** *22 42 53 974* **Fax** *22 42 53 986* **Rooms** *35* **Map** *6 E2*

Located in a quiet street lined with trees, this good value, historic hotel is in immaculate condition. The decor is simple, with whitewashed walls and good-quality wooden furnishings. Rooms are small but have en suite bathrooms with bath, shower and WC. A buffet breakfast is included in the price. **www.hotel-lunik.cz**

Maria Prag

Opletalova 21, Praha 1 **Tel** *22 22 11 229* **Fax** *22 22 40 229* **Rooms** *109* **Map** *4 E5*

The sleek, airy and bold design of the Maria Prag's lobby is a good indication of what's to come, with elegant rooms upstairs featuring Japanese accents. Staff, meanwhile, are friendly and there's a small but lovely wellness spa in the basement. Convenient location just off Wenceslas Square. **www.falkensteiner.com**

Na Zlatém Kříži

Jungmannovo náměstí 2, Praha 1 **Tel** *22 22 45 419* **Fax** *22 22 45 418* **Rooms** *8* **Map** *3 C5*

A challenger for the narrowest hotel in Prague award, the charming Golden Cross offers deceptively large, and rather luxurious double rooms and apartments, all with private bathrooms. A good buffet breakfast is served in the hotel's Gothic-style cellar. Transfers to and from the airport are possible. **www.antikhotels.com**

Opera

Těšnov 13, Praha 1 **Tel** *22 23 15 609* **Fax** *22 23 11 477* **Rooms** *67* **Map** *4 F2*

Although nowhere near the opera, this hotel is a classy Neo-Renaissance affair built in the late-19th century. Rooms are classically furnished and all have enormous windows with views of the small park opposite. The hotel bar is pure kitsch, with its 1950s-style booths, and shouldn't be missed. **www.hotel-opera.cz**

Pension Museum

Mezibranská 15, Praha 1 **Tel** *29 63 25 186* **Fax** *29 63 25 188* **Rooms** *12* **Map** *6 D1*

Large rooms, most with separate bedrooms and a small living area, are what distinguish the Pension Museum. Great service, an excellent breakfast and a super location at the top of Wenceslas Square, make this converted school just about the best value bed-and-breakfast in central Prague. **www.pension-museum.cz**

Tchaikovsky

Ke Karlovu 19, Praha 1 **Tel** *22 49 12 121* **Fax** *22 49 12 123* **Rooms** *19* **Map** *5 C2*

Ten-minutes' walk from Wenceslas Square on a quiet side street, the smart, Neo-Classical Tchaikovsky hits all the right notes with its simple charm and elegance. Rooms are well sized if low on frills, and bathrooms are huge and wonderfully decorated. A buffet breakfast is included in the price. **www.hoteltchaikovsky.com**

U Klenotníka

Rytířská 3, Praha 1 **Tel** *22 42 11 699* **Fax** *22 42 21 025* **Rooms** *11* **Map** *3 B4*

A small, but lovely hotel and restaurant in a converted house halfway between the Old Town Square and Wenceslas Square. Rooms are reasonably sized and offer great value for money. There is a small paternoster elevator for luggage. Excellent buffet breakfast is served in the downstairs restaurant. **www.uklenotnika.cz**

Best Western Premier Hotel Majestic

Štěpánská 33, Praha 1 **Tel** *22 14 86 100* **Fax** *22 14 86 486* **Rooms** *185* **Map** *5 C1*

Two renovated buildings, one Biedermeier style, the other Art Deco, were joined to form this hotel, offering small rooms but with all the modern amenities. Balconies and great views from the 7th floor add appeal to this well designed project just off Wenceslas Square. **www.hotel-majestic.cz**

Élite

Ostrovní 32, Praha 1 **Tel** *22 49 32 250* **Fax** *22 49 30 787* **Rooms** *78* **Map** *3 B5*

The Élite is housed in a building which dates from the late-14th century. Its cosy atmosphere is aptly augmented by a stylish grill club on the ground floor, offering excellent Mediterranean and Argentinian cuisine, as well as a cocktail bar providing jazz and Latino music. An open atrium contains a day-bar with a small garden. **www.hotelelite.cz**

Hotel Yasmin

Politických vězňů 12, Praha 1 **Tel** *23 41 00 121* **Fax** *23 41 00 101* **Rooms** *198* **Map** *4 D5*

Just a five-minute walk to Wenceslas Square, Hotel Yasmin is well run, with friendly staff and fresh, contemporary decor. Extra touches such as free WiFi in all rooms and luxurious bathrooms help to make it a cut above many others for the price. There's also a fine restaurant with a garden where you can dine in summer. **www.hotel-yasmin.cz**

Adria

Václavské náměstí 26, Praha 1 **Tel** *22 10 81 111* **Fax** *22 10 81 300* **Rooms** *87* **Map** *4 D5*

The Adria is bright and chic with an entrance on Wenceslas Square. Clever use of glass and mirrors makes the reception seem bigger than it is, and with plenty of gleaming brass the impression is light and up-beat. The bedrooms are bright, cheerful and smartly furnished. **www.adria.cz**

Carlo IV

Senovážné náměstí 13, Praha 1 **Tel** *22 45 93 111* **Fax** *22 45 93 000* **Rooms** *152*　　　**Map** *4 E4*

This magnificently decorated hotel with shimmering marble floors, intricate hand-painted frescos in a Neo-Classical building, is close to the centre. Part of the Boscolo Group, it is all startlingly wonderful, from the Box Block restaurant to the cigar bar, while the spa features one of Europe's best hotel swimming pools. **www.boscolohotels.com**

Esplanade

Washingtonova 19, Praha 1 **Tel** *22 45 01 111* **Fax** *22 42 29 306* **Rooms** *74*　　　**Map** *4 E5*

This imposing six-storey hotel opposite the opera house is known for its long history of luxury. The Art Nouveau façade hides an elegant interior, and all the rooms are well furnished. The hotel's café has a summer terrace, while the onsite French restaurant is world class. Service is exceptional. **www.esplanade.cz**

Marriott
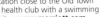

V celnici 8, Praha 1 **Tel** *22 28 88 888* **Fax** *22 28 88 889* **Rooms** *293*　　　**Map** *4 E3*

The Prague Marriott is one of the best hotels in the Marriott chain, and has a great location close to the Old Town gate. Every amenity and luxury imaginable is on offer in all the rooms. There is a great health club with a swimming pool, free to guests. The restaurants here are considered to be among the best in the city. **www.marriott.com**

Radisson SAS Alcron

Štěpánská 40, Praha 1 **Tel** *22 28 20 000* **Fax** *22 28 20 100* **Rooms** *206*　　　**Map** *6 D1*

The views from the upper floors of this exquisite hotel could be an attraction in themselves. But that would be to forget the other joys of staying at this Radisson hotel, including enormous bathrooms, divine chocolates at bedtime and plush carpets. Expensive but worth every penny. **www.radissonsas.com**

FURTHER AFIELD

Kafka

Cimburkova 24, Praha 3 **Tel** *22 27 80 431* **Fax** *22 27 81 333* **Rooms** *59*

A simple, clean but somewhat spartan and soulless hotel a 15-minute tram ride from Old Town. The building is a classic though, and a large number of triple and quad rooms make it a good choice for families on a budget. If you want to park in the hotel's car park you need to pre-book a space. **www.hotelkafka.cz**

Kavalír

Plzeňská 177, Praha 5 **Tel** *25 72 16 565* **Fax** *25 72 10 085* **Rooms** *50*

Cheapest hotel in the good value H&Hotels chain, this place is not without charm. Rooms are impressively large – some have two large double beds – and all the common areas are well kept, bright and breezy. Staff are friendly and communicate in a number of languages. It is some way from the city centre though. **www.europehotels.cz**

Abri

Jana Masaryka 36, Praha 2 **Tel** *72 28 11 097* **Fax** *22 50 91 925* **Rooms** *26*

Comfortable hotel in a quiet residential area of Prague, Vinohrady. Smallish rooms are well furnished and decorated, and all have private bathrooms. A small garden terrace is a pleasant place to unwind with a drink after a long day of sightseeing. Guarded parking and onsite restaurant. **www.abri.cz**

Anna

Budečská 17, Praha 2 **Tel** *22 25 13 111* **Fax** *22 25 15 158* **Rooms** *22*

Housed in an elegant Neo-Classical building with Art Nouveau interiors, this excellent value hotel is only a 10-minute walk from Wenceslas Square. Rooms are spacious and have large, comfortable beds, but some of the bathroms can be small. Staff are helpful, multilingual and very friendly. **www.hotelanna.cz**

Arcotel Teatrino

Bořivojova 53, Praha 3 **Tel** *22 14 22 111* **Fax** *22 14 22 222* **Rooms** *73*

Once a theatre, this design hotel is a well-priced, high-quality alternative to more expensive retreats. Located in residential Žižkov, its finest feature, besides the large, well-furnished rooms, is the spendid restaurant – situated in what was once the stalls – overlooked by the theatre's original balconies and boxes. **www.arcotel.at**

Ariston

Seifertova 65, Praha 3 **Tel** *22 27 82 517* **Fax** *22 27 80 347* **Rooms** *61*

Great value three-star hotel not too far from the city centre in a quiet residential area. Rooms are simple but clean and well-sized, with high ceilings and sturdy wooden desks. All have private bathrooms, and some larger rooms take a third bed. Non-smoking and disabled-friendly rooms are also available. **www.europehotels.cz**

Art Hotel Praha

Nad Královskou oborou 53, Praha 7 **Tel** *23 31 01 331* **Fax** *23 31 01 311* **Rooms** *24*

With its permanent display of Czech modern art, the Art Hotel is a cool, quiet place to escape the capital's tourist trail. Rooms are individually decorated, all with panache and taste. The lighting is a big feature: subtle and designed to catch your mood. Excellent buffet breakfast included in the price. **www.arthotel.cz**

Key to Price Guide *see p188* **Key to Symbols** *see back cover flap*

Julián
P 11 TV 目 & W &&

Elišky Peškové 11, Praha 5 **Tel** *25 73 11 150* **Fax** *25 73 11 149* **Rooms** *33*

Good value hotel where, though the rooms are on the small side, everything is done to make up for that one drawback. Service is fantastic, there is a sauna, solarium and a small fitness room, and children are especially welcome. Several rooms are accesible by wheelchair; one room has a specially adapted bathroom. **www.julian.cz**

Plaza Alta
P 11 8 目 & W &&

Ortenovo náměstí 22, Praha 7 **Tel** *22 04 07 082* **Fax** *22 04 07 091* **Rooms** *87*

The Alta offers large, very good value rooms just a little way out of Prague. The location is convenient to the Holešovice train station and the metro takes you to the centre of the city in just a couple of minutes. Excellent breakfast included in the price. **www.plazahotelalta.com**

U Blaženky
P 11 目 W &&

U Blaženky 1, Praha 5 **Tel** *25 15 64 532* **Fax** *25 15 63 529* **Rooms** *13*

You are guaranteed to feel special just arriving at this villa conversion in one of Prague's best residential districts. The excellent value – though by no means cheap – rooms are modern and spacious, full of extras and nice touches, while the dining room is home to fine local cuisine and an excellent winelist. **www.ublazenky.cz**

Ametyst
P 11 TV 目 & W &&&

Jana Masaryka 11, Praha 2 **Tel** *22 29 21 921* **Fax** *22 22 91 999* **Rooms** *84*   **Map** *6 F3*

Fine, modern townhouse-style hotel with air-conditioned rooms, all with private bath or shower and internet access. The attic rooms with sloping, beamed ceilings are especially attractive. Sauna and massage also available. Ametyst has a small restaurant with some fine decor. **www.hotelametyst.com**

Carlton
P 11 目 &   &&&

Táboritská 18, Praha 3 **Tel** *22 27 11 177* **Fax** *22 27 11 199* **Rooms** *49*

Not perfectly located, the Carlton is nevertheless a stylish, good-value hotel, offering large rooms at reasonable prices. The lofty celings and wooden beams make the top-floor rooms a preferred choice. Buffet breakfast served in a small cellar restaurant. One room is specially adapted for disabled visitors. **www.europehotels.cz**

Mövenpick
P 11 TV 8 目 & W &&&

Mozartova 1, Praha 5 **Tel** *25 71 51 111* **Fax** *25 71 53 131* **Rooms** *442*

Though not centrally located, this luxurious hotel situated in two buildings linked by a funicular is wonderful. All of the rooms – some of which are split over two levels – are large, comfortable and cater to all needs. The hotel's restaurants are well regarded, and it's also famous for ice cream. **www.movenpick-prague.com**

Corinthia Towers
P 11 TV 8 目 & W &&&&

Kongresová 1, Praha 4 **Tel** *26 11 91 111* **Fax** *26 12 25 011* **Rooms** *542*

Situated beside the Vyšehrad metro stop, the Corinthia Towers is only a few minutes from the city centre. Built in 1988 as a modern high-rise filled with glass, brass and marble, it has an impressive health centre and a beautiful indoor swimming pool. The good-sized bedrooms are well decorated and comfortable. **www.corinthia.cz**

Diplomat Praha
P 11 TV 8 目 & W &&&&

Evropská 15, Praha 6 **Tel** *29 65 59 213* **Fax** *29 65 59 215* **Rooms** *398*

This hotel is located right at the end of metro line A, but is only 12 minutes from the city centre. It opened in 1990 and still feels very new. Efficiently run by Austrians, it offers excellent facilities including a nightclub, numerous restaurants, shops and even a whirlpool in the health club. **www.diplomathotel.cz**

Mucha
11 TV 目 & W &&&&

Sokolovská 26, Praha 8 **Tel** *22 23 18 849* **Fax** *22 48 16 641* **Rooms** *39*   **Map** *4 F2*

Perhaps a little overpriced, the Mucha is nevertheless a good hotel, in a great location, minutes from the city centre. The legacy of Czech painter Alphonse Mucha for whom the hotel is named is not forgotten, with reproductions of his work all over the building, which is also something of an Art Deco masterpiece. **www.avehotels.cz**

Praha Hilton
P 11 TV 目 & W &&&&

Pobřeží 1, 186 00 Praha 8 **Tel** *22 48 41 111* **Fax** *22 48 42 378* **Rooms** *788*   **Map** *4 F2*

This is one of the biggest hotels in the country, and despite the huge size, it does have a certain style. The bedrooms are tastefully decorated with all the comforts you would expect to find in a large international hotel, while the cost of staying in one is lower than you may have thought. About 15 minutes' walk to the city. **www.hilton.com**

Praha Hotel
P 11 TV 8 目 & W &&&&

Sušická 20, Praha 6 **Tel** *22 43 41 111* **Fax** *22 43 11 218* **Rooms** *124*

When the Praha opened in 1981, it was regarded by its architects as the height of modernity, with its unique design, all curves and waves. Built to accommodate visiting heads of state and dignitaries, it is today open to all, though its secluded location still makes it a favourite of VIPs. **www.htlpraha.cz**

Riverside
P 11 目 & W &&&&

Janáčkovo nábřeží 15, Praha 5 **Tel** *23 47 05 155* **Fax** *23 47 05 158* **Rooms** *45*

Classy, and – as the name suggests – handy for the river, this hotel is certainly impressive, with small touches of elegance and fine living at every turn. From the basket of complimentary high-end toiletries in the bathrooms to the original, contemporary Czech art on the wall, your stay here will be enjoyable. **www.riversideprague.com**

RESTAURANTS, CAFÉS AND PUBS

Restaurants in Prague, just like the tourist economy, seem to be getting better. For 40 years state-licensed eating and drinking establishments had little incentive to experiment or improve. But attitudes are rapidly changing. Fuelled by the booming tourist industry, new restaurants are opening constantly, many of them foreign-owned, offering the discerning eater an ever-increasing choice. The restaurants described in this

The Good Soldier Švejk
at U Kalicha (see p207)

section reflect the change, though many only serve a limited range of standard Western dishes in addition to the staple Czech meals. *Choosing a Restaurant* on pages 202–7 summarizes the key features of the restaurants and cafés recommended in this guide, which are listed by area. Information on pubs, beer halls and bars appears on pages 208–9. Compared to Western prices, eating out in Prague is still cheap.

TIPS ON EATING OUT

Because of the huge influx of tourists, eating out has changed in character. The lunch hour is still early – between 11am and 1pm, and for most Czechs the normal time for the evening meal is around 7pm. However, many of the restaurants stay open late and it is possible to get a meal at any time from 10am until 11pm. Kitchens close 30 minutes to one hour earlier than stated closing times.

During spring and summer, the large numbers of visitors tend to put a strain on many of Prague's more popular restaurants. To be certain of a table, especially in the very well-known restaurants, it is advisable to book in

advance. The city centre is full of restaurants, and there are several off the normal tourist track. Prices also tend to be lower the further you go from the centre.

PLACES TO EAT

The importance of a stylish yet comfortable setting, and food which is inspired rather than just prepared, is slowly beginning to trickle down to Prague's better and more innovative restaurants. The places which follow this maxim are generally the best.

One of the simplest places to eat is the sausage stand, a utilitarian establishment which is very common in Central Europe. It offers Czech sausages, which can either be eaten standing at

Diners enjoying their meal at U Kalicha *(see p207)*

Modern Czech restaurant

the counter or taken away cold. For a late-night meal your best bet is often a falafel or pizza served from a street stand.

For greater comfort, head for a café *(kavárna)*. Cafés range from loud, busy main street locations to quieter bookstore establishments. All have fully stocked bars and serve a variety of food from simple pastries and sandwiches to full-blown meals. Opening hours differ widely, but many open early in the morning and are good for a quick, if not quite a Western-style, breakfast.

A restaurant may be called a *restaurace* or a *vinárna* (one that specialises in wine).

Plain Czech food is normally available at the local beer hall or pub *(pivnice)*, though the emphasis there is normally on drinking rather than eating.

READING THE MENU

Never judge a restaurant by the standard of its menu translations – mistakes are

Tourists eating at the outdoor cafés in the Old Town Square

common in every class of restaurant. Many menus still list the weight of meat served (a relic of communist bureaucracy). Bear in mind that most main courses come with potatoes, rice or dumplings. Salads and other side dishes must be ordered separately *(see pp198–9 for The Flavours of Prague.)*

THINGS TO BEWARE OF

In some restaurants or bars the waiter may bring nuts to your table. Yes, they are for you to eat, but at a price equal to, or higher than, an appetizer. You will not insult anybody by telling the waiter to take them away. The same applies to appetizers brought round by the waiter.

Restaurant sign

Check your bill carefully, because extra charges are often added – this is quite a common practice in Prague. However, legitimate extra costs do exist. Cover charges range from Kč10–25 and such basic items as milk, ketchup, bread and butter might be charged for. Finally, a 19% tax is normally included in the menu. Severe cases of food poisoning are rare in Prague, but mild cases are more common. Use common sense when buying food from street vendors and avoid any that appear not to be hygienic. In general, restaurants in Prague have a high standard of hygiene, equal to the rest of Europe.

ETIQUETTE

You don't have to wait to be seated in snack bars and smaller eateries. It is also quite normal for others to join your table if there is any room. No restaurant has an official dress code, but people tend to dress up when dining in up-market restaurants.

PAYMENT AND TIPPING

The average price for a full meal in the centre of Prague ranges from about Kč250 to Kč1,000, depending on the type of establishment. In some restaurants the waiter may write your order on a piece of paper and then leave it on your table for the per-

son who comes around when you are ready to pay. Levels of service vary, but generally a 10% tip is appropriate. Add the tip to the bill, do not leave the money on the table. More and more restaurants now accept major credit cards, but always ask before the meal to make sure. Traveller's cheques are not accepted.

VEGETARIANS

The situation for vegetarians in Prague is not ideal but is improving as awareness increases. Fresh vegetables are available throughout the year, including winter, and numerous restaurants offer vegetarian and vegan options. Nevertheless, even when a dish is described as meatless, it's always worth double-checking. Vegetarians should particularly beware of menu sections called *bezmasa* as, whilst the literal translation of this word is "without meat", its actual meaning is that meat is not the main ingredient in the dishes listed.

DISABLED

Many restaurants still do not cater specifically for the disabled. The staff will almost always try and help, but Prague's ubiquitous stairs and basements will defeat all but the most determined.

RESERVATIONS

There is generally no need to reserve a table at lunchtime or on weekday evenings in Prague. If you are planning to eat dinner on a Friday or Saturday evening, however, particularly in Prague's better known eating places, it is advisable to book in advance. Tables can be reserved in person or by telephone. Some restaurants also take bookings on the internet, through their website. Alternatively, online booking companies will make a free reservation for you at many of the city's restaurants. Your booking is confirmed by email and you pay as usual at the restaurant.

Fine dining amid stained-glass Art Deco splendour

The Flavours of Prague

While no visitor comes to Prague for the food, there is far more to contemporary Czech cuisine than the Central European norm of meat, potatoes and rice. Czech food remains based on seasonally available ingredients, while a simple, no-fuss approach allows natural flavours to dominate most dishes. The staples of Czech cooking are pork, beef, game and carp, which tend to be served grilled or roasted, accompanied by a light sauce and vegetables. They are also used in sour soups, known as *polévky*. It is also unlikely that you will leave Prague without tasting *knedlíky* (dumplings), either savoury or sweet.

Blueberries

Atmospheric U Pinkasů cellar bar and restaurant (see p206)

MEAT

The Czech favourite is pork *(vepřové)*. It appears in countless dishes, including soups, goulash and sausages, or can be served on its own, either grilled or (more commonly) roasted and served with sliced dumplings and sweet-sour cabbage *(Vepřo-knedlozelo)*. It also appears in other forms, notably as

Prague ham *(Pražska šunka)*, a succulent, lightly smoked meat usually eaten with bread at breakfast or with horseradish as a starter at suppertime.

Veal, occasionally served in the form of breadcrumbed, fried Wiener schnitzel *(sma-žený řízek)*, is popular.

Beef in the region has never been up to international standards, and needs to be prepared well to be edible.

The Prague favourite is *Svíčková*, sliced, roast sirloin, served in a cream sauce with dumplings and sliced lemon. If cooked well it can be tender and delicious. Beef is also used in goulash and stews. Most of the beef served in top restaurants is likely to be imported. Czech lamb *(jehněčí)* is not the best in the world, either, though for a short period from mid-March to mid-May there is

Apple strudel   **Trdelník (eclair)**   **Český koláč (plum jam bun)**
Honzova buchta (fruit buns)   **Čokoládový řez (chocolate cake)**
Bublanina (apple crumble tart)
Selection of typical Czech cakes and pastries

LOCAL DISHES AND SPECIALITIES

Knedlíky (dumplings), either savoury *(špekové)* in soups or sweet *(ovocné)* with fruits and berries, are perhaps Bohemia's best-known delicacy. Once a mere side dish they have now become a central feature of Czech cuisine, as Postmodern chefs rediscover their charms and experiment with new and different ways of cooking and serving them. Other specialities of the region include *Drštkova polévka*, a remarkably good tripe soup, which – although an acquired taste – has also seen something of a revival in recent years as better restaurants add it to their menus. Duck and pheasant remain popular in Prague and, with the city surrounded by fine hunting grounds, such game is always of top quality. Pork, though, is the city's (and the nation's) most popular food, served roasted on the bone, with red cabbage.

Stuffed eggs

Polévka s játrovými knedlíčky
Soup with liver dumplings is a common dish in the Czech Republic.

Wild chanterelle mushrooms from the forests around the city

way into supermarkets, many Czechs are unwilling to pay the higher prices these goods demand. As a result, the hardy cabbage remains the country's top vegetable, used in numerous different ways, such as raw as a salad, or boiled as an accompaniment to roast meats. The Czech version of *sauerkraut*, *kyselé zelí*, is ubiquitous. Mushrooms, too, are well liked, and find their way in to many sauces, especially those served with game.

good lamb available in Prague's markets, where it is usually sold whole, complete with the head which is used to make soup.

GAME

There is a wide variety of game to be found in the forests around Prague. Depending on the season (the best time is autumn) you will find duck, pheasant, goose, boar, venison, rabbit and hare on many menus. Duck is probably the most popular game dish, usually roasted with fruits, berries or sometimes with chestnuts, and served with red cabbage. Small pheasants, roasted whole with juniper and blueberries or cranberries, are also popular, while venison is often served grilled with mushrooms. Rabbit and hare are usually presented in spicy, goulash-style sauces.

VEGETABLES

Fresh vegetables are becoming more popular as an accompaniment to meals. Note, however, that Czechs tend to boil their vegetables into oblivion. While more and more imported, out-of-season produce is finding its

Fresh vegetables on a Prague market stall

BEST LOCAL SNACKS

Sausages Street stalls and snack bars all over the city sell traditional sausages (*klobásy* and *utopence*), frankfurters (*párky*) or bratwurst, served in a soft roll with mustard.

Chlebíčky Open sandwiches on sliced baguette are found in any delicatessen or snack bar in Prague. Toppings are usually ham, salami or cheese, always accompanied by a gherkin (*nakládaná okurka*).

Pivní sýr Beer cheese is soaked in ale until it becomes soft. It is served spread on bread and eaten with pickles or onions.

Syrečky These tasty cheese rounds have a pungent aroma and are served with beer and onions.

Palačinky Pancakes are filled with ice cream and/or fruits and jam, and are topped with lashings of sugar.

Pečený kapr s kyselou omáčkou *Carp with sour cream and lemon is popular, especially at Christmas.*

Vepřové s křenem *Pork is served roasted, on the bone, with red cabbage and either sauerkraut or horseradish.*

Ovocné knedlíky *Sweet dumplings are filled with fruits or berries, usually blueberries or plums.*

What to Drink in Prague

'Golden Tiger' beer mat

Czech beers are famous around the world, but nowhere are they drunk with such appreciation as in Prague. The Czechs take their beer *(pivo)* seriously and are very proud of it. Pilsner and its various relations originate in Bohemia. It is generally agreed that the best Pilsners are produced close to Pilsen – and all the top producers are not far from Prague. Beers can be bought in cans, in bottles, and best of all, on draught. Canned beer is made mostly for export, and no connoisseur would ever drink it. The Czech Republic also produces considerable quantities of wine, both red and white, mainly in Southern Moravia. Little of it is bottled for export. Mineral water can be found in most restaurants; Mattoni and Dobrá voda (meaning good water) are the two most widely available brands.

Gambrinus, legendary King of Beer, and trademark of a popular brand of Pilsner

Traditional copper brew-kettles in Plzeň

PILSNER AND BUDWEISER

The best-known Czech beer is Pilsner Urquell. Clear and golden, with a strong flavour of hops, Pilsner is made by the lager method: bottom-fermented and slowly matured at low temperatures. The word "Pilsner" (now a generic term for similar lagers brewed all over the world) is derived from Plzeň (in German, Pilsen), a town 80 km (50 miles) southwest of Prague, where this type of beer was first made in 1842. The brewery that developed the beer still makes it under the name Plzeňský prazdroj (original source), better known abroad as Pilsner Urquell. A slightly sweeter beer, Budweiser Budvar is brewed 150 km (100 miles) south of Prague in the town of České Budějovice (in German, Budweis). The American Budweiser's first brewer adopted the name after a visit to Bohemia in the 19th century.

Budweiser logo

Pilsner Urquell logo

This higher percentage refers to the original gravity, not the alcohol content

Světlé means light

Alcohol content

Reading a Beer Label

The most prominent figure on the label (usually 10% or 12%) does not refer to the alcohol content. It is a Czech measure of original gravity, indicating the density of malt and other sugars used in the brew. The percentage of alcohol by volume is usually given in smaller type. The label also states whether it is a dark or a light beer.

BEER AND BEER HALLS

| Staropramen | Gambrinus | Velkopopovický kozel | Budweiser Budvar | Plzeňský prazdroj (Pilsner Urquell) |

The real place to enjoy Czech beer is a pub or beer hall *(pivnice)*. Each pub is usually supplied by a single brewery *(pivovar)*, so only one brand of beer is available, but several different types are on offer. The major brands include Plzeňské and Gambrinus from Plzeň, Staropramen from Prague, and Velkopopovické from Velké Popovice, south of Prague. The usual drink is draught light beer *(světlé)*, but a number of beer halls, including U Fleků *(see p155)* and U Kalicha *(see p154)* also serve special strong dark lagers (ask for *tmavé*). Another type you may encounter is *kozel,* a strong light beer like a German *bock.*

A half litre of beer (just under a pint) is called a *velké* (large), and a third of a litre (larger than a half pint) is called a *malé* (small). The waiters bring beers and snacks to your table and mark everything you eat and drink on a tab. In some pubs there is a tacit assumption that all the customers want to go on drinking until closing time, so don't be surprised if more beers arrive without your ordering them. If you don't want them, just say no. The bill is totted up when you leave.

People enjoying a drink in one of Prague's beer gardens

WINES

Czech wine producers have not yet emulated the success of other East European wine-makers. The main wine-growing region is in Moravia, where most of the best wine is produced for local consumption. Some wine is also made in Bohemia, around Mělník, just north of Prague. The whites are made mostly from Riesling, Müller-Thurgau or Veltliner grapes *(polosuché* is demi-sec and *suché* is sec). Rulandské (Pinot) is an acceptable dry white. The reds are slightly

Rulandské, white and red

better, the main choices being Frankovka and Vavřinecké. In the autumn, a semi-fermented young, sweet white wine called *burčák* is sold and drunk across the capital.

CZECH SPIRITS AND LIQUEURS

In every restaurant and pub you'll find Becherovka, a bitter-sweet, amber herbal drink served both as an aperitif and a liqueur. It can also be diluted with tonic. Other local drinks include Borovička, a juniper-flavoured spirit, and plum brandy or Slivovice. The latter is clear and strong and rather an acquired taste. Imported spirits and cocktails are more expensive.

Becherovka

Choosing a Restaurant

These restaurants have been selected across a wide price range for their good value or exceptional cuisine; they are listed area by area, starting with Old Town and moving on to restaurants further outside the city. The entries appear alphabetically within each price category, and any special features are indicated by the symbols.

PRICE CATEGORIES
These have been calculated to represent the cost of an avarage three-course meal for one, including half a bottle of wine, and all unavoidable charges.

Ⓚ Under Kč400
ⓀⓀ Kč400–700
Ⓚ ⓀⓀ Kč700–1000
ⓀⓀ ⓀⓀ Over Kč1000

OLD TOWN

Beas
Ⓚ

Týnská 19 Praha 1, Praha 1 **Tel** *60 80 35 727*   **Map** *3 C3*

Spartan, cheap and tremendously popular vegetarian curry house. Food is served on rather utilitarian trays, yet it is good, hotter than the Prague norm, and comes with free water to alleviate the effect of the spices. As cheap as they come, this place attracts rich, poor and anyone who likes real Indian food.

Bohemia Bagel
Ⓚ

Masná 2, Praha 1 **Tel** *22 48 12 560*   **Map** *3 C3*

The best breakfast deal in Prague is available from 7am until 11pm (weekends 8am–11pm) at this always-busy bagel shop and café. High-speed Internet is also provided at reasonable rates throughout the day. It's become so popular, that several other branches have opened around central Prague.

Country Life
Ⓚ

Melantrichova 15, Praha 1 **Tel** *22 42 13 366*   **Map** *3 B4*

This is part of the international group of vegetarian restaurants, but few others anywhere in the world can compete with its sublimely picturesque setting. It gets crowded at lunchtimes with vegetarians and non-vegetarians alike, all hungry to try their excellent sandwiches, salads, soups and desserts.

Ariana
ⓀⓀ

Rámová 6, Praha 1 **Tel** *22 23 23 438*   **Map** *3 C2*

A cosy room of Persian rugs, brass lamps and carved wood welcomes visitors at this intimate Afghan family restaurant. Spicy aromas precede the arrival of tender lamb dishes and zesty soups. Aside from curries and kebabs, the genial staff bring on specials that make use of delicate cabbage, split pea, aubergine, minced mutton and yogurt.

Chez Marcel
ⓀⓀ

Haštalská 12, Praha 1 **Tel** *22 23 15 676*   **Map** *3 C2*

Chez Marcel is a touch of real France in the centre of Prague. This is where business people and students alike come for regional *plats du jour*, as well as steak *au poivre*, fresh mussels and probably the best French fries in the city. Surprisingly for such a good establishment, the food is reasonably priced.

Dahab
ⓀⓀ

Dlouhá 33, Praha 1 **Tel** *22 48 27 375*   **Map** *3 C3*

Right in the heart of the Old Town, Dahab is perhaps the only place in Prague where you can puff on a genuine *hookah* pipe after your meal. The combination of tearoom, patisserie, café and restaurant works well, and it has a nice selection of Middle Eastern dishes, including several vegetarian options.

Klub Architektů
ⓀⓀ

Betlémské náměstí 5A, Praha 1 **Tel** *22 44 01 214*   **Map** *3 B4*

This hidden jewel is tucked away in a warren of tunnels and arches, reached through a discreet courtyard close to the Bethlehem Chapel. The servings are hearty which is unusual for an inexpensive Prague dining room. The menu includes a good, varied vegetarian selection.

Kogo Pizzeria & Caffeteria
ⓀⓀ

Havelská 27, Praha 1 **Tel** *22 42 14 543*   **Map** *3 C4*

With its motto "taste the passion", it's clear that Kogo has set out to become Old Town's bellwether of style. Its clean, modern interior, sharp staff and Mediterranean menu attract a crowd that could have spilled from a glossy fashion magazine. Big, zesty salads, soups and starters precede the excellent seafood and pasta mains.

Kolkovna
ⓀⓀ

V kolkovně 8, Praha 1 **Tel** *22 48 19 701*   **Map** *3 C3*

Very good, authentic Czech dishes and excellent beer served from giant tanks combine the best attributes of a great Czech pub. The waiters can be a little standoffish, especially if you turn up on a crowded night without a reservation. The downstairs area is completely non-smoking.

Key to Symbols *see back cover flap*

Pizza Nuovo

Revoluční 1, Praha 1 **Tel** *22 18 03 308*

Map 4 D2

This informal pizzeria offers the city's best all-you-can-eat antipasti buffet of fresh fish, meats, cheese and salads. The thin-crust pizza is arguably the best in town. Pizza Diavolo – with spicy pepperoni and mozzarella – is worth the trip alone. The back room has a large play area that's perfect for families with small children.

Restaurace Století

Karoliny Světlé 21, Praha 1 **Tel** *22 22 20 008*

Map 3 A4

Arched ceilings, sepia prints and old china all evoke a gentler era in this quiet, intimate restaurant. The menu is inspired by the famous of yesteryear; for example, you can order a Marlene Dietrich (stuffed avocado with whipped Roquefort and marzipan) or an Al Capone (roast chicken leg with hot salsa and papaya).

Angel

V kolkovně 7, Praha 1 **Tel** *77 32 22 422*

Map 3 C3

Angel brings a burst of style and Asian fusion tastes to Prague without pretentious attitude or budget-busting prices. Veteran expat chef Sofia Smith has conceived the menu in this modernist, golden-hued dining room. Great-value lunches mix local dishes with exotic accents. The decadent desserts are a house speciality.

Red, Hot and Blues

Jakubská 12, Praha 1 **Tel** *22 23 14 639*

Map 3 C3

This popular Cajun-style restaurant was one of the first expat restaurants to open after the 1989 revolution and it's still going strong. Catering mainly to a rowdy mix of residents and tourists, the theme is French Quarter New Orleans and the menu is a fusion of southern US cooking, burgers and Tex-Mex. Live music some evenings.

Seven Angels

Jilská 20, Praha 1 **Tel** *22 42 34 381*

Map 3 B4

There has been a restaurant on this spot since the 13th century, but whatever the changes of management have been since then, Seven Angels remains one of the most charming, small dining rooms in Central Europe. The house speciality is traditional Bohemian cuisine, with a particular focus on game. A lively folk band plays Wed–Sun evenings.

Staroměstská

Staroměstské náměstí 19, Praha 1 **Tel** *22 42 32 534*

Map 3 C3

Housed in a medieval building in the heart of the Old Town Square, this popular restaurant has been an inn for over 50 years. Its classic Czech cuisine can be paired with the famous Pilsner beers. A small selection of Czech and other wines is also available. In summer, the outside tables offer a great view of the busy square (prices are higher though).

Amici Miei

Vězeňská 5, Praha 1 **Tel** *22 48 16 688*

Map 3 C2

A respected enclave for outstanding, authentic Italian cuisine, this small, romantic dining room features warm but slightly formal service from knowledgeable staff. From salad with langoustines and mango to classic Mediterranean seafood such as salt cod, the food is consistently excellent. Great Italian wines and seductive sweets.

Bellevue

Smetanovo nábřeží 2, Praha 1 **Tel** *22 22 21 443*

Map 3 A5

Situated by the river, Bellevue has a stunning view of the castle. The interior is an Art Deco triumph, all inlaid wood walls and marble floors. The menu includes Antipodean delicacies such as carpaccio of venison with truffle oil, which is yet to be seen on any other menu in Prague.

Francouzská Restaurace

Náměstí Republiky 5, Praha 1 **Tel** *22 20 02 770*

Map 4 D3

This fantastically ornate Art Nouveau restaurant is set in Prague's Municipal House. Service is formal, the wine list is impressive and the French cuisine has won a handful of awards from the Czech Republic's major food critics. Sunday jazz brunches win over guests with tender rosemary lamb and homemade sorbets.

La Provence

Štupartská 9, Praha 1 **Tel** *296 82 61 55*

Map 3 C3

Run by the Kampa Group, this upmarket French restaurant has an authentic (and slightly cheaper) brasserie on the ground floor and a cosy, countrified Provençal restaurant downstairs. It's an ideal spot for a romantic candlelit dinner but evening reservations are recommended.

Mlýnec

Novotného lávka 9, Praha 1 **Tel** *22 10 82 208*

Map 3 A4

Mlýnec has a stunning view out over Charles Bridge and an imaginative menu that includes both Czech staples like roast duck as well as more adventurous Asian and Japanese-inspired dishes such as mixed-fish tempura. Expect to pay a lot but the setting and food make it worthwhile.

U Modré Růže (The Blue Rose)

Rytířská 16, Praha 1 **Tel** *22 42 25 873*

Map 3 B4

There's something for everyone on the Czech and international menu of this upscale but very much underground restaurant, with beef, lamb, game, seafood and vegetarian dishes all vying for space. The setting is certainly unique, in beautifully restored 14th–15th-century catacombs.

JEWISH QUARTER

U Sádlů
Klimentská 2, Praha 1 **Tel** *22 48 13 874*   **Map** *4 D2*

The rather kitsch aspects of this medieval-themed restaurant are achieved with much aplomb. Every dish has a thematic name, including several under the heading "Meat from an Apocalyptic Piglet!" Cheerful staff, and a lively crowd most evenings make this a good choice for small groups of friends.

King Solomon
Široká 8, Praha 1 **Tel** *22 48 18 752*   **Map** *3 B3*

The light, pleasant interior of the King Solomon, in the heart of the Jewish Quarter, extends to its winter garden. The food is impeccably prepared and presented, complemented by kosher wines from the Czech Republic and beyond. They also deliver special Shabbat meals to hotels throughout Prague.

Le Café Colonial
Široká 6, Praha 1 **Tel** *22 48 18 322*   **Map** *3 B3*

A classy French-style place near Old Town's busy pedestrian streets, this local favourite succeeds with African and Asian decor and bold colours. There's a lively café on one side, with a full-on dining room on the other. The cuisine ranges from light spring rolls to exotic curries and seafood steaks. Cocktails are as popular as the select French wines.

Les Moules
Pařížská 19, Praha 1 **Tel** *22 23 15 022*   **Map** *3 B2*

Czechs claim otherwise, but some of the best beer in Prague is served here, and it's Belgian, not Bohemian. What really brings in the crowds though are the pots of tasty, steaming fresh mussels, flown in daily from Belgium. Other treats on the menu include young tender racks of lamb cooked in beer.

Barock
Pařížská 24, Praha 1 **Tel** *22 23 29 221*   **Map** *3 B2*

An eclectic and excellent range of modern European and Japanese cuisine is served by efficient staff in this perennially fashionable restaurant. But it's not merely a trendy venue – the food really is authentic, and more than up to international standards. Popularity means you should reserve a table to be sure of getting in.

La Bodeguita del Medio
Kaprova 5, Praha 1 **Tel** *22 48 13 922*   **Map** *3 B3*

Papa Hemingway stares down at diners enjoying seafood and Creole delights at this eclectic place. Once dinner is over in the downstairs restaurant, you can then head upstairs to enjoy original and classic cocktails and a great selection of Havana cigars until the early hours.

La Degustation (Boheme Bourgeoise)
Haštalská 18, Praha 1 **Tel** *22 23 11 234*   **Map** *3 C2*

Using ingredients from around Europe and combining it with traditional Czech dishes, this restaurant offers one of the most intriguing dining experiences in Prague with a choice of three, seven-course taster menus. Dishes range from ravioli filled with lobster and prawn in vanilla sauce to Argentinean organic entrecôte with foie gras parfait.

Pravda
Pařížská 17, Praha 1 **Tel** *22 23 26 203*   **Map** *3 B2*

A wonderful blend of old and new encompassing elegant gilt-and-white dining rooms and waiters in chic uniforms, Pravda will tempt the diner with its Asian- and Scandinavian-inspired fare. This includes relatively expensive seafood dishes such as Cajun crawfish and poached cod. The desserts are excellent.

PRAGUE CASTLE AND HRADČANY

Peklo (Hell)
Strahovské nádvoří 1, Praha 1 **Tel** *22 05 16 652*   **Map** *1 B4*

Peklo is near the Strahov Monastery, which belongs to the order of the Premonstratensians. They've been keeping wine in the cellars here since the 14th century. The restaurant offers fine Czech and international cuisine and, as you may expect, a fabulous array of wines.

Palffy Palace Restaurant
Valdštejnská 14, Praha 1 **Tel** *25 75 30 522*   **Map** *2 E2*

Enter at Valdštejnská 14, then climb the stone staircase to this wonderfully alternative restaurant, in what feels like an aristocrat's private rooms. Soft melodies seep through the walls from a musical academy on the premises, providing the perfect accompaniment to a regularly changing menu.

Key to Price Guide *see p202* **Key to Symbols** *see back cover flap*

LITTLE QUARTER

Café de Paris

Maltézské náměstí 4, Praha 1 **Tel** *60 31 60 718*   **Map** *2 E4*

This exceedingly cosy French-style café has a small but excellent value French menu and a very good wine list. The entrecôte steak here is served with a special "Café de Paris" sauce made from a secret recipe. The location, on a quiet square in the Little Quarter, is ideal.

Café Savoy

Vítězná 12, Praha 1 **Tel** *25 73 11 562*   **Map** *2 E5*

The setting here is the real selling point – a stunningly restored 19th-century coffee house just across the river from the National Theatre. The menu offers a good mix of Czech classics and international dishes. Rare for Prague, there's also a big and inventive breakfast menu. Open all day. Reservations recommended for dinner.

Cantina

Újezd 38, Praha 1 **Tel** *25 73 17 173*   **Map** *2 E5*

Everything is super-sized here, from the enormous margaritas to the massive portions of good value Tex-Mex food. All the usual favourites are on the menu, including super *burritos* and authentic tacos. The usual Czech problem of "not spicy enough" persists; ask for extra spices if you like hot food. Reservations required.

Mount Steak

Josefská 1, Praha 1 **Tel** *25 75 32 652*   **Map** *2 E3*

Very much a place for meat-lovers only, this restaurant offers over 60 different steaks, including boar, venison, kangaroo, shark and ostrich. All are cooked as you wish, either roasted on the bone or grilled, and served with hearty portions of potatoes and vegetables. Good side salads too.

Nebozízek (Little Auger)

Petřínské sady 411, Praha 1 **Tel** *25 73 15 329*   **Map** *2 D5*

During spring and summer, the outdoor patio at this renowned restaurant half-way up the Petřín funicular is very popular, offering wonderful views of Old and New Town. Inside, it is cosy and elegant. The menu is diverse, with seafood, Chinese and Czech dishes, steaks and more.

Sushi Bar

Zborovská 49, Praha 1 **Tel** *60 32 44 882*   **Map** *2 F5*

Sushi in Prague is often a disappointment but this stylish and contemporary locally run establishment is an exception. The mostly Czech chefs here have laboured hard to recreate Japanese sushi and sashimi classics, and the effort shows. Be sure to book ahead, since the dining room is small and has just a few tables.

U Patrona

Dražického náměstí 4, Praha 1 **Tel** *25 75 30 725*   **Map** *2 F3*

A leading culinary light for years, U Patrona still advances the standard on Prague's Left Bank, with an insistence on quality and old-world style. The cuisine focuses on traditional Czech fare, with boar, duck, lamb and beef taking starring roles, along with comforting soups. Book ahead to secure one of the two balcony tables.

U Tří Pštrosů (At the Three Ostriches)

Dražického náměstí 12, Praha 1 **Tel** *25 72 88 888*   **Map** *2 E3*

The dining room of At The Three Ostriches is somewhat reminiscent of a Bavarian hunting lodge, but the cuisine is 100 per cent bona-fide Czech. Adventurous diners may wish to try their ostrich specialities of goulash and hare with cream sauce and strawberry garnish, while there are simpler but equally good dishes for the less brave.

Cowboys

Nerudova 40, Praha 1 **Tel** *29 68 26 107*   **Map** *2 D3*

This is a sprawling complex of bars and dining rooms, serving slightly overpriced but always enjoyable steaks and seafood against a lavishly eccentric decor. The upper terrace, however, affords diners one of the best views of central Prague and fills up quickly in spring and summer. Reservations needed.

David

Tržiště 21, Praha 1 **Tel** *25 75 33 109*   **Map** *2 E3*

It's a steep incline up a cobblestone lane to David, but gourmets will find it worth the exertion. The set lunch is a serious two to three hour affair, with an interesting selection of Czech, European and New World wines on offer with which to wash down the supreme and intense flavours.

Kampa Park

Na Kampě 8b, Praha 1 **Tel** *29 68 26 112*   **Map** *2 F4*

The most famous contemporary restaurant in Prague, Kampa Park has been playing host to the great and good for many years. If you want to impress someone, then this is the place to come, if you can get a reservation. The fusion cuisine is mildly adventurous and always good.

U Malířů (At the Painter's)

Maltézské náměstí 11, Praha 1 **Tel** *25 75 30 318*　　　　　　　　**Map** *2 E4*

Established in 1543, this old-world inn has seen many changes over the years, most recently with the move to drop its traditional French menu. It now offers Central European game dishes and more Czech wines to counter the pricey French ones.

NEW TOWN

Himalaya 🏃 ♿　　　　　　⊗

Soukenická 2, Praha 1 **Tel** *23 33 53 594*　　　　　　　　**Map** *4 D2*

Authentic Bengali food in an unpretentious, casual two-level room translates into an affordable, spicy and appealing menu. Curries, vindaloo, vegetarian delights and tropical flavours are accompanied by friendly (if not the world's fastest) service. The result draws a following of local patrons who invariably enjoy eating and conversing for hours.

Jáma 　　　　　　⊗

V jámě 7, Praha 1 **Tel** *22 42 22 383*　　　　　　　　**Map** *5 C1*

Popular lunchtime spot serving great burgers – probably the city's best – and *burritos* to office workers and tourists alike. The evenings are very lively, when this becomes one of the city's top drinking spots, and getting a table can be difficult without a reservation. There's a small terrace at the rear.

Radost FX Café 🎵 🏃 ♿　　　　　⊗

Bělehradská 120, Praha 1 **Tel** *22 42 54 776*　　　　　　　　**Map** *6 E2*

Decent vegetarian food and a trendy, club-like atmosphere has won Radost FX a good local following for many years. There are three main dining areas – two at the back and a smaller café towards the street. Service can be slow on busy nights. A 15 per cent mandatory service charge is added to the bill.

Beograd 📋　　　　　⊗⊗

Vodičkova 5, Praha 1 **Tel** *22 49 12 084*　　　　　　　　**Map** *5 C1*

For years there was a Serb restaurant on this patch, and though the latest incarnation is pure Czech, the owners have kept the old name out of respect for the past. Somewhat more upmarket than the average Czech hostelry, prices are perhaps higher than the norm. The food is good, however, with game featured on the menu.

Buffalo Bill's 🏃 📋　　　　　⊗⊗

Vodičkova 9, Praha 1 **Tel** *22 49 48 624*　　　　　　　　**Map** *5 C1*

Quite the sensation when it opened in 1993, Buffalo Bill's Wild West-memorabilia covered cellar still draws locals, expat and tourists alike with its great mixture of Tex-Mex dishes and its wide range of ribs and wings from the American grill. Definitely child-friendly, with some of the best waiting staff in town.

Café Restaurant Louvre 🏃 📋 🖼　　　　⊗⊗

Národní třída 22, Praha 1 **Tel** *22 49 30 949*　　　　　　　　**Map** *3 B5*

An excellent place for a late and lazy breakfast on the terrace, Louvre has been in business since the early 1900s. A full restaurant menu of Czech and European cuisine, they also have an excellent selection of cakes, pastries and coffees. There's a smart billiards room on the premises.

Hotel Evropa Café 🏃 🖼　　　　⊗⊗

Václavské náměstí 25, Praha 1 **Tel** *22 42 15 387*　　　　　　　　**Map** *3 C5*

The café that remains perenially popular is an Art Nouveau classic, even if it is now slightly shabby around the edges. Still a favourite with the Prague literati, it simply oozes character, and the small terrace is one of the city's most popular. The food is distinctly average, but that is not why people come here.

Marie Teresie 📋　　　　⊗⊗

Na Příkopě 23, Praha 1 **Tel** *22 42 29 869*　　　　　　　　**Map** *3 C4*

A fluorescently lit shopping arcade is left behind on entering this spacious cellar restaurant, named after an Austrian Habsburg princess, who spent a great deal of time in these parts. The fare is traditional Czech, served with a silver service flourish. You can feel like royalty for very little money.

U Fleků 　　　　⊗⊗

Křemencova 11, Praha 1 **Tel** *22 49 34 019*　　　　　　　　**Map** *5 B1*

They've been brewing beer here for some 500 years, and that's a real draw to the legions of tourist coaches that pull up here nightly. That said, it's a convivial sort of tourist trap, with decent and affordable Czech food, excellent beer and the occasional sing-along – the language depending on the nationality of the tourist groups there.

U Pinkasů 🖼　　　⊗⊗

Jungmannovo nám. 16, Praha 1 **Tel** *22 11 11 150*　　　　　　　　**Map** *3 C5*

This has been a cheap and great value Czech beer hall since 1843. The food is simple but hearty, making this a very popular lunchtime destination. There are three levels: a traditional beerhouse in the basement, a bar area for light meals and snacks on the ground floor, and a more formal dining room upstairs.

Key to Price Guide *see p202* **Key to Symbols** *see back cover flap*

Café Imperial

Na Poříčí 15, Praha 1 **Tel** *24 60 11 440*

Map 4 D3

A long-needed renovation in 2007–8 restored this café to its early 20th-century Art Nouveau splendour. This is the perfect place to try local specialities like braised beef in cream sauce or veal schnitzel with mashed potatoes, in a setting that borders on theatrical.

U Kalicha (At the Chalice)

Na bojišti 12–14, Praha 1 **Tel** *22 49 12 557*

Map 6 D2

The look of this restaurant, including its cartooned walls, is based on the famous Czech novel *The Good Soldier Švejk*. Author Jaroslav Hašek set some of his novel's pivotal scenes here. Traditional Czech cuisine is available at prices aimed more at Western tourist budgets.

Zahrada v opeře

Legerova 75, Praha 1 **Tel** *22 42 39 685*

Map 6 E1

This clean, light, modern space off the top of Wenceslas Square features some of the city's top chefs, who excel at fusion food and creative conceptions. From exotic soups and interesting salads to delicate carpaccios, terrines and foie gras, the menu is as fresh and enticing as the design. Hard to find, so look for the restaurant's signs.

Zvonice

Jindřišská věž, Praha 1 **Tel** *22 42 20 009*

Map 4 D4

Installed in a Gothic belltower, circa 1518, and with the St Maria bell still intact, this unusual restaurant occupies the top three floors. It offers traditional Czech fare, with a strong emphasis on game dishes in hearty sauces. Meats are robust and tender, and local wines complement them well. Service does not always keep up but is improving.

Cicala

Žitná 43, Praha 1 **Tel** *22 22 10 375*

Map 5 C1

Cicala is a family run trattoria serving hearty Italian food. The extensive menu is divided into antipasti, pasta and meat courses and features simple but comforting dishes such as home-made spaghetti with garlic and chilli as well as more sophisticated offerings such as veal with white wine, sage and Parma ham. Service is friendly and informal.

FURTHER AFIELD

Žlutá Pumpa

Belgická 11, Praha 2 **Tel** *60 81 84 360*

This popular neighbourhood pub with street-side tables and friendly service is an affordable find and a great place to mix with locals. Try traditional Central European dishes, from schnitzel to goulash, with much-loved Bohemian lager, or take a chance on Czech conceptions of Mexican food. The setting is relaxed and low-key.

Ambiente

Mánesova 59, Praha 3 **Tel** *22 27 27 851*

Map 6 E1

This eclectic restaurant, which features everything from American Southwestern to Italian cuisine, is renowned for its salads, and probably serves the best Caesar salad in Prague. After a filling meal, take a stroll along handsome Mánesova, one of the prettiest streets in upscale Vinohrady.

Mozaika

Nitranská 13, Praha 3 **Tel** *22 42 53 011*

A bit out of the centre but worth seeking out, this neighbourhood favourite offers great value and outstanding service in a casual setting. The menu features lunch specials such as duck with orange sauce, and monkfish with vegetable lasagne. Veal and beef are particularly well executed. The wine list and outdoor tables add to the appeal.

Roca

Vinohradská 32, Praha 2 **Tel** *22 25 20 060*

This comfortable, friendly Italian restaurant will make you feel right at home with enticing seafood and pasta dishes, good wines and appetizing starters. Shellfish are a speciality, and the service is notoriously slick. Outside tables add to the charm on warm evenings, and make the most of the quiet Vinohrady district street.

U Marčanů

Veleslavínská 14, Praha 6 **Tel** *23 53 60 623*

Folk music, dancing and singing every night make this a favourite of visitors to Prague. A taxi-ride from the city centre, it is a pleasant villa in a residential area serving real Czech food to diners seated at long tables, enjoying huge portions and even bigger glasses of beer. Good times guaranteed. You will need to make a reservation.

Aromi

Mánesova 78, Praha 1 **Tel** *22 27 13 222*

Map 6 E1

One of Prague's finest Italian restaurants, Aromi offers an authentic taste of Italy in simple surroundings. The cream and brown decor is restrained and the atmosphere relaxed. Specialities here are seafood and pasta and there are also excellent wines from around the world. Not cheap but good value.

Pubs, Beer Halls and Bars

Prague suits practically everyone's taste, from sophisticated cocktail bars to traditional Czech cellar pubs. A new breed of pub, the themed Irish, English or sports bar, caters to the large number of young English men who travel to Prague on so-called stag weekends. The real charm of drinking in Prague is that it's possible to stroll around the Old Town and find places to drink and fraternize with Czechs and expatriates alike, regardless of the time. If you sit at an empty table, don't be surprised if others join you. In traditional Czech pubs a waiter will automatically bring more beer as soon as you appear close to finishing, unless you indicate otherwise. It pays to expect the unexpected in Prague – in some supposedly upmarket places, the waiters' attitude can be surly and unhelpful, while in the humblest pub you may find service to be efficient and courteous.

TRADITIONAL PUBS AND BEER HALLS

Traditionally, Czech pubs either serve food or are large beer halls dedicated to the mass consumption of beer. The words *hostinec* and *hospoda* used to indicate a pub with food, whereas a *pivnice* served only beer, but over time the distinctions have faded.

Recommended for the brave, **U Zlatého tygra** (The Golden Tiger) is a loud Czech literati pub, wall-to-wall with, mostly male, regulars. (This is where the Czech president, Vaclav Havel took Bill Clinton to show him local beer culture.) **U Fleků** has brewed its unique beer, Flekovské, since 1499. For authenticity, and Budvar, try **U Medvídků** which is not far away from the National Theatre *(see pp156–7)* and the Old Town Square. **U Vejvodů** is a former traditional Czech pub which has embraced tourism, with large tables and waiters who understand English. You lose something in authenticity but the beer is good, the food decent and there's usually a place to sit. The traditional *hospoda* scarcely comes more so than **U Pinkasů**, hidden behind Wenceslas Square in a quaint courtyard.

COCKTAIL BARS

Prague now has almost more cocktail bars than you could shake a swizzle stick at, but there are some that stand out. On Pařížská, Prague's Fifth Avenue, you'll find **Bugsy's**. This bar has even printed their own cocktail bible, though towards the end of the week it does become somewhat overtaken by burly men in long coats. That fate has yet to befall the neighbouring **Barock**, a cocktail bar and restaurant with a noticeably chic clientele. Nearby **Tretters** combines smart looks with a slightly more down-to-earth attitude.

IRISH PUBS AND THEME BARS

Prague now has theme bars in all shapes and sizes, with still the most common being the ubiquitous Irish pub. **Caffreys** is one of Prague's most popular – and pricier – Irish bars, located off the Old Town Square. **Rocky O'Reilly's** is the biggest Irish pub in town, and a rowdy place, packed to the rafters if there is a big football match on the television. **Jáma** is a lively pub with great bar food that serves Prague's best burger, among other attributes. Just a stone's throw away from Charles Bridge is possibly the only Irish-Cuban hybrid pub anywhere, the noisy and fun **O'Che's**.

There is karaoke at **Molotow Cocktail Bar**, while **La Casa Blu** is a South American bar where the Chilean, Peruvian, Mexican and Czech staff create a carnival-type atmosphere.

BOHEMIAN HANGOUTS

Not only in the geographical heart of Bohemia, these bars also represent the unconventional side of Prague citylife. **Al Capone's** is one of the most famous, not to say notorious, drinking dens in the Old Town, host to a parade of visitors and locals. **Chapeau Rouge** is a rowdy college joint that is a guaranteed all-nighter, with a street-level bar that's loads of fun and a downstairs club that's hopping most of the night. Over the Vltava in the Castle district you'll find **U Malého Glena** which translates roughly to "at Little Glen's", and is one of the longest surviving expatriate bars in the city. Not far away is **Jo's Bar & Garáž**, which has also stood the test of time as an expat hangout. It's a small, cavernous pub, Mexican eatery and disco, and becomes quickly packed. Over in Žižkov **Hapu** is a great neighbourhood bar with a cool but laid-back vibe.

SPORTS BARS

Sports bars have taken off in Prague, with places like **Legends**, a long, polished cellar bar with a deck of TV screens. The Wenceslas Square area is home to two popular places: **The Lions** and **Zlatá Hvězda**.

CAFÉ SOCIETY

The city is embedded in café society, ranging from old-fashioned smoky joints to cafés within bookstores, boutiques and billiard halls. Some are restaurants, others focus on drinking, but all serve alcohol. **Lávka** has the finest setting in the city. Situated at the foot of the Charles Bridge, it offers a great view of the castle. Other places to see and be seen are **Ebel** in the Old Town and **Slavia**, by the river opposite the National Theatre. For a perfect meeting place, try the **Grand Café Praha** opposite the clock tower in Old Town Square. **Globe** café and bookstore is a legend amongst Prague's expat community and serves the best cappuccino.

DIRECTORY

TRADITIONAL PUBS AND BEER HALLS

Kolkovna
Vítězná 7.
Map 2 E5.
Tel 25 15 11 080.
www.kolkovna.cz

The Beer House
PIVOVARSKÝ DŮM
Lípová 15.
Map 5 C2.
Tel 29 62 16 666. www.
gastroinfo.cz/pivodum

The Black Bull
U ČERNÉHO VOLA
Loretánské nám 1.
Map 1 B3.
Tel 22 05 13 481.

The Golden Tiger
U ZLATÉHO TYGRA
Husova 17.
Map 3 B4.
Tel 22 22 21 111.
www.uzlatehotygra.cz

The Shot Out Eye
U VYSTŘELENÝHO OKA
U Božích bojovníků 3.
Tel 22 62 78 714.

Trilobit
Palackého 15.
Map 3 C5.
Tel 22 49 46 065.
www.restauracetrilobit.cz

U Fleků
Křemencova 11.
Map 5 B1.
Tel 22 49 34 019.
www.ufleku.cz

U Kalicha
Na Bojišti 12–14.
Map 6 D3.
Tel 29 61 89 600.
www.ukalicha.cz

U Medvídků
Na Perštýně 7.
Map 3 B5.
Tel 22 42 11 916.
www.umedvidku.cz

U Pinkasů
Jungmannovo náměstí 15/16.
Map 3 C5.
Tel 22 11 11 150.
www.upinkasu.cz

U Vejvodů
Jilská 4.
Map 3 B4.
Tel 22 42 19 999.
www.restauraceu
vejvodu.cz

COCKTAIL BARS

Bar Bar
Všehrdova 17.
Map 2 E5.
Tel 25 73 12 246.
www.bar-bar.cz

Barock
Pařížská 24.
Map 3 B2.
Tel 22 23 29 221.
www.barockrestaurant.cz

Bugsy's
Pařížská 10. **Map** 3 B2.
Tel 22 48 10 287.
www.bugsysbar.cz

Cheers
Belgická 42. **Map** 6 F3.
Tel 22 25 13 108.
www.cheers-restaurant.cz

Tretters
V Kolkovně 3.
Map 3 C5.
Tel 22 48 11 165
www.tretters.cz

Ultramarin
Ostrovní 32. **Map** 3 B5.
Tel 22 49 32 249.
www.ultramarin.cz

Zanzibar
Lázeňská 6. **Map** 2 E4.
Tel 60 27 80 076.

IRISH PUBS AND THEME BARS

Caffreys
Staroměstské nám. 10.
Map 3 B3.
Tel 22 48 28 031.
www.caffreys.cz

George & Dragon
Staroměstské nám. 11.
Map 3 B3.
Tel 22 23 26 137.
www.georgeanddragon
prague.com

Jáma
V jámě 7. **Map** 5 C1.
Tel 22 42 22 383.
www.jamapub.cz

J.J. Murphy's
Tržiště 4. **Map** 2 E3.
Tel 25 75 35 575.
www.jjmurphys.cz

La Casa Blu
Kozí 15.
Map 3 C2.
Tel 22 48 18 270.
www.lacasablu.cz

Molly Malone's
U Obecního dvora 4.
Map 4 D3.
Tel 22 4 8 18 851.
www.mollymalones.cz

Molotow Cocktail Bar
Karlovo náměstí 31.
Map 5 B2.
Tel 60 32 51 275.
www.molotow.cz

O'Che's
Liliová 14. **Map** 3 C3.
Tel 22 22 21 178.
www.oches.com

Rocky O'Reilly's
Štěpánská 32. **Map** 3 A5.
Tel 22 22 31 060.
www.rockyoreillys.cz

BOHEMIAN HANGOUTS

Al Capone's
Bartolomějská 3.
Map 3 B5
Tel 22 4 2 12 192.
www.alcapone.cz

Chapeau Rouge
Jakubská 2. **Map** 3 C3.
Tel 22 23 16 328.
www.chapeaurouge.cz

Duende
Karolíny Světlé 30.
Map 3 A4.
Tel 77 51 86 077.
www.barduende.cz

Hapu
Orlická 8, Prague 3.
Tel 22 27 20 158.

Jet Set
Radlická 1, Prague 5.
Tel 25 73 27 251.
www.jetset.cz

Jo's Bar & Garáž
Malostranské nám 7.
Map 2 E3.
Tel 25 75 30 162.
www.josbar.cz

Merlin
Bělehradská 68A.
Map 6 E2.
Tel 22 25 22 054.
www.merlin-pub.cz

Mu Kafé
Mánesova 87.
Map 6 F1.
Tel 60 89 59 883.
www.mukafe.cz

U Malého Glena
Karmelitská 23.
Map 2 E4.
Tel 25 75 31 717.
www.malyglen.cz

SPORTS BARS

Legends
Týn 1. **Map** 3 C3.
Tel 22 48 95 404.
www.legends.cz

Sportbar Sparta ve Slavii
Smetanovo nábř. 1012/2.
Map 3 A5.
Tel 22 42 18 493.

The Lions
Krakovská 19. **Map** 6 D1.
Tel 72 02 16 204.
www.thelionsbar.cz

Zlatá Hvězda
Ve smečkách 12.
Map 6 D1.
Tel 29 62 22 292.
www.sportbar.cz

CAFÉ SOCIETY

Café Imperial
Na Poříčí 15. **Map** 4 D3.
Tel 24 60 11 440.

Ebel
Řetězova 9. **Map** 3 B4.
Tel 22 22 22 018.
www.ebelcoffee.cz

Globe
Pštrossova 6. **Map** 5 A1.
Tel 22 49 34 203.
www.globebookstore.cz

Grand Café Praha
Staroměstské nám. 22.
Map 3 B3.
Tel 22 16 32 522.
www.grandcafe.cz

Hotel Evropa Café
Václavské náměstí 25.
Map 3 C5.
Tel 22 42 15 387.
www.evropahotel.cz

Slavia
Smetanovo nábř 2.
Map 3 A5.
Tel 22 42 18 493.
www.cafeslavia.cz

Nightlife

Nightlife in Prague is now as lively as in other European cities. A constant stream of visitors and a spirited local crowd has seen to that. Cheap drink, cutting-edge performers, liberal gambling and prostitution laws all help pull in the crowds. Prague is also now firmly established as a tour-stop for major American and UK pop and rock acts, with arenas such as the Tesla and O2 arenas playing host to big names at least once a month.

On a more local level, Prague's club scene is a proven testing ground for up-and-coming bands, and the dance/music events, which are heavily influenced by that of nearby Berlin, is renowned for being experimental. Prague's gay and lesbian scene is buzzing, and the local population is among the most tolerant in mainland Europe. For similar reasons, Prague is also now well known for its adult venues.

DISCOS AND NIGHTCLUBS

The biggest club in the city is the **Lucerna Music Bar**, which offers a varied programme – either live local bands or a DJ playing classic hits – in an unusual basement ballroom in the beautiful, but run down, Lucerna building. It fills up quickly however, so make sure you get there early. **Karlovy Lázně** is another large club, which sometimes has live bands. **Zlatý Strom** offers techno/house together with 1970s, 80s and 90s dance tunes until 5am in a spectacular medieval cellar setting.

The trendier clubs, more likely to be playing cutting-edge music, include **Celnice** and **Radost FX**, where the city's most affluent are attracted by a constant diet of house music and plush decor, together with **XT3** and **Kulturní dům Vltavská**. The **Double Trouble** is popular with visiting stag parties, which means it can get quite rowdy. For genuinely experimental and original hardcore house and techno music, the best place to go is **Roxy**, where sets are often accompanied by art house video projections. Roxy regularly hosts live rock bands, including a number of big named bands.

If it is cabaret you are after, try **Tingl Tangl**, a club well known for its lively transvestite shows.

ROCK AND POP CLUBS

Lovers of live rock music are well served in Prague. One school of thought feels that the anarchic influence of Prague's pioneering 1980s rock bands helped – however inadvertently – bring down the communist regime. There are today a large number of popular rock venues – generally small clubs and cafés – which host a variety of different groups. The indigenous scene continues to thrive – Prague's own rock bands play both their own compositions as well as cover versions of more famous numbers, many singing in English. Higher-profile, more internationally renowned Western bands play in Prague regularly, usually at the **Tesla Arena** or **O2 Arena** (see p223).

The **Rock Café** and the **UZI Rock Bar**, both very popular venues, offer regular concerts followed by discos. Other venues include the **Futurum Rock Club**, open till the early hours. **Palác Akropolis** in Žižkov is great for visiting foreign bands. The Lucerna Music Bar and Roxy also host regular bands.

JAZZ

The roots of jazz in Prague can be traced not only to the American tradition but also to the pre-war heyday of Prague's famous jazz players, such as Jaroslav Ježek. Even during the communist period, Prague was an internationally renowned centre of jazz, never failing to attract the biggest names. Dizzy Gillespie, Stan Getz, Duke Ellington and Buddy Rich all played in Prague during the 1960s and 1970s.

Today, Prague's many jazz clubs play all forms, from Dixieland to swing. One of the leading and most popular jazz venues in the city is the **Jazz Club Reduta**, which has daily jazz concerts at around 9pm. When former US President Bill Clinton asked his Czech counterpart Vaclav Havel if he could play some jazz during a state visit to Prague in January 1994, the Czech president took him to the Jazz Club Reduta. The popular **Metropolitan Jazz Club** focuses on tried and true but fun oldies. At the **AghaRTA Jazz Centrum**, you can hear a high standard of playing. **U Malého Glena** has regular live blues, jazz and funk, while **Metropol Music Club** serves delicious international cuisine with jazz, swing or blues every night from 9pm. For serious enthusiasts, the International Jazz Festival (see p52) during October attracts talent from all over the world. **Blues Sklep** is a relative newcomer to Prague's jazz scene and offers an inventive and much appreciated schedule, showcasing acts from jazz, blues and other genres.

GAY AND LESBIAN VENUES

With even mainstream clubs such as **Radost FX** and **Mecca** holding regular gay nights, it is no wonder that Prague is considered one of Europe's hottest gay destinations. The scene is liberal and diverse. Clubs are split into various categories, with **Termix** being a loud and lively disco, and always packed. **Drake's Club** is a less in-your-face venue, and popular with visitors, while the city's most famous gay venue, **Friends**, is a cocktail bar. Friends has a steady following among expat and local men who are less interested in cruising than in just having a drink with like-minded folks. Temple, a gay centre, features a bar, disco, sex shop and hotel on the same premises.

The website www.prague. gayguide.net is a valuable resource for all things gay in Prague, including gay-friendly hotels, guesthouses and groups and associations.

ADULT PRAGUE

Like it or not, Prague has seen itself become the sex tourism capital of Europe since 1989, a result of cheap beer and the mistaken assumption that prostitution in the Czech Republic is legal. The law is, in fact, deliberately opaque, though the country's liberal ministers are keen to remove all doubt from the law and fully legalise the practice. For the time being, the emphasis remains on tolerance, and visitors are free to indulge themselves at any number of what are known as "Relax Clubs". Some are more respectable than others, and many are tourist traps which should be avoided.

DIRECTORY

DISCOS AND NIGHTCLUBS

Celnice
V Celnici 4. **Map** 4 D3.
Tel 77 75 02 505.
www.clubcelnice.com

Double Trouble
Melantrichova 17.
Map 3 B4.
Tel 221 632 414.
www.doubletrouble.cz

Karlovy Lázně
Novotného lávka.
Map 3 A4.
Tel 222 220 502.
www.karlovylazne.cz

Kulturní dům Vltavská
Bubenská 1.
Tel 220 879 683.
www.vltavska.cz

La Fabrique
Uhelný trh 2. **Map** 3 B4.
Tel 224 233 137.
www.lafabrique.cz

Lucerna Music Bar
Vodičkova 36.
Map 3 C5
Tel 224 217 108.
www.musicbar.cz

Misch Masch
Veletržní 61, Praha 7.
Tel 603 272 227.
www.mischmasch.cz

Radost FX
Bělehradská 120.
Map 6 E2.
Tel 22 42 54 776.
www.radostfx.cz

Tingl Tangl
Karolíny Světlé 12.
Map 3 A5.
Tel 224 238 278.
www.tingltangl.cz

Újezd
Újezd 18.
Map 2 E5.
Tel 257 316 537.

XT3
Rokycanova 29,
Praha 3.
Tel 222 783 463.
www.xt3.cz

Zlatý Strom
Karlova 6.
Map 3 A4.
Tel 222 220 441.
www.zlatystrom.cz

ROCK AND POP CLUBS

Futurum Music Bar
Zborovská 7,
Praha 5.
Map 2 F5.
Tel 257 328 571.
www.musicbar.cz

Klub Lávka
Novotného lávka 1.
Map 3 A4.
Tel 22 10 82 299.
www.lavka.cz

Palác Akropolis
Kubelíkova 27.
Tel 296 330 911.
www.palacakropolis.cz

Rock Café
Národní 20.
Map 3 B5.
Tel 224 933 947.
www.rockcafe.cz

Roxy
Dlouhá 33. **Map** 3 C3.
Tel 224 826 296.
www.roxy.cz

Tesla Arena
See p223.

UZI Rock Bar
Legerova 44.
Map 6 D3.
Tel 777 637 989.
www.demon.barr.cz/uzi

JAZZ CLUBS

AghaRTA Jazz Club
Železná 16.
Map 3 C4.
Tel 222 211 275.
www.agharta.cz

Blues Sklep
Liliová 10.
Map 3 B4.
Tel 221 466 138.

Jazz Club Reduta
Národni 20.
Map 3 B5
Tel 224 933 487.
www.redutajazzclub.cz

Metropol Music Club
Na Poříčí 12.
Map 4 D3.
Tel 222 314 071.
www.
prahaentertainment.com

Metropolitan Jazz Club
Jungmannova 14.
Map 3 C5.
Tel 224 947 777.

U Malého Glena
Karmelitská 23.
Map 2 E4.
Tel 257 531 717.
www.malyglen.cz

USP Jazz Lounge
Michalská 9.
Map 3 B4.
Tel 603 551 680.
www.jazzlounge.cz

GAY AND LESBIAN VENUES

Club Stella
Lužická 10,
Praha 2.
Tel 224 257 869.

Drake's Club
Zborovská 50,
Praha 5.
Map 2 F5
Tel 257 326 828.
www.drakes.cz

Friends
Bartolmějska 11.
Map 3 B5.
Tel 226 211 920.
www.friends-prague.cz

Heaven
Gorazdova 11.
Map 5 A3.
Tel 224 921 282.

Temple
Seifertova 3,
Praha 3.
Tel 222 710 773.

Termix
Třebízského 4a
Tel 222 710 462.
www.club-termix.cz

Valentino
Vinohradská 40.
Map 6 F1.
Tel 22 25 13 491.
www.club-valentino.cz

SHOPPING IN PRAGUE

With its wide, pedestrianised streets, classy shopping malls, souvenir shops and antiques *bazars*, Prague is now established as one of Europe's leading shopping destinations. Almost all of the major US and Western European retailers have established outlets in the city, and since 1989's Velvet Revolution, the quality of goods manufactured in the Czech Republic – always good – has improved considerably. Most of Prague's best shopping areas

Bohemian crystal

are in the centre of the city, and you can spend a whole day just diving in and out of small speciality shops and large department stores. For a different shopping experience, the few traditional markets in the city offer everything from vegetables to fresh fruit and to imported Russian caviar, toys, clothes, furniture, Czech crafts, electrical spare parts and even second-hand cars. Larger out-of-town malls are now also springing up, and are proving to be very popular.

OPENING HOURS

Most of Prague's shops open from 9am to 6pm Monday to Saturday, although supermarkets are open till late. However, shops are often more flexible than that, as many rely almost entirely on tourists for their trade. The more expensive gift shops have adapted their opening hours to the needs of their Western customers and tourists, often opening at 10am and closing much later in the evening. Many also open on Sundays as well.

Food stores open earlier, most of them at 7am – reflecting the early working day of many locals – and close at around 7pm. A few shops also take a break for lunch, which can vary from any time between noon and 2pm. Department stores and the big shopping centres and malls also open early but tend to close later, often around 10pm. Some open on Sundays.

All the shops are at their most crowded on Saturdays and for stress-free shopping it's often better to wander around them during the week. Prague's markets are

The antique shop in Bridge Street in the Little Quarter

generally open early every weekday morning but have varied closing times.

HOW TO PAY

Most staple goods, such as food, are cheaper than comparable items in the West, as long as they do not need to be imported. However, with more and more multinationals, such as Boss and Pierre Cardin, moving into the city, prices are slowly starting to rise.

The total price of goods should always include Value Added Tax (this is 19 per cent of the total price, depending on what is being sold), although all food is exempt from

this. Cash payments can usually only be made in Czech crowns, though some shops now take Euros, albeit at extortionate exchange rates. Smaller shops appreciate it if you pay the exact amount and at times may refuse to accept banknotes of Kč1,000 and above. All major credit and charge cards are widely accepted *(see p230)*.

Global Refund is a programme for non-EU residents that allows tax-free shopping for purchases exceeding Kč2,000. When you make a purchase at a shop displaying the Global Refund sign, ask at the cash till for a tax-free cheque. On leaving the country, show your items, receipts and cheques to customs officials, who will stamp the cheques, and you will get your VAT back. For more details, go to the Global Refund website (www.globalrefund.com).

A set of Russian dolls available from one of the many street shops

SALES AND BARGAINS

Following the examples of the Western stores, sales are becoming more popular. As a result, it is now quite normal for clothes to be sold off cheaper at the end of each season. There is also an increasing number of post-Christmas sales in the shops found around Old Town Square, Wenceslas Square, Na Příkopě and 28. října.

If you want vegetables, fruit, meat or other perishable produce, buy them at the beginning of the day, when the best quality goods are still on sale. There is no point in waiting till the end of the day in the hope of getting bargains, as is the case in Western shops that reduce prices to get rid of perishable items.

WHERE TO SHOP

Most of Prague's best shops are conveniently located in the city centre, especially in and around Wenceslas Square, though the souvenir shops lining Nerudova on the way up to the castle are also well worth your time. Many of these shopping areas have been pedestrianised, making for leisurely window-shopping, although they can get rather crowded. There are a number of department stores which sell an eclectic range of Czech and Western items, with more opening all the time. The best-known department store, **Kotva** (The Anchor), lies in the centre of the city. It was built in 1975

and its four storeys offer a wide range of Western goods, particularly fashion and electronics, with the bonus of an underground car park. But compared to Western department stores, Kotva has a smaller selection of goods than you may be accustomed to, and is now struggling to compete with the newer and more glamorous **Palladium** shopping mall (*see p217*) across the street. Prices for some of the more luxurious items on sale, such as perfumes, can often be equivalent to the Western ones.

Another popular store is **Tesco**. This has a good selection of Czech and Western products in a bland 1970s building in the centre of town. The city's oldest department store is **Bílá Labut'** (The White Swan) in Na Poříčí. It was opened shortly before the occupation of Czechoslovakia in 1939 and was the first building in Prague to have an escalator. It has since fallen on hard times and its future as a department store is uncertain.

Debenhams, another famous name from Western Europe, recently opened an enormous store on Wenceslas Square, and its home furnishings department on the third floor is very popular with locals.

The outskirts of Prague are now home to massive shopping parks, with large hypermarkets. Tesco has a huge branch at Zličín (at the end of metro line B), next to the equally enormous **IKEA**.

DIRECTORY

DEPARTMENT STORES

Bílá Labut'
Na Poříčí 23.
Map 4 E3.
Tel 224 811 364.

Debenhams
Václavské nám. 21.
Map 4 D5.
Tel 221 015 047.

Kotva
Václavské nám. 58.
Map 6 D1.
Tel 224 217 005.

Kotva
Nám. Republiky 8.
Map 4 D3.
Tel 224 237 503.

Marks & Spencer
Na Příkopě 19/21.
Map 3 C4.
Tel 224 235 735.

Tesco
Národní 26.
Map 3 B5.
Tel 222 003 111.

MARKETS AND MALLS

Prague city centre is not blessed with a great market for most of the year, though the Christmas Gift Market in Old Town Square is well worth visiting. The city's major central market, **Havelská tržnice** (*see p217*), sells mainly fresh produce and cheap souvenirs. A better option for something surprising is **Holešovice** in the north of the city (take the metro to Vltavská). The best of Prague's flea markets is **Buštěhrad Collectors Market**, a glorified car-boot sale close to Lidice.

Western-style shopping malls are now a common sight in Prague. The centre of the city is home to **Palladium** and **Slovanský dům** (*see p217*), while further afield **Flora Palace** (*see p217*) and the **Vinohradský Pavilion** (*see p217*) provide a genuinely Western European retail-therapy experience. Flora Palace is probably the better of the last two, offering three levels of stores and direct access from Flora metro station. There is also a large mall at Zličín, the **Metropole Mall**.

A second-hand bookshop in Prague

What to Buy in Prague

The massive selection of goods available in Prague's shops means that everyday items, such as food, books, camera film and toiletries are ubiquitous. Prague's more traditional products, such as Bohemian crystal, china, wooden toys and antiques, make great souvenirs, and there are still some real bargains to be picked up, though you will need to shop around. Increasingly popular are the more unusual, though less authentic, goods which are sold by many of Prague's street shops. These include Soviet army medals, Red Army uniforms and Russian dolls.

GLASS AND CHINA

Bohemian glass and china have always been ranked among the finest in the world. From huge, decorative vases to delicate glass figurines, the vast selection of glass and china items for sale is daunting. Crystal, glass and china can be quite different depending on where they are made. Lead crystal ranges in lead content from 14 to 24 per cent, for example. Always make sure you are fully aware of what you are buying.

Some of the best glass and china in Bohemia is produced at the Moser glassworks at Karlovy Vary and sold at **Moser**. The large Crystalex glassworks at Nový Bor and Poděbrady produce some of the most highly decorated glass, sold at **Art Glass**.

Other shops which sell a good selection of glass and china include **Crystal Porcelan, Dana-Bohemia** and two outlets called **Glass**. **Artěl** is a store selling mouth-blown glassware – designed by Karen Feldman – while **Arzenal** is another popular shop, with glass from the Czech's leading designer, Borek Šipek, whose collections are found in institutions ranging from MOMO in New York to the Design Museum in London. Billing itself as a cross-culture junction, there is a Thai restaurant on-site too.

However, prices for certain goods, especially classically designed vases, decanters and bowls are starting to reflect the increasing popularity of Bohemian crystal. The days when such goods could be purchased in Prague for half

the Western European price are over. Yet, value for money remains high, and you can still pick up bargains if you shop around carefully. Remember that many of the modern pieces are just as lovely and much cheaper.

Bohemian porcelain, while not as celebrated as Bohemian crystal, also makes an excellent gift or souvenir. **Český Porcelán**, the country's most famous factory, is in the town of Teplice, an hour's drive towards the German border from Prague, and its factory shop offers wonderful bargains. Other names worth looking out for include **Royal Dux Bohemia**, **Haas & Czjzek**, **A. Ruckl & Sons** and **Toner**.

Because of the fragile nature of the goods, many shops will pack anything you buy there. But if you go for a more expensive piece, it is worth looking into insurance before you leave Prague.

ANTIQUE SHOPS

Given its history as a major city in the Hapsburg empire, Prague is a great place to hunt for antiques. Hidden treasures seemingly lurk around every corner, and prices are still generally lower than in the West. Most of the city's shopping districts have a large number of antique shops: Old Town is full of them, as is the Royal Route from the castle. Look out for Bohemian furniture, glass and porcelain, as well as military and Soviet memorabilia.

Antique shops that are well worth exploring include **Dorotheum** and **Starožitnosti**. **Antique Clocks** sells exactly

what it says and **Military Antiques** is a haven for all army fanatics. For goods over Kč1,000, check with the shop whether you will need a licence to export them. You should watch out for an increasing number of fakes which are now appearing in the market.

Prague also has several *bazar* shops which stock a range of items at cheaper prices. Items are often unusual and good bargains can be found. **Bazar B & P** is a small, popular shop full of second-hand goods. For furniture bargains **Bazar nábytku** is well worth a visit.

TRADITIONAL CRAFTS

The traditional manufacture of high-quality, hand-crafted goods still survives. The variety of the merchandise available in the shops – hand-woven carpets, wooden toys, table mats, beautifully painted Easter eggs, baskets, figurines in folk costumes and ceramics – are all based on Czech and Moravian folk crafts and then enriched with modern elements. You can buy them from many market stalls as well as a fair number of shops.

Czech Traditional Handicrafts offers a huge choice of hand-carved decorative items. A jewellery shop known for using only the best Czech garnets mounted in stylish, contemporary settings is **Studio Šperk**. You should also look out for a new chain of shops called **Manufaktura** (Handmade), which sells goods made only in the Czech Republic. A number of street vendors around Old Town Square also sell handmade items including jewellery and puppets. Czech wooden items are also of the highest quality (*see* Speciality Shops, *pp216–17*).

BOOKS

There are numerous bookshops in Prague, reflecting its literary heritage, and many sell English-language books. One of the main bookshops is **Big Ben Bookshop**. Here, you'll find a range of English-language books (including Czech works which have been translated into English).

Maps and guides to Prague in English can be bought at **Academia**. Other specialist bookshops include **Palác knih**, **Kanzelberger** and **Fišer's Bookshop**.

Prague also has second-hand bookshops – look in Golden Lane and Karlova

Street – which stock some English-language books, and they all offer the visiting bibliophile hours of enjoyable browsing. **Antikvariát Dlážděná** is one of the best and has a vast selection. **Antikvariát Ztichlá Klika** deals in antiquarian books as well as 20th-century avant-garde works.

The legendary **Globe** café and bookstore has been a good place to find second-hand English books and enjoy the city's best cappuccino

since 1993, when the shop was opened in a poorer part of the capital by five entre-preneurial Americans. Now relocated to the city centre, the Globe hosts regular literary events, and art exhibitions, as does the newer **Shakespeare & Sons**, out in Vršovice, which is attempting to repeat the success of the Globe. **Anagram** is another great English bookstore, conveniently situated not far from Old Town Square.

DIRECTORY

GLASS AND CHINA

Art Glass
Karlova 11. **Map** 3 A4.
Tel 60 22 90 469.
One of several branches.

Artěl
Celetná 29.
Map 3 C3.
Tel 22 48 15 085.
www.artelshop.com

Arzenal
Valentinská 11.
Map 3 B3.
Tel 22 48 14 099.
www.arzenal.cz

Bohemia Crystal
ČESKE SKLO
Kozí 9.
Map 3 C2.
Tel 22 48 11 671.

Český Porcelán
Perlová 1.
Map 3 B4.
Tel 22 42 10 955.
www.cesky.porcelan.cz

Crystal Porcelan
Železná 10 . **Map** 3 C4.
Tel 22 42 11 175.

Dana-Bohemia
GLASS, CHINA, CRYSTAL
Národní 43.
Map 3 A5.
Tel 22 42 14 655.
One of several branches.

Dům Porcelánu
Jugoslavska 16.
Tel 22 15 05 320.
www.dumporcelanu.cz

Glass
SKLO
Malé náměstí 6.
Map 3 B4.
Tel 22 42 28 459.

Also at: Staroměstské náměstí 26–27.
Map 3 C3.
Tel 22 42 29 755.

Moser
Na příkopě 12.
Map 3 C4.
Tel 22 42 11 293.
www.moser-glass.com

ANTIQUE SHOPS

Antique Clocks
STAROŽITNOSTI UHLÍŘ
Mikulandská 8.
Map 3 B5.
Tel 22 49 30 572.

Antique Kaprova
Kaprova 12.
Map 3 B3.

A.D. Starožitnosti
Skořepka 8, Prague 1.
Map 3 B4.
Tel 224 238 599.

Bazar B & P
Nekázanka 17.
Map 4 D4.
Tel 22 42 10 550.
www.nekazanka.cz

Bazar nábytku
Libeňský ostrov.
Tel 266 310 726.
www.antik-bazar.cz

Dorotheum
Ovocný trh 2.
Map 3 C4.
Tel 22 42 22 001.
www.dorotheum.cz

Military Antiques
Charvátova 11.
Map 3 C5.
Tel 29 62 40 088.
One of several branches.

Starožitnosti
Námeští Kinských 7.
Tel 25 73 11 245.
www.antique-shop.cz

GIFTS AND SOUVENIRS

Czech Traditional Handicrafts
Karlova 26.
Map 3 A4.
Tel 221 632 480.

Handmade
MANUFAKTURA
Melantrichova 17.
Map 3 B4.
Tel 22 16 32 480.
www.manufaktura.biz
One of several branches.

Studio Šperk
Dlouhá 19. **Map** 3 C3.
Tel 22 48 15 161.

BOOKS

Anagram
Týn 4. **Map** 3 C3.
Tel 22 48 95 737.
www.anagram.cz

Antikvariát Dlážděná
Dlážděná 7.
Map 4 E4.
Tel 22 22 43 911.
www.adplus.cz

Antikvariát Ztichlá Klika
Betlémská 10–14.
Map 3 A5.
Tel 22 22 21 561.

Big Ben Bookshop
Malá Štupartská 5.
Map 3 C3.
Tel 22 48 26 565.

Fišer's Bookshop
FIŠEROVO KNIHKUPECTVÍ
Kaprova 10.
Map 3 B3.
Tel 22 23 20 733.

Franz Kafka Bookshop
Staroměstské nám. 11-12.
Map 3 B3.
Tel 22 23 21 454.

Globe
Pštrossova 6.
Map 5 A1.
Tel 22 49 34 203.
www.globebookstore.cz

Kanzelberger
Václavské náměstí 4.
Map 4 D5.
Tel 22 42 19 214.
www.dumknihy.cz

Knihkupectoí Academia
Václavské náměstí 34.
Map 4 D5.
Tel 22 42 23 511.

Palác knih
Václavské náměstí 41.
Map 4 D5.
Tel 22 11 11 364.

Shakespeare & Sons
Krymska 10, Prague 2.
Tel 27 17 40 839.
www.shakes.cz

Markets, Malls and Speciality Shops

Take your pick – super-modern mall or traditional market. Prague has them both, although do remember that Prague's main market is at some distance from the city centre at Holešovice. Malls are springing up everywhere in the city, and Prague has made a name for itself as a leading place to find all sorts of odd bits and pieces in any number of speciality stores. From Faberge eggs to Jewish *yarmulkas*, you'll find it in Prague.

MARKETS

Prague's markets offer a vast range of goods, although most are aimed at locals, offering fruit and vegetables, cheap clothing and electronics. The largest market in the city, **Prague Market**, is in Holešovice. It was converted from a former slaughterhouse. The market now sells fresh fruit and vegetables, all kinds of poultry as well as fish, textiles, flowers, electronics and even secondhand cars and vehicle parts. These are all sold in several large halls and in outdoor stalls. The market is generally open from Monday to Friday, 6am to 5pm.

In Havelská, right in the centre of the city, is **Havelská tržnice**, which mainly sells fruit, vegetables and cheap souvenirs. Other well-known markets in Prague include the **Smíchov Market** and a small one on the street V kotcích. Remember that some of the goods sold at all these markets, especially clothes and shoes, can be of very poor quality. Nevertheless, they are an excellent place to hunt for a bargain.

You will also enjoy foraging through the junk, antiques, furniture and military memorabilia (none of which comes with a promise of a refund or guarantee) at the out-of-town **Buštěhrad Collectors Market**, allegedly the third-largest market of its kind in Europe. You can get there by public transport, taking a bus from Dejvická metro station. The market is only open on the second and fourth Saturday of the month, from 8am to noon.

Old Town Square plays host to an excellent and very popular Christmas Gift Market from the end of November through the New Year's holiday. Besides the stalls selling gifts and toys, there are others selling hot wine and sausages, and there is also a small children's play area. The Square also hosts the city's Christmas tree and a number of open-air winter concerts.

MALLS

There is an increasing number of Western-style shopping malls in Prague, which are more popular and often much better than the old department stores, offering better value and a greater range of high-quality goods. **Vinohradský Pavilion** has been re-opened as a shopping mall, following extensive modernisation, as has **Koruna Palace**. In the very centre of town on Náměstí Republiky, the **Palladium** shopping centre has hundreds of shops and restaurants on five levels. Just down the street, on Na Příkopě, the upmarket **Slovanský dům** is home to a great number of chic boutiques, jewellery stores, the fabulous Kogo restaurant and a multiplex cinema, while **Myslbek**, across the road, is a deceptively large shopping centre with a better range of shops that are more accessible to the average pocket. Other shopping arcades include the enormous **Flora Palace** (Palác Flora: take the metro to Flora), which is home to hundreds of shops, and the slightly smaller **Nový Smíchov** (metro Anděl) home to Tesco and more.

Just outside Prague, at the Zličín terminus of the metro line B, is **Metropole**, Prague's biggest mall. It offers hundreds of stores, including a huge C&A, the biggest Kenvelo in Prague and a special children's area. There is also a ten-screen cinema, **Cinema City** *(see p221)*.

STREET STALLS

Street stalls and wandering vendors are not officially allowed to operate in most areas of Prague, though a number of vendors are permitted to sell souvenirs around Charles Bridge. Street stalls are allowed near the entrance to the Old Jewish Cemetery in the Jewish Quarter, and they also line the Old Castle Steps from Malostranská metro station up to the castle's eastern gate.

As most of these sellers are well vetted, the goods on sale tend to be reasonably good quality, though you are unlikely to find any real bargains, and much of what is on sale can be bought cheaper in souvenir stores.

SPECIALITY SHOPS

Bohemia and Moravia have long been known for their fine wooden toys. You will find a number of shops selling them throughout the city, especially in Old Town, but beware cheap imports. You can be sure of the genuine article at **Hračky** near the castle, Beruška in New Town and **Sparky's House of Toys**, just off Na Příkopě, a veritable treasure trove for children of all ages. Older children might also like **Games & Puzzles** on Wenceslas Square, which specializes in all sorts of mind teasers, including exquisite handmade wooden labyrinths.

If you are looking for something a little quirky, but very Czech, try **Botanicus** near Old Town Square, which sells all-natural and all-Czech health and beauty products, from soap to massage oil. Another popular store is **Qubus**, which sells anything and everything, as long as it is the height of modern design.

Most of the weird and wonderful things on sale were designed by young

Czechs. There are a number of other weird and wonderful stores in Prague. The **Spanish Synagogue Gift Shop** sells torah pointers, *yarmulkas*, watches and other Jewish gifts. **Le Patio** on Národní is a shop specializing in original illuminations and candelabra, as well as top-quality restored furniture imported from India, and tables and chairs made by some outstanding Czech blacksmiths. Another favourite for design fans is **de.fakto**, an upmarket version of IKEA, in the centre of the city. **Art Deco Galerie** is an upmarket junk shop with gor-geous period-pieces, glass, accessories, home furnishings and second-hand clothing. The prize for most bizarre shop in Prague must go to **American Heating**, a store specializing in the restoration of historic stoves.

FOOD AND DELICATESSENS

Prague's supermarkets are well stocked with the basic foodstuffs. **Delicacies-lahůdky** is a small shop with meat and fish counters. A specialist food shop, selling smoked sausage, cheeses and other local delicacies, is **Jan Paukert**. For freshly baked bread visit the bakers around Wenceslas Square and Karmelitská Street. **Paneria Pekařství** shops sell a good selection of patisseries and sandwiches.

For the best selection of local and international delicacies, however, try **Bake-shop** on Kozí just off Old Town Square. You'll find excellent breads and baked goods, as well as brownies, cookies and delicious sandwiches and salads. It's great for a snack, an informal lunch or to pick up supplies for a picnic.

DIRECTORY

MARKETS AND MALLS

Buštěhrad Collectors Market
Buštěhrad.

Flora Palace
PALÁC FLORA
Vinohradska 151.
Tel 25 57 41 712.
Map 6 F1.
www.palacflora.com

Havelská tržnice
Havelský trh.
Map 3 C3.

Koruna Palace
Václavské náměsti 1.
Map 3 C5.
Tel 22 42 19 526.
www.koruna-palace.cz

Metropole Mall
Zličín.
Tel 22 60 81 540.
www.metropole.cz

Myslbek
Na příkopě.
Map 3 C4
Tel 22 48 35 000.
www.myselbek.com

Nový Smíchov
Plzenská 8.
Tel 25 15 11 151.
www.novysmichov.eu

Palladium
Náměstí Republiky 1.
Map 4 D3.
Tel 22 57 70 250.
www.palladiumpraha.cz

Prague Market
Bubenské nábřeži 306.
Praha 7.
Tel 22 08 00 945.

Slovanský dům
Na příkopě 22.
Map 3 C4.
Tel 22 14 51 400.
www.slovanskydum.com

Smíchov Market
Náměsti 14. října 15.
Map 3 C4.
Tel 25 73 21 101.

Vinohradský Pavilion
Vinohradská 50.
Map 6 F1.
Tel 22 20 97 100.
www.pavilon.cz

SPECIALITY SHOPS

American Heating
Karmelitska 21.
Map 2 E4.
Tel 25 75 34 203.
www.starakamna.cz

Art Deco Galerie
Michalská 21.
Tel 22 42 23 076.
Map 3 B4.
www.artdecogalerie-mili.com

Beruška
Vodičkova 30. **Map** 3 C5.
Tel 22 10 14 607.

Botanicus
Týnská 3.
Map 3 C3.
Tel 23 47 67 446.
www.botanicus.cz

de.fakto
Vejvodova 3.
Map 3 B4.
Tel 22 42 33 815.
www.defakto.cz

Games & Puzzles
Václavské náměstí 38.
Map 6 D1.
Tel 22 49 46 506.
www.hras.cz

Hračky Traditional Toys
Loretánské náměsti 3.
Map 1 B3.
Tel 60 35 15 745.

Le Patio
Národní 22.
Map 3 A5.
Tel 22 49 34 402.
www.patium.com

Qubus
Rámová 3.
Map 3 C2.
Tel 22 23 13 151.
www.qubus.cz

Spanish Synagogue Gift Shop
Vĕžeňská 1. **Map** 3 B2.

Sparky's House of Toys
Havířská 2.
Map 3 C4.
Tel 22 42 39 309.
www.sparkys.cz

FOOD AND DELICATESSENS

Bakeshop
Kozí 1. **Map** 3 C2.
Tel 22 23 16 823.

Delicacies-lahůdky
ZLATÝ KŘÍŽ
Jungmannova náměstí 19.
Map 3 C5.
Tel 22 25 19 451.

Jan Paukert
Národní 17.
Map 3 B5.
Tel 22 42 14 968.

Paneria Pekařství
Valentinská 10/20.
Map 3 B3.
Tel 22 48 27 912.
www.paneria.cz
Also at: 28. října 10.
Map 3 C5; Nekázanka 19.
Map 4 D4; Vinohradská
23. **Map** 6 E1; Vodičkova
33. **Map** 3 C5.

PHARMACIES

*It is not usual for pharmacies to have individual names, so look out for **Léky** (drugs) or **Lékárna** (pharmacy).*

Belgická 37.
Map 6 E2.
Tel 22 25 13 396.

Národní 35.
Map 3 B5.
Tel 22 42 30 086.

Lékárna u Anděla
Stefanikova 6,
Prague 5.
Tel 25 73 20 918.
Open 24 hours.

Lékárna u Rotundy
Karoliny Svĕtlé 11.
Map 3 A4.
Tel 22 42 36 623.

ENTERTAINMENT IN PRAGUE

Since the Velvet Revolution in 1989, Prague's range of entertainment has become increasingly varied. Whether you prefer opera to jazz or minigolf to a football match, the city has plenty to offer. Movie buffs can choose from many of the latest Hollywood blockbusters, a lot of them in English with subtitles. For the adventurous, mime and fringe theatre are both thriving. Prague has a superb musical tradition, which includes symphony orchestras, opera, musicals, jazz and folk music. Concerts are performed throughout the year, in venues which range from Baroque palaces to public parks and gardens. Even if you don't speak Czech, you can still enjoy the city's cultural offerings. Some plays can be seen in English, and for many types of entertainment, music, dance and sport, a knowledge of the language isn't necessary at all.

Street musicians entertaining the crowds

PRACTICAL INFORMATION

The best place to look for information about what's on and where in Prague is in the English-language newspaper *The Prague Post (see p235)*. This provides details of the best entertainment and cultural events which will be of interest to an English-speaking audience. Those events that are in English or have translation facilities are marked. Other sources of information are the leaflets and City Guides given out at the ticket agencies in the city, such as **Ticketpro** or **PIS**. In addition there are two online bulletin boards in English, www.expats.cz and http://prague.tv, aimed at expats and visitors. You can also use the free booklet *Přehled*, printed in English and available from any PIS office. For a comprehensive rundown of events, buy *Culture in Prague*, a detailed monthly publication listing information on a variety of local exhibitions, concerts and theatre.

A performance of *Cosi Fan Tutte* at the Mozart Festival

BOOKING TICKETS

Tickets can be bought in advance from the box office at most venues. You can also book tickets in advance by writing to, or ringing, the venue. Remember that many of the city's box offices may not have any English speakers available. Tickets for the **opera** or for any of the performances at the **National Theatre** can also be booked online. The more popular events tend to become heavily booked up in advance by tour groups – particularly during the summer – and by season-ticket holders. However, standby tickets are usually available about an hour before the show. If this isn't practical and you want to be sure of a ticket on a particular day, it is better to

PUPPET THEATRE

Puppetry has a long tradition in Prague and is still strongly represented. The most famous puppet show in the city is held at the **Spejbl and Hurvínek Theatre** *(see p221)*. The show revolves around Daddy Spejbl and his reprobate son Hurvínek. Other puppet theatres include the **National Marionette Theatre** *(see p221)*, known for its entertaining puppet rendition of Mozart's *Don Giovanni*. The Theatre in the Old Town *(see p221)* and the **Puppet Empire** *(see p221)* also put on puppet shows occasionally. Check listings *(see p226)*.

Theatre puppets

buy them at a booking agency. The drawback to using agencies, however, is that commission on these tickets can be high, sometimes doubling the original price. Your hotel receptionist may also be able to get you tickets.

TICKET PRICES

Ticket prices are cheap compared to Western prices, except for certain performances, most notably during the Prague Spring Music Festival *(see p50)*. Prices range from around Kč100 for a small fringe production to up to Kč3,000 for a performance by an internationally famous orchestra. Paying by credit card is usually only acceptable at ticket agencies.

TICKET TOUTS

There has been a recent spate of counterfeit tickets on sale, especially for the larger rock concerts. To be safe, always buy your tickets at reputable agencies or at the venue itself.

LATE-NIGHT TRANSPORT

Prague's metro *(see pp242–3)* stops running shortly after midnight, while the normal bus and tram service ends around 11:30pm. Then the city's extensive night bus and tram service takes over. Timetables are displayed at each stop. Night trams and buses are regular and efficient and it is likely that there will be a

A view of the Rudolfinum auditorium *(see p223)*

The Neo-Classical Estates Theatre (Stavovské divadlo)

tram or bus stop near your hotel. Taxis provide the most certain form of late-night transportation, but beware of unscrupulous drivers trying to overcharge you *(see p245)*. It is often a good idea to try to walk a little way from the

Sparta Stadium *(see p223)*

theatre before you hail a cab; the fare will probably be a lot cheaper. Ask at your hotel before you go out to find out what the best transport options are.

MUSIC FESTIVALS

The most famous music festival of all is the Prague Spring Music Festival, held between May and June. Hundreds of international musicians come to Prague to take part in the celebrations. Other music festivals include the Mozart Festival *(see p51)*, held in the summer, the Prague Autumn Music Festival *(see p52)* and the International Jazz Festival *(see p52)*, that takes place in the autumn.

BOOKING AGENTS

Bohemia Ticket International
Malé Nàmèsti 13.
Map 3 B4.
Tel 22 42 27 832.
www.bohemiaticket.cz

Na Příkopě 16.
Map 4 D4.
Tel & ***Fax*** 22 42 15 031.
www.ticketsbti.cz

National Theatre tickets
www.narodni-divadlo.cz
Box office 22 49 01 448.

Opera tickets online
www.opera.cz

Prague Information Service (PIS)
Staroměstské náměstí 1.
Map 3 B3. ***Tel*** 12 444.

Ticket Art
Politických vězňů 9.
Map 4 D5.
Tel 22 28 97 552.
www.ticket-art.cz

Ticketpro
Štěpanská 61. **Map** 5 C1.
Tel 296 333 333.
Fax 234 704 204.
www.ticketpro.cz
Also at: Rytířská 12.
Map 3 B4.

Ticket Stream
Koubková 8.
Map 6 E3.
Tel 22 42 63 049.
www.ticketstream.cz

The Performing Arts

Prague has always been known for its artistic heritage. Theatre has played an important role in the city's cultural development, and recently the range of entertainment has expanded considerably. Even during the communist period Prague remained a centre of experimental theatre, not least the emergence of Black Light Theatre in the 1960s. Today, this tradition continues, with new theatre groups emerging all the time, ever more experimental. In general, the theatre season runs from September to June. During the summer, open-air performances are given in Prague's gardens and parks. For those who prefer to dance till dawn, relax to the sound of jazz or take in a movie – you will find plenty to entertain you in this city.

ENGLISH-LANGUAGE PERFORMANCES

Many theatres in Prague have started to stage a number of English-language productions, especially in the summer months. Even if the play is not performed in English, some venues use supertitles to provide a translation. For details, check the listings *(see p227)*.

MAJOR THEATRES

Prague's first permanent theatre was built in 1738, but the city's theatrical tradition dates from the Baroque and Renaissance periods.

The National Theatre *(see pp156–7)* is Prague's main venue for opera, ballet and plays. The neighbouring New Stage is another important venue. It is also the main stage for the multimedia **Laterna Magika** company, which is one of Prague's best-known theatre groups as well as being at the forefront of European improvisational theatre.

Other major theatres in the city include the "stone theatres." These gained importance during the 19th century and include the **Vinohrady Theatre**, the **Estates Theatre** *(see p65)* – one of the most respected in Prague – and the **Prague Municipal Theatre**, an acting company whose plays appear in turn at the **ABC Theatre**, the **Comedy Theatre** and the **Rokoko Studio of Drama**. The **Kolowrat Theatre** is based in the Kolowrat Palace.

FRINGE THEATRES

These originated during the 1960s and won renown for their fight against the status quo. The groups are still very innovative and largely experimental. They perform in small theatres, and many of Prague's best actors and actresses have developed their skills while working for some of these companies.

Fringe theatres include the **Dramatic Club**, well known for its supporting ensemble; the **Ypsilon Studio**, with one of the finest acting companies in the city; **Theatre Na Fidlovačce**, which stages a mix of musicals and straight drama; the large **Theatre Below Palmovka**, renowned for its mix of classical and modern plays; and the **Theatre in Celetná**. One of Prague's most spectacular theatrical and music venues is **Křižík's Fountain**, at the Exhibition Ground, where classical concerts are held and full orchestras perform to stunning lightshows. The **Semafor Theatre** is the home of the tremendously popular comedian, Jiří Suchý.

PANTOMIME, MIME AND BLACK LIGHT THEATRE

Some of the most popular theatre entertainment in Prague is Black Light Theatre, where black-clad actors move objects against a dark stage without being seen – a stunning visual spectacle, pantomime and mime. None of the three requires any understanding of Czech and all are strongly represented.

Jiří Srnec's Black Light Theatre is one of the major venues for Black Light Theatre performance. **Ta Fantastika** is another. These and others are listed in the directory *(see p221)*.

DANCE

In Prague, opera and ballet companies traditionally share the National Theatre, where the Czech Republic's best permanent ballet company is based. The **Prague State Opera** also has a resident ballet ensemble, and has in recent years, been keen to usurp the reputation of the **National Theatre** company as the city's best. The tickets for the ballet at both major venues are even lower than for opera performances. You can also watch ballet performances at the **Estates Theatre**. **Ponec** is an experimental performance dance space dedicated to modern dance, and hosts the annual Tanec Praha international festival of contemporary dance and movement theatre in June.

CINEMAS

Although Prague doesn't show all the latest Hollywood blockbusters, more than 80 per cent of the films shown are recent US productions, most in English with Czech subtitles. Multiplex cinemas are now big business. The largest of these – the **Cinema Cities** at Flora and Zličin – boasts 10 screens. **Světozor** is great for catching Czech films with English subtitles. **Bio Oko** is a fully restored art house cinema with a great café and an ambitious repertoire of contemporary Czech films as well as classics.

The listings magazines *(see p227)* show which films are on and in what language. There are still some major cinemas around Wenceslas Square, including **Lucerna** and **Slovanský Dům**; others are listed in the directory.

DIRECTORY

THEATRES

Animato Black Light Theatre
ČERNÉ DIVADLO ANIMATO
Na příkopě 10.
Map 3 C4.
Tel 28 19 32 665. **www.**animato.webpark.cz

Broadway
Na příkopě 31. **Map** 3 C4.
Tel 22 51 13 311. **www.**divadlo-broadway.cz.

Dramatic Club
ČINOHERNÍ KLUB
Ve Smečkách 26.
Map 6 D1.
Tel 29 62 22 123.
www.cinoherniklub.cz

Estates Theatre
STAVOVSKÉ DIVADLO
Ovocný trh. **Map** 3 C3.
Tel 22 42 28 503.
www.narodni-divadlo.cz

Jiří Srnec's Black Theatre
ČERNÉ DIVADLO JIŘÍHO SRNCE
U Lékárny 597, 15600
Praha 5.
Tel 25 79 21 835.
www.blacktheatresrnec.cz

Kolowrat Theatre
DIVADLO KOLOWRAT (IN ESTATES THEATRE)
Ovocný trh.
Map 3 C3.
Tel 22 49 01 448.
www.narodni-divadlo.cz

Křižík's Fountain
KŘIŽÍKOVA FONTÁNA
Výstaviště, Praha 7.
Tel 22 01 03 280.
www.krizikovafontana.cz

Laterna Magika
Národní 4.
Map 3 A5.
Tel 224 931 482.
www.laterna.cz

National Theatre
NÁRODNÍ DIVADLO
Národní 2.
Map 3 A5.
Tel 22 49 01 448.
www.narodni-divadlo.cz

National Marionette Theatre
NÁRODNÍ DIVADLO MARIONET
Žatecká 1. **Map** 3 B3.
Tel 22 48 19 322.
www.mozart.cz

Prague Municipal Theatre, ABC Theatre
MĚSTSKÁ DIVADLA PRAŽSKÁ, DIVADLO ABC
Vodičkova 28.
Map 3 C5.
Tel 22 42 15 943.
www.ecn.cz/abc

Prague Municipal Theatre, Comedy Theatre
MĚSTSKÁ DIVADLA PRAŽSKÁ, DIVADLO KOMEDIE
Jungmannova 1.
Map 5 B1.
Tel 22 42 22 734.
www.divadlokomedie.cz

Prague Municipal Theatre, Rokoko Studio of Drama
MĚSTSKÁ DIVADLA PRAŽSKÁ, DIVADLO ROKOKO
Václavské náměstí 38.
Map 4 D5.
Tel 22 42 17 113.
www.rokoko.cz

Puppet Empire
ŘÍŠE LOUTEK
Žatecká 1.
Map 3 B3.
Tel 22 23 24 568.
www.riseloutek.cz

Reduta Theatre
DIVADLO REDUTA
Národní 20. **Map** 3 B5.
Tel 22 49 33 487.
www.redutajazzclub.cz

Semafor Theatre
Divadlo Semafor,
Dejvická 27.
Tel 23 39 01 383.
www.semafor.cz

Spejbl and Hurvínek Theatre
DIVADLO SPEJBLA A HURVÍNKA
Dejvická 38.
Tel 22 43 16 784.
www.spejbl-hurvinek.cz

Ta Fantastika
Karlova 8. **Map** 3 A4.
Tel 22 22 21 366.
www.tafantastika.cz.

Theatre Below Palmovka
DIVADLO POD PALMOVKOU
Zenklova 34, Praha 8.
Tel 283 011 127.
www.divadlopodpalmovk ou.cz.

Theatre in Celetná
DIVADLO V CELETNÉ
Celetná 17.
Map 3 C3.
Tel 22 23 26 843.
www.divadlovceletne.cz

Theatre in the Old Town
DIVADLO V DLOUHÉ
Dlouhá 39.
Map 3 C3.
Tel 22 48 26 795.
www.divadlovdlouhe.cz

Theatre Na Fidlovačce
DIVADLO NA FIDLOVAČCE
Křesomyslova 625.
Map 6 E5.
Tel 24 14 04 040.
www.fidlovacka.cz

Vinohrady Theatre
DIVADLO NA VINOHRADECH
Náměstí Míru 7.
Map 6 F2.
Tel 22 42 57 601.
www.dnv-praha.cz

Ypsilon Studio
STUDIO YPSILON
Spálená 16.
Map 3 B5.
Tel 22 49 47 119.
www.ypsilonka.cz

DANCE

National Theatre
NÁRODNÍ DIVADLO BALET
Národní 2.
Map 3 A5.
Tel 22 49 01 448.
www.narodni-divadlo.cz

Prague State Opera
STÁTNÍ OPERA PRAHA
Wilsonova 4.
Map 6 E1.
Tel 22 42 27 266.
www.opera.cz

Ponec
Husitská 24a/899, Praha 3.
Tel 24 27 21 531.
www.divadloponec.cz

CINEMAS

Bio Oko
Františka Křižka 15,
Praha 7.
Tel 23 33 82 606.
www.biooko.cz

Cinema City Flóra
Vinohradská 149.
Praha 3.
Tel 25 57 42 021.
www.cinemacity.cz

Cinema City Zličín
Řevnická 1.
Praha 5.
Tel 25 79 51 966.
www.cinemacity.cz

Evald
Národní 28.
Map 3 B5.
Tel 22 11 05 225.
www.evald.cinemart.cz

Lucerna
Vodičkova 36.
Map 3 C5.
Tel 22 42 16 972.
www.lucerna.cz

Mat
Karlovo náměstí 19.
Map 5 B2.
Tel 22 49 15 765.
www.mat.cz

Multiplex Cinema Nový Smíchov
Plzeňská 8.
Tel 84 02 00 240.
www.palacecinemas.cz

Perštýn
Na Perštýně 6.
Map 3 B3.
Tel 22 16 68 432.

Slovanský Dům
Na Příkopě 22.
Map 3 C4.
Tel 84 02 00 240.
www.palacecinemas.cz

Světozor
Vodičkova 41.
Map 3 C5.
Tel 22 49 46 824.
www.kinosvetozor.cz

Village Cinemas Anděl
Radlická 1.Praha 5.
Tel 25 11 15 111.
www.villagecinemas.cz

Music and Sport

Prague may not match the vibrancy of Vienna or Budapest, but it certainly can hold its own among Europe's leading cultural destinations. Opera and ballet are well represented, while music is provided by some excellent orchestras. Prices offer good value.

Sports fans are well served too, with top-class ice hockey and Champions League football, both attracting crowds during the season, from September to May.

OPERA

Since Richard Wagner's *The Mastersingers of Nurnburg* officially opened Prague's State Opera House on 5 January 1888, Prague has been a centre of operatic excellence. Today, two highly competitive world-class opera companies give opera top billing on Prague's cultural calendar. And while the low Soviet-era prices of yore are now long gone, top-price seats range from Kč1,000 to 1,200, which makes opera in Prague more accessible than most cities in Europe.

The two major companies, the National and the State, both perform exclusively in their own theatres – the National Opera Company in the **National Theatre** *(see pp156–7)*; the State Opera Company at the **State Opera**. The latter presents a predominantly classical Italian repertoire, always in the orginal language, and performances are always popular. Tickets should be bought in advance. The National Opera Company has a more experimental repertoire, and most of its operas are performed in Czech.

To view a Czech opera, by Czech composers Smetana or Dvořák, the National Theatre is your best opportunity to do so. A lesser known opera company based at the **Estates Theatre** *(see p221)* performs mainly classical, Italian operas in the original language.

CLASSICAL MUSIC

The Czech Philharmonic Orchestra (CPO) has been based at the magnificent **Rudolfinum** *(see p84)* since giving its first concert there in January 1896, when it was conducted by no less a personality than Anton Dvořák, whose name the Rudolfinum's grand hall now carries. Finding immediate success with the public in Prague and abroad (the Philharmonic travelled to London on tour as early as 1902), the orchestra is today recognised by music lovers as one of the finest in the world.

The post of chief conductor of the CPO is one of the most revered appointments in classical music; currently the post is unfilled. Almost all contemporary Czech music, including the celebrated recent work *Requiem* by Milan Slavický, premiered at the Rudolfinum, though the programme is varied, and the works of Czech composers share the limelight with those of their foreign counterparts.

Besides the Rudolfinum, the main concert venue for classical music is the Smetana Hall, found in the **Municipal House** *(see p64)*. Other permanent concert halls include the **Atrium in Žižkov**, a converted chapel, the **Clementinum** and the imposing **Congress Centre Prague**. **Bertramka** is another venue with the added attraction of being the place where Mozart stayed when he was in Prague.

MUSIC IN CHURCHES AND PALACES

Concerts performed in the numerous churches and palaces around Prague are extremely popular. Many of these buildings are normally closed to the public, so this is the only chance to see them from inside. Major churches include the **Church of St James** *(see p65)*; the **Church of St Nicholas** *(see pp128–9)* in the Little Quarter; the **Church of St Nicholas** *(see p70)* in the Old Town; the **Church of St Francis** in Knights of the Cross Square *(see p79)*; St Vitus's Cathedral *(see p100)* and **St George's Basilica** *(see p98)*. Other important venues are the **National Museum** *(see p147)*; the **Lobkowicz Palace** *(see p99)* and the **Sternberg Palace** *(see pp112–13)*. It's worth checking the listings magazines *(p226)* for the specific dates and timings of concerts.

ETHNIC MUSIC

A small number of clubs and bars in Prague offer ethnic music. The **Palác Akropolis** hosts diverse performances daily in an atmospheric, converted 1920s-theatre building. The Akropolis hosts the likes of Ani Difranco, Apollo 440 and Transglobal Underground. A variety of bands can be seen from around the world in an unusual setting, at the **House of Culture**. Some of the better jazz clubs *(see pp210–11)* also feature ethnic musicians and bands on a regular basis. Another place worth checking out is **La Bodequita del Medio**, a Cuban restaurant that features Cuban performers some weekend evenings.

SPORTS

Czechs are crazy about most sports, and given their habit of winning international competitions in any number of events on a regular basis, it is not surprising. The biggest spectator sports are ice hockey and football, in that order of importance.

The main Czech ice hockey league has long been rated second only to the US NHL, and NHL rosters are filled with Czech players. Prague has two teams in the top division, Sparta and Slavia. Sparta plays its home games at the **Tesla Arena**, where tickets cost from Kč100 onwards. Slavia play at the **O2 Arena**, built for the 2004 Ice Hockey

World Championship, held in, but surprisingly not won by, the Czech Republic. Tickets here cost Kč140 and up. There are three games a week throughout the season, from September to May, so you should be able to catch a game.

Czech football has long been admired throughout the world, and the national team has often been among the world's best. The domestic league is less admired, as almost all of the country's top stars play in richer leagues elsewhere in Europe. The country's leading team, Sparta Prague, however, is a perennial qualifier for the European Champions League, which guarantees a procession of big-name opponents. Tickets for Champions League games (played September to December, depending on Sparta's progress) sell out quickly. Home matches of the Czech Republic are also played at **Sparta Stadium**, also known as the Axa Arena.

If you want to get active yourself, you may have to travel a little further out of town, as sports facilities are not extensive in central Prague. Squash, however, is currently all the rage, and there are number of courts in the city centre, including **ASB** on Wenceslas Square.

Golf, mini-golf or tennis are on offer at the **Motol**. The **Czech Lawn Tennis Club**, a little out of town on Štvanice Island, also offers 14 clay courts and six indoor courts that can be rented by the general public all day at the weekends and until 3pm on weekdays.

Swimming pools can also be found out of the city centre, including two at **Divoká Šárka** and **Kobylisy**. There are beautiful natural lakes for summertime swimming at **Lhotka** and **Šeberák**, and a whole range of watersports as well as golf are now on offer at **Hostivař Reservoir** and **Imperial Meadow**.

DIRECTORY

MUSIC VENUES

Academy of Music
HUDEBNÍ FAKULTA AMU
Malostranské náměstí 13.
Map 2 E3.
Tel 257 534 206.

Atrium in Žižkov
ATRIUM NA ŽIŽKOVĚ
Čajkovského 12, Praha 3.
Tel 222 721 838.
www.atriumzizkov.cz

Bertramka
BERTRAMKA MUZEUM
W A MOZARTA
Mozartova 169, Praha 5.
Tel 257 318 461.
www.bertramka.com

La Bodeguita del Medio
Kaprova 5. **Map** 3 B3.
Tel 224 813 922.
www.bodeguita.cz

Church of St James
KOSTEL SV. JAKUBA
Malá Štupartská.
Map 3 C3.

Church of St Nicholas (Old Town)
KOSTEL SV. MIKULÁŠE
Staroměstské náměstí.
Map 3 B3.

Church of St Nicholas
KOSTEL SV. MIKULÁŠE
Malostranské náměstí.
Map 2 E3.

Church of St Francis
KOSTEL SV. FRANTIŠKA
Křižovnické náměstí.
Map 3 A4.

Church of Sts Simon and Jude
KOSTEL SV. ŠIMONA
A JUDY
Dušní ulice.
Map 3 B2.
www.fok.cz

Clementinum
ZRCADLOVÁ SÍŇ
KLEMENTINA
Mariánské náměstí 10.
Map 3 B3.

Congress Centre Prague
KONGRESOVÉ CENTRUM
PRAHA
5. května 65, Prague 4.
Tel 261 171 111.
www.kcp.cz

Lobkowicz Palace
LOBKOVICKÝ PALÁC
Jiřská 3, Pražský hrad.
Map 2 E2.
Tel 233 312 925.

Music Theatre in Karlín
HUDEBNÍ DIVADLO KARLÍN
Křižíkova 10.
Map 4 F3.
Tel 22 18 68 666.
www.hdk.cz

National Museum
NÁRODNÍ MUZEUM
Václavské náměstí 68.
Map 6 D1.
Tel 224 497 111.

Prague State Opera
STÁTNÍ OPERA PRAHA
Wilsonova 4.
Map 6 E1.
Tel 224 227 266.
www.opera.cz

Rudolfinum – Dvořák Hall
RUDOLFINUM –
DVOŘÁKOVA SÍŇ
Alšovo nábřeží 12.
Map 3 A3.
Tel 227 059 227.
www.czech
philharmonic.cz

St George's Basilica
BAZILIKA SV. JIŘÍ
Jiřské náměstí,
Pražský hrad.
Map 2 E2.

St Vitus's Cathedral
KATEDRÁLA VÍTA
Pražský hrad.
Map 2 D2.

Sternberg Palace
ŠTERNBERSKÝ PALAC
Hradčanské náměstí 15.
Map 1 C3.
Tel 220 514 634.

ETHNIC MUSIC

House of Culture
KULTURNÍ DŮM VLTAVSKÁ
Bubenská 1.
Tel 220 879 683.
www.vltavska.cz

Palác Akropolis
Kubelíkova 27.
Tel 296 330 913.
www.palacakropolis.cz

SPORTING VENUES

ASB Squash
Václavské náměstí 13/15.
Tel 224 232 752.

Czech Lawn Tennis Club
Štvanice 38, Praha 7.
Tel 222 316 317.

Divoká Šárka
Praha 6.

Hostivař Reservoir
K Jezeru, Praha 10.

Imperial Meadow
CÍSAŘSKÁ LOUKA
Prague 5.

Kobylisy
Praha 8.

Lhotka
Praha 4.

Motol
V Úvalu 84, Praha 5.

O2 Arena
Ocelářská 460/2, Praha 9.
Tel 266 121 122.
www.O2arena.cz

Šeberák
K Šeberáku, Praha 4.

Sparta Stadium
AXA ARENA
Milady Horákové, Praha 7.
Tel 296 111 400.
www.sparta.cz

Tesla Arena
Za Elektrárnou 419,
Praha 7.
Tel 266 727 443.
www.hcsparta.cz

SURVIVAL GUIDE

PRACTICAL INFORMATION

Over the last 20 years, Prague has become more and more open to visitors. The city has responded well to the enormous influx of tourists, and facilities such as hotels, banks, restaurants and information centres have improved considerably. Even so, a little forward planning is always worthwhile. Reading up about a sight, checking if it is open and how best to get there, can save a lot of time and inconvenience.

A Martin Tour sightseeing bus

Prague's transport system is straightforward and most of the city's sights are within walking distance. In general, prices are still considerably lower than in the West, but a few of the more up-market restaurants and hotels are priced according to Western rather than Czech wallets. Despite a small increase in petty crime, especially pickpocketing, Prague is still safer than the majority of Western cities.

TOURIST INFORMATION

There are a number of tourist information offices and specialized agencies. These can provide advice on anything from accommodation and travel to restaurants and guided tours. Many employ English speakers and print English language publications. The efficient **Prague Information Service (PIS)** is the city's best tourist information point. It has three offices in the city centre and it provides visitors with maps, advice, listings (*see pp218–9*) and other types of information in English, German and Czech. To help you find your way around the city, **Kiwi** has a large selection of maps and guides in English.

Čedok street sign

TIPS FOR TOURISTS

In Prague, there are enough English speakers to make booking a room, buying a ticket or ordering a meal relatively simple. A smattering of German may also help, as many Czechs have a working knowledge of the language.

One of the best times to visit Prague is during the summer, although it can be rather crowded. Other busy

times of the year are Easter and major Catholic festivals (*see pp50–53*). The main sights, such as the Old Town Square, are always packed during these periods, but the crowds give Prague a carnival atmosphere. Street entertainers, buskers and small street stalls spring up around the most popular attractions. If the crowds do get too much, just turn off into one of the smaller streets and you are almost guaranteed peace and quiet. Bring a light raincoat for the summer and some warm, woolly clothes for the rest of the year.

OPENING HOURS

This guide lists the opening hours for the individual museums, galleries and churches. Most of the city's major sights can be seen throughout the year, but many of Prague's gardens and the castles outside the city are only

A branch of the Prague Information Service in Staroměstské Náměstí

Entry tickets for some of Prague's major tourist sights

open from 1 April to 31 October. Visiting hours are normally from 9am to 5pm, daily, but during the summer months opening times are extended to 6pm. Note that final admission times can often be as much as an hour earlier. Gardens stay open until 8pm in July and August. All museums and several castles are closed every Monday. The National Museum is closed on the first Tuesday of the month and the Jewish Museum is closed on Saturdays. Museum Night in June is an opportunity to visit collections between 7pm and 1am for free. A free transport service between the museums also operates.

Opening hours of Prague's shops vary widely. Some businesses are open between 7am and 6pm, Monday to Friday, and 8am to noon on Saturdays. Some department stores are open until 7pm on Saturdays and Sundays. Prague does not have any standard late-night shopping, although many of the more expensive tourist shops stay open until around 10pm.

◁ Street vendors and tourists on Charles Bridge

A horse-drawn carriage in the Old Town Square

Banks open from 8am to 4pm, Monday to Friday. Restaurants, cafés and bars all have varied opening hours *(see pp196–7)*. Most of the city's bars open from 10am and as there are no licensing laws, often stay open until everyone leaves.

LISTINGS AND TICKETS

There are dozens of galleries and museums scattered throughout the city, and to find out what's on it is best to look in a listings paper. The English-language newspaper *The Prague Post* gives detailed listings of most events and exhibitions. Available from newsstands in the city centre, it also gives tips for the visitor and informative articles on Prague, its politics and its people. The **PIS** has a free monthly English-language listings booklet entitled *Přehled* which is also useful.

The price of entry tickets for museums varies widely, from Kč60 to around Kč300. Most churches are free, with a collection box at the door. Tickets for entertainment events can be bought from the booking agencies in the city, or at the venue itself. Some of Prague's hotels can get you tickets, or try a large travel agent in the centre.

SIGHTSEEING TIPS

A good way to see Prague is to take a sightseeing tour. Many firms offer trips around Prague's major sights as well as outings to castles such as Karlstein and Konopiště *(see pp168–9)*. Tours usually start from Náměstí Republiky (Republic Square) and from the upper part of Václavské náměstí (Wenceslas Square). These trips can be expensive but prices vary, so it is worth checking what's on offer before you make a booking. The Jewish Museum *(see p87)* organizes trips around the Jewish Quarter. For those on a tight budget, **PIS** offers some of the cheapest tours.

A trip on tram No. 91, run by the Museum of Municipal Mass Transport, is one of the cheapest and best city centre tours. It starts off at the Exhibition Ground *(see pp178–9)* and travels around the Old Town, the New Town and the Jewish Quarter. It runs from Easter to the middle of November every weekend and public holiday. Tickets can be bought on board. Trams 22 and 23 will take you from the city up to the castle. Sightseeing trips in horse-drawn carriages (fiacres) are run from the Old Town Square, and in summer, a "fun train" from Mostecká Street runs through some of the loveliest parts of Hradčany and the Little Quarter.

A Czech signpost located in the Old Town Square

DIRECTORY

INFORMATION CENTRES AND TOUR OPERATORS

Akasi
28.října. **Map** 3 C5.
Tel 22 22 43 067.
Fax 22 42 37 235.

Na Příkopě 3–5. **Map** 3 C4.
Tel 22 42 36 118.
Fax 22 42 37 235.

American Express
Václavské náměstí 56.
Map 6 D1.
Tel 22 28 00 111.
Fax 22 22 11 131.
www.americanexpress.com

Čedok
Na Příkopě 18. **Map** 3 C4.
Tel 22 14 47 242.
Fax 22 42 16 324.

Rytířská 16. **Map** 3 C4.
Tel 24 22 77 23.
www.cedok.cz

Czech Republic Information Centre
Staroměstské náměstí 5.
Map 3 B3.
Tel 22 48 61 476.
www.czechtourism.cz

Kiwi
Jungmannova 23. **Map** 3 C5.
Tel 22 49 48 455.
www.kiwick.cz

Martin Tour Praha
Štěpánská 61. **Map** 5 C1.
Tel 22 42 12 473.
Fax 22 42 39 752.

Corner of Staroměstské náměstí/
Pařížská 1. **Map** 3 B5.
www.martintour.cz

Prague Information Service – PIS
Staroměstské náměstí 1.
Map 3 B3.
Tel 22 17 14 444.

Main station, Hlavní Nádraží.
Map 4 E5. **www**.prague-info.cz

Precious Legacy
Široká 9. **Map** 3 B3.
Tel 22 23 21 951.
www.legacytours.net

Premiant
Palackého 1.
Map 3 C5.
Tel 29 62 46 070.
www.premiant.cz

Personal Security and Health

Compared to many Western cities, Prague is relatively safe. Though you may not need emergency help from the police, you should feel free to approach them at any time for advice of any kind; they are generally very helpful to the tourist population. If you should need emergency medical care during you stay in Prague, it will be given free. There is also a number of English-speaking services available, including health centres, pharmacies and dentists, as well as US and British information centres.

A Prague police sign

ADVICE FOR VISITORS

Prague is a safe and unthreatening city to walk around. Violence and robbery are rare in the city centre and crimes against tourists are usually limited to petty pilfering from cars and hotels, and the only really prevalent issue – pickpockets. Using your common sense should help you to avoid trouble. Always remember to keep your bag in sight and avoid carrying your passport, wallet and valuables in your back pocket or an open bag. Thieves do tend to operate around the popular sights, such as Charles Bridge, and many use diversionary tactics, one knocking into you while the other steals your belongings. It is very unlikely that

Municipal police badge

State police badge

anything stolen will ever be recovered. Never leave anything of value in your car. Car alarms have proved not to be a deterrent. Try and park your car in an underground car park, especially if you are driving a foreign make. Always take out adequate insurance before you arrive as it is difficult to arrange once there. Report any thefts to the police for future insurance claims.

Women travelling on their own may encounter a few unwanted stares and comments, but this is as far as sexual harassment will go. However, one place to try and avoid at night if you are a woman alone is Wenceslas Square as men may assume you are one of the city's prostitutes.

Unfortunately, Prague has too few reputable bars and cafés that stay open into the early hours. The words "nonstop" and "herna" are synonymous with shady characters; the latter are filled with slotmachines and gambling addicts. See our bars and cafés listings for recommended places (see pp208–9) to visit instead.

It is an unwritten law that you should carry your passport at all times and although you are unlikely to be asked to produce it, having it could save a lot of problems. Before you travel take photocopies of all essential documents as replacing them can be difficult and time-consuming.

THE POLICE AND SECURITY SERVICES

In Prague you will come across several kinds of policemen and women and members of various security services. Report any problems to a uniformed state police officer at a police station. The main stations are marked on the Street Finder maps (see pp246–57). The state police carry guns and can arrest a suspect. They patrol the streets on foot or drive green and white patrol cars. The municipal police are the other main security force and are divided into different sections. A new branch specifically for tourists are set to be in force by 2010. They will patrol the main tourist zones between Wenceslas Square, Old Town and around Prague Castle between 10am and midnight targeting petty criminals such as pickpockets and money exchange fraudsters. Special mobile stations will also be set up and staffed by English- and German-speaking officers to enable tourists to report crimes and seek on-the-spot

A male state police officer

A municipal police officer

A female state police officer

A "black sheriff"

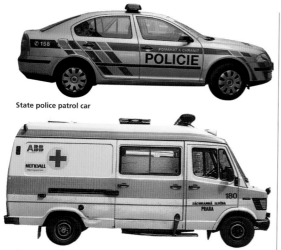

State police patrol car

Prague ambulance

advice. Traffic police regulate parking including clamping and issuing fines *(see pp240–41)*, speeding and drink driving. It is illegal to drive with any alcohol in your bloodstream and if you are caught the penalties are severe. If you have a serious traffic accident, you must immediately ring the police. It is against the law to move anything before the police get there.

There are also a number of private security guards. These are often called "black sheriffs" (many of them actually wear black uniforms) and tend to guard banks and be used as security at football matches. They are not armed.

HEALTH CARE

All EU nationals are entitled to free health care in the Czech Republic. To claim medical treatment, visitors must have a European Health Insurance Card (formerly form E111) which should be presented to the physician along with a valid form of identification. Not all treatments are covered by the card so additional medical insurance is a good idea.

Your hotel should be able to put you in touch with a local doctor if necessary, but

Pharmacy sign

if you need immediate help Prague's emergency services are available 24 hours a day so you can call an ambulance in an emergency. Hospitals with casualty units are marked on the Street Finder maps *(see pp246–57)*.

There are also 24-hour pharmacies (lékárna) *(see p217)* with staff who are qualified to give advice and administer simple remedies. If you want an English-speaking doctor, visit the **Diplomatic Health Centre** for foreigners at Na Homolce. Alternatively, try the **Canadian Medical Center** or, for dental care, the **American Dental Associates**. You will need to take a passport and a means of payment with you if you wish to use these services.

Those with respiratory problems should be aware that between October and March sulphur dioxide levels in Prague occasionally exceed the World Health Organization's accepted levels. With increasing car ownership in the city and a lack of money for alternative fuels, this situation seems unlikely to improve in the near future, so if you are likely to be affected be sure to take any medication you might need with you.

DIRECTORY

EMERGENCY NUMBERS

Ambulance
Rychlá lékařská pomoc
Tel 155.

Police
Tísňové volání policie
Tel 158.

Fire
Tísňové volání hasičů
Tel 150.

Emergency Operator
Tel 112 (in English).

MEDICAL CENTRES

American Dental Associates
V celnici 4. **Map** 4 D3.
(8am–6pm Mon–Fri, 8am–noon Sat.)
Tel 22 11 81 121.

Canadian Medical Center
Veleslavínská 1.
Tel 23 53 60 133.
www.cmcpraha.cz

Diplomatic Health Centre
Nemocnice Na Homolce
Roentgenova 2.
Tel 25 72 71 111.
www.homolka.cz

24-hour Pharmacy
Palackého 5.
Tel 22 49 46 982. **Map** 3 C5.

Lékárna U Svaté Ludmily
Belgická 37.
Tel 22 42 37 207.
Map 6 F3.

GENERAL HELP

American Centre
Americké středisko
US Embassy, Tržistě 13. **Map** 2 E3.
Tel 25 75 30 640.
www.usembassy.cz

British Council
Britské kulturní středisko
Politických Vězňů13. **Map** 4 D5.
Tel 22 19 91 160.
www.britishcouncil.cz

Car Breakdown Service/Road Accidents
Tel 1230.

Lost and Found
Ztráty a nálezy
Karoliny Světlé 5. **Map** 3 A5.
Tel 22 42 35 085.

Money, Banks and Currency Exchange Offices

A bureau de change sign in Prague

Compared to many European cities, Prague is a relatively cheap city to visit. Hundreds of banks and bureaux de change have been established, some staying open all night. For the lowest charges and, unfortunately, the longest queues, it is best to change money in a bank. Credit cards are becoming more and more accepted. Traveller's cheques can only be changed in banks.

BANKING

Hundreds of private banks and bureaux de change have been opened in Prague since 1989. The large, modern banks – generally found in the city centre – all open between 8am and 5pm Monday to Friday. The banks may not close at lunch. There are always long queues at the exchange tills so make sure you get there well before closing time. Hundreds of bureaux de change are found in tiny shops throughout the city. However, despite sometimes offering better exchange rates than the banks, their commission charges are huge, often as high as 12% compared to the bank's 1–5%. But there is a minimum bank commission of Kč20–50. The main advantage of these exchange offices is their convenience. Many are open late every day, some offer a 24-hour service, and queues are rare.

Most of the larger hotels will also change foreign currency for you, but again commission rates may be very high. If you find you have some Czech currency left over from your stay, you can reconvert your money. All banks will reconvert your extra crowns for a small commission. Finally, never change your money on the

black market. As well as being illegal the rate is not any higher than banks or exchanges and it is likely you'll be given notes that are not legal tender.

There are also may ATM machines in the centre of Prague. Some of these are in the entrance to banks and are open when the branch is

An automatic teller machine for dispensing cash

closed. They accept most major credit and debit cards, and information is in English, German, French or Czech.

CREDIT CARDS

Paying by credit card is becoming more popular in Prague but even if a shop or restaurant window sports a credit card sign, do not assume they will accept all types of card as payment; if in a restaurant, it is always better to ask before you eat your meal to avoid difficulties later. The cards most often accepted are: American Express, VISA and MasterCard. Most banks will allow cash advances (up to your limit) on your card.

Façade of the Československá Obchodní bank

DIRECTORY

BANKS

Česká Národní Banka
Na příkopě 28. **Map** 3 C4.
Tel 22 44 11 111.
Fax 22 44 12 404.
www.cnb.cz

Česká Spořitelna
Rytířská 29. **Map** 3 C4.
Tel 22 14 60 801.
www.csas.cz

Commercial Bank
KOMERČNI BANKA
Spálená 51. **Map** 3 B5.
Tel 22 24 11 111.
www.kb.cz
One of several branches.

Czechoslovak Commercial Bank
ČESKOSLOVENSKÁ OBCHODNÍ BANKA
Na příkopě 18. **Map** 3 C4.
Tel 26 13 51 111.
www.csob.cz

GE Money Bank
Opletalova 4. **Map** 4 D5.
Tel 22 44 90 630.
www.gemoney.cz

Unicredit Bank
Revoluční 7. **Map** 4 D2.
Tel 22 11 19 768.
Fax 22 11 19 796.
www.unicreditbank.cz

BUREAUX DE CHANGE

American Express
Václavské náměstí 56.
Map 3 C5.
Tel 22 28 00 237.
Fax 22 22 11 131.
www.americanexpress.com

Exact Change
Na Poříčí 13.
Map 4 D3.
Tel 22 48 19 744.
One of several branches.

Interchange
Železná 1. **Map** 3 C4.
Tel 22 42 21 839.
One of several branches.

CASH AND TRAVELLER'S CHEQUES

The currency in Prague is the Czech crown. Hellers (of which there are theoretically 100 to the crown) began being phased out in 2008. It is legal to bring Czech currency into and out of the Czech Republic. Traveller's cheques are the safest alternative to carrying cash. It is recommended that you take well-known brands – American Express, Thomas Cook, for example – although it is unlikely that the major banks will refuse any. However, traveller's cheques are not accepted as currency by any shops or restaurants and must be changed at exchanges or banks. The American Express office sells and cashes traveller's cheques. They don't charge commission for cashing their own cheques.

Banknotes

*Czech banknotes are now in circulation in the denominations Kč50, Kč100, Kč200, Kč500, Kč1,000, Kč2,000 and Kč5,000.***Kč50 note**

Coins

Coins come in the following denominations: Kč1, Kč2, Kč5, Kč10, Kč20 and Kč50. All the coins have the Czech emblem, a lion rampant, on one side.

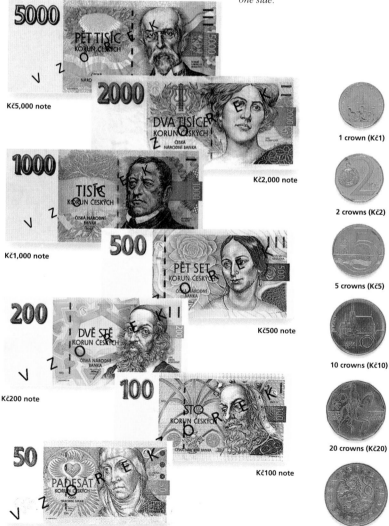

Kč5,000 note

Kč2,000 note

Kč1,000 note

Kč500 note

Kč200 note

Kč100 note

Kč50 note

1 crown (Kč1)

2 crowns (Kč2)

5 crowns (Kč5)

10 crowns (Kč10)

20 crowns (Kč20)

50 crowns (Kč50)

Communications

The Czech telephone and postal service, Telecom, has undergone a major modernization programme. Digital phones have replaced the older coin-operated ones, and the postal service has become much more efficient. There were some problems in the transition, but the upgrading and improvements have been completed and few problems should be experienced.

USING A PHONECARD TELEPHONE

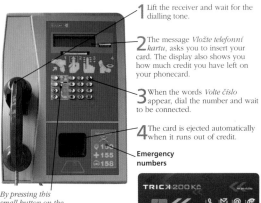

1 Lift the receiver and wait for the dialling tone.

2 The message *Vložte telefonní kartu*, asks you to insert your card. The display also shows you how much credit you have left on your phonecard.

3 When the words *Volte číslo* appear, dial the number and wait to be connected.

4 The card is ejected automatically when it runs out of credit.

Emergency numbers

By pressing this small button on the phone at any time during your call, you can have an English translation of the instructions.

The multi-purpose TRICK phonecard

REACHING THE RIGHT NUMBER

	Dial
• Internal (Czech) directory enquiries	1180
• Prague directory enquiries and the operator	1180
• International exchange and to make a collect call *(ask for an English-speaker)*	1181
• International call followed by the country code	00
• International directory enquiries	1181
• **In case of emergencies (Police)**	**158**
• **Emergency operator (English)**	**112**

USING PUBLIC TELEPHONES

With the growing use of mobile phones, there are fewer public phones but you will still find them on busy street corners and in metro stations. You can also find them in post offices, where you have to leave a deposit, make the call, and then pay what you owe to the attendant. In hotels, you can usually get a direct line but commission charges on the calls are

often exorbitant. Remember also that international calls are extremely expensive, no matter what time of day you phone. But they are at least somewhat cheaper after 7pm, and also on Saturdays and Sundays. The cheapest way to call abroad is after 5pm and on weekends via Telecom's Xcall service (ring 970 00).

You will need a phonecard to use a public phone in Prague. You can buy phonecards *(Telefonní karta)* from most tabáks and newsstands,

and from post offices, supermarkets and petrol stations. Two very popular cards are Karta X, a pre-paid calling card which allows you to make national and international calls from any phone, and TRICK, a multifunctional card which can be used to pay for telephone calls and internet services. On all phones in the country the dialling tone is a short note followed by a long one; the ringing tone consists of long regular notes, and the engaged signal has short and rapid notes.

PROBLEM NUMBERS

If you have problems getting through to a number in Prague, it is very likely that the number has changed due to the modernization of the phone system. To check, ring the directory enquiries number and ask for an English speaker.

MOBILE PHONES

Czech mobile phones operate on a GSM band of 900/1800 MHz, the same standard in use throughout Europe, but different from that used in the United States. US cell phones will work provided they are tri-band phones and that the service provider allows for international roaming. To avoid high roaming fees, you can also buy local pay-as-you-go SIM cards, which give you a temporary telephone number and allow you to make calls and send text messages on the local network.

Pay-as-you-go cards are quite reasonably priced, starting at around Kč200 for the basic card. The three main mobile phone operators are Telefonica O2 (www.cz.o2. com), Vodaphone (www. vodafone.cz) and T-Mobile (www.t-mobile.cz). All offer some form of pay-as-you-go service. Buy the cards at phone stores or newsagents around town.

INTERNET ACCESS

Most hotels offer guests some form of in-room Internet access, through either a wireless or a LAN connection.

Wireless connections may not be reliable, depending on how far your room is from the router. If Internet access is important to you, it's best to mention this at the hotel reception when checking in and request a room with a strong wireless signal.

Most hotels will usually also have a public computer terminal for guests to surf the Internet or, failing that, will allow guests to quickly check email on the hotel computer. The receptionist should know the location of the nearest Internet café.

Internet cafés are relatively common in Prague. One of the best is **Káva Káva Káva** in the New Town area. Rates at most Internet cafés are reasonable, at from Kč1 to Kč2 per minute. Just because the word "café" is part of the name, don't assume they will serve coffee or that the coffee will be drinkable if they do. It is also worth bearing in mind that more and more cafés, bars and restaurants are offering customers with laptops free wireless access. Look for a "wi-fi hotspot" sticker on the door. Connections are usually straightforward and pretty fast. If there's a password, the staff should be able to tell you what it is.

Post Office sign

POST OFFICES

There are a number of post offices in Prague *(see Street Finder on pp246–57)*. The best and largest one is the **Main Post Office** in Jindřišská, just off Wenceslas Square. It has a huge variety of services, including a large phone room where you can make international calls. This service operates from 7am to 11pm. The main post office has undergone a complete

Tobacconist's, where you can also buy stamps and phonecards

refurbishment, and is now modern and straightforward to use, with easy-access information in English, and swift and efficient service. Take a ticket when you enter the building and then follow the number on it to the correct booth, which will be indicated by an electronic display.

The main post office on Jindřišská is open from 2am to midnight. Most other post offices offer more regular business hours from 9am to 5pm or 6pm Monday to Friday, and from 9am until noon on Saturday.

SENDING A LETTER

The postal service is now fast, but prices for all the post office services are expected to increase slightly in the future.

There is no first or second class mail in the Czech Republic, but the majority of letters usually arrive at their destination within a few days.

If you want to send something more valuable through the post, use the registered mail service, which is reliable and efficient. Aerogrammes abroad do not exist.

Postcards or letters can be posted in the many orange post boxes scattered around Prague. Both take around five working days to arrive in the UK and about a week to get to America. Stamps can

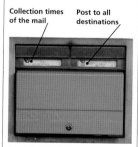

Collection times of the mail

Post to all destinations

A standard post box

be bought from post offices, newsagents or tabáks – who will also tell you what stamps you need. All parcels and registered letters need to be handed in at a post office.

For emergency parcels and packages which need to arrive quickly, you can use an international courier service, such as **DHL**, rather than the post office.

POSTE RESTANTE

Post restante letters are delivered to the Main Post Office in Jindřišská Street. Go to window 1 or 2 (open Monday to Friday 7am to 8pm and Saturday 7am to noon) with your passport or other official identification. The **American Express** office will also hold mail and parcels for up to a month for anyone who is a registered card holder.

DIRECTORY

USEFUL ADDRESSES

Main Post Office
Jindřišská 14. **Map** 4 D5.
Tel 22 11 31 111. **Tel** 800 10
44 10 (general information).
Open 2am–midnight daily.
www.cpost.cz

American Express
Václavské náměstí 56.
Map 4 D5.
Tel 22 28 00 237.
Fax 22 22 11 131.
www.americanexpress.com

DHL
Václavské náměstí 47.
Map 4 D5. **Tel** 800 103 000.
www.dhl.cz

Káva Káva Káva
Národní 37. **Map** 3 B5.
Tel 22 42 28 862.
Open 7am–10pm daily
(from 9am Sat & Sun).
www.kava-coffee.cz

Additional Information

Visitors shopping and relaxing on Na Příkopě

You can take in as much foreign currency as you like, however, it is illegal to take more than Kč350,000 out of the Czech Republic. To export authentic antiques you need to obtain a special licence *(see Shopping p214)*. VAT (value added tax) can be claimed back on items totalling Kč2,000 or more which are carried out of the country within 30 days of purchase.

STUDENT INFORMATION

If you are entitled to an International Student Identity Card (ISIC), it is worth getting one before travelling to Prague. Admission charges into most of Prague's major tourist sights are cheaper on production of a valid ISIC card. Students can also get cheaper coach and train travel. If you are looking for somewhere cheap to stay, there are a couple of youth hostels in the centre of the city that provide good value accommodation for young people *(see Where to Stay, pp186–7)*.

DISABLED TRAVELLERS

Facilities for the disabled are few and far between in Prague. The prevalence of narrow streets and uneven paving, especially in the historic centre, can also contribute to problems. Occasionally you will come across a ramp at the entrance to a building to allow the disabled easier access, but this is the exception rather than the rule. Newer hotels usually have better facilities, however, and there are some organizations that campaign for the disabled. Unfortunately, those that do are currently hampered by both public inertia and a lack of funding.

Despite, this, these attitudes are slowly changing and, although transport around the city is a major problem, groups do now exist who can help you with advice, sightseeing tours, accommodation and getting around the city. Two of the best organizations to contact in advance of your trip are the **Czech Association of Persons with Disabilities** and the **Prague Wheelchair Association**.

Czech Association of Persons with Disabilities
Karlínské náměstí 12.
Map 5 B2.
Tel 22 23 17 489.
www.svaztp.cz

Prague Wheelchair Association
Benediktská 6.
Map 4 D3.
Tel 22 48 27 210.
Fax 22 48 26 079.
www.pov.cz

CUSTOMS REGULATIONS AND IMMIGRATION

A valid passport or, where applicable, an ID card is needed when entering the Czech Republic from countries outside the Schengen Zone of 25 European nations. Visitors are advised to contact the Czech embassy or consulate, or check details with their travel agent to confirm visa requirements before travelling. British nationals must have a valid passport or identity card, but visas are not required (www.czechembassy.org.uk/consular.htm). Visitors from the United States, Canada, Australia and New Zealand need a valid passport with a minimum of 90 days remaining on it, and can stay for up to three months without a visa. If you require a visa you can obtain one from your nearest Czech embassy or consulate.

For non-EU visitors, customs allowances per person are 2 litres (3.6 pints) of wine, 1 litre (1.8 pints) of spirits, 200 cigarettes or equivalent tobacco products. Goods under 175 euros in value can be imported duty-free.

EMBASSIES AND CONSULATES

Australian Consulate
Klimentská 10. **Map** 4 D2.
Tel 29 65 78 350. **Open**
9am–1pm, 2–5pm Mon–Fri.

Canadian Embassy
Muchova 6.
Tel 27 21 01 800. **Open**
8.30am–12.30pm Mon–Fri.
www.canada.cz

New Zealand Consulate
Tel 22 25 14 672. **Fax** *22 42 54 640. (Can be unattended. Lost passport: contact UK Embassy; in emergency: call Consulate in Berlin: 00 49 30 20 62 10 or 00 49 17 27 20 69 92 out of hours).*

United Kingdom Embassy
Thunovská 14. **Map** 2 E3.
Tel 25 74 02 111.
Open *9–11:30am Mon–Fri.*
www.britain.cz

United States Embassy
Tržiště 15. **Map** 2 E3. *Tel 25 70 22 000.* **Open** *9am–4:30pm Mon–Fri.* **www**.usembassy.cz

English-language newspaper published in Prague

NEWSPAPERS, TV, RADIO

Prague has a number of newspapers including a weekly English-language one, *The Prague Post*. It is well produced and provides useful tips for visitors to the city as well as up-to-date and informative pieces on Prague, its people and politics. It also includes a good leisure supplement, *Night and Day*.

Most of the newsstands that are around Wenceslas Square and other popular tourist spots sell the main quality European newspapers such as *The Times*, the *Guardian*, *El País* and *Die Zeit*, as well as US papers such as the *International Herald Tribune*.

These days there is a larger choice of television in Prague than ever before. Western films are interspersed with well-made nature programmes and classic Czech films. Various satellite

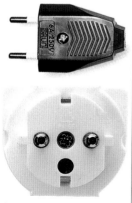

A two-prong and a three-prong plug adaptor for use in Prague

channels are also available, plus numerous programmes in English, including the daily news.

You can listen to the BBC World Service on 101.1FM, but one of the most popular radio stations is Europe II on 88.2MHz playing a blend of mainstream pop. Other stations include Radio I on 91.9MHz and Radio Bonton on 99.7MHz. You can also listen to the BBC on the Internet by logging on to www.bbc.co.uk.

CONVERSION CHART

Imperial to Metric
1 inch = 2.54 centimetres
1 foot = 30 centimetres
1 mile = 1.6 kilometres
1 ounce = 28 grams
1 pound = 454 grams
1 pint = 0.6 litre
1 gallon = 4.6 litres

Metric to Imperial
1 millimetre = 0.04 inch
1 centimetre = 0.4 inch
1 metre = 3 feet 3 inches
1 kilometre = 0.6 mile
1 gram = 0.04 ounce
1 kilogram = 2.2 pounds
1 litre = 1.8 pints

ELECTRICAL ADAPTORS

The electricity supply in Prague is 230V AC and two-pin plugs are used. For British or US plugs, an adaptor is needed. Adaptors may not be easily found in Prague and it is wise to bring one with you if you plan to use your own electrical items.

PRAGUE TIME

Prague is on Central European time, which is Greenwich Mean Time (GMT) plus 1 hour. Summer time runs effectively from the end of March up until the end of October – this is GMT plus 2 hours. New York is 6 hours behind Prague, and Los Angeles 9 hours behind. Sydney is 8 hours ahead (10 in summer), while Moscow and Johannesburg are 3 and 2 hours ahead respectively.

RELIGIOUS SERVICES

Anglican
St. Clement's; Klimentská 5.
Map 4 D2. 🕆 *11am Sun.*

Baptist
International Baptist Church of Prague; Vinohradská 68.
Map 6 F1.
***Tel** 73 17 78 735.* 🕆 *11am Sun.*

Hussite Church
Church of St. Nicholas; Staroměstské náměstí. **Map** 3 C3.
***Tel** 23 47 60 058.* 🕆 *10:30am Sun.* **www**.husiti.cz

Interdenominational
International Church; Peroutkova 57. ***Tel** 29 63 92 338.* **www**.internationalchurchof prague.cz
🕆 *(in English) 10:30am Sun.*

Jewish
Old-New Synagogue (see pp88–9). Jerusalem Synagogue; Jeruzalémská 7. **Map** 4 E4. **www**.kehilaprag.cz ✡ *(in Hebrew) Sundown Fri; 9am Sat.*

Methodist-Evangelical
Ječná 19. **Map** 5 C2.
***Tel** 22 25 05 020.* **www**.praguefellowship.cz
🕆 *4:30pm Sun.*

Roman Catholic
Services are held in many churches. Some are: Church of the Infant Jesus of Prague, Karmelitská 9.
Map 2 E4. ***Tel** 25 75 33 646.* **www**.apha.cz 🕆 *(in English)* noon Sun. Church of St. Thomas, Josefská 8. **Map** 2 E3. ***Tel** 25 75 32 675. 5 (in English) 11am Sun.*

A Roman Catholic service

GETTING TO PRAGUE

Prague is located at the heart of Europe and – apart from the Czech Republic's lack of motorways – has good transport connections with the rest of the continent. There are direct flights every day from most of Europe's major cities and, via ČSA and Delta Airlines, to selected cities in the USA. However, there are no direct flights from Australia. International coach transport is efficient and cheap but journey times can be off-putting. International rail transport is a popular method of travelling to Prague, but trains tend to get booked up early, especially in the summer. The main train station (Hlavní nádraží) is close to Wenceslas Square and the city centre and, except for the airport, other major points of arrival are also fairly central.

ČSA logo

AIR TRAVEL

There are 50 international airlines which now fly to Prague airport. If you are flying from the United States, **Delta Air** operates a limited number of non-stop flights from Atlanta and New York. There are no Australian or New Zealand carriers flying to Prague, although you can fly **British Airways** with a stop in London. Other major airlines include **Air France**, **KLM**, **Alitalia**, **Lufthansa** and **Czech Airlines (ČSA)**. It takes about one and a half hours to fly from London to Prague and about nine hours from the east coast of America.

DISCOUNT FARES

Prague has become increasingly popular with budget carriers, both as a hub and a destination. Both **Easy Jet** and **Ryanair** fly regularly between Prague and cities in the UK. **Sky Europe**, **Smart Wings** and **German Wings** are popular budget carriers that connect Prague to destinations around the rest of Europe.

APEX (advanced purchase) tickets can be good buys, but they have stringent conditions attached to them. These include having to book your ticket at least a month in advance and severe penalties if you cancel your flight.

If you ring well in advance, airlines will quote you the standard fare, but the price may be lowered nearer the time if seats remain unsold – this is rarely the case in the summer months, however, as Prague is such a popular destination. You may get a better deal in winter. Students, senior citizens and regular business travellers may all be able to get discounts at any time of year. Children under two (who do not occupy a separate seat) pay 10% of the adult fare. Fares are more expensive in July and August. If you do get a cheap deal, ensure that you will get a refund if your agent goes out of business.

Porters at Prague Airport

AIRLINE OFFICES

Air France
Ruzyně Airport. **Map** 3 C5.
Tel 22 01 13 737. www.airfrance.com

British Airways
Ruzyně Airport. *Tel 23 90 00 299*
www.britishairways.com

Czech Airlines (ČSA)
V Celnici 5. **Map** 4 D3.
Tel 23 90 07 007. www.csa.cz

Delta Airlines
Národní 32. **Map** 3 B5.
Tel 23 47 23 260. www.delta-air.cz

Easy Jet
www.easyjet.com

German Wings
www.germanwings.com

KLM
Ruzyně Airport. **Map** 3 C5.
Tel 23 30 90 933. www.klm.com

Lufthansa
Ruzyně Airport. *Tel 23 40 08 234.*
www.lufthansa.com

Ryanair
www.ryanair.com

Sky Europe
www.skyeurope.com

Smart Wings
www.smartwings.com

Terminal North 2 at Prague Airport

PRAGUE AIRPORT

Prague's only international airport is at Ruzyně, 15 km (9 miles) northwest of the city centre. The airport is modern, clean, efficient and functional. It offers all that you would expect from an international air-

PASOVÁ KONTROLA
PASSPORT CONTROL
Sign for passport control

port: 24-hour exchange facilities; car rental offices; a duty-free shop; post office and a left-luggage office.

The airport was thoroughly modernized at the start of the millennium, including the addition of a new terminal, opened in 2006. The North 1 terminal is used for inter-continental flights, including those to the UK, North America, the Middle East, Africa and Asia. Flights within the EU and other European destinations are served by the new North 2 terminal. Other changes include a new business class lounge and catering facility.

TRANSPORT FROM THE AIRPORT TO THE CITY

The airport is linked to the city centre by a regular mini-bus service run by **CEDAZ**. For the return trip to the airport, these can be picked up at V celnici street, a short distance from Náměstí Republiky. Buses leave every 30 minutes from 5:30am to 9:30pm and tickets cost Kč120 per person. **CEDAZ** also offers a mini-bus service on demand to and from the airport. For a group of one to four people, the trip into town costs Kč480; for five to eight people it is Kč960. The buses can also take you to

CEDAZ bus operating between the airport and the city

addresses outside the city, and can even be used to tour the Czech Republic.

There is also a regular public bus service to the airport from Dejvická metro (bus 119) and from Zličín metro (bus 100).

Alternatively, there is always a rank of taxis waiting in front of the terminal. Ask at the information booth about the price you should expect to pay for a taxi into town; it is likely to be about Kč600.

CEDAZ
Tel *22 01 14 296 or 22 42 81 005.*
Fax *22 01 14 286.*
www.cedaz.cz

The airport forecourt, from which buses and taxis can be taken into town

PRAGUE'S EUROPEAN AIR CONNECTIONS

Prague, situated at the centre of Europe, has good flight connections to most major European cities. It can be reached in less than two and a half hours on direct flights from all the airports marked on the map.

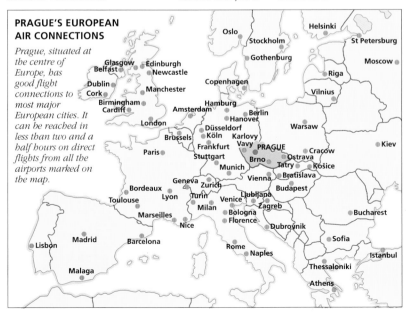

Oslo
Helsinki
Stockholm
St Petersburg
Gothenburg
Moscow
Glasgow   Edinburgh
Belfast   Newcastle
Riga
Dublin
Copenhagen
Cork   Manchester
Vilnius
Birmingham   Hamburg
Cardiff   Amsterdam   Berlin
Hanover   Warsaw
London   Düsseldorf
Brussels   Köln   Karlovy
Frankfurt   Vavy   PRAGUE   Kiev
Paris   Stuttgart   Craçow
Munich   Brno   Ostrava
Tatry   Košice
Geneva   Vienna   Bratislava
Bordeaux   Zurich
Lyon   Turin   Ljubljana   Budapest
Toulouse   Venice   Zagreb
Marseilles   Milan
Nice   Bologna   Bucharest
Florence
Dubrovnik
Lisbon   Madrid   Barcelona
Rome   Sofia
Naples
Malaga   Thessaloniki
Istanbul
Athens

The spacious interior of the railway station, Masarykovo Nádraži

TRAVELLING BY TRAIN

Prague is connected by rail to all the major capitals of Europe. Rail travel can be an enjoyable, if rather slow, way to travel to and from Prague. International trains have dining cars and couchettes, and tickets are cheaper than air fares. The railways in the Czech Republic are run by the State (České Dráhy – ČD).

The façade of Hlavní nádraží

There are information offices at stations, and these usually have English speakers, so you shouldn't have any trouble booking a ticket. PIS and Čedok (see p227) will help you with timetables and prices. There are four types of train run by ČD. These are the *rychlík* (express) trains; the *osobní* (passenger) trains, which form a local service and stop at all stations, often travelling as slowly as 30 km/h (20 mph); the EX, or national express; and the EC (Eurocity) or international express. International trains are

the fastest. Tickets can be bought in advance or on the day at stations or at the **Travel Agency of Czech Railways** *(see p186)*, however, trains tend to get booked up quickly. If you do want to buy a ticket just before your train leaves, be warned that queues at ticket booths can be long. When you buy your ticket, specify exactly where and when you want to go, whether you want a single or return and what class of ticket you want. First class carriages exist on most trains and guarantee you a seat. In the timetable, an 'R' in a box by a train number means you must have a seat reserved on that train. An 'R' without a box means a reservation is recommended. If you are caught in the wrong carriage, you have to pay an on-the-spot fine.

TRAIN STATIONS

The biggest and busiest railway station in Prague is Hlavní nádraží which is only a five-minute walk from the city centre. In 2008 work started on a thorough renovation of the station to clean it up and reverse the insensitive restoration carried out in

the 1970s. Work is expected to be finished by 2011. The station is large, with a good-sized, inexpensive, 24-hr left-luggage office in the basement. The nearby luggage lockers are convenient and very cheap. There are also food stalls, bureaux de change and a number of booking and information services in the departure hall.

The other rail stations in the city are Masarykovo nádraží – Prague's oldest terminal, the Holešovice Station and the smallest, Smíchov Station.

TRAVELLING BY COACH

Coach connections from Prague to many of the major European cities can be infrequent and are often booked up. However, many of these coach routes are much cheaper, and often faster, than the slower trains. The city's main bus terminal is Florenc, situated on the eastern edge of the New Town. During the summer months there are hundreds of coach trips to all the major coastal resorts in southern Europe. These get booked up quickly by Czechs, so buy your ticket in advance and be sure to reserve yourself a seat. International bus timetables are confusing; check with PIS *(see p227)* for more detailed information. Coach travel is cheap, but long-haul journeys can be uncomfortable and are slower than air.

A uniformed ČD railway porter

Passengers boarding a long-haul coach

PRAGUE'S MAJOR RAIL AND COACH STATIONS

The major points of arrival by train and coach are all fairly central and easily accessible by metro – the nearest metro to each terminal is shown in the boxes along with more detailed travel information.

KEY

🚆 Railway

●— station

Ⓜ Metro station

🚌 Coach

○ station

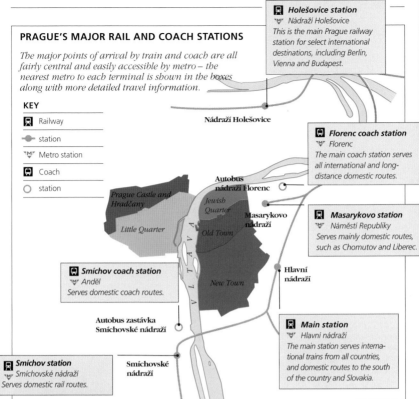

🚆 Holešovice station
Ⓜ *Nádraží Holešovice*
This is the main Prague railway station for select international destinations, including Berlin, Vienna and Budapest.

🚌 Florenc coach station
Ⓜ *Florenc*
The main coach station serves all international and long-distance domestic routes.

🚆 Masarykovo station
Ⓜ *Náměstí Republiky*
Serves mainly domestic routes, such as Chomutov and Liberec.

🚌 Smíchov coach station
Ⓜ *Anděl*
Serves domestic coach routes.

🚆 Main station
Ⓜ *Hlavní nádraží*
The main station serves international trains from all countries, and domestic routes to the south of the country and Slovakia.

🚆 Smíchov station
Ⓜ *Smíchovské nádraží*
Serves domestic rail routes.

Nádraží Holešovice

Prague Castle and Hradčany

Jewish Quarter

Little Quarter

Old Town

Masarykovo nádraží

Autobus nádraží Florenc

Hlavní nádraží

New Town

V L T A V A

Autobus zastávka Smíchovské nádraží

Smíchovské nádraží

A Czech motorway sign

TRAVELLING BY CAR

To drive a car in the Czech Republic you must be at least 18. Most foreign driving licences, including Canadian, US and EC ones, are honoured – New Zealand and Australian drivers should get an International Driving Licence. If you bring your own car to Prague, by law you must carry the following with you at all times: a valid driver's licence, vehicle registration card, a hire certificate or, if you are borrowing the car, a letter signed by the owner and authorized by a recognized body, such as the AA or RAC, giving you permission to drive it and a Green Card (an international motoring certificate for insurance). If you drive on the motorway, you will also need to display a special highway sticker available at the border, petrol stations and post offices. Other items you have to carry at all times are a set of replacement bulbs, red warning triangles and a first-aid kit. You also have to display a national identification sticker. Headlights must be used even during daylight hours between November and April, and whenever visibility is poor. It is compulsory to wear seatbelts if fitted, and children under 12 are not allowed in the front seat. When you are driving it is strictly forbidden to have any alcohol in your blood and to use a mobile phone.

There are now good connections to all the major cities in the Czech Republic, including Plzeň and Brno, and many more are currently under construction.

The speed limit on motorways is 130 km/h (81 mph); on dual and single carriageways 90 km/h (56 mph) and in urban areas 50 km/h (31 mph). The traffic police patrolling the roads are very vigilant, and any infringements are dealt with harshly. There are also occasional road blocks to catch drunken drivers.

The popular, Czech-made Škoda car

GETTING AROUND PRAGUE

The centre of Prague is conveniently small and most of the sights can be reached comfortably on foot. But to cross the city quickly or visit a more remote sight, the public transport is efficient, clean and cheap. It is based on trams, buses and the underground (metro) system, all of which are run by the Prague Transport Corporation (Dopravní podnik). Throughout this guide, the best method of transport

Walking around the city

is given for each sight. The metro and trams serve the city centre, while buses are used to reach the suburbs. The entire system is simple to use – only one ticket is needed for all three forms of transport. Bus, tram and metro routes are found on city maps, available at most city centre tabáks, bookshops and newsagents; or refer to the map on the inside back cover of this guide.

DRIVING A CAR

Most visitors are better off not driving around the centre of Prague. The city's complex web of one-way streets, the large number of pedestrianized areas around the historic core of the city and a very severe shortage of parking spaces make driving very difficult. Prague's public transport system is a much more efficient way of travelling around the city centre.

If you do decide to use a car, remember that on-the-spot fines for traffic violations are common, especially if you are caught driving in one of the city's restricted areas, such as Wenceslas Square. Prague's motorists have become less disciplined and caution is often needed, You must drive on the right and the law states that both driver and front- and back-seat passengers should wear seat belts, if they are fitted. The speed limit in the city is 50 km/h (31 mph) unless a sign indicates otherwise. Traffic signs are similar

One-way traffic and No stopping except for supply lorries

to those in Western Europe. Cars can be useful for seeing sights outside the city. Car rental is inexpensive, but public transport is almost as efficient getting out of the city as in it (see pp236–9).

PARKING

Car parking spaces in the city centre are scarce and the penalties for illegal parking, harsh. Many parking spaces are reserved for residents and marked with a blue line.

Pedestrian zone

Pedestrian crossing

PRAGUE ON FOOT

Walking around Prague is the most enjoyable way to see the city. Some pedestrian crossings are controlled by traffic lights, but be sure to cross only when the green man is showing, and even then, check the road carefully. It is now illegal for drivers to ignore pedestrian crossings, but for years they were allowed to do so, and old habits die hard. Those crossings without lights are still ignored by drivers. Remember that trams run in the centre of the road and go in both directions, which can be confusing. They also travel at high speeds, occasionally coming upon you with little warning. With the uneven cobbled streets, steep hills and a mass of tram lines, flat comfortable shoes are strongly recommended.

Street or square name and Prague district

Street number

City registration number

Brown street signs with tourist information

Parking meters are rare. To use them, insert coins for the amount of time you need and display your receipt prominently on the dashboard. Unfortunately, car theft is rife, and expensive Western cars are a favourite target. It is safer to park in an official – preferably underground – car park *(see the Street Finder pp246–57)*. But these are expensive and tend to get full early on in the morning. Many parking spaces are reserved for office workers and disabled drivers. Parking at central hotels is limited, with only a few spaces allocated. It is better to park at one of the guarded car parks at the edge of the city and use public transport to get in.

Parking sign

TOWING AND CLAMPING

Many Prague locals park on the pavement. But ignoring *No Parking* signs may well mean that you find your car has been towed away or clamped. Both the municipal and the private firms that patrol the city are vigilant and ruthless with illegally parked cars, especially with foreign cars. If your car has disappeared, ring 158 to find out if it has been towed away or stolen. To reclaim your towed-away car, you have to go to one of the parking lots (the police will tell you which one) and pay a hefty fine before the car is released. Wheel clamping is becoming

Prague's colourful clamp, also known as the Denver Boot

very popular. You must pay a fine of 1,300 crowns at a police station (the ticket on your windscreen will tell you the address) and return to your car to wait for the clamp to be removed.

THE TRANSPORT SYSTEM

The best way to get around the city centre is by metro or tram. Prague's rush hours are between 6am and 8am and 3pm and 5pm, Monday to Friday. But more trains, trams and buses run at these times, so crowding is not usually a problem. Some bus routes to the suburbs only run during peak hours. There are information offices at Muzeum and Můstek metro stations (open 7am–9pm daily), at Ruzyně Airport (open 7am–10pm daily) and at Nádraží Holešovice; staff are friendly and helpful, and English is spoken.

One of the many newsstands in Wenceslas Square

TICKETS

Paying on the transport system relies on the honour system. Be aware, however, that periodic checks are carried out by plain-clothes ticket inspectors who levy an on-the-spot and large fine if you don't have a valid ticket. A transfer ticket covers the entire system – bus, tram and metro – and allows 75 minutes of travel after validation on weekdays and 90 minutes at the weekend. Buy the ticket before you travel and validate it in the machines provided, or you will be travelling illegally. You can buy single ride tickets, valid for 20 minutes of travel on trams and buses or for five stations on metro lines. Transfers are not allowed with single ride tickets. You can also buy longer-term tickets, which are often more convenient and a good idea if you are visiting Prague for one or more days and planning on seeing many

tourist sights around the city. Longer-term tickets offer unlimited rides on buses, trams and the metro for periods ranging from 24 hours to five days.

Three-day pass   **Transfer ticket**

Travelling by Metro

The underground railway, known as the metro, is the quickest and most comfortable form of transport in Prague. Managed by the Prague Transport Corporation *(see p240)*, its construction began in 1967. It has three lines, A, B and C. The straightforward layout and clear signs make finding your way around the system very easy. Trains run between 5am and midnight.

**The metro sign for
Můstek metro station**

FINDING YOUR WAY AROUND THE METRO

Metro entrances are not always easy to spot. Look for a sign displaying the 'M' within an upside-down triangle *(see right)*. The street entrance will normally lead you down a flight of steps. A high-pitched bleep (for the blind) at some entrances can also help to guide you.

Once you have purchased your ticket and passed through the unmanned ticket barriers, continue down the fast-moving escalators to the trains. At the bottom of each escalator is a long central corridor with a platform on either side for trains travelling in either direction. Signs suspended from the ceiling indicate the direction of the trains *(see opposite page)*. The edges

The spacious interior of Můstek metro station

of the platforms are marked with a white, broken line which should not be crossed until the train stops. Most of the metro doors open and close automatically (you may have to push a button on some trains), giving a recorded message when they are about to close. During the journey the name of the next station is announced in Czech.

Maps of the underground system can be found above each metro door.

Line A is the most useful for tourists, because it covers all the main areas of the city centre – Prague Castle, the Little Quarter, the Old Town and the New Town – as well as the main shopping area around Wenceslas Square.

Displayed above some seats are disabled signs. These seats should be given up for the elderly, disabled, and those with small children.

AUTOMATIC TICKET MACHINES

You can buy transport tickets at designated ticket sellers *(see p241)* or at the automatic ticket machines in the metro station. The ticket machines, and tickets themselves, may vary in design and colour, but they are still applicable to all forms of transport. The machine offers a choice of tickets at varying prices, for adults, children, bicycles and other bulky items. Once it has been validated, a single-journey ticket is valid for an hour.

1 Check which price band is the right one to meet your requirements, then press the appropriately labelled button.

3 If you are happy that you have selected the right type of ticket, then press the *výdej* button to confirm your choice. (If you are unsure, press the button labelled *storno* and start the process again.)

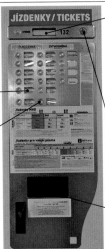

2 The visual display unit confirms which type of ticket you are in the process of selecting.

4 When you have confirmed your choice of ticket, insert coins into this slot. Most machines give change.

5 Collect your ticket, and any change that may be due to you, from the large slot at the base of the machine.

MAKING A JOURNEY BY METRO

1 The letters, each in a different colour, indicate the three metro lines. The number above the letter is the time it takes to get from one end of the line to the other.

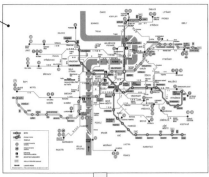

This metro map can be bought from most metro stations, tabáks and newsagents. A metro map has also been included at the end of this book.

2 To decide which line to take, find your destination on the *Street Finder (see pp252–7)*, its nearest metro station and then plot your route on a metro map.

3 Two types of standard metro ticket are available *(left)*. The more expensive tickets allow for transfers. You can also buy tickets that allow for unlimited travel within a 24-hour period *(below)* or for periods of 1, 3 or 5 days.

The central corridor with platforms either side and signs indicating the direction of trains

4 Before going down the escalators, you must stamp a single-journey ticket in one of these machines. If the ticket has not been stamped, it is not valid and you will have to pay a fine if caught.

5 This sign, hanging from the ceiling, is visible when you come down the escalator. It shows the direction of the trains on each platform. This one says that the train's final station *(Stanice)* on the left is Háje, so from the metro map you know the train is travelling south.

"Stanice" means station

"Směr" means direction

Kolej	Směr	Směr	Kolej
2	Stanice	Stanice	**1**
	Háje	Letňany	

Name of station

The red circle indicates which station you are in

6 This sign along the central platform indicates the station on line C where you are (red circle) and those stations where you can transfer to the other lines (A and B). For stations to the left of the red circle follow the arrow to the left, and vice-versa for stations to the right.

7 Once you are at your stop, follow the exit signs *(Výstup)* leading out of the metro system.

⬆ Výstup ⬆

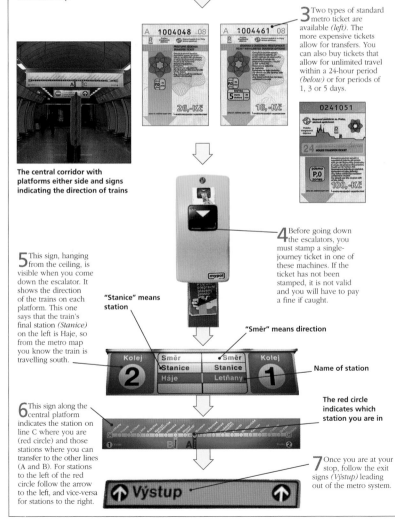

Travelling by Tram

Trams are Prague's oldest method of public transport. Horse-drawn trams appeared on the streets in 1879, but by 1891 the first electric tram was in operation. After the metro, the tram system is the fastest and most efficient way of getting around the city. Some lines only operate in the rush hour and there are a number of night trams, all of which pass by Lazarská in the New Town.

TRAM TICKETS

The tram system is run by the Prague Transport Corporation (see p240). Tram tickets are also valid for the metro and buses (see p242).

You have to buy your ticket before you board a tram. Once you have entered, you will see two or three small punching machines on metal poles just inside the door. Insert your ticket and it will be stamped automatically.

If you do not punch your ticket it is not valid and, if you are caught by a ticket inspector, you will have to pay an on-the-spot fine (see p241). A single-journey ticket is valid for one journey only (see p241), however long.

Each tram stop has a timetable – the stop underlined is where you are standing. The stops below that line indicate where that tram is heading.

Trams run every five to 20 minutes. Doors either open and close automatically or by pushing a button and each stop is announced in Czech. After the metro closes, a small number of night trams run every 30 minutes or so. These trams (numbers 51 to 58) are marked by blue numbers at the tram stop. For more information see www.dp-praha.cz.

Tram Signs
These are found at every tram stop and tell you which trams stop there, and in what direction each tram is going.

Name of the tram stop

Tram logo

The direction each tram is heading in

Numbers indicate which trams stop here

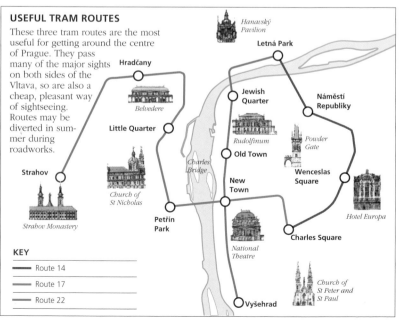

A busy tram on the streets of Prague

USEFUL TRAM ROUTES

These three tram routes are the most useful for getting around the centre of Prague. They pass many of the major sights on both sides of the Vltava, so are also a cheap, pleasant way of sightseeing. Routes may be diverted in summer during roadworks.

Hanavský Pavilion

Letná Park

Hradčany

Belvedere

Jewish Quarter

Náměstí Republiky

Little Quarter

Rudolfinum

Powder Gate

Old Town

Charles Bridge

Strahov

Church of St Nicholas

New Town

Wenceslas Square

Hotel Europa

Strahov Monastery

Petřín Park

National Theatre

Charles Square

Church of St Peter and St Paul

Vyšehrad

KEY

▬▬ Route 14

▬▬ Route 17

▬▬ Route 22

Travelling by Bus

You are unlikely to use a bus unless you want to visit the outer suburbs. By law, buses are not allowed in the city centre (they produce noxious fumes and the streets are too narrow), so they transport people from the suburbs to tram and metro stops outside the centre.

Bus stop logo

BUS TICKETS

A typical public bus in Prague

Unless you have small change, you must buy a ticket before you board a bus. Tickets are available from all the usual agents *(see p241).*

Again, you must validate your ticket in the punching machine on the bus. If you buy a single-journey ticket, it is only valid for one journey. Each time you change bus, you will have to buy a new ticket, unless you have a transfer ticket *(see p241).* The doors open and close automatically and the end of the boarding period is signalled by a high-pitched signal. You are expected to give up your seat for the elderly and disabled.

Bus timetables are located at every stop. They have the numbers of all the buses that stop there and the timetable for each route. The frequency of buses varies considerably. In the rush hour there may be 12 to 15 buses an hour, at other times as few as three.

Throughout the night there are 12 buses which go to the outer areas not served by the tram and metro system. For more information see www.dpp.cz.

Travelling by Taxi

For visitors to Prague taxis are a useful but often frustrating form of transport. After decades of public ownership, all taxis are now privately owned, but there are many unscrupulous drivers who are out to charge as much as they can get away with. For this reason it's worth taking a few simple precautions. For a start, find out how much a fare should cost.

An illuminated taxi sign

TAXI FARES

One of the many taxi ranks in the centre of the town

As soon as you enter a taxi there is a minimum charge. After that, by law the fare should increase at a set rate per kilometre. However, this set charge is rarely, if ever, adhered to and taxis can be a very expensive way of getting around the city. Taxi meters can be set at four different rates but for journeys in the city it should be set at one (the cheapest). However, rather than depend on the meters –

they are often rigged – it is a wise move to negotiate a fare you think is reasonable before you enter the cab. Vigorous bargaining can often bring the price down. Few taxi drivers speak more than the most rudimentary English, so communication can be difficult. Unless your Czech pronunciation is good, write down your destination for them in Czech. Be sure surcharges are included in the figure you negotiate before-

Taxi receipts, if requested, are required to be given by law.

The distance travelled — Amount charged

eb european business solutions

hand. If problems do arise at the end of the journey, ask for a receipt before you pay. This will normally deter drivers from trying to overcharge you. Avoid taxis around the main tourist sights, these can often be the worst offenders. If possible, order a taxi by phone from a reliable operator such as AAA Radiotaxi (tel. 14 014), or ask your hotel receptionist or one of the restaurant staff to call one for you.

The meter displays your fare and surcharges.

Fare   Surcharges   Rate

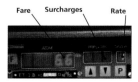

STREET FINDER

The map references given for all the sights, hotels, restaurants, bars, shops and entertainment venues described in this book refer to the maps in this section. A complete index of street names and all the places of interest marked, can be found on the following pages. The key map (right) shows the area of Prague covered by the *Street Finder*. This map includes sightseeing areas, as well as districts for hotels, restaurants, pubs and entertainment venues.

In keeping with Czech maps, none of the street names in the index or on the Street Finder have the Czech word for street, *ulice*, included (though you may see it on the city's street signs). For instance, Celetná ulice appears as Celetná in both the index and the Street Finder. The numbers preceding some street names are dates. In our index we ignore the numbers, so that 17. listopadu (17 November), is listed under 'L'.

KEY TO STREET FINDER

	Major sight
	Places of interest
	Other building
Ⓜ	Metro station
🚂	Train station
🚌	Coach station
🚊	Tram stop
🚋	Funicular railway
⛴	River boat boarding point
🚕	Taxi rank
P	Car park
ℹ	Tourist information office
✚	Hospital with casualty unit
🚓	Police station
✝	Church
✡	Synagogue
⊠	Post office
==	Railway line
—	City wall
⋯	Pedestrian street

SCALE OF MAP PAGES

0 metres	200
	1:8,400
0 yards	200

View of the Little Quarter, Hradčany and Prague Castle from the Old Town Bridge Tower

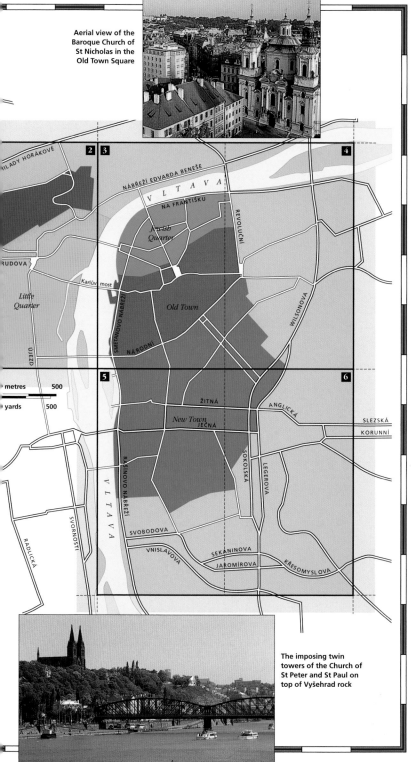

Aerial view of the Baroque Church of St Nicholas in the Old Town Square

The imposing twin towers of the Church of St Peter and St Paul on top of Vyšehrad rock

Street Finder Index

The order of the names in the index is affected by the *háček*, the accent like an inverted circumflex (*háček* means "little hook"). In the Czech alphabet, **č**, **ř**, **š** and **ž** are treated as separate letters. Street names beginning with **ř**, for example, are listed after those beginning with **r** without an accent.

Churches, buildings, museums and monuments are marked on the Street Finder maps with their English and Czech names. In the index, both forms are listed. However, English names for streets and squares, such as Wenceslas Square, do not appear on the maps. Where they are listed in the index, the Czech name is given in brackets in the form that appears on the map.

USEFUL WORDS	
dům	house
hrad	castle
kostel	church
klášter	convent, monastery
most	bridge
nábřeží	embankment
nádraží	station
náměstí	square
sady	park
schody	steps
třída	avenue
ulice	street
ulička	lane
zahrada	garden

A

Albertov	5 C4
Alšovo nábřeží	3 A3
Americká	6 F3
Anenská	3 A4
Anenské náměstí	3 A4
Anežská	3 C2
Anglická	6 E2
Anny Letenské	6 F1
Apolinářská	5 C4
Archbishop's Palace	2 D3
Arcibiskupský palác	2 D3
At St Thomas's	2 E3
At the Three Ostriches	2 F3
autobusové nádraži Praha, Florenc	4 F3
autobusové zast. Hradčanská	2 D1

B

Badeniho	2 F1
Balbínova	6 E2
Bartolomějská	3 B5
Barvířská	4 E2
Bazilika sv. Jiří	2 E2
Bělehradská	6 E2
Belgická	6 F3
Bělohorská	1 A4
Belvedér	2 E1
Belvedere	2 E1
Benátská	5 B3
Benediktská	4 D3
Besední	2 E5
Bethlehem Chapel	3 B4
Betlémská	3 A5
Betlémské kaple	3 B4
Betlémské náměstí	3 B4
Bílkova	3 B2
Biskupská	4 E2
Biskupský dvůr	4 E2
Blanická	6 F2

Bolzanova	4 E4
Boršov	3 A4
Botanical Gardens	5 B3
Botanická zahrada	5 B3
Botič	6 D5
Botičská	5 B4
Boženy Němcové	6 D4
Bridge Street (Mostecká)	2 E3
Bruselská	6 E3
Brusnice	1 C2
Břehová	3 A2
Břetislavova	2 D3

C

Capuchin Monastery	1 B2
Carolinum	3 C4
Celetná	3 C3
Chaloupeckého	1 B5
Chalice Restaurant	6 D3
Charles Bridge (Karlův most)	2 F4
continues	3 A4
Charles Square (Karlovo náměstí)	5 B2
Charles Street (Karlova)	2 A4
continues	3 B4
Charvátova	3 B5
Chodecká	1 A5
Chotkova	2 E1
Chotkovy sady	2 F1
Chrám sv. Víta	2 D2
Church of Our Lady before Týn	3 C3
Church of Our Lady beneath the Chain	2 E4
Church of Our Lady of the Snows	3 C5
Church of Our Lady Victorious	2 D4
Church of St Castullus	3 C2

Church of St Catherine	5 C3
Church of St Cyril and St Methodius	5 B2
Church of St Gall	3 C4
Church of St Giles	3 B4
Church of St Ignatius	5 C2
Church of St James	3 C3
Church of St John on the Rock	5 B3
Church of St Lawrence	1 C5
Church of St Martin in the Wall	3 B5
Church of St Nicholas (Little Quarter)	2 D3
Church of St Nicholas (Old Town)	3 B3
Church of St Simon and St Jude	3 B2
Church of St Stephen	5 C2
Church of St Thomas	2 E3
Church of St Ursula	3 A5
Church of the Holy Ghost	3 B3
Cihelná	2 F3
Clam-Gallas Palace	3 B4
Clam-Gallasův palác	3 B4
Clementinum	3 A4
Cubist Houses	3 B2
Cukrovarnická	1 A1

Č

Čechův most	3 B2
Čelakovského sady	6 E1
continues	6 D1
Černá	5 B1
Černín Palace	1 B3
Černínská	1 B2
Černínský palác	1 B3
Čertovka	2 F4
Červená	3 B3

D

Dalibor Tower	2 E2
Daliborka	2 E2
Dělostřelecká	1 A1
Diskařská	1 A5
Dittrichova	5 A2
Divadelní	3 A5
Dlabačov	1 A4
Dlážděná	4 E4
Dlouhá	3 C3
Dražického	2 F3
Dražického náměstí	2 E3
Dřevná	5 A3
Dům pánů z Kunštátu	3 B4
Dům U Dvou zlatých medvědů	3 B4
Dušní	3 B2
Dvořák Museum	6 D2
Dvořákovo nábřeží	3 A2

E

Elišky Krásnohorské	3 B2
Estates Theatre	3 C4

F

Faust House	5 B3
Faustův dům	5 B3
Florenc (metro)	4 F3
Franciscan Garden	3 C5
Francouzská	6 F2
Františkánská zahrada	3 C5
Fričova	6 E5
Fügnerovo náměstí	6 D3
Funicular Railway	2 D5

G

Gogolova	2 F1
Golden Lane (Zlatá ulička)	2 E2
Golz-Kinský Palace	3 C3

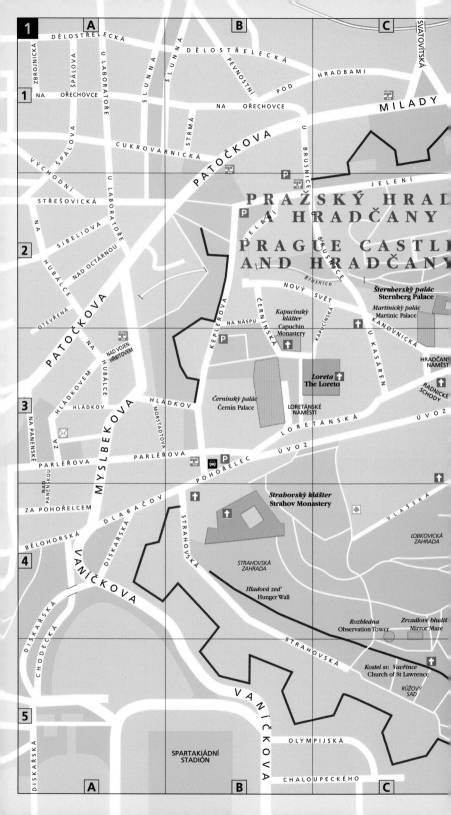

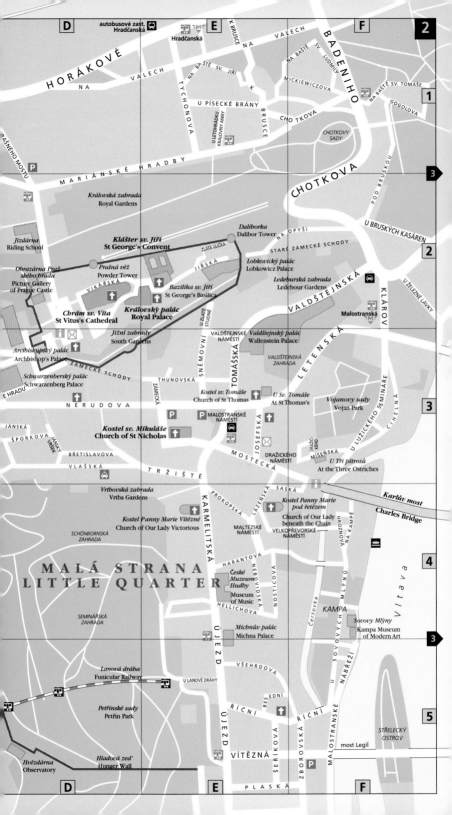

3
A
B
P **C**
LETENSKÝ

1

Letenské sady
Letná Park

BENEŠE

2

EDVARDA

NÁBŘEŽÍ

Čechův most

FRANTIŠKU

Řásnovka

MALÁ KLÁŠTERSKÁ

KA

2

Vltava

NÁMĚSTÍ
CURIEOVÝCH

NA
ŘÁSNOKOVSKÉ

DUŠNÍ

Klášter sv. Anežky
St Agnes's Convent

Kostel sv. Simona a Judy
Church of St Simon and St Jude

KLÁŠTERSKÁ

DVOŘÁKOVO NÁBŘEŽÍ

PAŘÍŽSKÁ

U MILOSRDNÝCH

DVORA

ZA

HAŠTALEM

HAŠTALSKÁ

J O S E F O V

Kubistické domy
Cubist Houses

HAŠTALSKÉ
NÁMĚSTÍ

KOSÁRKOVO NÁBŘEŽÍ

U PLOVÁRNY

BŘEHOVÁ

17. LISTOPADU

U STARÉHO HŘBITOVA

BÍLKOVA

ELIŠKY KRÁSNOHORSKÉ

J E W I S H   Q U A R T E R

KOZÍ

U OBECNÍHO DVORA

Kostel sv. Haštala
Church of St Castullus

RÁMOVÁ

RYBNÁ

Starý židovský hřbitov
Old Jewish Cemetery

NA REJDIŠTI

Klausová synagóga
Klausen Synagogue

Staronová synagóga
Old-New Synagogue

U STARÉ

ŠKOLY

VĚŽEŇSKÁ

Španělská synagóga
Spanish Synagogue

KOZÍ

DLOUHÁ

MASNÁ

MASNÁ

Uměleckoprůmyslové muzeum
Museum of Decorative Arts

Rudolfinum

MÁNESŮV most

NÁMĚSTÍ JANA
PALACHA

Pinkasova synagóga
Pinkas Synagogue

ALŠOVO NÁBŘEŽÍ

VALENTINSKÁ

MAISELOVA

ČERVENÁ

ŠIROKÁ

Vysoká synagóga
High Synagogue

Židovská radnice
Jewish Town Hall

U KOSTELA

Maiselova synagóga
Maisel Synagogue

Staroměstská

MAISELOVA

SIROKÁ

U RADNICE

ŽATECKÁ

KAPROVA

VELESLAVÍNOVA

PLATNÉŘSKÁ

MARIÁNSKÉ
NÁMĚSTÍ

SALVÁTORSKÁ

DLOUHÁ

TÝNSKÁ ULIČKA

MALÁ ŠTUPARTSKÁ

*Kostel sv.
Jakuba*
Church of St
James

JAKUBSKÁ

*Palác Golz-
Kinských*
Golz-Kinský
Palace

*Pomník Jana
Husa*
Jan Hus
Monument

*Kostel Panny Marie
před Týnem*
Church of Our
Lady before Týn

ŠTUPARTSKÁ

Kostel sv. Mikuláše
Church of St Nicholas

STAROMĚSTSKÉ
NÁMĚSTÍ

Staroměstská radnice
Old Town Hall

CELETNÁ

3

KŘIŽOVNICKÁ

KARLŮV most

KŘIŽOVNICKÉ
NÁMĚSTÍ

Klementinum
Clementinum

SEMINÁŘSKÁ

HUSOVA

LINHARTSKÁ

MALÉ
NÁMĚSTÍ

MELANTRICHOVA

ŽELEZNÁ

KAMZÍKOVÁ

OVOCNÝ
TRH

Karolinum
Carolinum

Stavovské divadlo
Estates Theatre

KARLOVA

Clam-Gallasův palác
Clam-Gallas Palace

KARLOVA

HLAVSOVA

JILSKÁ

JALOVCOVÁ

*Dům U Dvou
zlatých medvědů*
House at the Two
Golden Bears

KOŽNÁ

HAVELSKÁ

Kostel sv. Havla
Church of St Gall

HAVÍŘSKÁ

NA PŘÍKOPĚ

*Muzeum Bedřicha
Smetany*
Smetana
Museum

NOVOTNÉHO
LÁVKA

NÁPLAVNÍ

ŘETĚZOVÁ

Dům pánů z Kunštátu
Palace of the Lords of Kunštát

ANENSKÁ

ANENSKÉ
NÁMĚSTÍ

ZLATÁ

LILIOVÁ

VEJVODOVA

MICHALSKÁ

Kostel sv. Jiljí
Church of St Giles

HAVELSKÁ

U KOTCŮ

V KOTCÍCH

RYTÍŘSKÁ

NA MŮSTKU

PROVAZNICKÁ

PROVAZNICKÁ

i

Můstek

4

SMETANOVO NÁBŘEŽÍ

KAROLÍNY

U ZÁBRADLÍ

TŘÍBRÁŽ

NÁPRSTKOVA

BORŠOV

BETLÉMSKÁ

KONVIKTSKÁ

Betlémská kaple
Bethlehem Chapel

BETLÉMSKÉ
NÁMĚSTÍ

Náprstkovo muzeum
Náprstek Museum

BARTOLOMĚJSKÁ

SKOŘEPKA

NA PERŠTÝNĚ

MARTINSKÁ

S T A R É   M Ě S T O

UHELNÝ
TRH

PERLOVÁ

28. ŘÍJNA

O L D   T O W N

VÁCLAVSKÉ

JUNGMANNOVO
NÁMĚSTÍ

Kostel Panny Marie Sněžné
Church of Our Lady of the Snows

2

SVĚTLÉ

DIVADELNÍ

KROCÍNOVA

SVĚTLÉ

NÁRODNÍ

MIKULANDSKÁ

Kostel sv. Martina ve zdi
Church of St Martin in the Wall

SPÁLENÁ

Františkánská zahrada
Franciscan Garden

5

most Legií

NÁRODNÍ

Kostel sv. Voršily
Church of St Ursula

OSTROVNÍ

VORŠILSKÁ

**Národní
třída**

VLADISLAVOVA

CHARVÁTOVA

PURKYŇOVA

PALACKÉHO

N O V É   M Ě S T O

N E W   T O W N

JUNGMANNOVA

VODIČKOVA

Národní divadlo
National Theatre

A

5

B

C

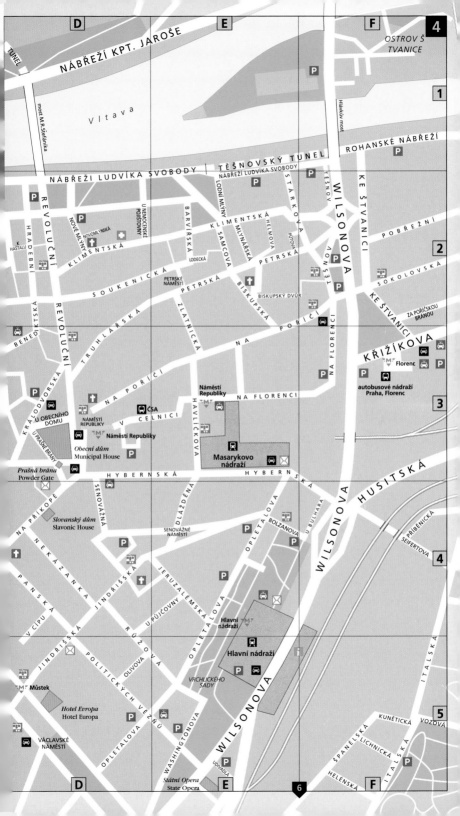

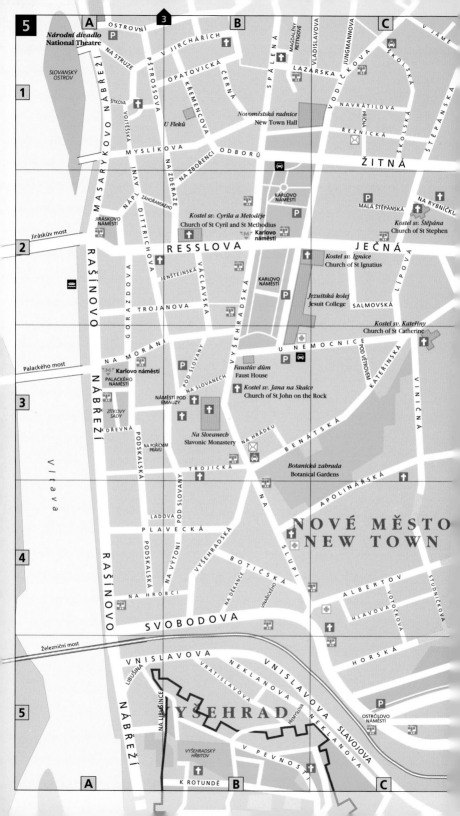

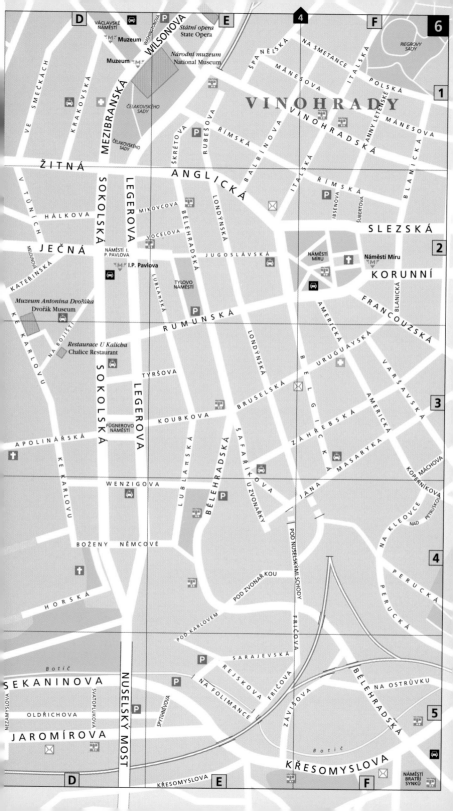

General Index

Acknowledgments

Dorling Kindersley wishes to thank the following people who contributed to the preparation of this book.

Main Contributor

Vladimír Soukup was born in Prague in 1949. He worked for the daily newpaper, *Evening Prague*, for 20 years, eventually becoming Deputy Chief Editor. He has written a wide range of popular guides to Prague.

Additional Contributors

Ben Sullivan, Lynn Reich.

Editorial and Design

Managing Editor Carolyn Ryden; *Managing Art Editor* Steve Knowlden; *Senior Editor* Georgina Matthews; *Senior Art Editor* Vanessa Courtier; *Editorial Director* David Lamb; *Art Director* Anne-Marie Bulat; *Production Controller* Hilary Stephens; *Picture Research* Ellen Root; *Designer* Nicola Erdpresser, Sangita Patel; *Consultant* Helena Svojsikova; *Maps* Caroline Bowie, Simon Farbrother, James Mills-Hicks, David Pugh (DKCartography); *Revisions Editorial and Design* Emma Anacootee, Mark Baker, Claire Baranowski, Russell Davies, Stephanie Driver, Fay Franklin, Alistair Gunn, Elaine Harries, Charlie Hawkings, Jan Kaplan, Juliet Kenny, Dr Tomáš Kleisner, Jude Ledger, Susannah Marriott, Helen Partington, Marianne Petrou, Robert Purnell, Marian Sucha, Daphne Trotter, Conrad Van Dyk, Christopher Vinz.

Additional Photography

Mark Baker, DK Studio/Steve Gorton, Ian O'Leary, Otto Palan, M Soskova, Clive Streeter, Alan Williams, Peter Wilson.

t = top; tl = top left; tc = top centre; tr = top right; cla = centre left above; ca = centre above; cra = centre right above; cl = centre left; c = centre; cr = centre right; clb = centre left below; cb = centre below; crb = centre right below; bl = bottom left; b = bottom; bc = bottom centre; br = bottom right; d = detail.

Works of art on the pages detailed have been reproduced with the permission of the following copyright holders: Aristide Maillol *Pomona* 1910 © ADAG, Paris, and DACS, London, 2006: 164bc. Gustav Makarius Tauc (An der Aulenkaut 31, Wiesbaden, Germany) under commission of the Minorite Order in Rome: 35bc.

The publishers are grateful to the following individuals, companies and picture libraries for permission to reproduce photographs or to photograph at their establishments: ALAMY IMAGES: Frank Chmura 236bl; Chris Fredriksson 199c; PjrFoto.com/Phil Robinson 227bc; Profimedia International S. R.O/Michaela Dusíková 179bl; Robert Harding Picture Library 10bl; ARCHEOLOGICKÝ ÚSTAV ČESKÉ AKADEMIE VĚD: 20t; ARCHIV FÜR KUNST UND GESCHICHTE, BERLIN: 17b, 18tl (d), 18tr, 18bc(d), 18br(d), 19tl(d), 19tc(d), 19tr(d), 19c(d), 19bc(d), 20clr, 20bl, 23cb(d), 29cla(d), 32t(d), 32bl, 34ca(d), 34tr(d), 43tl, 50b(d), 105cr, 118t, Erich Lessing 28ca(d), 31bl(d), 88c, 89cb; ARCHIV HLAVNÍHO MESTA. PRAHY (CLAM-GALLASŮV PALÁC): 23cl, 24bl, 28bl, 28br, 30b, 33clb, 33bc, 72t, 136br, 137br(d), 138ca, 168c. BILDARCHIV

PREUSSISCHER KULTURBESITZ: 4t(d), 19bl(d), 29br, 34bc, 68tr, 104bl(d); BRIDGEMAN ART LIBRARY, London: Prado, Madrid 29t; Rosegarten Museum, Constance 26ca. CEDAZ, LTD: 237tr; ČESKÁ TISKOVÁ KANCELÁŘ: 19br, 35cbr, 203cr; COMSTOCK: George Gerster 12cla; JEAN-LOUP CHARMET: 18bl(d), 21c, 31br, 33t, 33bl, 33br(d), 34cbr(d), 34bl, 62c, 69tc; ZDENEK CHRAPPEK: 50c; CORBIS: Gail Mooney 199tl; JOE CORNISH: 58–9, 60, 148br; CZECH AIRLINES: 236ca; CZECH NATIONAL BANK: 239. MARY EVANS PICTURE LIBRARY: 9, 59, 138cb, 183, 225. GRAFOPRINT NEUBERT: 31clb, 38clb, 116c. ROBERT HARDING PICTURE LIBRARY: Michael Jenner 128tl; Christopher Rennie 24ca, 103tr; Peter Scholey 30t, 129tl; HIDDEN PLACES RESIDENCES & BOUTIQUE HOTELS: 187bl; HUTCHISON LIBRARY: Libuše Taylor 51b, 52t, 177tl, 205c. THE IMAGE BANK: Andrea Pistolesi 14b; Courtesy of ISIC, UK: 242c. KANCELÁŘ PREZIDENTA REPUBLIKY: 20–1, 21tr, 21bl, 21br, 22c; KAPLAN PRODUCTIONS: 117t; OLDRICH KARASEK: 11tr 56cb, 62tr, 101bl; 101crb, 134t, 135b; 176t, 201c, 219t, 233cl, 240bc; KARLŠTEJN: 25tl; Vladimír Hyhlík 24–5, KAREL KESTNER: 35bl; KLEMENTINUM: 23tl; Prokop Paul 22t; THE KOBAL COLLECTION: 34cra; DALIBOR KUSÁK: 164bl, 168–9 all, 170-1 all. IVAN MALÝ: 218t, 218c; LEONADO MEDIABANK: 184br; MUZEÚM HLAVNÍHO MĚSTA PRAHY 32–3; MUZEUM POŠTOVNÍ ZNÁMKY: 149cl. NÁRODNÍ GALERIE V PRAZE: 24br, 40b; Grafická sbírka 26t, 27bl, 31t, 67b, 69c, 100t, 102b, 121t, 125cb, 129br, 138b, 157cb, 175b, 180b; Klášter sv. Anežky 39tr, 83t, 92–3 all, 133b; Klášter sv. Jiří 16, 37br, 38t, 39tr, 97clb, 106–7 all, 108–9 all, Šternbersky palác 38ca, 112–3 all, 114–5 all, Veletržní Palac 164–5 all; Zbraslav 40b; NÁRODNÍ MUZEUM, PRAHA: 147b; NÁRODNÍ MUZEUM V PRAZE: Vlasta Dvořáková 20clb, 26–7, 26bl, 26bc, 26br, 27t, 27cl, 27cr, 27br, 29bl, 39cb, 75b, 72b, Jarmila Kutová 20c, 22bl, Dagmar Landová 28bc, 126c, Muzeum Antonína Dvořáka 39b, Muzeum Bedřicha Smetany 32ca, Prokop Paul 75b, Tyršovo Muzeum; 149bl; NÁRODNÍ TECHNICKÉ MUZEUM: Gabriel Urbánek 41t. OBRAZÁRNA PRAŽSKÉHO HRADU: 98b; ÖSTERREICHISCHE NATIONALBIBLIOTHEK, WIEN: 25clb, 26cb. PHOTO- GRAPHERS DIRECT: Chris Barton 10cra, Eddie Gerald 11bl; PIVOVARSKÉ MUZEUM: 200tr, 200c; PRAGUE INFORMATION SERVICE: www.prague-info.cz 226bc; BOHUMÍR PROKŮPEK: 25bl, 30t, 120c, 121c, 121bl, 163b. REX FEATURES LTD: Alfred 35tr, Richard Gardener 240t. SCIENCE PHOTO LIBRARY: Geospace 13, 38crb; SOTHEBY'S/ THAMES AND HUDSON: 104c; STÁTNÍ ÚSTŘEDNI ARCHIV: 23b; STÁTNÍ ÚSTAV PAMÁTKOVÉ PÉČE: 23tc; STÁTNÍ ŽIDOVSKÉ MUZEUM: 39ca, 85t, 85c, 90t; LUBOMÍR STIBUREK, www.czfoto.cz: 55b, 145ca, 163t, 176c, 243cl, 244cr, 251bca, 252cr; MARIAN SUCHA: front endpaper Lbl, 55t, 56cb, 94, 127b, 174t, 205bl, 205t, 233bc, 245c; SVATOVÍTSKÝ POKLAD, PRAŽSKÝ HRAD: 14t, 21tl, 24t, 24cb, 28t, 40tr. MARTIN TOUR, PRAHA: 226tr; UMĚLECKOPRŮMYSLOVÉ MUZEUM V PRAZE: 39tl, 40tl, 149c, 149br, Gabriel Urbánek 28clb, 41b; UNIVERZITA KARLOVA: 25tr. U PINKASU RESTAURANT: 198cla; PETER WILSON: 4b, 197tl, 224-5, 246. ZEFA: 33cra.

Front endpaper: all special or additional photography except (centre) JOE CORNISH. JACKET: Front - CORBIS: Dallas and John Heaton main image; DK IMAGES: Jiri Kopriva bl. Back – JOE CORNISH: bl, tl; DK IMAGES: Jiri Dolezal cla; Jiri Kopriva clb. Spine – CORBIS: Dallas and John Heaton t; DK IMAGES: Peter Wilson b. All other images © Dorling Kindersley. For further information, see: www.dkimages.com

Phrase Book

In Emergency

Help!	Pomoc!	po-mots
Stop!	Zastavte!	za-stav-te
Call a	Zavolejte	za-vo-ley-te
doctor!	doktora!	dok-to-ra!
Call an	Zavolejte	za-vo-ley-te
ambulance!	sanitku!	sa-nit-ku!
Call the	Zavolejte	za-vo-ley-te
police!	policii!	poli-tsi-yi!
Call the fire	Zavolejte	za-vol-ey-te
brigade!	hasiče	ha-si-che
Where is the	Kde je	gde ye
telephone?	telefón?	tele-fohn?
the nearest	nejbližší	ney-blish-ee
hospital?	nemocnice?	ne-mots-nyitse?

Communication Essentials

Yes/No	Ano/Ne	ano/ne
Please	Prosím	pro-seem
Thank you	Děkuji vám	dye-ku-ji vahm
Excuse me	Prosím vás	pro-seem vahs
Hello	Dobrý den	do-bree den
Goodbye	Na shledanou	na s-hle-da-no
Good evening	Dobrý večer	dob-ree vech-er
morning	ráno	rah-no
afternoon	odpoledne	od-po-led-ne
evening	večer	ve-cher
yesterday	včera	vche-ra
today	dnes	dnes
tomorrow	zítra	zeet-ra
here	tady	ta-di
there	tam	tam
What?	Co?	tso?
When?	Kdy?	gdi?
Why?	Proč?	proch?
Where?	Kde?	gde?

Useful Phrases

How are you?	Jak se máte?	yak-se mah-te?
Very well,	Velmi dobře	vel-mi dob-rzhe
thank you.	děkuji.	dye kuyi
Pleased to meet you.	Těší mě.	tyesh-ee mye
See you soon.	Uvidíme se	u-vi-dyee-me-se-
	brzy.	br-zi
That's fine.	To je v	to ye vpo-
	pořádku.	rzhahdku
Where is/are…?	Kde je/jsou …?	gde ye/yso …?
How long does	Jak dlouho to trvá	yak dlo ho to tr-va
it take to get to?	se dostat do..?	se do-stat do…?
How do I get to…?	Jak se	yak se
	dostanu k..?	do-sta-nu k …?
Do you speak	Mluvíte	mlu-vee-te
English?	anglicky?	an-glits-ki?
I don't understand.	Nerozumím.	ne-ro-zu-meem
Could you speak	Mohl(a)* byste	mohl- (a) bis-te
more slowly?	mluvit trochu	mlu-vit tro-khu
	pomaleji?	po-maley?
Pardon?	Prosím?	pro-seem?
I'm lost.	Ztratil(a)*	stra-tyil (a)
	jsem se.	ysem se.

Useful Words

big	velký	vel-kee
small	malý	mal-ee
hot	horký	hor-kee
cold	studený	stu-den-e•
good	dobrý	dob-ree
bad	špatný	shpat-nee
well	dobře	dob-rzhe
open	otevřeno	ot-ev-rzhe-no
closed	zavřeno	zav-rzhe-no
left	do leva	do le-va
right	do prava	do pra-va
straight on	rovně	rov-nye
near	blízko	blee-sko
far	daleko	da-le-ko
up	nahoru	na-ho-ru
down	dolů	do-loo
early	brzy	br-zi
late	pozdě	poz-dye
entrance	vchod	vkhod
exit	východ	vee-khod
toilets	toalety	toa-leti
free, unoccupied	volný	vol-nee
free, no charge	zdarma	zdar-ma

Making a Telephone Call

I'd like to place a	Chtěl(a)* bych	khtyel(a) bikh
call.	volat	vo-lat
I'd like to make a	Chtěl(a)* bych	khtyel(a) bikh
reverse-charge call.	volat na účet	volat na oo-chet
	volaného.	volan-eh-ho
I'll try again later.	Zkusím to	skus-eem to
	později.	poz-dyey
Can I leave	Mohu nechat	mo-hu ne-khat
a message?	zprávu?	sprah-vu?
Hold on.	Počkejte.	poch-key-te
Could you speak	Mohl(a)* byste	mo-hl (a) bis-te
up a little, please?	mluvit hlasitěji?	mluvit hla-si-tyey?
local call	místní hovor	meest-nyee hov-or

Sightseeing

art gallery	galerie	ga-ler-riye
bus stop	autobusová	au-to-bus-o-vah
	zastávka	za-stah-vka
church	kostel	kos-tel
garden	zahrada	za hra-da
library	knihovna	knyi-hov-na
museum	muzeum	muz-e-um
railway station	nádraží	nah-dra-zhee
tourist	turistické	tooristi-tske
information	informace	in-for-ma-tse
closed for the	státní	staht-nyee
public holiday	svátek	svah-tek

Shopping

How much does	Co to stojí?	tso to sto-yee?
this cost?		
I would like …	Chtěl(a)* bych ….	khtyel(a) bikh…
Do you have …?	Máte …?	maa-te …?
I'm just looking.	Jenom se dívám.	ye-nom se
		dyee-vahm
Do you take	Berete kreditní	be-re-te kred-it
credit cards?	karty?	nyee karti?
What time do	V kolik	v ko-lik
you open/	otevíráte/	o-te-vee-rah-te/
close?	zavíráte?	za vee rah-te?
this one	tento	ten-to
that one	tamten	tam-ten
expensive	drahý	dra-hee
cheap	levný	lev-nee
size	velikost	vel-ik-ost
white	bílý	bee-lee
black	černý	cher-nee
red	červený	cher-ven-ee
yellow	žlutý	zhlu-tee
green	zelený	zel-en-ee
blue	modrý	mod-ree
brown	hnědý	hnyed-ee

Types of Shop

antique shop	starožitnictví	sta-ro zhit--
		nyits-tvee
bank	banka	bank a
bakery	pekárna	pe-kahr-na
bookstore	knihkupectví	knih-kupets-tvee
butcher	řeznictví	rzhez-nyits-tvee
camera shop	obchod	op-khot
	s fotoaparáty	sfoto-aparahti
chemist		
(prescriptions etc)	lékárna	leh-kah-rna
chemist (cosmetics,		
toiletries etc)	drogerie	drog-erye
delicatessen	lahůdky	la-hoo-dki
department store	obchodní dům	op-khod-nyee doom
grocery	potraviny	pot-ra-vini
glass	sklo	sklo
hairdresser		
(ladies)	kadeřnictví	ka-derzh-nyits-tvee
(mens)	holič	ho-lich
market	trh	trkh
newsstand	novinový	no-vi-novee
	stánek	stah-nek
post office	pošta	posh-ta
supermarket	samoobsluha	sa-mo-ob-slu-ha
tobacconist	tabák	ta-bahk
travel	cestovní	tses-tov-nyi
agency	kancelář	kantse-laarzh

* Alternatives for a female speaker are shown in brackets.

Staying in a Hotel

Do you have a vacant room?	Máte volný pokoj?	mah-te vol-nee po-koy?
double room	dvoulůžkový pokoj	dvo-loozb-kovee po-koy
with double bed	s dvojitou postelí	sdvoy-to pos-telee
twin room	pokoj s dvěma postelemi	po-koy sdvye-ma pos-tel-emi
room with a bath	pokoj s koupelnou	po-koy s ko-pel-no
porter	vrátný	vraht-nee
hall porter	nosič	nos-ich
key	klíč	kleech
I have a reservation.	Mám reservaci.	mahm rez-ervatsi

Eating Out

Have you got a table for ...?	Máte stůl pro ...?	mah-te stool pro ...?
I'd like to reserve a table.	Chtěl(a)* bych rezervovat stůl.	khtyel(a) bikh rez-er-vov-at stool
breakfast	snídaně	snyee-danye
lunch	oběd	ob-yed
dinner	večeře	vech e-rzhe
The bill, please.	Prosím, účet.	pro-seem oo-chet
I am a vegetarian.	Jsem vegetarián(ka)*.	ysem veghe-tariahn(ka)
waitress!	slečno	slech-no
waiter!	pane vrchní!	pane vrkh-nyee!
fixed price menu	standardní menu	stan-dard-nyee men-u
dish of the day	nabídka dne	nab-eed-ka dne
starter	předkrm	przhed-krm
main course	hlavní jídlo	hlav-nyee yeed-lo
vegetables	zelenina	zel-en-yin-a
dessert	zákusek	zah-kusek
cover charge	poplatek	pop-la-tek
wine list	nápojový lístek	nah-po-yo-vee lee-stek
rare (steak)	krvavý	kr-va-vee
medium	středně udělaný	strzhed-nye ud-yel-an-ee
well done	dobře udělaný	dobrzhe-ud-yel-an-ee
glass	sklenice	sklen-yitse
bottle	láhev	lah-hev
knife	nůž	noozh
fork	vidlička	vid-lich-ka
spoon	lžíce	lzhee-tse

Menu Decoder

biftek	bif-tek	steak
bílé víno	bee-leh vee-no	white wine
bramborové knedlíky	bram-bo-ro-veh kne-dleeki	potato dumplings
brambory	bram-bo-ri	potatoes
chléb	khlehb	bread
cibule	tsi-bu-le	onion
citrónový džus	tsi-tron-o-vee dzhuus	lemon juice
cukr	tsukr	sugar
čaj	chay	tea
čerstvé ovoce	cher-stveb-o-vo-ce	fresh fruit
červené víno	cher-ven-eb vee-no	red wine
česnek	ches-nek	garlic
dort	dort	cake
fazole	fa-zo-le	beans
grilované	gril-ov-a-neb	grilled
houby	ho-bi	mushrooms
houska	hous-ka	roll
houskové knedlíky	ho-sko-veh kne-dleeki	bread dumplings
hovězí	hov-ye-zee	beef
hranolky	hran-ol-ki	chips
husa	hu-sa	goose
jablko	ya-bl-ko	apple
jahody	ya-ho-di	strawberries
jehněčí	ye-bnye-chee	lamb
kachna	kakh-na	duck
kapr	ka-pr	carp
káva	kah-va	coffee
krevety	krev-et-í	prawns
kuře	ku-rzhe	chicken
kyselé zelí	kis-eh-leh zel-ee	sauerkraut
maso	ma-so	meat
máslo	mah-slo	butter
minerálka perliva/ neperliva	min-er-abl-ka purl-i-vab/ ne-purl i-vab	mineral water fizzy/ still

mléko	mleh-ko	milk
mořská jídla	morzh-skab-yeed-la-	seafood
ocet	ots-et	vinegar
okurka	o-ku-rka	cucumber
olej	oley	oil
párek	paa-rek	sausage/frankfurter
pečené	petsh-en-eb	baked
pečené	pech-en-eb	roast
pepř	peprzh	pepper
polévka	pol-eb-vka	soup
pomeranč	po-me-ranch	orange
pomerančový džus	po-me-ran-ch-- o-vee dzhuus	orange juice
pivo	pi-vo	beer
rajské	rayskeh	tomato
ryba	rib-a	fish
rýže	ree-zhe	rice
salát	sal-at	salad
sůl	sool	salt
sýr	seer	cheese
šunka	shun-ka	ham
vařená /uzená	varzh-enab u-zenab	cooked smoked
telecí	te-le-tsee	veal
tuna	tu-na	tuna
vajíčko	va-yee-cbko	egg
vařené	varzh-en-eb	boiled
vepřové	vep-rzbo-veb	pork
voda	vo-da	water
vývar	vee-var	broth
zelí	zel-ee	cabbage
zelenina	zel-enyina	vegetables
zmrzlina	zmrz-lin-a	ice cream

Numbers

1	jedna	yed-na
2	dvě	dvye
3	tři	trzhi
4	čtyři	chti-rzbi
5	pět	pyet
6	šest	shest
7	sedm	sedm
8	osm	osm
9	devět	dev-yet
10	deset	des-et
11	jedenáct	ye-de-nabtst
12	dvanáct	dva-nabtst
13	třináct	trzhi-nabtst
14	čtrnáct	chtr-nabtst
15	patnáct	pat-nabtst
16	šestnáct	shest-nabtst
17	sedmnáct	sedm-nabtst
18	osmnáct	osm-nabtst
19	devatenáct	de-va-te-nabtst
20	dvacet	dva-tset
21	dvacet jedna	dva-tset yed-na
22	dvacet dva	dva-tset dva
23	dvacet tři	dva-tset-trzhi
24	dvacet čtyři	dva-tset chti-rzbi
25	dvacet pět	dva-tset pyet
30	třicet	trzhi-tset
40	čtyřicet	chti-rzbi-tset
50	padesát	pa-de-sabt
60	šedesát	she-de-sabt
70	sedmdesát	sedm-de-sabt
80	osmdesát	osm-de-sabt
90	devadesát	de-va-de-sabt
100	sto	sto
1,000	tisíc	tyi-seets
2,000	dva tisíce	dva tyi-see-tse
5,000	pět tisíc	pyet tyi-seets
1,000,000	milión	mi-li-obn

Time

one minute	jedna minuta	yed-na min-uta
one hour	jedna hodina	yed-na hod-yin-a
half an hour	půl hodiny	pool hod-yin-i
day	den	den
week	týden	tee-den
Monday	pondělí	pon-dye-lee
Tuesday	úterý	oo-ter-ee
Wednesday	středa	strzhe-da
Thursday	čtvrtek	chtvr-tek
Friday	pátek	pah-tek
Saturday	sobota	so-bo-ta
Sunday	neděle	ned-yel-e

* Alternatives for a female speaker are shown in brackets.

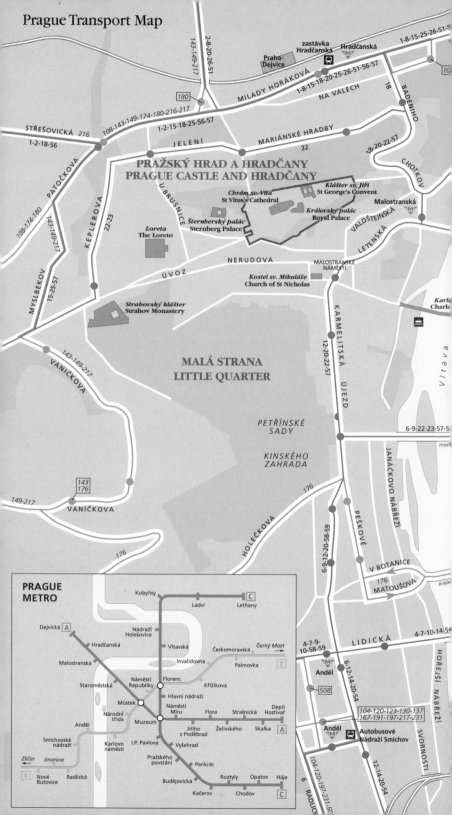